MODERN PAINTERS

VOLUME V

"Accuse me not
Of arrogance, ...
If, having walked with Nature,
And offered, far as frailty would allow,
My heart a daily sacrifice to Truth,
I now affirm of Nature and of Truth,
Whom I have served, that their Divinity
Revolts, offended at the ways of men,
Philosophers, who, though the human soul
Be of a thousand faculties composed,
And twice ten thousand interests, do yet prize
This soul, and the transcendent universe,
No more than as a mirror that reflects
To proud Self-love her own intelligence."

WORDSWORTH

Painted by Fra Angelico   Drawn by J. Ruskin   Engd. by W. Holl

Ancilla Domini

Modern Painters

Vol. V

By

John Ruskin

London: George Allen

November 1904

PREFACE

1. THE disproportion between the length of time occupied in the preparation of this volume, and the slightness of apparent result, is so vexatious to me, and must seem so strange to the reader, that he will perhaps bear with my stating some of the matters which have employed or interrupted me between 1855 and 1860. I needed rest after finishing the fourth volume, and did little in the following summer. The winter of 1856 was spent in writing the "Elements of Drawing," for which I thought there was immediate need; and in examining with more attention than they deserved, some of the modern theories of political economy, to which there was necessarily reference in my addresses at Manchester. The Manchester Exhibition then gave me some work, chiefly in its magnificent Reynolds' constellation; and thence I went on into Scotland, to look at Dumblane and Jedburgh, and some other favourite sites of Turner's; which I had not all seen, when I received notice from Mr. Wornum that he had obtained for me permission, from the Trustees of the National Gallery, to arrange, as I thought best, the Turner drawings belonging to the nation; on which I returned to London immediately.

2. In seven tin boxes in the lower room of the National Gallery I found upwards of nineteen thousand pieces of paper, drawn upon by Turner in one way or another. Many on both sides; some with four, five, or six subjects on each side (the pencil point digging spiritedly through from the foregrounds of the front into the tender pieces of sky on the back); some in chalk, which the touch of the

finger would sweep away ;[1] others in ink, rotted into holes ; others (some splendid coloured drawings among them) long eaten away by damp and mildew, and falling into dust at the edges, in capes and bays of fragile decay ; others worm-eaten, some mouse-eaten, many torn, half-way through ; numbers doubled (quadrupled, I should say,) up into four, being Turner's favourite mode of packing for travelling ; nearly all rudely flattened out from the bundles in which Turner had finally rolled them up and squeezed them into his drawers in Queen Anne Street. Dust of thirty years' accumulation, black, dense, and sooty, lay in the rents of the crushed and crumpled edges of these flattened bundles, looking like a jagged black frame, and producing altogether unexpected effects in brilliant portions of skies, whence an accidental or experimental finger mark of the first bundle-unfolder had swept it away.

About half, or rather more, of the entire number con-sisted of pencil sketches, in flat oblong pocket-books, dropping to pieces at the back, tearing laterally whenever opened, and every drawing rubbing itself into the one opposite. These first I paged with my own hand ; then unbound ; and laid every leaf separately in a clean sheet of perfectly smooth writing paper, so that it might receive no farther injury. Then, enclosing the contents and boards of each book (usually ninety-two leaves, more or less drawn on both sides, with two sketches on the boards at the beginning and end,) in a separate sealed packet, I returned it to its tin box. The loose sketches needed more trouble. The dust had first to be got off them ; (from the chalk ones it could only be blown off ;) then they had to be variously flattened ; the torn ones to be laid down, the loveliest guarded, so as to prevent all future friction ; and four hundred of the most characteristic framed and glazed, and cabinets constructed for them which would admit of their free use by the public.

---

[1] The best book of studies for his great shipwrecks contained about a quarter of a pound of chalk débris, black and white, broken off the crayons with which Turner had drawn furiously on both sides of the leaves ; every leaf, with peculiar foresight, and consideration of diffi-culties to be met by future mounters, containing half of one subject on the front of it, and half of another on the back.

With two assistants, I was at work all the autumn and winter of 1857, every day, all day long, and often far into the night.

3. The manual labour would not have hurt me; but the excitement involved in seeing unfolded the whole career of Turner's mind during his life, joined with much sorrow at the state in which nearly all his most precious work had been left, and with great anxiety, and heavy sense of responsibility besides, were very trying; and I have never in my life felt so much exhausted as when I locked the last box, and gave the keys to Mr. Wornum, in May, 1858. Among the later coloured sketches, there was one magnificent series, which appeared to be of some towns along the course of the Rhine on the north of Switzerland. Knowing that these towns were peculiarly liable to be injured by modern railroad works, I thought I might rest myself by hunting down these Turner subjects, and sketching what I could of them, in order to illustrate his compositions.

As I expected, the subjects in question were all on or near that east and west reach of the Rhine between Constance and Basle. Most of them are of Rheinfelden, Säckingen, Lauffenburg, Schaffhausen, and the Swiss Baden.

4. Having made what notes were possible to me of these subjects in the summer (one or two are used in this volume), I was crossing Lombardy in order to examine some points of the shepherd character in the Vaudois valleys, thinking to get my book finished next spring; when I unexpectedly found some good Paul Veroneses at Turin. There were several questions respecting the real motives of Venetian work that still troubled me not a little, and which I had intended to work out in the Louvre; but seeing that Turin was a good place wherein to keep out of people's way, I settled there instead, and began with Veronese's Queen of Sheba;—when, with much consternation, but more delight, I found that I had never got to the roots of the moral power of the Venetians, and that they needed still another and a very stern course of study. There was nothing for it but to give up the book for that year. The winter was spent mainly in trying to get at the

mind of Titian ; not a light winter's task ; of which the issue,
being in many ways very unexpected to me (the reader will
find it partly told towards the close of this volume), neces-
sitated my going in the spring to Berlin, to see Titian's
portrait of Lavinia there, and to Dresden to see the Tribute
Money, the elder Lavinia, and girl in white, with the flag
fan. Another portrait, at Dresden, of a lady in a dress of
rose and gold, by me unheard of before, and one of an
admiral, at Munich, had like to have kept me in Germany
all summer.

5. Getting home at last, and having put myself to
arrange materials of which it was not easy, after so much
interruption, to recover the command ;—which also were
now not reducible to a single volume—two questions
occurred in the outset, one in the section on vegetation,
respecting the origin of wood ; the other in the section on
sea, respecting curves of waves ; to neither of which, from
botanists or mathematicians, any sufficient answer seemed
obtainable.

In other respects also the section on the sea was wholly
unsatisfactory to me : I knew little of ships, nothing of
blue open water. Turner's pathetic interest in the sea,
and his inexhaustible knowledge of shipping, deserved more
complete and accurate illustration than was at all possible
to me ; and the mathematical difficulty lay at the beginning
of all demonstration of facts. I determined to do this
piece of work well, or not at all, and threw the proposed
section out of this volume. If I ever am able to do what
I want with it (and this is barely probable), it will be a
separate book ; which on other accounts, I do not regret,
since many persons might be interested in studies of the
shipping of the old Nelson times, and of the sea-waves and
sailor character of all times, who would not care to encum-
ber themselves with five volumes of a work on Art.

The vegetation question had, however, at all cost, to be
made out as best might be ; and again lost me much time.
Many of the results of this inquiry, also, can only be given,
if ever, in a detached form.

6. During these various discouragements, the preparation of the Plates could not go on prosperously. Drawing

is difficult enough, undertaken in quietness: it is impossible to bring it to any point of fine rightness with half-applied energy.

Many experiments were made in hope of expressing Turner's peculiar execution and touch by facsimile. They cost time, and strength, and, for the present, have failed; many elaborate drawings, made during the winter of 1858, having been at last thrown aside. Some good may afterwards come of these; but certainly not by reduction to the size of the page of this book, for which, even of smaller subjects, I have not prepared the most interesting, for I do not wish the possession of any effective and valuable engravings from Turner to be contingent on the purchasing a book of mine.[1]

Feebly and faultfully, therefore, yet as well as I can do it under these discouragements, the book is at last done; respecting the general course of which, it will be kind and well if the reader will note these few points that follow.

7. The first volume was the expansion of a reply to a magazine article; and was not begun because I then thought myself qualified to write a systematic treatise on Art; but because I at least knew, and knew it to be demonstrable, that Turner was right and true, and that his critics were wrong, false, and base. At that time I had seen much of nature, and had been several times in Italy, wintering once in Rome; but had chiefly delighted in northern art, beginning, when a mere boy, with Rubens and Rembrandt. It was long before I got quit of a boy's

---

[1] To Mr. Armytage, Mr. Cuff, and Mr. Cousen, I have to express my sincere thanks for the patience, and my sincere admiration of the skill, with which they have helped me. Their patience, especially, has been put to severe trial by the rewardless toil required to produce facsimiles of drawings in which the slightness of subject could never attract any due notice to the excellence of workmanship.

Aid, just as disinterested, and deserving of as earnest acknowledgment, has been given me by Miss Byfield, in her faultless facsimiles of my careless sketches; by Miss O. Hill, who prepared the copies which I required from portions of the pictures of the old masters; and by Mr. G. Allen, in accurate line studies from nature, of which, though only two are engraved in this volume, many others have been most serviceable both to it and to me.

veneration for Rubens' physical art-power; and the reader will, perhaps, on this ground forgive the strong expressions of admiration for Rubens, which, to my great regret, occur in the first volume.

Finding myself, however, engaged seriously in the essay, I went, before writing the second volume, to study in Italy; where the strong reaction from the influence of Rubens threw me at first too far under that of Angelico and Raphael; and, which was the worst harm that came of that Rubens influence, blinded me long to the deepest qualities of Venetian art; which, the reader may see by expressions occurring not only in the second, but even in the third and fourth volumes, I thought, however powerful, yet partly luxurious and sensual, until I was led into the final inquiries above related.

8. These oscillations of temper, and progressions of discovery, extending over a period of seventeen years, ought not to diminish the reader's confidence in the book. Let him be assured of this, that unless important changes are occurring in his opinions continually, all his life long, not one of those opinions can be on any questionable subject true. All true opinions are living, and show their life by being capable of nourishment; therefore of change. But their change is that of a tree—not of a cloud.

In the main aim and principle of the book, there is no variation, from its first syllable to its last. It declares the perfectness and eternal beauty of the work of God; and tests all work of man by concurrence with, or subjection to that. And it differs from most books, and has a chance of being in some respects better for the difference, in that it has not been written either for fame, or for money, or for conscience-sake, but of necessity.

It has not been written for praise. Had I wished to gain present reputation, by a little flattery adroitly used in some places, a sharp word or two withheld in others, and the substitution of verbiage generally for investigation, I could have made the circulation of these volumes tenfold what it has been in modern society. Had I wished for future fame I should have written one volume, not five. Also, it has not been written for money. In this wealth-producing country, seventeen years' labour could hardly have been invested with less chance of equivalent return.

Also, it has not been written for conscience-sake. I had no definite hope in writing it; still less any sense of its being required of me as a duty. It seems to me, and seemed always, probable, that I might have done much more good in some other way. But it has been written of necessity. I saw an injustice done, and tried to remedy it. I heard falsehood taught, and was compelled to deny it. Nothing else was possible to me. I knew not how little or how much might come of the business, or whether I was fit for it; but here was the lie full set in front of me, and there was no way round it, but only over it. So that, as the work changed like a tree, it was also rooted like a tree—not where it would, but where need was; on which, if any fruit grow such as you can like, you are welcome to gather it without thanks; and so far as it is poor or bitter, it will be your justice to refuse it without reviling.

wealth producing country, stubborn yellow labour could hardly have been invested with such chance of equivalent gains.

And, if it has not been written for compensation, I had no lucrative hope in writing it; it will bear any sense of reward you can attach to it, to a day. It seems to me, and I cannot think it probable, that I might have done much more good in some other way. But it has been written sincerely. I am no illusative dog, and tried to remedy it. I mean falsehood, naught, and was compelled to deny me. Nothing else was possible to me. I knew not how little or how much might come of the business, or whether I was fit for it; but here was the jar full set in order, and there was no way round it, but only over it. So that, as the world changed like a street, it was also melted to a tree—not where it would, but where head was; of which, if any fruit grow such as you can like, you are welcome to gather it without thanks; and so far as it prove bitter, it will be your justice to refuse it without blame.

TABLE OF CONTENTS

PART VI

OF LEAF BEAUTY

PART VII

OF CLOUD BEAUTY

PART VIII

OF IDEAS OF RELATION :—FIRST, OF INVENTION FORMAL

PART IX

OF IDEAS OF RELATION :—SECOND, OF INVENTION SPIRITUAL

LIST OF PLATES TO VOL. V.

The above Illustrations are, in this edition, printed from half-tone reproductions of the original plates.

MODERN PAINTERS

PART VI

OF LEAF BEAUTY

CHAPTER I

THE EARTH-VEIL

§ 1. "To dress it and to keep it."

That, then, was to be our work. Alas! what work have we set ourselves upon instead! How have we ravaged the garden instead of kept it—feeding our war-horses with its flowers, and splintering its trees into spear-shafts!

"And at the East a flaming sword."

Is its flame quenchless? and are those gates that keep the way indeed passable no more? or is it not rather that we no more desire to enter? For what can we conceive of that first Eden which we might not yet win back, if we chose? It was a place full of flowers, we say. Well: the flowers are always striving to grow wherever we suffer them; and the fairer, the closer. There may, indeed, have been a Fall of Flowers, as a Fall of Man; but assuredly creatures such as we are can now fancy nothing lovelier than roses and lilies, which would grow for us side by side, leaf overlapping leaf, till the Earth was white and red with them, if we cared to have it so. And Paradise was full of pleasant shades and fruitful avenues. Well: what hinders us from covering as much of the world as we like with pleasant shade, and pure blossom, and goodly fruit? Who forbids its valleys to be covered over with corn till they laugh and sing? Who prevents its dark forests, ghostly and un-inhabitable, from being changed into infinite orchards, wreathing the hills with frail-floreted snow, far away to the half-lighted horizon of April, and flushing the face of all the autumnal earth with glow of clustered food? But Paradise was a place of peace, we say, and all the animals were gentle servants to us. Well: the world would yet be a place of peace if we were all peacemakers, and gentle service should we have of its creatures if we gave them gentle mastery. But so long as we make sport of slaying bird and beast, so long as we choose to contend rather with our fellows than with our faults, and make battle-field of our meadows instead of pasture—so long, truly, the Flaming Sword will still turn every way, and the gates of Eden remain barred close enough, till we have sheathed the sharper flame of our own passions, and broken down the closer gates of our own hearts.

§ 2. I have been led to see and feel this more and more, as I considered the service which the flowers and trees, which man was at first appointed to keep, were in-tended to render to him in return for his care; and the services they still render to him, as far as he allows their influence, or fulfils his own task towards them. For what infinite wonderfulness there is in this vegetation, considered, as indeed it is, the means by which the earth becomes the companion of man—his friend and his teacher! In the conditions which we have traced in its rocks, there could only be seen preparation for his existence;—the characters which enable him to live on it safely, and to work with it easily—in all these it has been inanimate and passive; but vegetation is to it as an imperfect soul, given to meet the soul of man. The earth in its depths must remain dead and cold, incapable except of slow crystalline change; but at its surface, which human beings look upon and deal with, it ministers to them through a veil of strange intermediate being: which breathes, but has no voice; moves, but cannot leave its appointed place; passes through life without con-sciousness, to death without bitterness; wears the beauty of youth, without its passion; and declines to the weakness of age, without its regret.

§ 3. And in this mystery of intermediate being, entirely
subordinate to us, with which we can deal as we choose,
having just the greater power as we have the less responsibility for our treatment of the unsuffering creature, most
of the pleasures which we need from the external world are
gathered, and most of the lessons we need are written, all
kinds of precious grace and teaching being united in this
link between the Earth and Man ; wonderful in universal
adaptation to his need, desire, and discipline ; God's daily
preparation of the earth for him, with beautiful means of
life.   First, a carpet to make it soft for him ; then, a
coloured fantasy of embroidery thereon ; then, tall spreading of foliage to shade him from sun heat, and shade also
the fallen rain, that it may not dry quickly back into the
clouds, but stay to nourish the springs among the moss.
Stout wood to bear this leafage : easily to be cut, yet tough
and light, to make houses for him, or instruments (lance-
shaft, or plough-handle, according to his temper) ; useless
it had been, if harder ; useless, if less fibrous ; useless, if
less elastic.   Winter comes, and the shade of leafage falls
away, to let the sun warm the earth ; the strong boughs
remain, breaking the strength of winter winds.   The seeds
which are to prolong the race, innumerable according to the
need, are made beautiful and palatable, varied into infinitude
of appeal to the fancy of man, or provision for his service :
cold juice, or glowing spice, or balm, or incense, softening
oil, preserving resin, medicine of styptic, febrifuge, or lulling
charm : and all these presented in forms of endless change.
Fragility or force, softness and strength, in all degrees
and aspects ; unerring uprightness, as of temple pillars,
or unguided wandering of feeble tendrils on the ground ;
mighty resistances of rigid arm and limb to the storms of
ages, or wavings to and fro with faintest pulse of summer
streamlet.   Roots cleaving the strength of rock, or binding
the transience of the sand ; crests basking in sunshine of
the desert, or hiding by dripping spring and lightless cave ;
foliage far tossing in entangled fields beneath every wave of
ocean—clothing, with variegated, everlasting films, the peaks
of the trackless mountains, or ministering at cottage doors
to every gentlest passion and simplest joy of humanity.

§ 4. Being thus prepared for us in all ways, and made beautiful, and good for food, and for building, and for instruments of our hands, this race of plants, deserving boundless affection and admiration from us, becomes, in proportion to their obtaining it, a nearly perfect test of our being in right temper of mind and way of life; so that no one can be far wrong in either who loves the trees enough, and every one is assuredly wrong in both who does not love them, if his life has brought them in his way. It is clearly possible to do without them, for the great companionship of the sea and sky are all that sailors need; and many a noble heart has been taught the best it had to learn between dark stone walls. Still if human life be cast among trees at all, the love borne to them is a sure test of its purity. And it is a sorrowful proof of the mistaken ways of the world that the "country," in the simple sense of a place of fields and trees, has hitherto been the source of reproach to its inhabitants, and that the words "countryman, rustic, clown, paysan, villager," still signify a rude and untaught person, as opposed to the words "townsman" and "citizen." We accept this usage of words, or the evil which it signifies, somewhat too quietly; as if it were quite necessary and natural that country-people should be rude, and townspeople gentle. Whereas I believe that the result of each mode of life may, in some stages of the world's progress, be the exact reverse; and that another use of words may be forced upon us by a new aspect of facts, so that we may find ourselves saying: "Such and such a person is very gentle and kind—he is quite rustic; and such and such another person is very rude and ill-taught—he is quite urbane."

§ 5. At all events, cities have hitherto gained the better part of their good report through our evil ways of going on in the world generally: chiefly and eminently through our bad habit of fighting with each other. No field, in the middle ages, being safe from devastation, and every country lane yielding easier passage to the marauders, peacefully-minded men necessarily congregated in cities, and walled themselves in, making as few cross-country roads as possible: while the men who sowed and reaped

the harvests of Europe were only the servants or slaves of
the barons.   The disdain of all agricultural pursuits by the
nobility, and of all plain facts by the monks, kept educated
Europe in a state of mind over which natural phenomena
could have no power; body and intellect being lost in the
practice of war without purpose, and the meditation of
words without meaning.   Men learned the dexterity with
sword and syllogism, which they mistook for education,
within cloister and tilt-yard; and looked on all the broad
space of the world of God mainly as a place for exercise
of horses, or for growth of food.

§ 6. There is a beautiful type of this neglect of the perfectness of the Earth's beauty, by reason of the passions of
men, in that picture of Paul Uccello's of the battle of Sant'
Egidio,[1] in which the armies meet on a country road beside
a hedge of wild roses; the tender red flowers tossing above
the helmets, and glowing between the lowered lances.   For
in like manner the whole of Nature only shone hitherto for
man between the tossing of helmet-crests; and sometimes
I cannot but think of the trees of the earth as capable
of a kind of sorrow, in that imperfect life of theirs, as they
opened their innocent leaves in the warm spring-time, in vain
for men; and all along the dells of England her beeches
cast their dappled shade only where the outlaw drew his
bow, and the king rode his careless chase; and by the sweet
French rivers their long ranks of poplar waved in the
twilight, only to show the flames of burning cities on the
horizon, through the tracery of their stems; amidst the
fair defiles of the Apennines, the twisted olive-trunks hid
the ambushes of treachery; and on their valley meadows,
day by day, the lilies which were white at the dawn were
washed with crimson at sunset.

§ 7. And indeed I had once purposed, in this work, to
show what kind of evidence existed respecting the possible
influence of country life on men; it seeming to me, then,
likely that here and there a reader would perceive this to
be a grave question, more than most which we contend

---

[1] In our own National Gallery.   It is quaint and imperfect, but of
great interest.

about, political or social, and might care to follow it out with me earnestly.

The day will assuredly come when men will see that it *is* a grave question ; at which period, also, I doubt not, there will arise persons able to investigate it. For the present, the movements of the world seem little likely to be influenced by botanical law ; or by any other considerations respecting trees, than the probable price of timber. I shall limit myself, therefore, to my own simple woodman's work, and try to hew this book into its final shape, with the limited and humble aim that I had in beginning it, namely, to prove how far the idle and peaceable persons, who have hitherto cared about leaves and clouds, have rightly seen, or faithfully reported of them.

CHAPTER II

THE LEAF-ORDERS

§ 1. As in our sketch of the structure of mountains it seemed advisable to adopt a classification of their forms, which, though inconsistent with absolute scientific precision, was convenient for order of successive inquiry, and gave useful largeness of view ; so, and with yet stronger reason, in glancing at the first laws of vegetable life, it will be best to follow an arrangement easily remembered and broadly true, however incapable of being carried out into entirely consistent detail. I say, "with yet stronger reason," because more questions are at issue among botanists than among geologists ; a greater number of classifications have been suggested for plants than for rocks ; nor is it unlikely that those now accepted may be hereafter modified. I take an arrangement, therefore, involving no theory ; serviceable enough for all working purposes, and sure to remain thus serviceable, in its rough generality, whatever views may hereafter be developed among botanists.

§ 2. A child's division of plants is into "trees and flowers." If, however, we were to take him in spring, after he had gathered his lapful of daisies, from the lawn into the orchard, and ask him how he would call those wreaths of richer floret, whose frail petals tossed their foam of promise between him and the sky, he would at once see the need of some intermediate name, and call them, perhaps, "tree-flowers." If, then, we took him to a birch-wood, and showed him that catkins were flowers, as well as cherry-blossoms, he might, with a little help, reach so far as to divide all flowers into two classes ; one, those that grew on ground ; and another, those that grew on trees.

The botanist might smile at such a division; but an artist would not. To him, as to the child, there is something specific and distinctive in those rough trunks that carry the higher flowers. To him, it makes the main difference between one plant and another, whether it is to tell as a light upon the ground, or as a shade upon the sky. And if, after this, we asked for a little help from the botanist, and he were to lead us, leaving the blossoms, to look more carefully at leaves and buds, we should find ourselves able in some sort to justify, even to him, our childish classification. For our present purposes, justifiable or not, it is the most suggestive and convenient. Plants are, indeed, broadly referable to two great classes. The first we may, perhaps, not inexpediently call TENTED PLANTS. They live in encampments, on the ground, as lilies; or on surfaces of rock, or stems of other plants, as lichens and mosses. They live—some for a year, some for many years, some for myriads of years; but, perishing, they pass as the tented Arab passes: they leave *no memorials of themselves*, except the seed, or bulb, or root which is to perpetuate the race.

§ 3. The other great class of plants we may perhaps best call BUILDING PLANTS. These will *not* live on the ground, but eagerly raise edifices above it. Each works hard with solemn forethought all its life. Perishing, it leaves its work in the form which will be most useful to its successors—its own monument, and their inheritance. These architectural edifices we call "Trees."

It may be thought that this nomenclature already involves a theory. But I care about neither the nomenclature, nor about anything questionable in my description of the classes. The reader is welcome to give them what names he likes, and to render what account of them he thinks fittest. But to us, as artists, or lovers of art, this is the first and most vital question concerning a plant: "Has it a fixed form or a changing one? Shall I find it always as I do to-day —this Parnassia palustris—with one leaf and one flower? or may it some day have incalculable pomp of leaves and unmeasured treasure of flowers? Will it rise only to the height of a man—as an ear of corn—and perish like a

man; or will it spread its boughs
to the river, and enlarge its circle of s
thousand years?"

§ 4. This, I repeat, is the *first* question
plant. And as it answers, I range it on one side
other, among those that rest or those that toil; te
dwellers, who toil not, neither do they spin; or tree-
builders, whose days are as the days of a people. I find
again, on farther questioning these plants who rest, that
one group of them does indeed rest always, contentedly,
on the ground, but that those of another group, more
ambitious, emulate the builders; and though they cannot
build rightly, raise for themselves pillars out of the remains
of past generations, on which they themselves, living the
life of St. Simeon Stylites, are called, by courtesy, Trees;
being, in fact, many of them (palms, for instance) quite
as stately as real trees.[1]

These two classes we might call earth-plants, and pillar-
plants.

§ 5. Again, in questioning the true builders as to their
modes of work, I find that they also are divisible into
two great classes. Without in the least wishing the reader
to accept the fanciful nomenclature, I think he may yet
most conveniently remember these as "Builders with the
shield," and "Builders with the sword."

Builders with the shield have expanded leaves, more
or less resembling shields, partly in shape, but still more
in office; for under their lifted shadow the young bud
of the next year is kept from harm. These are the
gentlest of the builders, and live in pleasant places, pro-
viding food and shelter for man. Builders with the sword,
on the contrary, have sharp leaves in the shape of swords,
and the young buds, instead of being as numerous as the

---

[1] I am not sure that this is a fair account of palms. I have never
had opportunity of studying stems of Endogens, and I cannot understand the descriptions given of them in books, nor do I know how far
some of their branched conditions approximate to real tree-structure.
If this work, whatever errors it may involve, provokes the curiosity of
the reader so as to lead him to seek for more and better knowledge, it
will do all the service I hope from it.

leaf-shadow, are few in
...h in the midst of a sheaf
...in savage places, are sternly
...hey give much help to man
...ength, they (with few exceptions)
...imperfect shelter. Their mode of
...han that of the shield-builders, and
...ys resemble the pillar-plants of the oppo-
...we call them generally "Pines."
...ur work, in this section, will lie only among the
shield-builders, sword-builders, and plants of rest. The
Pillar-plants belong, for the most part, to other climates.
I could not analyze them rightly: and the labour given
to them would be comparatively useless for our present
purposes. The chief mystery of vegetation, so far as
respects external form, is among the fair shield-builders.
These, at least, we must examine fondly and earnestly.

CHAPTER III

THE BUD

§ 1. IF you gather, in summer time, an outer spray of any shield-leaved tree, you will find it consists of a slender rod, throwing out leaves, perhaps on every side, perhaps on two sides only, with usually a cluster of closer leaves at the end. In order to understand its structure, we must reduce it to a simple general type. Nay, even to a very inaccurate type. For a tree-branch is essentially a complex thing, and no "simple" type can, therefore, be a right one.

§ 2. This type I am going to give you is full of fallacies and inaccuracies; but out of these fallacies we will bring the truth by casting them aside one by one.

Let the tree spray be represented under one of these two types, A or B, Fig. 1, the cluster at the end being in each case supposed to consist of three leaves only (a most impertinent supposition, for it must at least have four, only the fourth would be in a puzzling perspective in A, and hidden behind the central leaf in B). So, receive this false type patiently. When leaves are set on the stalk one after another as in A, they are called "alternate;" when placed as in B, "opposite." It is necessary you should remember this not very difficult piece of nomenclature.

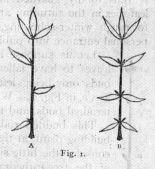

Fig. 1.

If you examine the branch you have gathered, you will
see that for some little way below the full-leaf cluster at
the end, the stalk is smooth, and the leaves are set regularly
on it.   But at six, eight, or ten inches down, there comes
an awkward knot ; something seems to have gone wrong,
perhaps another spray branches off there ; at all events, the
stem gets suddenly thicker, and you may break it there
(probably) easier than anywhere else.

That is the junction of two stories of the building.   The
smooth piece has all been done this summer.   At the knot
the foundation was left during the winter.

The year's work is called a "shoot."   I shall be glad
if you will break it off to look at, as my A and B types are
supposed to go no farther down than the knot.

The alternate form A is more frequent than B, and some
botanists think includes B.   We will, therefore, begin with it.

§ 3.   If you look close at the figure, you will see small
projecting points at the roots of the leaves.   These represent buds, which you may find, most probably, in the
shoot you have in your hand.   Whether you find them or
not, they are there—visible, or latent, does not matter.
Every leaf has assuredly an infant bud to take care of, laid
tenderly, as in a cradle, just where the leaf-stalk forms a
safe niche between it and the main stem.   The child-bud
is thus fondly guarded all summer ; but its protecting
leaf dies in the autumn ; and then the boy-bud is put out
to rough winter-schooling, by which he is prepared for
personal entrance into public life in the spring.

Let us suppose autumn to have come, and the
leaves to have fallen.   Then our A of Fig. 1, the
buds only being left, one for each leaf, will appear
as A B, in Fig. 2.   We will call the buds grouped at B,
terminal buds, and those at a, b, and c, lateral buds.

This budded rod is the true year's work of the
building plant, at that part of its edifice.   You may
consider the little spray, if you like, as one pinnacle
of the tree-cathedral, which has taken a year to
fashion ; innumerable other pinnacles having been
built at the same time on other branches.

Fig. 2.

§ 4.   Now, every one of these buds, a, b, and c, as well

J. Ruskin

J. C. Armytage

51. The Dryad's Toil.

as every terminal bud, has the power and disposition to
raise himself, in the spring, into just such another pinnacle
as A B is.

This development is the process we have mainly to study
in this chapter; but, in the outset, let us see clearly what
it is to end in.

Each bud, I said, has the power and disposition to make
a pinnacle of himself, but he has not always the opportunity.
What may hinder him we shall see presently.   Meantime,
the reader will, perhaps,
kindly allow me to assume
that the buds a, b, and
c, come to nothing, and
only the three terminal
ones build forward. Each
of these producing the
image of the first pinnacle,
we have the type for our
next summer bough of
Fig. 3; in which observe
the original shoot A B has
become thicker; its lateral
buds having proved abor-
tive, are now only seen as
little knobs on its sides.
Its terminal buds have
each risen into a new
pinnacle. The central or
strongest one, B C, has

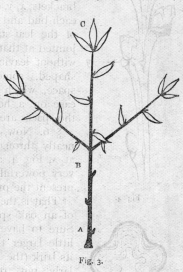

Fig. 3.

become the very image of what his parent shoot, A B, was
last year. The two lateral ones are weaker and shorter,
one probably longer than the other.   The joint at B is
the knot or foundation for each shoot above spoken of.

Knowing now what we are about, we will go into closer
detail.

§ 5. Let us return to the type in Fig. 2, of the fully
accomplished summer's work: the rod with its bare buds.
Plate 51, opposite, represents, of about half its real size, an
outer spray of oak in winter. It is not growing strongly,
and is as simple as possible in ramification.   You may

easily see, in each branch, the continuous piece of shoot
produced last year. The wrinkles which make these shoots
look like old branches are caused by drying, as the stalk
of a bunch of raisins is furrowed (the oak-shoot fresh
gathered is round as a grape stalk). I
draw them thus, because the furrows are
important clues to structure. Fig. 4 is
the top of one of these oak sprays
magnified for reference. The little
brackets, *x*, *y*, etc., which project beneath
each bud and sustain it, are the remains
of the leaf-stalks. Those stalks were
jointed at that place, and the leaves fell
without leaving a scar, only a crescent-
shaped, somewhat blank-looking flat
space, which you may study at your
ease on a horse-chestnut stem, where
the spaces are very large.

§ 6. Now, if you cut your oak spray
neatly through, just above a bud, as
at A, Fig. 4, and look at it with a not
very powerful magnifier, you will find it
present the pretty section, Fig. 5.

Fig. 4.

That is the proper or normal section
of an oak spray. Never quite regular.
Sure to have one of the projections a
little larger than the rest, and to have
its bark (the black line) not quite regularly put round it, but exquisitely
finished, down to a little white star in
the very centre, which I have not drawn,
because it would look in the woodcut
black, not white; and be too conspicuous.

Fig. 5.

The oak spray, however, will not keep this form unchanged for an instant. Cut it through a little way above
your first section, and you will find the largest projection
is increasing, till, just where it opens [1] at last into the

---

[1] The added portion, surrounding two of the sides of the pentagon,
is the preparation for the stalk of the leaf, which, on detaching itself
from the stem, presents variable sections, of which those numbered 1

leaf-stalk, its section is Fig. 6. If, therefore, you choose to consider every interval between bud and bud as one story of your tower or pinnacle, you find that there is literally not a hair's-breadth of the work in which the *plan* of the tower does not change. You may see in Plate 51 that every shoot is affected by a subtle (in nature an *infinitely* subtle) change of contour between bud and bud.

Fig. 6.

§ 7. But farther, observe in what succession those buds are put round the bearing stem. Let the section of the stem be represented

1   2   3   4

Fig. 7.

by the small central circle in Fig. 8 ; and suppose it surrounded by a *nearly* regular pentagon (in the figure it is quite regular for clearness' sake). Let the first of any ascending series of buds be represented by the curved projection filling the nearest angle of the pentagon at 1. Then the next bud, above, will fill the angle at 2 ; the next above at 3, the next at 4, the next at 5. The sixth will come nearly over the first. That is to say, each projecting portion of the section, Fig. 5, expands into its bud, not successively, but by leaps, always to the *next but one ;* the buds being thus placed in a nearly regular spiral order.

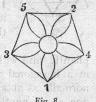

Fig. 8.

§ 8. I say nearly regular—for there are subtleties of variation in plan which it would be merely tiresome to

to 4, Fig. 7, are examples. I cannot determine the proper normal form. The bulb-shaped spot in the heart of the uppermost of the five projections in Fig. 6 is the root of the bud.

enter into. All that we need care about is the general law, of which the oak spray furnishes a striking example,—that the buds of the first great group of alternate builders rise in a spiral order round the stem (I believe, for the most part, the spiral proceeds from right to left). And this spiral succession very frequently approximates to the pentagonal order, which it takes with great accuracy in an oak; for, merely assuming that each ascending bud places itself as far as it can easily out of the way of the one beneath, and yet not quite on the opposite side of the stem, we find the interval between the two must generally approximate to that left between 1 and 2, or 2 and 3, in Fig. 8.[1]

§ 9. Should the interval be consistently a little *less* than

that which brings out the pentagonal structure, the plant seems to get at first into much difficulty. For, in such case, there is a probability of the buds falling into a triangle, as at A, Fig. 9; and then the fourth must come over the first, which would be inadmissible (we shall soon see why). Nevertheless, the plant seems to like the triangular result for its outline, and sets itself to get out of the difficulty with much ingenuity, by methods of succession which I will examine farther in the next chapter: it being enough for us to know at present that the puzzled but persevering vegetable *does* get out of its difficulty, and issues trium-

Fig. 9.

phantly, and with a peculiar expression of leafy exultation, in a hexagonal star, composed of two distinct triangles, normally as at B, Fig. 9. Why the buds do not like to be one above another, we shall see in next chapter. Meantime I must shortly warn the reader of what we shall then discover, that, though we have spoken of the projections of our pentagonal tower as if they were first built to sustain each its leaf, they are themselves chiefly built by the leaf they seem to sustain. Without troubling ourselves about

[1] For more accurate information the reader may consult Professor Lindley's *Introduction to Botany* (Longman, 1848), vol. i. p. 245, *et seqq.*

this yet, let us fix in our minds broadly the effective aspect of the matter, which is all we want, by a simple practical illustration.

§ 10. Take a piece of stick half-an-inch thick, and a yard or two long, and tie large knots, at any *equal* distances you choose, on a piece of pack-thread. Then wind the pack-thread round the stick, with any number of equidistant turns you choose, from one end to the other, and the knots will take the position of buds in the general type of alternate vegetation. By varying the number of knots and the turns of the thread, you may get the system of any tree, with the exception of one character only, viz., that since the shoot grows faster at one time than another, the buds run closer together when the growth is slow. You cannot imitate this structure by closing the coils of your string, for that would alter the positions of your knots irregularly. The intervals between the buds are, by this gradual acceleration or retardation of growth, usually varied in lovely proportions. Fig. 10 shows the elevations of the buds on five

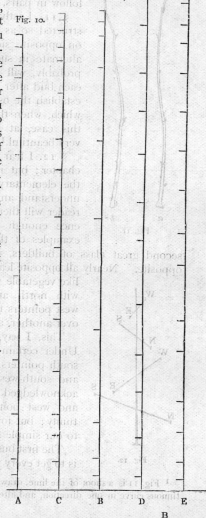

Fig. 10.

A   C   B   D   E

different sprays of oak; A and B being of the real size (short shoots); C, D, and E, on a reduced scale. I have not traced the cause of the apparent tendency of the buds to follow in pairs, in these longer shoots.

§ 11. Lastly: if the spiral be constructed so as to bring the buds nearly on opposite sides of the stem, though alternate in succession, the stem, most probably, will shoot a little away from each bud after throwing it off, and thus establish the oscillatory form *b*, Fig. 11, which, when the buds are placed, as in this case, at diminishing intervals, is very beautiful.[1]

§ 12. I fear this has been a tiresome chapter; but it is necessary to master the elementary structure, if we are to understand anything of trees; and the reader will therefore, perhaps, take patience enough to look at one or two examples of the spray structure of the second great class of builders, in which the leaves are opposite. Nearly all opposite-leaved trees grow, normally, like vegetable weathercocks run to seed, with north and south, and east and west pointers thrown off alternately one over another, as in Fig. 12.

a   b

Fig. 11

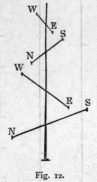

Fig. 12.

This, I say, is the normal condition. Under certain circumstances, north and south pointers set themselves north-east and south-west; this concession being acknowledged and imitated by the east and west pointers at the next opportunity; but for the present, let us keep to our simple form.

The first business of the budding stem, is to get every pair of buds set accurately

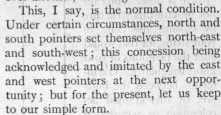

[1] Fig. 11 is a shoot of the lime, drawn on two sides, to show its continuous curve in one direction, and alternated curves in another. The

at right angles to the one below.   Here are some examples
of the way it contrives this.   A, Fig. 13, is the section
of the stem of a spray of box, magnified eight or nine

Fig. 13.

times, just where it throws off two of its leaves, suppose
on north and south sides.   The crescents below and
above are sections through the leaf-stalks thrown off on
each side.   Just above this joint, the section of the stem
is B, which is the normal section of a box-stem, as Fig. 5
is of an oak's.   This, as it ascends, becomes C, elongating
itself now east and west; and the section next to C would
be again A turned that way; or, taking the succession completely through two joints, and of the real size, it would
be thus : Fig. 14.

C   B   A   C   B   A   C

Fig. 14.

The stem of the spotted aucuba is normally hexagonal,
as that of the box is normally square.   It is very dexterous
and delicate in its mode of transformation to the two sides.

buds, which may be seen to be at equal heights in the two figures,
are exquisitely proportioned in their distances.   There is no end to the
refinement of system, if we choose to pursue it.

Through the joint it is A, Fig. 15. Above joint, B, normal
passing on into C, and D for the next joint.

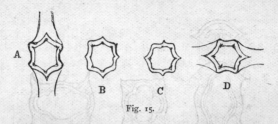

Fig. 15.

While in the horse-chestnut, a larger tree, and, as we
shall see hereafter, therefore less regular in conduct, the
section, normally hexagonal, is much rounded and softened

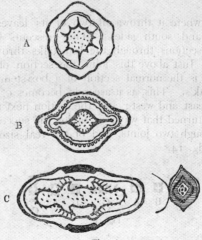

Fig. 16.

into irregularities; A, Fig. 16, becoming, as it buds, B and
c. The dark diamond beside c is a section through a
bud, in which, however small, the quatrefoil disposition
is always seen complete: the four little infant leaves with
a queen leaf in the middle, all laid in their fan-shaped

feebleness, safe in a white cloud of miniature woollen blanket.

§ 13. The elementary structure of all important trees may, I think, thus be resolved into three principal forms : three-leaved, Fig. 9; four-leaved, Figs. 13 to 16; and five-leaved, Fig. 8. Or, in well-known terms, trefoil, quatrefoil, cinqfoil. And these are essential classes, more complicated forms being usually, it seems to me, resolvable into these, but these not into each other. The simplest arrangement (Fig. 11), in which the buds are nearly opposite in position, though alternate in elevation, cannot, I believe, constitute a separate class, being only an accidental condition of the spiral. If it did, it might be called difoil; but the important classes are three :—

> Trefoil,   Fig.   9 : Type, Rhododendron.
> Quatrefoil, Fig. 13 : Type, Horse-chestnut.
> Cinqfoil,   Fig.   5 : Type, Oak.

§ 14. The coincidences between beautiful architecture and the construction of trees must more and more have become marked in the reader's mind as we advanced; and if he will now look at what I have said in other places of the use and meaning of the trefoil, quatrefoil, and cinqfoil, in Gothic architecture, he will see why I could hardly help thinking and speaking of all trees as builders. But there is yet one more subtlety in their way of building which we have not noticed. If the reader will look carefully at the separate shoots in Plate 51, he will see that the furrows of the stems fall in almost every case into continuous spiral curves, carrying the whole system of buds with them. This superinduced spiral action, of which we shall perhaps presently discover the cause, often takes place vigorously, producing completely twisted stems of great thickness. It is nearly always existent slightly, giving farther grace and change to the whole wonderful structure. And thus we have, as the final result of one year's vegetative labour on any single spray, a twisted tower, not similar at any height of its building : or (for, as we shall see presently, it loses in diameter at each bud) a twisted spire, correspondent somewhat in principle to the twisted spire of Dijon, or twisted

fountain of Ulm, or twisted shafts of Verona. Bossed as
it ascends with living sculpture, chiselled, not by diminution
but through increase, it rises by one consistent impulse from
its base to its minaret, ready, in spring-time, to throw round
it at the crest at once the radiance of fresh youth and the
promise of restoration after that youth has passed away. A
marvellous creation ; nay, might we not almost say, a marvellous creature, full of prescience in its infancy, foreboding
even, in the earliest gladness of its opening to sunshine, the
hour of fainting strength and falling leaf, and guarding under
the shade of its faithful shields the bud that is to bear its
hope through winter's shieldless sleep ?

Men often look to bring about great results by violent
and unprepared effort. But it is only in fair and forecast
order, "as the earth bringeth forth her bud," that righteousness and praise may spring forth before the nations.

CHAPTER IV

THE LEAF

§ 1. HAVING now some clear idea of the position of the bud, we have next to examine the forms and structure of its shield—the leaf which guards it. You will form the best general idea of the flattened leaf of shield-builders by thinking of it as you would of a mast and sail. More consistently with our classification, we might perhaps say, by thinking always of the arm sustaining the shield; but we should be in danger of carrying fancy too far, and the likeness of mast and sail is closer, for the mast tapers as the leaf-rib does, while the hand holding the uppermost strap of the buckler clenches itself. Whichever figure we use, it will cure us of the bad habit of imagining a leaf composed of a short stalk with a broad expansion at the end of it. Whereas we should always think of the stalk as running right up the leaf to its point, and carrying the expanded, or foliate part, as the mast of a lugger does its sail. To some extent, indeed, it has yards also, ribs branching from the innermost one; only the yards of the leaf will not run up and down, which is one essential function of a sailyard.

§ 2. The analogy will, however, serve one step more. As the sail must be on one side of the mast, so the expansion of a leaf is on one side of its central rib, or of its system of ribs. It is laid over them as if it were stretched over a frame, so that on the upper surface it is comparatively smooth; on the lower, barred. The understanding of the broad relations of these parts is the principal work we have to do in this chapter.

§ 3. First, then, you may roughly assume that the section

of any leaf-mast will be a crescent, as at *a*, Fig. 17 (compare

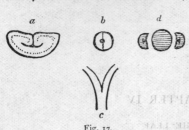

Fig. 7 above). The flat side is the uppermost, the round side underneath, and the flat or upper side carries the leaf. You can at once see the convenience of this structure for fitting to a central stem. Suppose the central stem

Fig. 17.

has a little hole in the centre, *b*, Fig. 17, and that you cut it down through the middle (as terrible knights used to cut their enemies in the dark ages, so that half the head fell on one side, and half on the other) : Pull the two halves separate, *c*, and they will nearly represent the shape and position of opposite leaf-ribs. In reality the leaf-stalks have to fit themselves to the central stem, *a*, and as we shall see presently, to lap round it ; but we must not go too fast.

§ 4. Now, *a*, Fig. 17, being the general type of a leaf-stalk, Fig. 18 is the general type of the way it expands

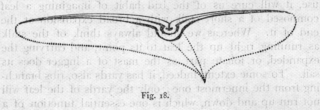

Fig. 18.

into and carries its leaf ;[1] this figure being the enlargement of a typical section right across any leaf, the dotted lines show the under surface foreshortened. You see I have made one side broader than the other. I mean that. It is typically so. Nature cannot endure two sides of a leaf to be alike. By encouraging one side more than the other,

---

[1] I believe the undermost of the two divisions of the leaf represents vegetable tissue *returning* from the extremity. See Lindley's *Introduction to Botany* (1848), vol. i. p. 253.

either by giving it more air or light, or perhaps in a chief degree by the mere fact of the moisture necessarily accumulating on the lower edge when it rains, and the other always drying first, she contrives it so, that if the essential form or idea of the leaf be *a*, Fig. 19, the actual form will always be *c*, or an approximation to it; one half being pushed in advance of the other, as at *b*, and all reconciled by soft curvature, *c*. The effort of the leaf to keep itself symmetrical rights it, however, often at the point, so that the insertion of the stalk only makes the inequality manifest. But it follows that the sides of a straight section across the leaf are unequal all the way up, as in my drawing, except at one point.

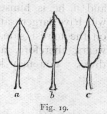

Fig. 19.

§ 5. I have represented the two wings of the leaf as slightly convex on the upper surface. This is also on the whole a typical character. I use the expression "wings of the leaf," because, supposing we exaggerate the main rib a little, the section will generally resemble a bad painter's type of a bird (*a*, Fig. 20). Sometimes the outer edges curl up, *b*, but an entirely concave form, *c*, is rare. When *b* is strongly developed, closing well in, the leaf gets a good deal the look of a boat with a keel.

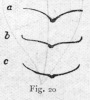

Fig. 20

§ 6. If now you take this oblique form of sail, and cut it into any required number of pieces down to its mast, as in Fig. 21, A, and then suppose each of the pieces to contract into studding-sails at the side, you will have whatever type of divided leaf you choose to shape it for. In Fig. 21, A, B, I have taken the rose, as the simplest type. The leaf is given in separate contour at C; but that of the mountain ash, A, Fig. 22, suggests the original oval form which encloses all the subdivisions much more beautifully. Each of the studding-sails in this ash-leaf looks much at first as if he were himself a mainsail. But you may know him always to be a subordinate, by observing that the inequality of the two sides, which is brought about

by accidental influences in the mainsail, is an organic law
in the studding-sail. The real leaf tries to set itself evenly
on its mast; and the inequality is only a graceful concession to circumstances. But the subordinate or studding-
sail is always *by law* larger at one side than the other;
and if he is himself again divided into smaller sails, he
will have larger sails on the lowest side, or one more sail
on the lowest side, than he has on the other. He always
wears, therefore, a servant's, or, at least, subordinate's
dress. You may know him anywhere as not the master.

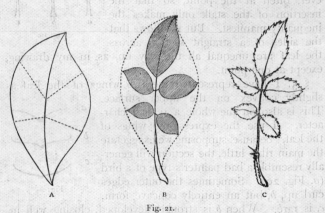

Fig. 21.

Even in the ash leaflet, of which I have outlined one
separately, B, Fig. 22, this is clearly seen; but it is much
more distinct in more finely divided leaves.[1]

§ 7. Observe, then, that leaves are broadly divisible
into mainsails and studding-sails; but that the word *leaf*
is properly to be used only of the mainsail; leaflet is the
best word for minor divisions; and whether these minor
members are only separated by deep cuts, or become complete stalked leaflets, still they are always to be thought of
merely as parts of a true leaf.

It follows from the mode of their construction that

[1] For farther notes on this subject, see my *Elements of Drawing*,
p. 286, [§ 214, new ed.]

leaflets must always lie more or less *flat*, or edge to edge,
in a continuous plane.   This position distinguishes them
from true leaves as much as their oblique form, and distinguishes them with the same delicate likeness of system ;
for as the true leaf takes, accidentally and partially, the

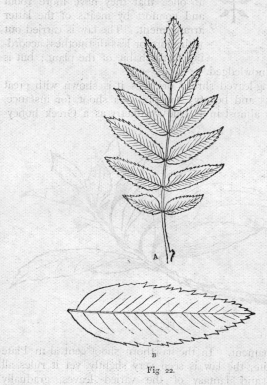

Fig 22.

oblique outline which is legally required in the subordinate,
so the true leaf takes accidentally and partially the flat disposition which is legally required in the subordinate.   And
this point of position we must now study.   Henceforward,
throughout this chapter, the reader will please note that I
speak only of true *leaves*, not of *leaflets*.

§ 8. LAW I. THE LAW OF DEFLECTION.—The first

law, then, respecting position in true leaves, is that they
fall gradually back from the upper-
most one, or uppermost group. They
are never set as at *a*, Fig. 23, but
always as at *b*. The reader may see
at once that they have more room
and comfort by means of the latter
arrangement. The law is carried out
with more or less distinctness according to the habit of the plant; but is
always acknowledged.

a   *b*

Fig. 23.

In strong-leaved shrubs or trees it is shown with great
distinctness and beauty: the phillyrea shoot, for instance,
Fig. 24, is almost in as true symmetry as a Greek honey-

Fig. 24.

suckle ornament. In the hawthorn shoot central in Plate
52, opposite, the law is seen very slightly, yet it rules all
the play and fantasy of the varied leaves, gradually
depressing their lines as they are set lower. In crowded
foliage of large trees, the disposition of each separate leaf
is not so manifest. For there is a strange coincidence in
this between trees and communities of men. When the
community is small, people fall more easily into their places,
and take, each in his place, a firmer standing than can
be obtained by the individuals of a great nation. The

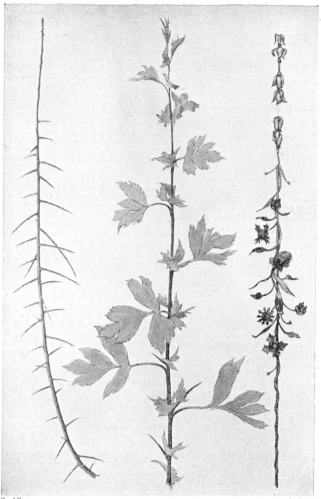

G Allen

G. Cook

52. Spirals of Thorn

members of a vast community are separately weaker, as an aspen or elm leaf is thin, tremulous, and directionless, compared with the spear-like setting and firm substance of a rhododendron or laurel leaf. The laurel and rhododendron are like the Athenian or Florentine republics; the aspen like England—strong-trunked enough when put to proof, and very good for making cartwheels of, but shaking pale with epidemic panic at every breeze. Nevertheless, the aspen has the better of the great nation, in that if you take it bough by bough, you shall find the gentle law of respect and room for each other truly observed by the leaves in such broken way as they can manage it; but in the nation you find every one scrambling for his neighbour's place.

This, then, is our first law, which we may generally call the Law of Deflection, or, if the position of the leaves with respect to the root be regarded, of Radiation. The second is more curious, and we must go back over our ground a little to get at it.

§ 9. LAW II. THE LAW OF SUCCESSION.—From what we saw of the position of buds, it follows that in every tree the leaves at the end of the spray, taking the direction given them by the uppermost cycle or spiral of the buds, will fall naturally into a starry group, expressive of the order of their growth. In an oak we shall have a cluster of five leaves, in a horse-chestnut of four, in a rhododendron of six, and so on. But observe, if we draw the oak-leaves

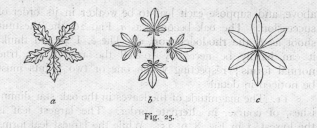

a   *b*   *c*

Fig. 25.

all equal, as at *a*, Fig. 25, or the chestnuts (*b*), or the rhododendron's (*c*), you instantly will feel, or ought to feel, that something is wrong; that those are not foliage forms —not even normally or typically so—but dead forms, like

crystals of snow. Considering this, and looking back to
last chapter, you will see that the buds which throw out
these leaves do not grow side by side, but one above
another. In the oak and rhododendron, all five and all
six buds are at different heights; in the chestnut, one
couple is above the other couple.

§ 10. Now, so surely as one bud is above another, it
must be stronger or weaker than that other. The shoot
may either be increasing in strength as it advances, or
declining; in either case, the buds must vary in power,
and the leaves in size. At the top of the shoot, the last or
uppermost leaves are mostly the smallest; of course always
so in spring as they develope.

Let us then apply these conditions to our formal figure

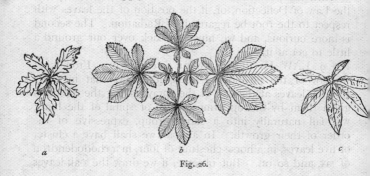

Fig. 26.

above, and suppose each leaf to be weaker in its order of
succession. The oak becomes as *a*, Fig. 26, the chestnut
shoot as *b*, the rhododendron, *c*. These, I should think,
it can hardly be necessary to tell the reader, are true
normal forms; respecting which one or two points must
be noticed in detail.

§ 11. The magnitude of the leaves in the oak star dimin-
ishes, of course, in alternate order. The largest leaf is
the lowest, 1 in Fig. 8, p. 15. While the largest leaf forms
the bottom, next it, opposite each other, come the third
and fourth, in order and magnitude, and the fifth and
second from the top. An oak star is, therefore, always an
oblique star; but in the chestnut and other quatrefoil trees,

though the uppermost couple of leaves must always be smaller than the lowermost couple, there appears no geometrical reason why the opposite leaves of each couple should vary in size. Nevertheless, they always do, so that

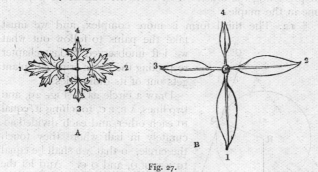

Fig. 27.

the quatrefoil becomes oblique as well as the cinqfoil, as you see it is in Fig. 26.

The normal of four-foils is therefore as in Fig. 27, A

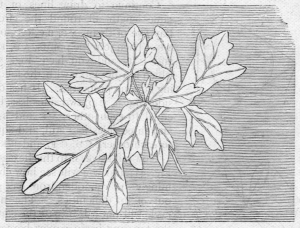

Fig. 28.

(maple), with magnitudes, in order numbered; but it often happens that an opposite pair agree to become largest and smallest; thus giving the pretty symmetry, Fig. 27, B, (spotted aucuba). Of course the quatrefoil in reality is always less formal, one pair of leaves more or less hiding or preceding the other. Fig. 28 is the outline of a young one in the maple.

§ 12. The third form is more complex, and we must take the pains to follow out what we left unobserved in last chapter respecting the way a triplicate plant gets out of its difficulties.

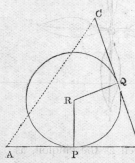

Fig. 29.

Draw a circle as in Fig. 29, and two lines, A B, B C, touching it, equal to each other, and each divided accurately in half where they touch the circle, so that A P shall be equal to P B, B Q, and Q C. And let the lines A B and B C be so placed that a dotted line A C, joining their extremities, would not be much longer than either of them.

Continue to draw lines of the same length all round the circle. Lay five of them, A B, B C, C D, D E, E F. Then join the points, A D, E B, and C F, and you have Fig. 30, which is a hexagon, with the following curious properties. It has one side largest, C D, two sides less, but equal to each other, A E and B F; and three sides less still, and equal to each other, A D, C F, and B E.

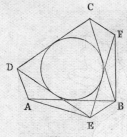

Fig. 30.

Now put leaves into this hexagon, Fig. 31, and you will see how charmingly the rhododendron has got out of its difficulties. The next cycle will put a leaf in at the gap at the top, and begin a new hexagon. Observe, however, this geometrical figure is only to the rhododendron

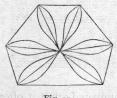

Fig. 31.

what the *a* in Fig. 25 is to the oak, the icy or dead form.

To get the living normal form we must introduce our law
of succession. That is to say, the five
lines A B, B C, etc., must continually
diminish, as they proceed, and therefore,
continually approach the centre; roughly
as in Fig. 32.

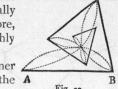

§ 13. I dread entering into the finer
properties of this construction, but the **A**
reader cannot now fail to feel their

Fig. 32.

B

beautiful result either in the cluster in Fig. 26, or here
in Fig. 33, which is a richer and more oblique one. The

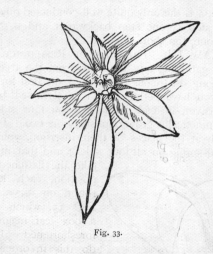

Fig. 33.

three leaves of the uppermost triad are perfectly seen,
closing over the bud; and the general form is clear,
though the lower triads are confused to the eye by unequal development, as in these complex arrangements is
almost always the case. The more difficulties are to be
encountered the more license is given to the plant in
dealing with them, and we shall hardly ever find a rhododendron shoot fulfilling its splendid spiral as an oak does
its simple one.

Here, for instance, is the actual order of ascending leaves in four rhododendron shoots which I gather at random.

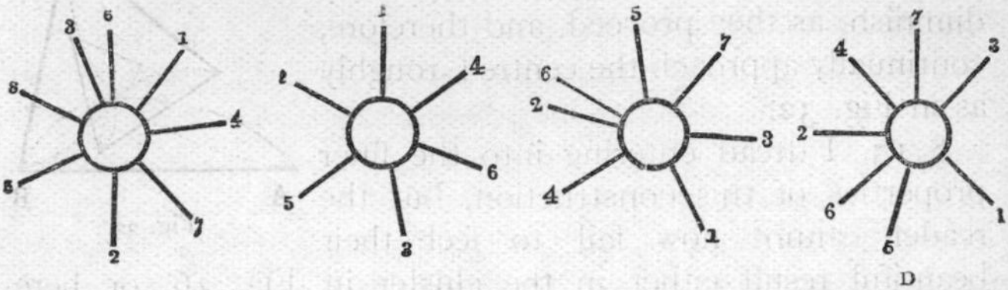

Fig. 34.

Of these, A is the only quite well-conducted one ; B takes one short step, C, one step backwards, and D, two steps back, and one, too short, forward.

§ 14. LAW III. THE LAW OF RESILIENCE.—If you have been gathering any branches from the trees I have named among quatrefoils (the box is the best for exemplification), you have perhaps been embarrassed by finding that the leaves, instead of growing on four sides of the stem, did practically grow oppositely on two. But if you look closely at the places of their insertion, you will find they indeed spring on all four sides ; and that in order to

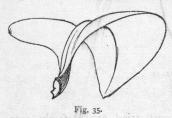

Fig. 35.

take the flattened opposite position, each leaf twists round on its stalk, as in Fig. 35, which represents a box-leaf magnified and foreshortened. The leaves do this in order to avoid growing downwards, where the position of the bough and bud would, if the leaves regularly kept their places, involve downward growth. The leaves always rise up on each side from beneath, and form a flattened group, more or less distinctly in proportion to the horizontality of the bough, and the contiguity of foliage below and above. I shall not trouble myself to illustrate this law, as you have only to gather a few tree-sprays to see its effect. But you must note the resulting characters on *every* leaf; namely, that not one leaf in a thousand grows without a fixed turn in its stalk, warping and varying the whole of the curve on the two edges throughout its length, and thus producing the loveliest conditions of its form. We shall presently trace the law of resilience farther on a larger scale: meanwhile, in summing the results of our inquiry thus far, let us remember that every one of these laws is observed with varying accuracy and gentle equity, according not only to the strength and fellowship of foliage on the spray itself, but according to the place and circumstances of its growth.

§ 15. For the leaves, as we shall see immediately, are the feeders of the plant. Their own orderly habits of succession must not interfere with their main business of finding food. Where the sun and air are, the leaf must go, whether it be out of order or not. So, therefore, in any group, the first consideration with the young leaves is much like that of young bees, how to keep out of each other's way, that every one may at once leave its neighbours as much free-air pasture as possible, and obtain a relative freedom for itself. This would be a quite simple matter, and produce other simply balanced forms, if each branch, with open air all round it, had nothing to think of but reconcilement of interests among its own leaves. But every branch has others to meet or to cross, sharing with them, in various advantage, what shade, or sun, or rain is to be had. Hence every single leaf-cluster presents the general aspect of a little family, entirely at unity among themselves, but obliged to get their living by various shifts, concessions, and infringements of the family rules, in order not to invade the privileges of other people in their neighbourhood.

§ 16. And in the arrangement of these concessions there is an exquisite sensibility among the leaves. They do not grow each to his own liking, till they run against one another, and then turn back sulkily; but by a watchful instinct, far apart, they anticipate their companions' courses, as ships at sea, and in every new unfolding of their edged tissue, guide themselves by the sense of each other's remote presence, and by a watchful penetration of leafy purpose in

the far future. So that every shadow which one casts on
the next, and every glint of sun which each reflects to the
next, and every touch which in toss of storm each receives
from the next, aid or arrest the development of their advancing form, and direct, as will be safest and best, the
curve of every fold and the current of every vein.

§ 17. And this peculiar character exists in all the structures thus developed, that they are always visibly the result
of a volition on the part of the leaf, meeting an external
force or fate, to which it is never passively subjected. Upon
it, as on a mineral in the course of formation, the great
merciless influences of the universe, and the oppressive
powers of minor things immediately near it, act continually.
Heat and cold, gravity and the other attractions, windy
pressure, or local and unhealthy restraint, must, in certain
inevitable degrees, affect the whole of its life. But it is
life which they affect;—a life of progress and will,—not a
merely passive accumulation of substance. This may be
seen by a single glance. The mineral—suppose an agate
in the course of formation—shows in every line nothing
but a dead submission to surrounding force. Flowing, or
congealing, its substance is here repelled, there attracted,
unresistingly to its place, and its languid sinuosities follow
the clefts of the rock that contains them, in servile deflexion
and compulsory cohesion, impotently calculable, and cold.
But the leaf, full of fears and affections, shrinks and seeks,
as it obeys. Not thrust, but awed into its retiring; not
dragged, but won to its advance; not bent aside, as by a
bridle, into new courses of growth : but persuaded and con-
verted through tender continuance of voluntary change.

§ 18. The mineral and it differing thus widely in separate
being, they differ no less in modes of companionship. The
mineral crystals group themselves neither in succession,
nor in sympathy; but great and small recklessly strive for
place, and deface or distort each other as they gather into
opponent asperities. The confused crowd fills the rock
cavity, hanging together in a glittering, yet sordid heap, in
which nearly every crystal, owing to their vain contention,
is imperfect, or impure. Here and there one, at the cost
and in defiance of the rest, rises into unwarped shape or

unstained clearness.   But the order of the leaves is one of soft and subdued concession.   Patiently each awaits its appointed time, accepts its prepared place, yields its required observance.   Under every oppression of external accident, the group yet follows a law laid down in its own heart ; and all the members of it, whether in sickness or health, in strength or languor, combine to carry out this first and last heart law ; receiving, and seeming to desire for themselves and for each other, only life which they may communicate, and loveliness which they may reflect.

CHAPTER V

LEAF ASPECTS

§ 1. BEFORE following farther our inquiry into tree structure, it will rest us, and perhaps forward our work a little, to make some use of what we know already.

It results generally from what we have seen, that any group of four or five leaves, presenting itself in its natural position to the eye, consists of a series of forms connected by exquisite and complex symmetries, and that these forms will be not only varied in themselves, but every one of them seen under a different condition of foreshortening.

The facility of drawing the group may be judged of by a comparison. Suppose five or six boats, very beautifully built, and sharp in the prow, to start all from one point, and the first bearing up into the wind, the other three or four to fall off from it in succession an equal number of points,[1] taking each, in consequence, a different slope of deck from the stem of the sail. Suppose, also, that the bows of these boats were transparent, so that you could see the under sides of their decks, as well as the upper ;— and that it were required of you to draw all their five decks, the under or upper side, as their curve showed it, in true foreshortened perspective, indicating the exact distance each boat had reached at a given moment from the central point they started from.

If you can do that, you can draw a rose-leaf. Not otherwise.

§ 2. When, some few years ago, the pre-Raphaelites began to lead our wandering artists back into the eternal

---

[1] I don't know that this is rightly expressed ; but the meaning will be understood.

paths of all great Art, and showed that whatever men drew at all, ought to be drawn accurately and knowingly; not blunderingly nor by guess (leaves of trees, among other things): as ignorant pride on the one hand refused their teaching, ignorant hope caught at it on the other. "What!" said many a feeble young student to himself. "Painting is not a matter of science then, nor of supreme skill, nor of inventive brain. I have only to go and paint the leaves of the trees as they grow, and I shall produce beautiful landscapes directly."

Alas! my innocent young friend. "Paint the leaves as they grow!" If you can paint *one* leaf, you can paint the world. These pre-Raphaelite laws, which you think so light, lay stern on the strength of Apelles and Zeuxis; put Titian to thoughtful trouble; are unrelaxed yet, and unrelaxable for ever. Paint a leaf indeed! Above-named Titian has done it: Correggio, moreover, and Giorgione: and Leonardo, very nearly, trying hard. Holbein, three or four times, in precious pieces, highest wrought. Raphael, it may be, in one or two crowns of Muse or Sibyl. If any one else, in later times, we have to consider.

§ 3. At least until recently, the perception of organic leaf form was absolutely, in all painters whatsoever, proportionate to their power of drawing the human figure. All the great Italian designers drew leaves thoroughly well, though none quite so fondly as Correggio. Rubens drew them coarsely and vigorously, just as he drew limbs. Among the inferior Dutch painters, the leaf-painting degenerates in proportion to the diminishing power in figure. Cuyp, Wouvermans, and Paul Potter, paint better foliage than either Hobbima or Ruysdael.

§ 4. In like manner the power of treating vegetation in sculpture is absolutely commensurate with nobleness of figure design. The quantity, richness, or deceptive finish may be greater in third-rate work; but in true understanding and force of arrangement the leaf and the human figure show always parallel skill. The leaf-mouldings of Lorenzo Ghiberti are unrivalled, as his bas-reliefs are, and the severe foliage of the Cathedral of Chartres is as grand as its queen-statues.

§ 5. The greatest draughtsmen draw leaves, like every-thing else, of their full-life size in the nearest part of the picture. They cannot be rightly drawn on any other terms. It is impossible to reduce a group so treated without losing much of its character; and more painfully impossible to represent by engraving any good workman's handling. I intended to have inserted in this place an engraving of the cluster of oak-leaves above Correggio's Antiope in the Louvre, but it is too lovely; and if I am able to engrave it at all, it must be separately, and of its own size. So I draw roughly, instead, a group of oak-leaves on a young shoot, a little curled with autumn frost: Plate 53. I could not draw them accurately enough if I drew them in spring. They would droop and lose their relations. Thus roughly drawn, and losing some of their grace, by withering, they, nevertheless, have enough left to show how noble leaf-form is; and to prove, it seems to me, that Dutch dmughts-men do not wholly express it. For instance, Fig 3, Plate 54, is a facsimile of a bit of the nearest oak foliage out of Hobbima's Scene with the Water-mill, No. 131, in the Dulwich Gallery. Compared with the real forms of oak-leaf, in Plate 53, it may, I hope, at least enable my readers to understand, if they choose, why, never having ceased to rate the Dutch painters for their meanness or minuteness, I yet accepted the leaf-painting of the pre-Raphaelites with reverence and hope.

§ 6. No word has been more harmfully misused than that ugly one of "niggling." I should be glad if it were entirely banished from service and record. The only essential question about drawing is whether it be right or wrong; that it be small or large, swift or slow, is a matter of convenience only. But so far as the word may be legiti-mately used at all, it belongs especially to such execution as this of Hobbima's — execution which substitutes, on whatever scale, a mechanical trick or habit of hand for true drawing of known or intended forms. So long as the work is thoughtfully directed, there is no niggling. In a small Greek coin the muscles of the human body are as grandly treated as in a colossal statue; and a fine vignette of Turner's will show separate touches often more extended

J Ruskin
53 The Dryad's Crown
J. C. Armytage

Cuyp and Hobbima   J. Cousen

54. Dutch Leafage

in intention, and stronger in result, than those of his
largest oil pictures. In the vignette of the picture of
Ginevra, at page 90 of Rogers's Italy, the forefinger touching the lip is entirely and rightly drawn, bent at the two
joints, within the length of the thirtieth of an inch, and the
whole hand within the space of one of those "niggling"
touches of Hobbima. But if this work were magnified, it
would be seen to be a strong and simple expression of a
hand by thick black lines.

§ 7. Niggling, therefore, essentially means disorganized
and mechanical work, applied on a scale which may deceive
a vulgar or ignorant person into the idea of its being true:
a definition applicable to the whole of the leaf-painting
of the Dutch landscapists in distant effect, and for the
most part to that of their near subjects also. Cuyp and
Wouvermans, as before stated, and others, in proportion to
their power over the figure, drew leaves better in the foreground, yet never altogether well; for though Cuyp often
draws a single leaf carefully (weedy ground-vegetation especially, with great truth), he never felt the connection of
leaves, but scattered them on the boughs at random. Fig. 1
in Plate 54 is nearly a *facsimile* of part of the branch on
the left side in our National Gallery picture. Its entire
want of grace and organization ought to be felt at a glance,
after the work we have gone through. The average conditions of leafage-painting among the Dutch are better
represented by Fig. 2, Plate 54, which is a piece of the
foliage from the Cuyp in the Dulwich Gallery, No. 163.
It is merely wrought with a mechanical play of brush in
a well-trained hand, gradating the colour irregularly and
agreeably, but with no more feeling or knowledge of leafage
than a paper-stainer shows in graining a pattern. A bit of
the stalk is seen on the left; it might just as well have
been on the other side, for any connection the leaves have
with it. As the leafage retires into distance, the Dutch
painters merely diminish their *scale* of touch. The touch
itself remains the same, but its effect is falser; for though
the separate stains or blots in Fig. 2 do not rightly represent the forms of leaves, they may not inaccurately
represent the number of leaves on that spray. But in

distance, when, instead of one spray, we have thousands in sight, no human industry, nor possible diminution of touch, can represent their mist of foliage, and the Dutch work becomes doubly base, by reason of false form, and lost infinity.

§ 8. Hence what I said in our first inquiry about foliage (Vol. I., p. 214). "A single dusty roll of Turner's brush is more truly expressive of the infinitude of foliage than the niggling of Hobbima could have rendered his canvas, if he had worked on it till doomsday." And this brings me to the main difficulty I have had in preparing this section. That infinitude of Turner's execution attaches not only to his distant work, but in due degree to the nearest pieces of his trees. As I have shown in the chapter on mystery, he perfected the system of art, as applicable to landscape, by the introduction of this infiniteness. In other qualities he is often only equal, in some inferior, to great preceding painters; but in this mystery he stands alone. He could not paint a cluster of leaves better than Titian; but he could a bough, much more a distant mass of foliage. No man ever before painted a distant tree rightly, or a full-leaved branch rightly. All Titian's distant branches are ponderous flakes, as if covered with seaweed, while Veronese's and Raphael's are conventional, being exquisitely ornamental arrangements of small perfect leaves. See the background of the Parnassus in Volpato's plate. It is very lovely, however.

§ 9. But this peculiar execution of Turner's is entirely uncopiable; least of all to be copied in engraving. It is at once so dexterous and so keenly cunning, swiftest play of hand being applied with concentrated attention on every movement, that no care in facsimile will render it. The delay in the conclusion of this work has been partly caused by the failure of repeated attempts to express this execution. I see my way now to some partial result; but must get the writing done, and give undivided care to it before I attempt to produce costly plates. Meanwhile, the little cluster of foliage opposite, from the thicket which runs up the bank on the right-hand side of the drawing of Richmond, looking up the river, in the Yorkshire series,

J. M. W. Turner

J. C. Armytage

55. By the Wayside

will give the reader some idea of the mingled definiteness
and mystery of Turner's work, as opposed to the mechanism
of the Dutch on the one side, and the conventional severity
of the Italians on the other. It should be compared with
the published engraving in the Yorkshire series ; for just
as much increase, both in quantity and refinement, would
be necessary in every portion of the picture, before any
true conception could be given of the richness of Turner's
designs. A fragment of distant foliage I may give farther
on ; but, in order to judge rightly of either example, we
must know one or two points in the structure of branches,
requiring yet some irksome patience of inquiry, which I am
compelled to ask the reader to grant me through another
two chapters.

CHAPTER VI

THE BRANCH

§ 1. WE have hitherto spoken of each shoot as either straight or only warped by its spiral tendency; but no shoot of any length, except those of the sapling, ever can be straight; for, as the family of leaves which it bears are forced unanimously to take some given direction in search of food or light, the stalk necessarily obeys the same impulse, and bends itself so as to sustain them in their adopted position, with the greatest ease to itself and comfort for them.

In doing this, it has two main influences to comply or contend with: the first, the direct action of the leaves in drawing it this way or that, as they themselves seek particular situations; the second, the pressure of their absolute weight after they have taken their places, depressing each bough in a given degree; the leverage increasing as the leaf extends. To these principal forces may frequently be added that of some prevalent wind, which, on a majority of days in the year, bends the bough, leaves and all, for hours together, out of its normal position. Owing to these three forces, the shoot is nearly sure to be curved in at least two directions;[1] that is to say, not merely as the rim of a wine-glass is curved (so that, looking at it horizontally, the circle becomes a straight line), but as the edge of a lip or an eyebrow is curved, partly upwards, partly forwards, so that in no possible perspective can it be seen as a straight line. Similarly, no perspective will usually

---

[1] See the note on Fig. 11, at page 18, which shows these two directions in a shoot of lime.

bring a shoot of a free-growing tree to appear a straight line.

§ 2. It is evident that the more leaves the stalk has to sustain, the more strength it requires. It might appear, therefore, not unadvisable that every leaf should, as it grew, pay a small tax to the stalk for its sustenance; so that there might be no fear of any number of leaves being too oppressive to their bearer. Which, accordingly, is just what the leaves do. Each, from the moment of his complete majority, pays a stated tax to the stalk; that is to say, collects for it a certain quantity of wood, or materials for wood, and sends this wood, or what ultimately will become wood, *down* the stalk to add to its thickness.

§ 3. "Down the stalk?" yes, and down a great way farther. For as the leaves, if they did not thus contribute to their own support, would soon be too heavy for the spray, so if the spray, with its family of leaves, contributed nothing to the thickness of the branch, the leaf-families would soon break down their sustaining branches. And, similarly, if the branches gave nothing to the stem, the stem would soon fall under its boughs. Therefore by a power of which I believe no sufficient account exists,[1] as each leaf adds to the thickness of the shoot, so each shoot to the branch, so each branch to the stem, and that with so perfect an order and regularity of duty, that from every leaf in all the countless crowd at the tree's summit, one slender fibre, or at least fibre's thickness of wood, descends through shoot, through spray, through branch, and through stem; and having thus added, in its due proportion, to form the strength of the tree, labours yet farther and more painfully to provide for its security; and thrusting forward

---

[1] I find that the office and nature of cambium, the causes of the action of the sap, and the real mode of the formation of buds, are all still under the investigation of botanists. I do not lose time in stating the doubts or probabilities which exist on these subjects. For us, the mechanical fact of the increase of thickness by every leaf's action is all that needs attention. The reader who wishes for information as accurate as the present state of science admits, may consult Lindley's *Introduction to Botany*, and an interesting little book by Dr. Alexander Harvey on *Trees and their Nature* (Nisbet and Co., 1856), to which I owe much help.

into the root, loses nothing of its mighty energy until, mining through the darkness, it has taken hold in cleft of rock or depth of earth, as extended as the sweep of its green crest in the free air.

§ 4. Such at least is the mechanical aspect of the tree. The work of its construction, considered as a branched tower, partly propped by buttresses, partly lashed by cables, is thus shared in by every leaf. But considering it as a living body to be nourished, it is probably an inaccurate analogy to speak of the leaves being taxed for the enlargement of the trunk. Strictly speaking, the trunk enlarges by sustaining them. For each leaf, however far removed from the ground, stands in need of nourishment derived from the ground, as well as of that which it finds in the air; and it simply sends its root down along the stem of the tree, until it reaches the ground and obtains the necessary mineral elements. The trunk has been therefore called by some botanists a " bundle of roots," but I think inaccurately. It is rather a messenger to the roots.[1] A root, properly so called, is a fibre, spongy or absorbent at the extremity, which secretes certain elements from the earth. The stem is by this definition no more a cluster of roots than a cluster of leaves, but a channel of intercourse between the roots and the leaves. It can gather no nourishment. It only carries nourishment, being, in fact, a group of canals for the conveyance of marketable commodities, with an electric telegraph attached to each, transmitting messages from leaf to root, and root to leaf, up and down the tree. But whatever view we take of the operative causes, the external and visible fact is simply that every leaf does send down from its stalk a slender thread of woody matter along the sides of the shoot it grows upon; and that the increase of thickness in stem, proportioned to the advance of the leaves, corresponds with an increase of thickness in roots, proportioned to the advance of their outer fibres. How far interchange of elements takes place between root and leaf, it is not our work here to examine; the general and broad idea is this, that the whole tree is fed partly by the earth, partly by the air; strengthened and

[1] In the true sense, "a mediator" ($\mu\epsilon\sigma\ell\tau\eta\varsigma$).

sustained by the one, agitated and educated by the other; all of it which is best, in substance, life, and beauty, being drawn more from the dew of heaven than the fatness of the earth. The results of this nourishment of the bough by the leaf in external aspect, are the object of our immediate inquiry.

§ 5. Hitherto we have considered the shoot as an ascending body, throwing off buds at intervals. This it is indeed ; but the part of it which ascends is not seen externally. Look back to Plate 51. You will observe that each shoot is furrowed, and that the ridges between the furrows rise in slightly spiral lines, terminating in the armlets under the buds which bore last year's leaves. These ridges, which rib the shoot so distinctly, are not on the ascending part of it. They are the contributions of each successive leaf thrown out as it ascended. Every leaf sent down a slender cord, covering and clinging to the shoot beneath, and increasing its thickness. Each, according to his size and strength, wove his little strand of cable, as a spider his thread ; and cast it down the side of the springing tower by a marvellous magic—irresistible ! The fall of a granite pyramid from an Alp may perhaps be stayed ; the descending force of that silver thread shall not be stayed. It will split the rocks themselves at its roots, if need be, rather than fail in its work.

So many leaves, so many silver cords. Count—for by just the thickness of one cord, beneath each leaf, let fall in fivefold order round and round, the shoot increases in thickness to its root :—a spire built downwards from the heaven.

And now we see why the leaves dislike being above each other. Each seeks a vacant place, where he may freely let fall the cord. The turning aside of the cable to avoid the buds beneath, is one of the main causes of spiral curvature, as the shoot increases. It required all the care I could give to the drawing, and all Mr. Armytage's skill in engraving Plate 51, to express, though drawing them nearly of their full size, the principal courses of curvature in even this least graceful of trees.

§ 6. According to the structure thus ascertained, the body of the shoot may at any point be considered as formed by a central rod, represented by the shaded inner circle, *a*, Fig. 36, surrounded by as many rods of descending external wood as there are leaves above the point where the section is made. The first five leaves above send down the first dark rods; and the next above send down those between, which, being from younger leaves, are less, but yet fill the interstices; then the third group sending down the smallest, it will be seen at a glance how a spiral action is produced. But it would lead us into too subtle detail if I traced the forces of this gradual superimposition. I must be content to let the reader pursue this part of the subject for himself, if it amuses him, and proceed to larger questions.

Fig. 36.

§ 7. Broadly and practically, we may consider the whole cluster of woody material in Fig. 36 as one circle of fibrous substance formed round a small central rod. The real appearance in most trees is approximately as in *b*, Fig. 36, the radiating structure becoming more distinct in proportion to the largeness and compactness of the wood.[1]

Now the next question is, how this descending external coating of wood will behave itself when it comes to the forking of the shoots. To simplify the examination of this, let us suppose the original or growing shoot (whose section is the shaded inner circle in Fig. 36) to have been in the form of a letter Y, and no thicker than a stout iron wire, as in Fig. 37. Down the arms of this letter Y, we have two fibrous streams running in the direction of the arrows. If the depth or thickness of these streams be such as at *b* and *c*, what will their thickness be when they unite at *e*? Evidently, the quantity of wood surrounding the vertical wire at *e* must be twice as great as that surrounding the wires *b* and *c*.

Fig. 37.

[1] The gradual development of this radiating structure, which is organic and essential, composed of what are called by botanists medullary rays, is still a great mystery and wonder to me.

§ 8. The reader will, perhaps, be good enough to take it on my word (if he does not know enough of geometry to ascertain), that the large circle, in Fig. 38, contains twice as much area as either of the two smaller circles. Putting these circles in position, so as to guide us, and supposing the trunk to be bounded by straight lines, we have for the outline of the fork that in Fig. 38. How, then, do the two minor circles change into one large one? The section of the stem at *a* is a circle; and at *b*, is a circle; and at *c*, a circle. But what is it at *e*? Evidently, if the two circles merely united gradually, without change of form through a series of figures, such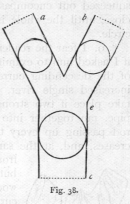

Fig. 38.

as those at the top of Fig. 39, the quantity of wood, instead of remaining the same, would diminish from the

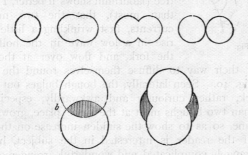

Fig. 39.

contents of two circles to the contents of one. So for every loss, which the circles sustain at this junction, an equal quantity of wood must be thrust out somehow to the side. Thus, to enable the circles to run into each other, as far as shown at *b*, in Fig. 39, there must be a loss between them of as much wood as the shaded space.

Therefore, half of that space must be added, or rather pushed out on each side, and the section of the uniting branch becomes approximately as in *c*, Fig. 39; the wood squeezed out encompassing the stem more as the circles close, until the whole is reconciled into one larger single circle.

§ 9. I fear the reader would have no patience with me, if I asked him to examine, in longitudinal section, the lines of the descending currents of wood as they eddy into the increased single river. Of course, it is just what would take place if two strong streams, filling each a cylindrical pipe, ran together into one large cylinder, with a central rod passing up every tube. But, as this central rod increases, and, at the same time, the supply of the stream

Fig. 40

from above, every added leaf contributing its little current, the eddies of wood about the fork become intensely curious and interesting; of which thus much the reader may observe in a moment by gathering a branch of any tree (laburnum shows it better, I think, than most), that the two meeting currents, first wrinkling a little, then rise in a low wave in the hollow of the fork, and flow over at the side,

making their way to diffuse themselves round the stem, as in Fig. 40. Seen laterally, the bough bulges out below the fork, rather curiously and awkwardly, especially if more than two boughs meet at the same place, growing in one plane, so as to show the sudden increase on the profile. If the reader is interested in the subject, he will find strangely complicated and wonderful arrangements of stream when smaller boughs meet larger (one example is given in Plate 3, Vol. III., where the current of a smaller bough, entering upwards, pushes its way into the stronger rivers of the stem). But I cannot, of course, enter into such detail here.

§ 10. The little ringed accumulation, repelled from the wood of the larger trunk at the base of small boughs, may be seen at a glance in any tree, and needs no illustration;

but I give one from Salvator, Fig. 41 (from his own etching,

Fig. 41.

Democritus omnium Derisor), which is interesting, because

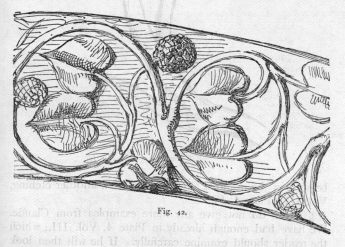

Fig. 42.

it shows the swelling at the bases of insertion, which yet,

Salvator's eye not being quick enough to detect the law of descent in the fibres, he, with his usual love of ugliness, fastens on this swollen character, and exaggerates it into an appearance of disease. The same bloated aspect may

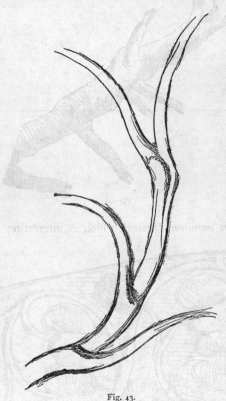

Fig. 43.

be seen in the example already given from another etching, Vol. III., Plate 4, Fig. 8.

§ 11. I do not give any more examples from Claude. We have had enough already in Plate 4, Vol. III., which the reader should examine carefully. If he will then look forward to Fig. 61 here, he will see how Turner inserts branches, and with what certain and strange instinct of fidelity he marks the wrinkled enlargement and sinuous eddies of the wood rivers where they meet.

And remember always that Turner's greatness and rightness in all these points successively depend on no scientific knowledge. He was entirely ignorant of all the laws we have been developing. He had merely accustomed himself to see impartially, intensely, and fearlessly.

§ 12. It may, perhaps, be interesting to compare, with the rude fallacies of Claude and Salvator, a little piece of earliest art, wrought by men who could see and feel. The scroll, Fig. 42, is a portion of that which surrounds the arch in San Zeno of Verona, above the pillar engraved in the *Stones of Venice*, Plate 17, Vol. I. It is, therefore, twelfth, or earliest thirteenth-century work. Yet the foliage is already full of spring and life; and in the part of the stem, which I have given of its real size[1] in Fig. 43, the reader will perhaps be surprised to see at the junctions the laws of vegetation, which escaped the sight of all the degenerate landscape-painters of Italy, expressed by one of her simple architectural workmen six hundred years ago.

We now know enough, I think, of the internal conditions which regulate tree-structure to enable us to investigate, finally, the great laws of branch and stem aspect. But they are very beautiful; and we will give them a separate chapter.

---

[1] [Reduced for this edition.]

CHAPTER VII

THE STEM

§ 1 WE must be content, in this most complex subject, to advance very slowly; and our easiest, if not our only way, will be to examine, first, the conditions under which boughs would form, supposing them all to divide in one plane, as your hand divides when you lay it flat on the table, with the fingers as wide apart as you can. And then we will deduce the laws of ramification which follow on the real structure of branches, which truly divide, not in one plane, but as your fingers separate if you hold a large round ball with them.

The reader has, I hope, a clear idea by this time of the main principle of tree-growth; namely, that the increase is by addition, or superimposition, not extension. A branch does not stretch itself out as a leech stretches its body. But it receives additions at its extremity, and proportional additions to its thickness. For although the actual living shoot, or growing point, of any year, lengthens itself gradually until it reaches its terminal bud, after that bud is formed, its length is fixed. It is thenceforth one joint of the tree, like the joint of a pillar, on which other joints of marble may be laid to elongate the pillar, but which will not itself stretch. A tree is thus truly edified, or built, like a house.

§ 2. I am not sure with what absolute stringency this law is observed, or what slight lengthening of substance may be traceable by close measurement among inferior branches. For practical purposes, we may assume that the law is final, and that if we represent the state of a plant, or extremity of branch, in any given year under the simplest possible type, Fig. 44, *a*, of two shoots, with terminal buds, springing from one stem, its growth next year may be expressed by the type, Fig. 44, *b*, in which, the original stems not changing or increasing, the terminal buds have built up each another story of plant, or repetition of the original form; and, in order to support this new edifice, have sent down roots all the way to the ground, so as to enclose and thicken the inferior stem.

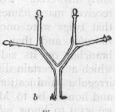

Fig. 44.

But if this is so, how does the original stem, which never lengthens, ever become the tall trunk of a tree? The arrangement just stated provides very satisfactorily for making it stout, but not for making it tall. If the ramification proceeds in this way, the tree must assuredly become a round compact ball of short sticks, attached to the ground by a very stout, almost invisible, stem, like a puff-ball.

For if we take the form above, on a small scale, merely to see what comes of it, and carry its branching three steps farther, we get the successive conditions in Fig. 45, of which the last comes already round to the ground.

"But those forms really look something like trees!"

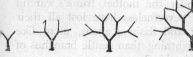

Fig. 45.

Yes, if they were on a large scale. But each of the little shoots is only six or seven inches long; the whole cluster would but be three or four feet over, and touches the ground already at its extremity. It would enlarge if it went on growing, but never rise from the ground.

§ 3. This is an interesting question: one, also, which, I

fear, we must solve, so far as yet it can be solved, with
little help.   Perhaps nothing is more curious in the history of human mind than the way in which the science of
botany has become oppressed by nomenclature.   Here is
perhaps the first question which an intelligent child would
think of asking about a tree : " Mamma, how does it make
its trunk ? " and you may open one botanical work after
another, and good ones too, and by sensible men,—you
shall not find this child's question fairly put, much less
fairly answered.   You will be told gravely that a stem has
received many names, such as *culmus*, *stipes*, and *truncus ;*
that twigs were once called *flagella*, but are now called
ramuli ; and that Mr. Link calls a straight stem, with
branches on its sides, a *caulis excurrens ;* and a stem,
which at a certain distance above the earth breaks out into
irregular ramifications, a *caulis deliquescens*.   All thanks
and honour be to Mr. Link !   But at this moment, when
we want to know *why* one stem breaks out " at a certain
distance," and the other not at all, we find no great help
in those splendid excurrencies and deliquescencies.   " At
a certain distance ? "   Yes : but why not before ? or why
then ?   How was it that, for many and many a year, the
young shoots agreed to construct a vertical tower, or, at
least, the nucleus of one, and then, one merry day, changed
their minds, and built about their metropolis in all directions, nobody knows where, far into the air in free delight ?
How is it that yonder larch-stem grows straight and true,
while its branches, constructed by the same process as
the mother trunk, and under the mother trunk's careful
inspection and direction, nevertheless have lost all their
manners, and go forking and flashing about, more like
cracklings of spitefullest lightning than gentle branches of
trees that dip green leaves in dew ?

§ 4. We have probably, many of us, missed the point
of such questions as these, because we too readily associated
the structure of trees with that of flowers.   The flowering
part of a plant shoots out or up, in some given direction,
until, at a stated period, it opens or branches into perfect
form by a law just as fixed, and just as inexplicable, as
that which numbers the joints of an animal's skeleton,

and puts the head on its right joint. In many forms of
flowers—foxglove, aloe, hemlock, or blossom of maize—
the structure of the flowering part so far assimilates itself
to that of a tree, that we not unnaturally think of a tree
only as a large flower, or large remnant of flower, run to
seed. And we suppose the time and place of its branching to be just as organically determined as the height of
the stalk of straw, or hemlock pipe, and the fashion of its
branching just as fixed as the shape of petals in a pansy
or cowslip.

§ 5. But that is not so; not so in anywise. So far
as you can watch a tree, it is produced throughout by
repetitions of the same process, which repetitions, however,
are arbitrarily directed so as to produce one effect at one
time, and another at another time. A young sapling has
his branches as much as the tall tree. He does not shoot
up in a long thin rod, and begin to branch when he is
ten or fifteen feet high, as the hemlock or foxglove does
when each has reached its ten or fifteen inches. The
young sapling conducts himself with all the dignity of a
tree from the first;—only he so manages his branches as
to form a support for his future life, in a strong straight
trunk, that will hold him well off the ground. Prudent
little sapling!—but how does he manage this? how keep
the young branches from rambling about, till the proper
time, or on what plea dismiss them from his service if
they will not help his provident purpose? So again,
there is no difference in mode of construction between
the trunk of a pine and its branch. But external circumstances so far interfere with the results of this repeated
construction, that a stone pine rises for a hundred feet
like a pillar, and then suddenly bursts into a cloud. It
is the knowledge of the mode in which such change may
take place which forms the true natural history of trees;—
or, more accurately, their moral history. An animal is
born with so many limbs, and a head of such a shape.
That is, strictly speaking, not its history, but one fact in
its history: a fact of which no other account can be given
than that it was so appointed. But a tree is born without
a head. It has got to make its own head. It is born

like a little family from which a great nation is to spring;
and at a certain time, under peculiar external circumstances,
this nation, every individual of which remains the same in
nature and temper, yet gives itself a new political constitution, and sends out branch colonies, which enforce
forms of law and life entirely different from those of the
parent state. That is the history of the state. It is also the
history of a tree.

§ 6. Of these hidden histories, I know and can tell you
as little as I did of the making of rocks. It will be enough
for me if I can put the difficulty fairly before you, show you
clearly such facts as are necessary to the understanding of
great Art, and so leave you to pursue, at your pleasure,
the graceful mystery of this imperfect leafage life.

I took in the outset the type of a *triple* bud as the most
general that could be given of all trees, because it represents
a prevalently upright main tendency, with a capacity of

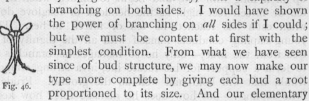

branching on both sides. I would have shown
the power of branching on *all* sides if I could;
but we must be content at first with the
simplest condition. From what we have seen
since of bud structure, we may now make our
type more complete by giving each bud a root
proportioned to its size. And our elementary
type of tree plant will be as in Fig. 46.

Fig. 46.

§ 7. Now these three buds, though differently placed,
have all one mind. No bud has an oblique mind. Every
one would like, if he could, to grow upright, and it is
because the midmost one has entirely his own way in this
matter, that he is largest. He is an elder brother;—his
birthright is to grow straight towards the sky. A younger
child may perhaps supplant him, if he does not care for
his privilege. In the meantime all are of one family, and
love each other,—so that the two lateral buds do not stoop
aside because they like it, but to let their more favoured
brother grow in peace. All the three buds and roots have
at heart the same desire;—which is, the one to grow as
straight as he can towards bright heaven, the other as deep
as he can into dark earth. Up to light and down to shade;
—into air and into rock:—that is their mind and purpose

for ever. So far as they can, in kindness to each other, and by sufferance of external circumstances, work out that destiny, they will. But their beauty will not result from their working it out,—only from their maintained purpose and resolve to do so, if it may be. They will fail—certainly two, perhaps all three of them : fail egregiously ;—ridiculously ;—it may be, agonizingly. Instead of growing up, they may be wholly sacrificed to happier buds above, and have to grow *down*, sideways, roundabout ways, all sorts of ways. Instead of getting down quietly into the convent of the earth, they may have to cling and crawl about hardest and hottest angles of it, full in sight of man and beast, and roughly trodden under foot by them ;—stumbling-blocks to many.

Yet out of such sacrifice, gracefully made—such misfortune, gloriously sustained—all their true beauty is to arise. Yes, and from more than sacrifice—more than misfortune : from *death*. Yes, and more than death : from the worst kind of death : not natural, coming to each in its due time ; but premature, oppressed, unnatural, misguided —or so it would seem—to the poor dying sprays. Yet, without such death, no strong trunk were ever possible ; no grace of glorious limb or glittering leaf ; no companionship with the rest of nature or with man.

§ 8. Let us see how this must be. We return to our poor little threefold type, Fig. 46, above. Next year he will become as in Fig. 47. The two lateral buds keeping as much as may be out of their brother's way, and yet growing upwards with a will, strike diagonal lines, and in moderate comfort accomplish their year's life and terminal buds. But what is to be done next ? Forming the triple terminal head on this diagonal line, we find that one of our next year's buds, *c*, will have to grow down again, which is very hard ; and another, *b*, will run right against the lateral branch of the upper bud, A, which must not be allowed under any circumstances.

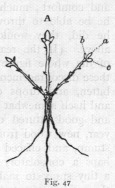

Fig. 47

What are we to do?

§ 9. The best we can. Give up our straightness, and
some of our length, and consent to grow short, and crooked.

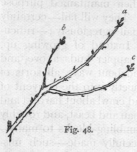

Fig. 48.

Bud *b* shall be ordered to stoop
forward and keep his head out
of the great bough's way, as in
Fig. 48, and grow as he best may,
with the consumptive pain in his
chest. To give him a little more
room, the elder brother, *a*, shall
stoop a little forward also, re-
covering himself when he has got
out of *b*'s way; and bud *c* shall
be encouraged to bend himself
bravely round and up, after his first start in that disagree-
able downward direction. Poor *b*, withdrawn from air and
light between *a* and A, and having to live stooping besides, cannot make much of himself, and is stunted and
feeble; *c*, having free play for his energies, bends up with a
will, and becomes handsomer, to our minds, than if he had
been straight, and *a* is none the worse for his concession
to unhappy *b* in early life.

So far well for this year. But how for next? *b* is already
too near the spray above him, even for his own strength
and comfort; much less, with his weak constitution, will
he be able to throw up any strong new shoots. And if
he did, they would only run into those of the bough
above. (If the reader will proceed in the construction
of the whole figure he will see that this is so.) Under
these discouragements and deficiencies, *b* is probably frost-
bitten, and drops off. The bough proceeds, mutilated,
and itself somewhat discouraged. But it repeats its sincere
and good-natured compliances, and at the close of the
year, new wood from all the leaves having concealed the
stump, and effaced the memory of poor lost *b*, and perhaps a consolatory bud lower down having thrown out
a tiny spray to make the most of the vacant space near
the main stem, we shall find the bough in some such shape
as Fig. 49.

§ 10. Wherein we already see the germ of our irregularly

bending branch, which might ultimately be much the
prettier for the loss of *b*. Alas! the Fates have forbidden
even this. While the low bough is making all these exertions, the boughs
of A, above him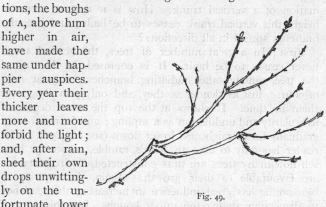
higher in air,
have made the
same under hap-
pier auspices.
Every year their
thicker leaves
more and more
forbid the light;
and, after rain,
shed their own
drops unwitting-
ly on the un-
fortunate lower

Fig. 49.

bough, and prevent the air or sun from drying his bark
or checking the chill in his medullary rays. Slowly a
hopeless languor gains upon him. He buds here or there,
faintly, in the spring; but the flow of strong wood from
above oppresses him even about his root, where it joins
the trunk. The very sap does not turn aside to him,
but rushes up to the stronger, laughing leaves far above.
Life is no more worth having; and abandoning all effort,
the poor bough drops, and finds consummation of destiny
in helping an old woman's fire.

When he is gone, the one next above is left with greater
freedom, and will shoot now from points of its sprays
which were before likely to perish. Hence another condition of irregularity in form. But that bough also will
fall in its turn, though after longer persistence. Gradually thus the central trunk is built, and the branches by
whose help it was formed cast off, leaving here and there
scars, which are all effaced by years, or lost sight of among
the roughness and furrows of the aged surface. The work
is continually advancing, and thus the head of foliage on
any tree is not an expansion at a given height, like a
flower-bell, but the collective group of boughs, or workmen,

who have got up so far, and will get up higher next year, still losing one or two of their number underneath.

§ 11. So far well. But this only accounts for the formation of a vertical trunk. How is it that at a certain height this vertical trunk ceases to be built; and irregular branches spread in all directions?

First: In a great number of trees, the vertical trunk never ceases to be built. It is confused, at the top of the tree, among other radiating branches, being at first, of course, just as slender as they, and only prevailing over them in time. It shows at the top the same degree of irregularity and undulation as a sapling; and is transformed gradually into straightness lower down (see Fig. 50). The reader has only to take an hour's ramble, to see for himself how many trees are thus constructed, if circumstances are favourable to their growth. Again, the mystery of blossoming has great influence in increasing the tendency to dispersion among the upper boughs; but this part of vegetative structure I cannot enter into; it is too subtle, and has, besides, no absolute bearing on our subject; the principal conditions which produce the varied play of branches being purely mechanical. The point at which they show a determined tendency to spread is generally to be conceived as a place of *rest* for the tree, where it has reached the height from the ground at which ground-mist, imperfect circulation of air, etc., have ceased to operate injuriously on it, and where it has free room, and air, and light for its growth.

§ 12. I find there is quite an infinite interest in watching the different ways in which trees part their sprays at this resting-place, and the sometimes abrupt, sometimes gentle and undiscoverable, severing of the upright stem into the wandering and wilful branches; but a volume, instead of a chapter or two, and quite a little gallery of plates would be needed to illustrate the various grace of this division, associated as it is with an exquisitely subtle effacing of undulation in the thicker stems, by the flowing down of the wood from above; the curves which are too violent in the branches being filled up, so that what was as at *a*, Fig. 50, becomes as at *b*, and when the main stem is old, passes at last into straightness by almost imperceptible curves, a continually gradated emphasis of curvature being carried to the branch extremities.

§ 13. Hitherto we have confined ourselves entirely to examination of stems in one plane. We must glance —though only to ascertain how impossible it is to do more than glance — at the conditions of form which result from the throwing out of branches, not in one plane, but on all sides. "As your fingers divide when they hold a ball," I said: or, better, a large cup, without a handle. Consider how such ramification will appear in one of the bud groups, that of our old friend the oak. We saw it opened usually into five shoots. Imagine then (Fig. 51), a five-sided cup or funnel with a stout rod running through the centre of it. In the figure it is seen from above, so as partly to show the inside, and a little obliquely, that the central rod may not hide any of the angles. Then let us suppose that, where the angles of this cup were, we have, instead, five rods, as in Fig. 52, A, like the ribs of a pentagonal umbrella turned inside out by the wind.

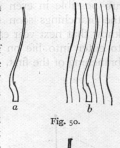

Fig. 50.

Fig. 51.

I dot the pentagon which connects their extremities, to keep their positions clear. Then these five rods, with the central one, will represent the five shoots, and the leader, from a vigorous young oak-spray. Put the leaves on each; the five-foiled star at its extremity, and the others, now not quite formally, but still on the whole as in Fig. 3 above, and we have the result, Fig. 52, B—rather a pretty one.

§ 14. By considering the various aspects which the five rods would take in Fig. 52, as the entire group was seen from below or above, and at different angles and distances, the reader may find out for himself what changes of aspect are possible in even so regular a structure as this. But the branchings soon take more complex symmetry. We know that next year each of these five subordinate rods is to enter into life on its own account, and to repeat the branching of the first. Thus, we shall have five pentagonal

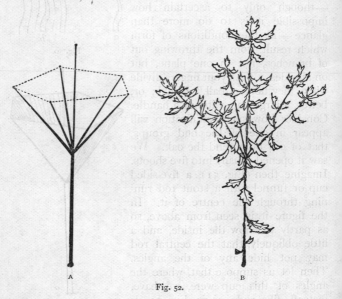

Fig. 52.

cups surrounding a large central pentagonal cup. This figure, if the reader likes a pretty perspective problem, he may construct for his own pleasure :—which having done, or conceived, he is then to apply the great principles of subjection and resilience, not to three branches only, as in Fig. 49, but to the five of each cup ;—by which the cups get flattened out and bent up, as you may have seen vessels of Venetian glass, so that every cup actually takes something the shape of a thick aloe or artichoke leaf ; and they surround the central one, not as a bunch of grapes surrounds a grape at the end of it, but as the petals grow round the centre of a rose. So that any one of these lateral branches—though, seen from above, it would present a symmetrical figure, as if it were not flattened (A, Fig. 53)

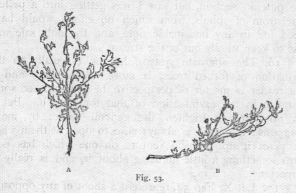

Fig. 53.

—seen sideways, or in profile, will show itself to be at least as much flattened as at B.

§ 15. You may thus regard the whole tree as composed of a series of such thick, flat, branch-leaves; only incomparably more varied and enriched in framework as they spread; and arranged more or less in spirals round the trunk. Gather a cone of a Scotch fir; begin at the bottom of it, and pull off the seeds, so as to show one of the spiral rows of them continuously, from the bottom to the top, leaving enough seeds above them to support the row. Then the gradual lengthening of the seeds from the root, their spiral arrangement, and their limitation within a curved, convex form, furnish the best *severe* type you can have of the branch system of all stemmed trees; and each seed of the cone represents, not badly, the sort of flattened solid leaf-shape which all complete branches have. Also, if you will try to draw the spiral of the fir-cone, you will understand something about tree-perspective, which may be generally useful. Finally, if you note the way in which the seeds of the cone slip each farther and farther over each other, so as to change sides in the middle of the cone, and obtain a reversed action of spiral lines in the upper half, you may imagine what a piece of work it

would be for both of us, if we were to try to follow the
complexities of branch order in trees of irregular growth,
such as the rhododendron. I tried to do it, at least, for
the pine, in section, but saw I was getting into a perfect
maelström of spirals, from which no efforts would have
freed me, in any imaginable time, and the only safe way
was to keep wholly out of the stream.

§ 16. The alternate system, leading especially to the
formation of forked trees, is more manageable; and if
the reader is master of perspective, he may proceed some
distance in the examination of that for himself. But I
do not care to frighten the general reader by many
diagrams : the book is always sure to open at them when
he takes it up. I will venture on one which has perhaps something a little amusing about it, and is really of
importance.

§ 17. Let X, Fig. 54, represent a shoot of any opposite-
leaved tree. The mode in which it will grow into a tree

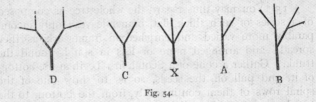

D   C   X   A   B

Fig. 54.

depends, mainly, on its disposition to lose the leader or
a lateral shoot. If it keeps the leader, but drops the
lateral, it takes the form A, and next year by a repetition
of the process, B. But if it keeps the laterals, and drops
the leader, it becomes, first, C, and next year, D. The
form A is almost universal in spiral or alternate trees ;
and it is especially to be noted as bringing about this
result, that in any given forking, one bough always goes
on in its own direct course, and the other leaves it softly :
they do not separate as if one was repelled from the other.
Thus in Fig. 55, a perfect and nearly symmetrical piece
of ramification, by Turner (lowest bough but one in the
tree on the left in the " Château of La belle Gabrielle "),

J. Ruskin

J. Emslie

56. Sketch by a Clerk of the Works

the leading bough, going on in its own curve, throws off, first, a bough to the right, then one to the left, then two small ones to the right, and proceeds itself, hidden by leaves, to form the farthest upper point of the branch.

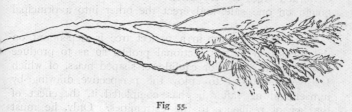

Fig 55.

The lower secondary bough—the first thrown off— proceeds in its own curve, branching first to left, then to right.

The upper bough proceeds in the same way, throwing off first to left, then to right. And this is the commonest and most graceful structure. But if the tree loses the leader, as at C, Fig. 54 (and many opposite trees have a trick of doing so), a very curious result is arrived at, which I will give in a geometrical form.

§ 18. The number of branches which die, so as to leave the main stem bare, is always greatest low down, or near the interior of the tree. It follows that the lengths of stem which do not fork diminish gradually to the extremities, in a fixed proportion. This is a general law. Assume, for example's sake, the stem to separate always into two branches, at an equal angle, and that each branch is three-quarters of the length of the preceding one. Diminish their thicknesses in proportion, and carry out the figure any extent you like. In Plate 56, opposite, Fig. 1, you have it at its ninth branch; in which I wish you to notice, first, the delicate curve formed by every complete line of the branches (compare Vol. IV. Fig. 91); and, secondly, the very curious result of the top of the tree being a broad flat line, which passes at an angle into lateral shorter lines, and so down to the extremities. It is this property which renders the contours of tops of trees so intensely difficult to draw rightly, without making their curves too smooth and insipid.

Observe, also, that the great weight of the foliage being thrown on the outside of each main fork, the tendency of forked trees is very often to droop and diminish the bough on one side, and erect the other into a principal mass.[1]

§ 19. But the form in a perfect tree is dependent on the revolution of this sectional profile, so as to produce a mushroom-shaped or cauliflower-shaped mass, of which I leave the reader to enjoy the perspective drawing by himself, adding, after he has completed it, the effect of the law of resilience to the extremities. Only, he must note this : that in real trees, as the branches rise from the ground, the open spaces underneath are partly filled by subsequent branchings, so that a real tree has not so much the shape of a mushroom, as of an apple, or, if elongated, a pear.

§ 20. And now you may just begin to understand a little of Turner's meaning in those odd pear-shaped trees of his, in the " Mercury and Argus," and other such compositions : which, however, before we can do completely, we must gather our evidence together, and see what general results will come of it respecting the hearts and fancies of trees, no less than their forms.

---

[1] This is Harding's favourite form of tree. You will find it much insisted on in his works on foliage. I intended to have given a figure to show the results of the pressure of the weight of all the leafage on a great lateral bough, in modifying its curves, the strength of timber being greatest where the leverage of the mass tells most. But I find nobody ever reads things which it takes any trouble to understand, so that it is of no use to write them.

CHAPTER VIII

THE LEAF MONUMENTS

§ 1. AND now, having ascertained in its main points the
system on which the leaf-workers build, let us see, finally,
what results in aspect, and appeal to human mind, their
building must present. In some sort it resembles that of
the coral animal, differing, however, in two main points.
First, the animal which forms branched coral, builds, I
believe, in calm water, and has few accidents of current,
light, or heat to contend with. He builds in monotonous
ramification, untormented, therefore unbeautiful. Secondly,
each coral animal builds for himself, adding his cell to
what has been before constructed, as a bee adds another
cell to the comb. He obtains no essential connection with
the root and foundation of the whole structure. That
foundation is thickened clumsily, by a fused and encumber-
ing aggregation, as a stalactite increases ;—not by threads
proceeding from the extremities to the root.

§ 2. The leaf, as we have seen, builds in both respects
under opposite conditions. It leads a life of endurance,
effort, and various success, issuing in various beauty ; and
it connects itself with the whole previous edifice by one
sustaining thread, continuing its appointed piece of work
all the way from top to root. Whence result three great
conditions in branch aspect, for which I cannot find good
names, but must use the imperfect ones of " Spring,"
" Caprice," " Fellowship."

§ 3. I. SPRING: or the appearance of elastic and progres-
sive power, as opposed to the look of a bent piece of cord.
—This follows partly on the poise of the bough, partly on

its action in seeking or shunning. Every branch-line expresses both these. It takes a curve accurately showing the relations between the strength of the sprays in that position (growing downward, upward, or laterally), and the weight of leaves they carry; and again, it takes a curve expressive of the will or aim of those sprays, during all their life, and handed down from sire to son, in steady inheritance of resolution to reach forward in a given direction, or bend away from some given evil influence.

And all these proportionate strengths and measured efforts of the bough produce its loveliness, and ought to be felt, in looking at it, not by any mathematical evidence, but by the same fine instinct which enables us to perceive, when a girl dances rightly, that she moves easily, and with delight to herself; that her limbs are strong enough, and her body tender enough, to move precisely as she wills them to move. You cannot say of any bend of arm or foot what precise relations of their curves to the whole figure manifest, in their changeful melodies, that ease of motion; yet you feel that they do so, and you feel it by a true instinct. And if you reason on the matter farther, you may know, though you cannot see, that an absolute mathematical necessity proportions every bend of the body to the rate and direction of its motion, and that the momentary fancy and fire of the will measure themselves, even in their gaily-fancied freedom, by stern laws of nervous life, and material attraction, which regulate eternally every pulse of the strength of man, and every sweep of the stars of heaven.

§ 4. Observe, also, the balance of the bough of a tree is quite as subtle as that of a figure in motion. It is a balance between the elasticity of the bough and the weight of leaves, affected in curvature, literally, by the growth of *every* leaf; and besides this, when it moves, it is partly supported by the resistance of the air, greater or less, according to the shape of leaf;—so that branches float on the wind more than they yield to it; and in their tossing do not so much bend under a force, as rise on a wave, which penetrates in liquid threads through all their sprays.

§ 5. I am not sure how far, by any illustration, I can exemplify these subtle conditions of form. All my plans have been shortened, and I have learned to content myself with yet more contracted issues of them after the shortening, because I know that nearly all in such matters must be said or shown, unavailably. No saying will teach the truth. Nothing but doing. If the reader will draw boughs of trees long and faithfully, giving previous pains to gain the power (how rare!) of drawing *anything* faithfully, he will come to see what Turner's work is, or any other right work; but not by reading, nor thinking, nor idly looking. However, in some degree, even our ordinary instinctive perception of grace and balance may serve us, if we choose to pay any accurate attention to the matter.

§ 6. Look back to Fig. 55. That bough of Turner's is exactly and exquisitely poised, leaves and all, for its present horizontal position. Turn the book so as to put the spray upright, with the leaves at the top. You ought to see they would then be wrong;—that they must, in that position, have adjusted themselves more directly above the main stem, and more firmly, the curves of the lighter sprays being a deflection caused by their weight in the horizontal position. Again, Fig. 56 represents, enlarged to four times the size of the original, the two Scotch firs in Turner's etching of Inverary.[1] These are both in perfect poise, representing a double action : the warping of the trees away from the sea-wind, and the continual growing out of the boughs on the right-hand side, to recover the balance.

Turn the page so as to be horizontal, and you ought to feel that, considered now as branches, both would be out of balance. If you turn the heads of the trees to your right, they are wrong, because gravity would have bent them more downwards ; if to your left, wrong, because the law of resilience would have raised them more at the extremities.

---

[1] They are enlarged, partly, in order to show the care and minuteness of Turner's drawing on the smallest scale, partly to save the reader the trouble of using a magnifying glass, partly because this woodcut will print safely ; while if I had facsimiled the fine Turner etching, the block might have been spoiled after a hundred impressions. [Reduced for this edition.]

§ 7. Now take two branches of Salvator's, Figs. 57 and

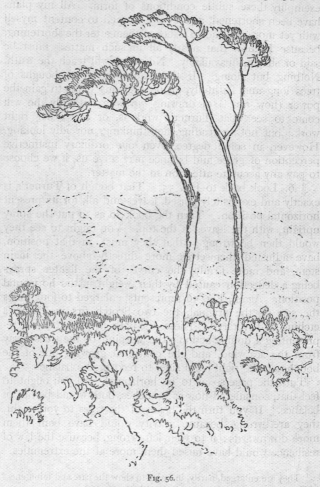

Fig. 56.

58.[1] You ought to feel that these have neither poise nor

[1] Magnified to twice the size of the original, but otherwise facsimiled from his own etchings of Œdipus, and the School of Plato. [Reduced for this edition.]

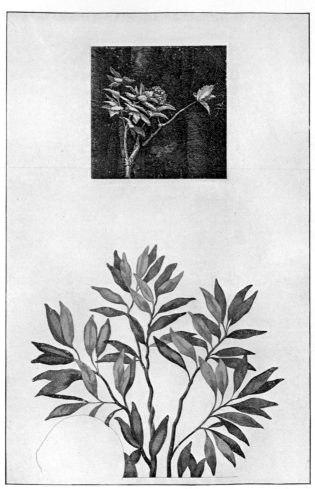

57. Leafage by Dürer and Veronese

spring; their leaves are incoherent, ragged, hanging together in decay.

Immediately after these, turn to Plate **57** opposite. The branch at the top is facsimiled from that in the hand of Adam, in Dürer's Adam and Eve.[1] It is full of the most exquisite vitality and spring in every line. Look at

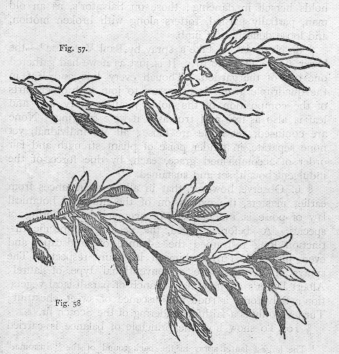

Fig. 57.

Fig. 58

it for five minutes carefully. Then turn back to Salvator's, Fig. 57. Are you as well satisfied with it? You ought to feel that it is not strong enough at the origin to sustain the leaves; and that if it were, those leaves themselves are in broken or forced relations with each other. Such relations

---

[1] The parrot perched on it is removed, which may be done without altering the curve, as the bird is set where its weight would not have bent the wood. [This Plate, and Figs. 57, 58, 60, and 61, reduced for this edition.]

might, indeed, exist in a partially withered tree, and one of these branches is intended to be partially withered, but the other is not; and if it were, Salvator's choice of the withered tree is precisely the sign of his preferring ugliness to beauty, decrepitude and disorganization to life and youth. The leaves on the spray, by Dürer, hold themselves as the girl holds herself in dancing; those on Salvator's, as an old man, partially palsied, totters along with broken motion, and loose deflection of limb.

§ 8. Next, let us take a spray by Paul Veronese [1]—the lower figure in Plate 57. It is just as if we had gathered one out of the garden. Though every line and leaf in the quadruple group is necessary to join with other parts of the composition of the noble picture, every line and leaf is also as free and true as if it were growing. None are confused, yet none are loose; all are individual, yet none separate, in tender poise of pliant strength and fair order of accomplished grace, each, by due force of the indulgent bough, set and sustained.

§ 9. Observe, however, that in all these instances from earlier masters, the expression of the universal botanical law of poise is independent of accuracy in rendering of species. As before noticed, the neglect of specific distinction long restrained the advance of landscape, and even hindered Turner himself in many respects. The sprays of Veronese are a conventional type of laurel; Albert Dürer's an imaginary branch of paradisiacal vegetation; Salvator's, a rude reminiscence of sweet chestnut; Turner's only is a faithful rendering of the Scotch fir.

§ 10. To show how the principle of balance is carried

---

[1] The largest laurel spray in the background of the " Susanna," Louvre—reduced to about a fifth of the original. The drawing was made for me by M. Hippolyte Dubois, and I am glad it is not one of my own, lest I should be charged with exaggerating Veronese's accuracy.

This group of leaves is, in the original, of the life-size; the circle which interferes with the spray on the right being the outline of the head of one of the elders; and, as painted for distant effect, there is no care in completing the stems :—they are struck with a few broken touches of the brush, which cannot be imitated in the engraving, and much of their spirit is lost in consequence.

out by Nature herself, here is a little terminal upright spray

Fig. 59.

of willow, the most graceful of English trees (Fig. 59). I have drawn it carefully; and if the reader will study its curves, or, better, trace and pencil them with a perfectly fine point, he will feel, I think, without difficulty, their finished relation to the leaves they sustain. Then, if we turn suddenly to a piece of Dutch branch-drawing (Fig. 60), facsimiled from No. 160, Dulwich Gallery (Berghem), he will understand, I believe, also the qualities of that, without comment of mine. It is of course not so dark in the original, being drawn with the chance dashes of a brush loaded with brown, but the contours are absolutely as in the woodcut. This Dutch design is a very characteristic example of two faults in tree-drawing; namely, the loss not

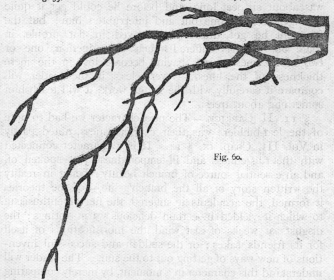

Fig. 60.

only of grace and spring, but of woodiness. A branch is not elastic as steel is, neither as a carter's whip is. It is a combination, wholly peculiar, of elasticity with half-dead and sapless stubbornness, and of continuous curve with pauses of knottiness, every bough having its blunted, affronted, fatigued, or repentant moments of existence, and mingling crabbed rugosities and fretful changes of mind with the main tendencies of its growth. The piece of pollard willow (Fig. 61), facsimiled from Turner's etching of "Young Anglers," in the Liber Studiorum, has all these characters in perfectness, and may serve for sufficient study of them. It is impossible to explain in what the expression of the woody strength consists, unless it be felt. One very obvious condition is the excessive fineness of curvature, approximating continually to a straight line. In order to get a piece of branch curvature given as accurately as I could by an unprejudiced person, I set one of my pupils at the Working Men's College (a joiner by trade) to draw, last spring, a lilac branch of its real size, as it grew, before it budded. It was about six feet long, and before he could get it quite right, the buds came out and interrupted him; but the fragment he got drawn is engraved in flat profile, in Plate 58. It has suffered much by reduction, one or two of its finest curves having become lost in the mere thickness of the lines. Nevertheless, if the reader will compare it carefully with the Dutch work, it will teach him something about trees.

§ 11. II. CAPRICE.—The next character we had to note of the leaf-builders was their capriciousness, noted partly in Vol. III. Chap. IX. § 14. It is a character connected with the ruggedness and ill-temperedness just spoken of, and an essential source of branch beauty: being in reality the written story of all the branch's life,—of the theories it formed, the accidents it suffered, the fits of enthusiasm to which it yielded in certain delicious warm springs; the disgusts at weeks of east wind, the mortifications of itself for its friends' sakes; or the sudden and successful inventions of new ways of getting out to the sun. The reader will understand this character in a moment, by merely comparing

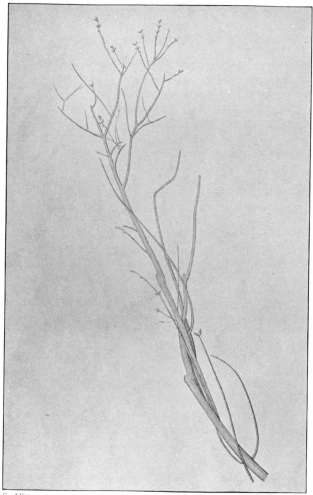

G Allen

G. Cock

53. Branch Curvature

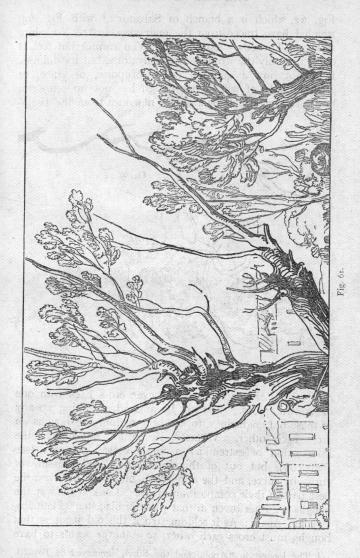

Fig. 61.

Fig. 62, which is a branch of Salvator's,[1] with Fig. 63, which I have traced from the engraving, in the Yorkshire series, of Turner's "Aske Hall." You cannot but feel at once, not only the wrongness of Salvator's, but its dulness. It is not now a question either of poise, or grace, or gravity; only of wit. That bough has got no sense; it has not been struck by a single new idea from the begin-

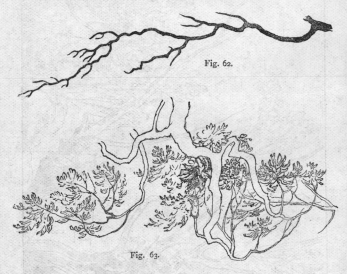

Fig. 62.

Fig. 63.

ning of it to the end; dares not even cross itself with one of its own sprays. You will be amazed, in taking up any of these old engravings, to see how seldom the boughs *do* cross each other. Whereas, in nature, not only is the intersection of extremities a mathematical necessity (see Plate 56), but out of this intersection and crossing of curve by curve, and the opposition of line it involves, the best part of their composition arises. Look at the way the boughs are interwoven in that piece of lilac stem (Plate 58).

§ 12. Again: As it seldom struck the old painters that boughs must cross each other, so it never seems to have

[1] The longest in "Apollo and the Sibyl," engraved by Boydell. (Reduced one-half.)

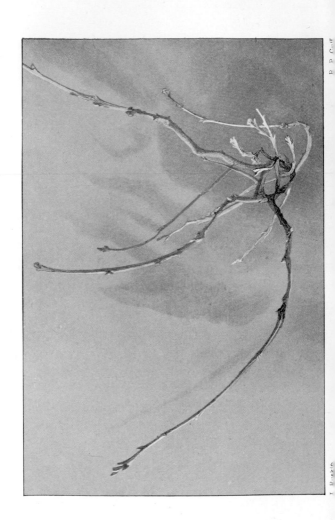

occurred to them that they must be sometimes foreshortened.
I chose this bit from "Aske Hall," that you might see
at once, both how Turner fore-
shortens the main stem, and
how, in doing so, he shows the
turning aside, and outwards, of
the one next to it, to the left,
to get more air.[1]   Indeed, this
foreshortening lies at the core
of the business; for unless it
be well understood, no branch-
form can ever be rightly drawn.
I placed the oak spray in
Plate 51, so as to be seen as
nearly straight on its flank as
possible.   It is the most uninteresting position in which a
bough can be drawn; but it
shows the first simple action
of the law of resilience.   I will
now turn the bough with its
extremity towards us, and foreshorten it (Plate 59), which
being done, you perceive another
tendency in the whole branch,
not seen at all in the first Plate,
to throw its sprays to its own right (or to your left), which
it does to avoid the branch next it, while the *forward*
action is in a sweeping curve round to your right, or to
the branch's left: a curve which it takes to recover position after its first concession.   The lines of the nearer and
smaller shoots are very nearly—thus foreshortened—those
of a boat's bow.   Here is a piece of Dutch foreshortening
for you to compare with it, Fig. 64.[2]

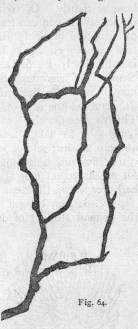

Fig. 64.

---

[1] The foreshortening of the bough to the right is a piece of great
audacity; it comes towards us two or three feet sharply, after forking,
so as to look suddenly half as thick again as at the fork; then bends
back again, and outwards.

[2] Hobbima. Dulwich Gallery, No. 131. Turn the book with its
outer edge down.

§ 13. In this final perfection of bough-drawing, Turner stands *wholly alone*. Even Titian does not foreshorten his boughs rightly. Of course he could, if he had cared to do so; for if you can foreshorten a limb or a hand, much more a tree branch. But either he had never looked at a tree carefully enough to feel that it was necessary, or, which is more likely, he disliked to introduce in a background elements of vigorous projection. Be the reason what it may, if you take Lefèvre's plates of the Peter Martyr and St. Jerome—the only ones I know which give any idea of Titian's tree-drawing, you will observe at once that the boughs lie in flakes, artificially set to the right and left, and are not intricate or varied, even where the foliage indicates some foreshortening;—completing thus the evidence for my statement long ago given, that no man but Turner had ever drawn the stem of a tree. (Vol. I. p. 417.)

§ 14. It may be well also to note, for the advantage of the general student of design, that, in foliage and bough

Fig. 65.

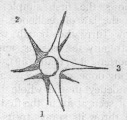

Fig. 66.

drawing, all the final grace and general utility of the study depend on its being well foreshortened; and that, till the power of doing so quite accurately is obtained, no landscape-drawing is of the least value; nor can the character of any tree be known at all until not only its branches, but its minutest extremities, have been drawn in the severest fore-shortening, with little accompanying plans of the arrange-ments of the leaves or buds, or thorns, on the stem. Thus Fig. 65 is the extremity of a single shoot of spruce fir, foreshortened, showing the resilience of its swords from beneath; and Fig. 66 is a little ground-plan, showing the position of the three lowest triple groups of thorn on a shoot of gooseberry.[1] The fir shoot is carelessly drawn; but it is not worth while to do it better, unless I engraved it on steel, so as to show the fine relations of shade.

§ 15. III. FELLOWSHIP.—The compactness of mass presented by this little sheaf of pine-swords may lead us to the consideration of the last character I have to note of boughs; namely, the mode of their association in masses. It follows, of course, from all the laws of growth we have ascertained, that the terminal outline of any tree or branch must be a simple one, containing within it, at a given height or level, the series of leaves of the year; only we have not yet noticed the kind of form which results, in each branch, from the part it has to take in forming the mass of the tree. The systems of branching are indeed infinite, and could not be exemplified by any number of types; but here are two common types, in section, which will enough explain what I mean.

§ 16. If a tree branches with a concave tendency, it is apt to carry its boughs to the outer curve of limitation, as at A, Fig. 67, and if with a convex tendency, as at B. In either case the vertical section, or profile, of a bough will give a triangular mass, terminated by curves, and elongated at one extremity. These triangular masses you may see at a glance, prevailing in the branch system of any tree in winter. They may, of course, be mathematically reduced to the four types a, b, c, and d, Fig. 67, but are capable of endless variety of expression in action, and in the adjustment of their weights to the bearing stem.

§ 17. To conclude, then, we find that the beauty of these buildings of the leaves consists, from the first step of it to the last, in its showing their perfect fellowship; and a single aim uniting them under circumstances of various distress, trial, and pleasure. Without the fellowship, no

---

[1] Their change from groups of three to groups of two, and then to single thorns at the end of the spray, will be found very beautiful in a real shoot. The figure on the left in Plate 52 is a branch of blackthorn with its spines (which are a peculiar condition of branch, and can bud like branches, while thorns have no root nor power of development). Such a branch gives good practice without too much difficulty.

beauty; without the steady purpose, no beauty; without trouble, and death, no beauty; without individual pleasure,

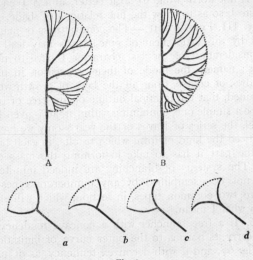

Fig. 67.

freedom, and caprice, so far as may be consistent with the universal good, no beauty.

§ 18. Tree-loveliness might be thus lost or killed in many ways. Discordance would kill it—of one leaf with another; disobedience would kill it—of any leaf to the ruling law; indulgence would kill it, and the doing away with pain; or slavish symmetry would kill it, and the doing away with delight. And this is so, down to the smallest atom and beginning of life: so soon as there is life at all, there are these four conditions of it;—harmony, obedience, distress, and delightsome inequality. Here is the magnified section of an oak-bud, not the size of a wheat grain (Fig. 68). Already its nascent leaves are seen arranged under the perfect law of resilience, preparing for stoutest work on the right side. Here is a dog-wood bud just opening into life

Fig. 68.

(Fig. 69). Its ruling law is to be four square, but see how the uppermost leaf takes the lead, and the lower bends up, already a little distressed by the effort. Overleaf is a birch-

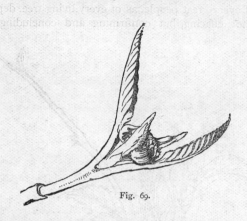

Fig. 69.

bud, farther advanced (Fig. 70). Who shall say how many humours the little thing has in its mind already; or how many adventures it has passed through? And so to the end. Help, submission, sorrow, dissimilarity, are the sources of all good;—war, disobedience, luxury, equality, the sources of all evil.

§ 19. There is yet another and a deeply laid lesson to be received from the leaf-builders, which I hope the reader has already perceived. Every leaf, we have seen, connects its work with the entire and accumulated result of the work of its predecessors. Their previous construction served it during its life, raised it towards the light, gave it more free sway and motion in the wind, and removed it from the noxiousness of earth exhalation. Dying, it leaves its own small but well-laboured thread, adding, though imperceptibly, yet essentially, to the strength, from roof to crest, of the trunk on which it had lived, and fitting that trunk for better service to succeeding races of leaves.

We men, sometimes, in what we presume to be humility, compare ourselves with leaves; but we have as yet no right to do so. The leaves may well scorn the comparison

We, who live for ourselves, and neither know how to use nor keep the work of past time, may humbly learn,—as from the ant, foresight,—from the leaf, reverence. The power of every great people, as of every living tree, depends on its not effacing, but confirming and concluding, the

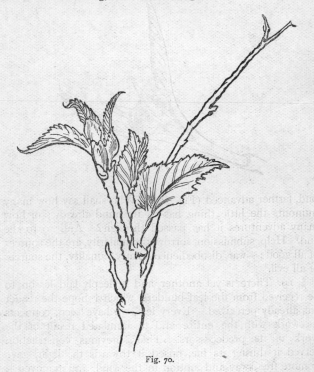

Fig. 70.

labours of its ancestors. Looking back to the history of nations, we may date the beginning of their decline from the moment when they ceased to be reverent in heart, and accumulative in hand and brain; from the moment when the redundant fruit of age hid in them the hollowness of heart, whence the simplicities of custom and sinews of tradition had withered away. Had men but guarded the righteous laws, and protected the precious works of their fathers, with half the industry they have given to change and to ravage, they would not now have been seeking vainly, in millennial visions and mechanic servitudes, the accomplishment of the promise made to them so long ago : " As the days of a tree are the days of My people, and Mine elect shall long enjoy the work of their hands ; they shall not labour in vain, nor bring forth for trouble ; for they are the seed of the blessed of the Lord, and their offspring with them."

§ 20. This lesson we have to take from the leaf's life. One more we may receive from its death. If ever, in autumn, a pensiveness falls upon us as the leaves drift by in their fading, may we not wisely look up in hope to their mighty monuments ? Behold how fair, how far prolonged, in arch and aisle, the avenues of the valleys ; the fringes of the hills ! So stately,—so eternal ; the joy of man, the comfort of all living creatures, the glory of the earth,—they are but the monuments of those poor leaves that flit faintly past us to die. Let them not pass, without our understanding their last counsel and example : that we also, careless of monument by the grave, may build it in the world—monument by which men may be taught to remember, not where we died, but where we lived.

CHAPTER IX

THE LEAF SHADOWS

§ 1. It may be judged, by the time which it has taken to arrive at any clear idea of the structure of shield-builders, what a task would open to us if we endeavoured to trace the more wonderful forms of the wild builders with the sword. Not that they are more complex; but they are more definite, and cannot be so easily generalized. The conditions which produce the spire of the cypress, and flaked breadth of the cedar, the rounded head of the stone pine, and perfect pyramid of the black spruce, are far more distinct, and would require more accurate and curious diagrams to illustrate them, than the graceful, but in some degree monotonous, branching of shield-builders. In broad principle they are, however, alike. The leaves construct the sprays in the same accumulative way : the only essential difference being that in the sword-builders the leaves are all set close, and at equal intervals. Instead of admitting extended and variable spaces between them, the whole spray is one tower of leaf-roots, set in a perfect spiral. Thus, Fig. 71, at A, represents a fragment of spray of Scotch fir of its real size. B is the same piece magnified, the diamond-like spaces being the points on which the leaves grew. The dotted lines show the regularity of the spiral. As the minor stems join in boughs, the scars left by the leaves are gradually effaced, and a thick, but broken and scaly bark forms instead.

§ 2. A sword-builder may therefore be generally con-sidered as a shield-builder put under the severest military restraint. The graceful and thin leaf is concentrated into a strong, narrow, pointed rod ; and the insertion of these

rods on the stem is in a close and perfectly timed order.
In some ambiguous trees connected with the tribe (as the
arbor vitæ) there is no proper stem to the outer leaves, but
all the extremities form a kind of coralline leaf, flat and
fern-like, but articulated like a crustacean animal, which

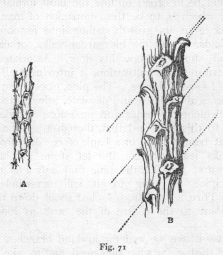

Fig. 71

gradually concentrates and embrowns itself into the stem.
The thicker branches of these trees are exquisitely fantastic;
and the mode in which the flat system of leaf first produces an irregular branch, and then adapts itself to the
symmetrical cone of the whole tree, is one of the most
interesting processes of form which I know in vegetation.

§ 3. Neither this, however, nor any other of the pine
formations, have we space here to examine in detail; while
without detail, all discussion of them is in vain. I shall
only permit myself to note a few points respecting my
favourite tree, the black spruce, not with any view to art
criticism (though we might get at some curious results by
a comparison of popular pine-drawing in Germany, America,
and other dark-wooded countries, with the true natural
forms), but because I think the expression of this tree has
not been rightly understood by travellers in Switzerland,

and that with a little watching of it, they might easily obtain a juster feeling.

§ 4. Of the many marked adaptations of nature to the mind of man, it seems one of the most singular, that trees intended especially for the adornment of the wildest mountains should be in broad outline the most formal of trees. The vine, which is to be the companion of man, is waywardly docile in its growth, falling into festoons beside his cornfields, or roofing his garden-walks, or casting its shadow all summer upon his door. Associated always with the trimness of cultivation, it introduces all possible elements of sweet wildness. The pine, placed nearly always among scenes disordered and desolate, brings into them all possible elements of order and precision. Lowland trees may lean to this side and that, though it is but a meadow breeze that bends them, or a bank of cowslips from which their trunks lean aslope. But let storm and avalanche do their worst, and let the pine find only a ledge of vertical precipice to cling to, it will nevertheless grow straight. Thrust a rod from its last shoot down the stem ; it shall point to the centre of the earth as long as the tree lives.

§ 5. Also it may be well for lowland branches to reach hither and thither for what they need, and to take all kinds of irregular shape and extension. But the pine is trained to need nothing, and to endure everything. It is resolvedly whole, self-contained, desiring nothing but rightness, content with restricted completion. Tall or short, it will be straight. Small or large, it will be round. It may be permitted also to these soft lowland trees that they should make themselves gay with show of blossom, and glad with pretty charities of fruitfulness. We builders with the sword have harder work to do for man, and must do it in close-set troops. To stay the sliding of the mountain snows, which would bury him ; to hold in divided drops, at our sword-points, the rain which would sweep away him and his treasure-fields ; to nurse in shade among our brown fallen leaves the tricklings that feed the brooks in drought ; to give massive shield against the winter wind, which shrieks through the bare branches of the plain :—such service must we do him

stedfastly while we live.   Our bodies, also, are at his
service : softer than the bodies of other trees, though our
toil is harder than theirs.   Let him take them as pleases
him, for his houses and ships.   So also it may be well for
these timid lowland trees to tremble with all their leaves,
or turn their paleness to the sky, if but a rush of rain
passes by them ; or to let fall their leaves at last, sick
and sere.   But we pines must live carelessly amidst the
wrath of clouds.   We only wave our branches to and fro
when the storm pleads with us, as men toss their arms in
a dream.

And finally, these weak lowland trees may struggle fondly
for the last remnants of life, and send up feeble saplings
again from their roots when they are cut down.   But we
builders with the sword perish boldly ; our dying shall be
perfect and solemn, as our warring : we give up our lives
without reluctance, and for ever.[1]

§ 6. I wish the reader to fix his attention for a moment
on these two great characters of the pine, its straightness
and rounded perfectness ; both wonderful, and in their
issue lovely, though they have hitherto prevented the tree
from being drawn.   I say, first, its straightness.   Because
we constantly see it in the wildest scenery, we are apt to
remember only as characteristic examples of it those which
have been disturbed by violent accident or disease.   Of
course such instances are frequent.   The soil of the pine
is subject to continual change ; perhaps the rock in which
it is rooted splits in frost and falls forward, throwing the
young stems aslope, or the whole mass of earth round it
is undermined by rain, or a huge boulder falls on its stem
from above, and forces it for twenty years to grow with
weight of a couple of tons leaning on its side.   Hence,
especially at edges of loose cliffs, about waterfalls, or at
glacier banks, and in other places liable to disturbance,
the pine may be seen distorted and oblique ; and in
Turner's " Source of the Arveron," he has, with his usual
unerring perception of the main point in any matter,

---

[1] " Crœsus, therefore, having heard these things, sent word to the
people of Lampsacus that they should let Miltiades go ; and, if not, he
would cut them down like a pine-tree."—*Herod.* vi. 37.

fastened on this means of relating the glacier's history.
The glacier cannot explain its own motion; and ordinary
observers saw in it only its rigidity; but Turner saw that
the wonderful thing was its non-rigidity. Other ice is
fixed, only this ice stirs. All the banks are staggering
beneath its waves, crumbling and withered as by the blast
of a perpetual storm. He made the rocks of his foreground loose—rolling and tottering down together; the
pines smitten aside by them, their tops dead, bared by
the ice wind.

§ 7. Nevertheless, this is not the truest or universal
expression of the pine's character. I said long ago (Vol. I.
p. 135), even of Turner: "Into the spirit of the pine he
cannot enter." He understood the glacier at once; he
had seen the force of sea on shore too often to miss the
action of those crystal-crested waves. But the pine was
strange to him, adverse to his delight in broad and flowing
line; he refused its magnificent erectness. Magnificent!—
nay, sometimes almost terrible. Other trees, tufting crag
or hill, yield to the form and sway of the ground, clothe
it with soft compliance, are partly its subjects, partly its
flatterers, partly its comforters. But the pine rises in
serene resistance, self-contained; nor can I ever without
awe stay long under a great Alpine cliff, far from all house
or work of men, looking up to its companies of pines, as
they stand on the inaccessible juts and perilous ledges
of the enormous wall, in quiet multitudes, each like the
shadow of the one beside it—upright, fixed, spectral, as
troops of ghosts standing on the walls of Hades, not
knowing each other—dumb for ever. You cannot reach
them, cannot cry to them;—those trees never heard
human voice; they are far above all sound but of the
winds. No foot ever stirred fallen leaf of theirs. All
comfortless they stand, between the two eternities of the
Vacancy and the Rock: yet with such iron will, that the
rock itself looks bent and shattered beside them—fragile,
weak, inconsistent, compared to their dark energy of
delicate life, and monotony of enchanted pride:—un-
numbered, unconquerable.

§ 8. Then note, farther, their perfectness. The impression

on most people's minds must have been received more from pictures than reality, so far as I can judge :—so ragged they think the pine; whereas its chief character in health is green and full *roundness*. It stands compact, like one of its own cones, slightly curved on its sides, finished and quaint as a carved tree in some Elizabethan garden; and instead of being wild in expression, forms the softest of all forest scenery; for other trees show their trunks and twisting boughs : but the pine, growing either in luxuriant mass or in happy isolation, allows no branch to be seen. Summit behind summit rise its pyramidal ranges, or down to the very grass sweep the circlets of its boughs; so that there is nothing but green cone and green carpet. Nor is it only softer, but in one sense more cheerful than other foliage; for it casts only a pyramidal shadow. Lowland forest arches overhead, and chequers the ground with darkness; but the pine, growing in scattered groups, leaves the glades between emerald-bright. Its gloom is all its own; narrowing into the sky, it lets the sunshine strike down to the dew. And if ever a superstitious feeling comes over me among the pine-glades, it is never tainted with the old German forest fear; but is only a more solemn tone of the fairy enchantment that haunts our English meadows; so that I have always called the prettiest pine-glade in Chamouni, "Fairies' Hollow." It is in the glen beneath the steep ascent above Pont Pelissier, and may be reached by a little winding path which goes down from the top of the hill; being, indeed, not truly a glen, but a broad ledge of moss and turf, leaning in a formidable precipice (which, however, the gentle branches hide) over the Arve. An almost isolated rock promontory, many-coloured, rises at the end of it. On the other sides it is bordered by cliffs, from which a little cascade falls, literally, down among the pines, for it is so light, shaking itself into mere showers of seed pearl in the sun, that the pines don't know it from mist, and grow through it without minding. Underneath, there is only the mossy silence, and above, for ever, the snow of the Nameless Aiguille.

§ 9. And then the third character which I want you to notice in the pine is its exquisite fineness. Other trees

rise against the sky in dots and knots, but this in fringes.[1]
You never see the edges of it, so subtle are they; and
for this reason, it chiefly of trees, is capable of the fiery
change which we saw before had been noticed by Shake-
spere. When the sun rises behind a ridge crested with
pine, provided the ridge be at a distance of about two miles,
and seen clear, all the trees, for about three or four degrees
on each side of the sun, become trees of light, seen in clear
flame against the darker sky, and dazzling as the sun itself.
This is owing to the lustre of the leaves, and their minute
division. It seems as if these trees, living always among
the clouds, had caught part of their glory from them; and
themselves the darkest of vegetation, could yet add splendour
to the sun itself.

§ 10. Yet I have been more struck by their character of
finished delicacy at a distance from the central Alps, among

---

[1] Keats (as is his way) puts nearly all that may be said of the pine
into one verse, though they are only figurative pines of which he is
speaking. I have come to that pass of admiration for him now, that I
dare not read him, so discontented he makes me with my own work:
but others must not leave unread, in considering the influence of trees
upon the human soul, that marvellous ode to Psyche. Here is the
piece about pines :—

> " Yes, I will be thy priest, and build a fane
>   In some untrodden region of my mind,
>   Where branchèd thoughts, new grown with pleasant pain,
>   Instead of pines, shall murmur in the wind :
>   Far, far around shall those dark-clustered trees
>   *Fledge the wild-ridgèd mountains*, steep by steep ;
>   And there by zephyrs, streams, and birds, and bees,
>   The moss-lain Dryads shall be lull'd to sleep ;
>   And in the midst of this wide quietness
>   A rosy sanctuary will I dress
>   With the wreath'd trellis of a working brain,
>   With buds, and bells, and stars without a name,
>   With all the Gardener Fancy e'er could feign,
>   Who, breeding flowers, will never breed the same.
>   And there shall be for thee all soft delight
>   That shadowy thought can win ;
>   A bright torch, and a casement ope, at night,
>   To let the warm Love in."

the pastoral hills of the Emmenthal, or lowland districts of Berne, where they are set in groups between the cottages, whose shingle roofs (they also of pine) of deep gray blue, and lightly carved fronts, golden and orange in the autumn sunshine,[1] gleam on the banks and lawns of hill-side,— endless lawns, mounded, and studded, and bossed all over with deeper green hay-heaps, orderly set, like jewellery (the mountain hay, when the pastures are full of springs, being strangely dark and fresh in verdure for a whole day after it is cut). And amidst this delicate delight of cottage and field, the young pines stand delicatest of all, scented as with frankincense, their slender stems straight as arrows, and crystal white, looking as if they would break with a touch like needles ; and their arabesques of dark leaf pierced through and through by the pale radiance of clear sky, opal blue, where they follow each other along the soft hill-ridges, up and down.

§ 11. I have watched them in such scenes with the deeper interest, because of all trees they have hitherto had most influence on human character. The effect of other vegetation, however great, has been divided by mingled species ; elm and oak in England, poplar in France, birch in Scotland, olive in Italy and Spain, share their power with inferior trees, and with all the changing charm of successive agriculture. But the tremendous unity of the pine absorbs and moulds the life of a race. The pine shadows rest upon a nation. The Northern peoples, century after century, lived under one or other of the two great powers of the Pine and the Sea, both infinite. They dwelt amidst the forests, as they wandered on the waves, and saw no end, nor any other horizon ; still the dark green trees, or the dark green waters, jagged the dawn with their fringe or their foam. And whatever elements of imagination, or of warrior strength, or of domestic justice, were brought down by the Norwegian and the Goth against the dissoluteness or degradation of

[1] There has been much cottage-building about the hills lately, with very pretty carving, the skill in which has been encouraged by travellers ; and the fresh-cut larch is splendid in colour under rosy sunlight.

the South of Europe, were taught them under the green
roofs and wild penetralia of the pine.

§ 12. I do not attempt, delightful as the task would
be, to trace this influence (mixed with superstition) in
Scandinavia, or North Germany; but let us at least note
it in the instance which we speak of so frequently, yet
so seldom take to heart. There has been much dispute
respecting the character of the Swiss, arising out of the
difficulty which other nations had to understand their
simplicity. They were assumed to be either romantically
virtuous, or basely mercenary, when in fact they were
neither heroic nor base, but were true-hearted men, stubborn
with more than any recorded stubbornness; not much
regarding their lives, yet not casting them causelessly away;
forming no high ideal of improvement, but never relaxing
their grasp of a good they had once gained; devoid of all
romantic sentiment, yet loving with a practical and patient
love that neither wearied nor forsook; little given to
enthusiasm in religion, but maintaining their faith in a
purity which no worldliness deadened, and no hypocrisy
soiled; neither chivalrously generous nor pathetically
humane, yet never pursuing their defeated enemies, not
suffering their poor to perish; proud, yet not allowing
their pride to prick them into unwary or unworthy
quarrel; avaricious, yet contentedly rendering to their
neighbour his due; dull, but clear-sighted to all the
principles of justice; and patient, without ever allowing
delay to be prolonged by sloth, or forbearance by fear.

§ 13. This temper of Swiss mind, while it animated
the whole confederacy, was rooted chiefly in one small
district which formed the heart of their country, yet lay
not among its highest mountains. Beneath the glaciers
of Zermatt and Evolena, and on the scorching slopes of
the Valais, the peasants remained in an aimless torpor,
unheard of but as the obedient vassals of the great
Bishopric of Sion. But where the lower ledges of cal-
careous rock were broken by the inlets of the Lake Lucerne,
and bracing winds penetrating from the north forbade
the growth of the vine, compelling the peasantry to adopt
an entirely pastoral life, was reared another race of men.

Their narrow domain should be marked by a small green spot on every map of Europe. It is about forty miles from east to west; as many from north to south; yet on that shred of rugged ground, while every kingdom of the world around it rose or fell in fatal change, and every multi- tudinous race mingled or wasted itself in various disper- sion and decline, the simple shepherd dynasty remained changeless. There is no record of their origin. They are neither Goths, Burgundians, Romans, nor Germans. They have been for ever Helvetii, and for ever free. Voluntarily placing themselves under the protection of the House of Hapsburg, they acknowledged its supremacy, but resisted its oppression; and rose against the unjust governors it appointed over them, not to gain, but to redeem, their liberties. Victorious in the struggle by the Lake of Egeri, they stood the foremost standard-bearers among the nations of Europe in the cause of loyalty and life—loyalty in its highest sense, to the laws of God's helpful justice, and of man's faithful and brotherly fortitude.

§ 14. You will find among them, as I said, no subtle wit nor high enthusiasm, only an undeceivable common sense, and an obstinate rectitude. They cannot be per- suaded into their duties, but they feel them; they use no phrases of friendship, but do not fail you at your need. Questions of creed, which other nations sought to solve by logic or reverie, these shepherds brought to practical tests; sustained with tranquillity the excommunication of abbots who wanted to feed their cattle on other people's fields, and, halbert in hand, struck down the Swiss Refor- mation, because the Evangelicals of Zurich refused to send them their due supplies of salt. Not readily yielding to the demands of superstition, they were patient under those of economy; they would purchase the remission of taxes, but not of sins; and while the sale of indulgences was arrested in the church of Ensiedeln as boldly as at the gates of Wittenberg, the inhabitants of the valley of Frutigen[1] ate no meat for seven years, in order peacefully

---

[1] This valley is on the pass of the Gemmi in Canton Berne, but the people are the same in temper as those of the Waldstätten.

to free themselves and their descendants from the seigniorial claims of the Baron of Thurm.

§ 15. What praise may be justly due to this modest and rational virtue, we have perhaps no sufficient grounds for defining. It must long remain questionable how far the vices of superior civilization may be atoned for by its achievements, and the errors of more transcendental devotion forgiven to its rapture. But, take it for what we may, the character of this peasantry is, at least, serviceable to others and sufficient for their own peace ; and in its consistency and simplicity, it stands alone in the history of the human heart. How far it was developed by circumstances of natural phenomena may also be disputed ; nor should I enter into such dispute with any strongly held conviction. The Swiss have certainly no feelings respecting their mountains in anywise correspondent with ours. It was rather as fortresses of defence, than as spectacles of splendour, that the cliffs of the Rothstock bare rule over the destinies of those who dwelt at their feet ; and the training for which the mountain children had to thank the slopes of the Muotta-Thal, was in soundness of breath, and steadiness of limb, far more than in elevation of idea. But the point which I desire the reader to note is, that the character of the scene which, if any, appears to have been impressive to the inhabitant, is not that which we ourselves feel when we enter the district. It was not from their lakes, nor their cliffs, nor their glaciers—though these were all peculiarly their possession, that the three venerable cantons or states received their name. They were not called the States of the Rock, nor the States of the Lake, but the States of the *Forest*. And the one of the three which contains the most touching record of the spiritual power of Swiss religion, in the name of the convent of the " Hill of Angels," has, for its own, none but the sweet childish name of " Under the Woods."

§ 16. And indeed you may pass under them if, leaving the most sacred spot in Swiss history, the Meadow of the Three Fountains, you bid the boatman row southward a little way by the shore of the Bay of Uri. Steepest there on its western side, the walls of its rocks ascend to heaven.

Far in the blue of evening, like a great cathedral pavement, lies the lake in its darkness; and you may hear the whisper of innumerable falling waters return from the hollows of the cliff, like the voices of a multitude praying under their breath. From time to time the beat of a wave, slow lifted, where the rocks lean over the black depth, dies heavily as the last note of a requiem. Opposite, green with steep grass, and set with châlet villages, the Frohnalp rises in one solemn glow of pastoral light and peace; and above, against the clouds of twilight, ghostly on the gray precipice, stand, myriad by myriad, the shadowy armies of the Unterwalden pine.[1]

I have seen that it is possible for the stranger to pass through this great chapel, with its font of waters, and mountain pillars, and vaults of clouds, without being touched by one noble thought, or stirred by any sacred passion; but for those who received from its waves the baptism of their youth, and learned beneath its rocks the fidelity of their manhood, and watched amidst its clouds the likeness of the dream of life, with the eyes of age—for these I will not believe that the mountain shrine was built, or the calm of its forest-shadows guarded by their God, in vain.

[1] The cliff immediately bordering the lake is in Canton Uri; the green hills of Unterwalden rise above. This is the grandest piece of the shore of Lake Lucerne; the rocks near Tell's Chapel are neither so lofty nor so precipitous.

CHAPTER X

LEAVES MOTIONLESS

§ 1. It will be remembered that our final inquiry was to be into the sources of beauty in the tented plants, or flowers of the field; which the reader may perhaps suppose one of no great difficulty, the beauty of flowers being somewhat generally admitted and comprehended.

Admitted? yes. Comprehended? no; and, which is worse, in all its highest characters, for many a day yet, incomprehensible: though with a little steady application, I suppose we might soon know more than we do now about the colours of flowers,—being tangible enough, and staying longer than those of clouds. We have discovered something definite about colours of opal and of peacock's plume; perhaps, also, in due time we may give some account of that true gold (the only gold of intrinsic value) which gilds buttercups; and understand how the spots are laid, in painting a pansy.

Art of interest, when we may win any of its secrets; but to such knowledge the road lies not up brick streets. And howsoever that flower-painting may be done, one thing is certain, it is not by machinery.

§ 2. Perhaps, it may be thought, if we understood flowers better, we might love them less.

We do not love them much, as it is. Few people really care about flowers. Many, indeed, are fond of finding a new shape of blossom, caring for it as a child cares about a kaleidoscope. Many, also, like a fair service of flowers in the greenhouse, as a fair service of plate on the table. Many are scientifically interested in them, though even these in the nomenclature rather than the flowers. And a few enjoy their gardens : but I have never heard of a piece of land, which would let well on a building lease, remaining unlet because it was a flowery piece. I have never heard of parks being kept for wild hyacinths, though often of their being kept for wild beasts. And the blossoming time of the year being principally spring, I perceive it to be the mind of most people, during that period, to stay in towns.

§ 3. A year or two ago, a keen-sighted and eccentrically-minded friend of mine, having taken it into his head to violate this national custom, and go to the Tyrol in spring, was passing through a valley near Landeck, with several similarly headstrong companions. A strange mountain appeared in the distance, belted about its breast with a zone of blue, like our English Queen. Was it a blue cloud? a blue horizontal bar of the air that Titian breathed in youth, seen now far away, which mortal might never breathe again? Was it a mirage—a meteor? Would it stay to be approached? (ten miles of winding road yet between them, and the foot of its mountain). Such questioning had they concerning it. My keen-sighted friend alone maintained it to be substantial : whatever it might be, it was not air, and would not vanish. The ten miles of road were overpassed, the carriage left, the mountain climbed. It stayed patiently, expanding still into richer breadth and heavenlier glow—a belt of gentians. Such things may verily be seen among the Alps in spring, and in spring only. Which being so, I observe most people prefer going in autumn.

§ 4. Nevertheless, without any special affection for them, most of us, at least, languidly consent to the beauty of flowers, and occasionally gather them, and prefer them from among other forms of vegetation. This, strange to say, is precisely what great painters do *not*.

Every other kind of object they paint, in its due place and office, with respect ;—but, except compulsorily and imperfectly, never flowers. A curious fact this ! Here are men whose lives are spent in the study of colour, and the one thing they will not paint is a flower ! Anything but that. A furred mantle, a jewelled zone, a silken gown, a brazen corslet, nay, an old leathern chair, or a wall-paper if you will, with utmost care and delight;—but a flower by no manner of means, if avoidable. When the thing has perforce to be done, the great painters of course do it rightly. Titian, in his early work, sometimes carries a blossom or two out with affection, as the columbines in our Bacchus and Ariadne. So also Holbein. But in his later and mightier work, Titian will only paint a fan or wristband intensely, never a flower. In his portrait of Lavinia, at Berlin, the roses are just touched finely enough to fill their place, with no affection whatever, and with the most subdued red possible; while in the later portrait of her, at Dresden, there are no roses at all, but a belt of chased golden balls, on every stud of which Titian has concentrated his strength, and I verily believe forgot the face a little, so much has his mind been set on them.

§ 5. In Paul Veronese's Europa, at Dresden, the entire foreground is covered with flowers, but they are executed with sharp and crude touches like those of a decorative painter. In Correggio's paintings, at Dresden, and in the Antiope of the Louvre, there are lovely pieces of foliage, but no flowers. A large garland of oranges and lemons, with their leaves, above the St. George, at Dresden, is connected traditionally with the garlanded backgrounds of Ghirlandajo and Mantegna, but the studious absence of flowers renders it almost disagreeably ponderous. I do not remember any painted by Velasquez, or by Tintoret, except compulsory Annunciation lilies. The flowers of Rubens are gross and rude; those of Vandyck vague, slight, and subdued in colour, so as not to contend with the flesh. In his portraits of King Charles's children, at Turin, an enchanting picture, there is a rose-thicket, in which the roses seem to be enchanted the wrong way, for their leaves are all gray, and the flowers dull brick-red. Yet it is right.

§ 6. One reason for this is that all great men like their inferior forms to follow and obey contours of large surfaces, or group themselves in connected masses. Patterns do the first, leaves the last; but flowers stand separately.

Another reason is that the beauty of flower-petals and texture can only be seen by looking at it close; but flat patterns can be seen far off, as well as gleaming of metal-work.

All the great men calculate their work for effect at some distance, and with that object, know it to be lost time to complete the drawing of flowers. Farther, the forms of flowers being determined, require a painful attention, and restrain the fancy; whereas, in painting fur, jewels, or bronze, the colour and touch may be varied almost at pleasure, and without effort.

Again, much of what is best in flowers is inimitable in painting; and a thoroughly good workman feels the feebleness of his means when he matches them fairly with Nature, and gives up the attempt frankly—painting the rose dull red, rather than trying to rival its flush in sunshine.

And, lastly, in nearly all good landscape-painting, the breadth of foreground included implies such a distance of the spectator from the nearest object as must entirely prevent his seeing flower detail.

§ 7. There is, however, a deeper reason than all these; namely, that flowers have no sublimity. We shall have to examine the nature of sublimity in our following and last section, among other ideas of relation. Here I only note the fact briefly, that impressions of awe and sorrow being at the root of the sensation of sublimity, and the beauty of separate flowers not being of the kind which connects itself with such sensation, there is a wide distinction, in general, between flower-loving minds and minds of the highest order. Flowers seem intended for the solace of ordinary humanity: children love them; quiet, tender, contented ordinary people love them as they grow; luxurious and disorderly people rejoice in them gathered: they are the cottager's treasure; and in the crowded town, mark, as with a little broken fragment of rainbow, the windows of the workers in whose heart rests the covenant of peace. Passionate or religious minds contemplate them with fond, feverish intensity; the affection is seen severely calm in the works of many old religious painters, and mixed with more open and true country sentiment in those of our own Pre-Raphaelites. To the child and the girl, the peasant and the manufacturing operative, to the grisette and the nun, the lover and monk, they are precious always. But to the men of supreme power and thoughtfulness, precious only at times; symbolically and pathetically often to the poets, but rarely for their own sake. They fall forgotten from the great workmen's and soldiers' hands. Such men will take, in thankfulness, crowns of leaves, or crowns of thorns—not crowns of flowers.

§ 8. Some beautiful things have been done lately, and more beautiful are likely to be done, by our younger painters, in representing blossoms of the orchard and the field in mass and extent. I have had something to do with the encouragement of this impulse; and truly, if pictures are to be essentially imitative rather than inventive, it is better to spend care in painting hyacinths than dead leaves, and roses rather than stubble. Such work, however, as I stated in my first essay on this subject, in the year 1851,[1] can only connect itself with the great schools by becoming inventive instead of copyist; and for the most part, I believe these young painters would do well to remember that the best beauty of flowers being wholly inimitable, and their sweetest service unrenderable by art, the picture involves some approach to an unsatisfying mockery in the cold imagery of what Nature has given to be breathed with the profuse winds of spring, and touched by the happy footsteps of youth.

§ 9. Among the greater masters, as I have said, there is little laborious or affectionate flower-painting. The utmost that Turner ever allows in his foregrounds is a water-lily or two, a cluster of heath or fox-glove, a thistle sometimes, a violet or daisy, or a bindweed-bell; just enough to lead the eye into the understanding of the rich mystery of his more distant leafage. Rich mystery, indeed, respecting which these following facts about the foliage of tented plants must be noted carefully.

§ 10. Two characters seem especially aimed at by nature in the earth-plants; first, that they should be characteristic and interesting; secondly, that they should not be very visibly injured by crushing.

---

[1] *Pre-Raphaelitism*: p. 28, and the note at p. 27; compare p. 63. (See now On the Old Road, Vol. I. Part 1, § 185 and note, and § 219.) The essay contains some important notes on Turner's work, which, therefore, I do not repeat in this volume.

I say, first, characteristic. The leaves of large trees
take approximately simple forms, slightly monotonous.
They are intended to be seen in mass. But the leaves
of the herbage at our feet take all kinds of strange shapes,
as if to invite us to examine them. Star-shaped, heart-
shaped, spear-shaped, arrow-shaped, fretted, fringed, cleft,
furrowed, serrated, sinuated; in whorls, in tufts, in spires,
in wreaths, endlessly expressive, deceptive, fantastic, never

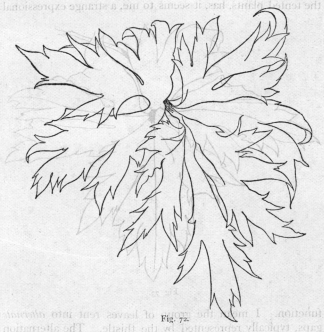

Fig. 72.

the same from footstalk to blossom; they seem perpetually
to tempt our watchfulness, and take delight in outstripping
our wonder.

§ 11. Secondly, observe, their forms are such as will
not be visibly injured by crushing. Their complexity is
already disordered: jags and rents are their laws of being;
rent by the footstep, they betray no harm. Here, for
instance (Fig. 72), is the mere outline of a buttercup-leaf

in full free growth; which, perhaps, may be taken as a
good common type of earth foliage. Fig. 73 is a less
advanced one, placed so as to show its symmetrical bound-
ing form. But both, how various;—how delicately rent
into beauty! As in the aiguilles of the great Alps, so in
this lowest field-herb, where rending is the law of being, it
is the law of loveliness.

§ 12. One class, however, of these torn leaves, peculiar to
the tented plants, has, it seems to me, a strange expressional

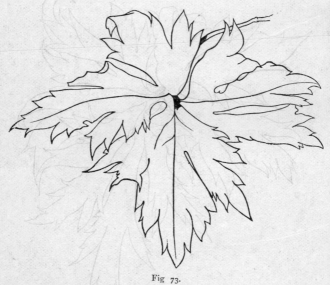

Fig 73.

function. I mean the group of leaves rent into *alternate*
gaps, typically represented by the thistle. The alternation
of the rent, if not absolutely, is, effectively, peculiar to the
earth-plants. Leaves of the builders are rent symmetrically,
so as to form radiating groups, as in the horse-chestnut, or
they are irregularly sinuous, as in the oak; but the earth-
plants continually present forms such as those in the
opposite Plate: a kind of web-footed leaf, so to speak; a
continuous tissue, enlarged alternately on each side of the
stalk. Leaves of this form have necessarily a kind of

J. Ruskin

J. Cousen

60 The Rending of Leaves

limping gait, as if they grew not all at once, but first a
little bit on one side, and then a little bit on the other,
and wherever they occur in quantity, give the expression to
foreground vegetation which we feel and call "ragged."

§ 13. It is strange that the mere alternation of the rent
should give this effect; the more so, because alternate leaves,
completely separate from each other, produce one of the
most graceful types of building plants. Yet the fact is
indeed so, that the alternate rent in the earth-leaf is the
principal cause of its ragged effect. However deeply it
may be rent symmetrically, as in the alchemilla, or butter-
cup, just instanced, and however finely divided, as in the
parsleys, the result is always a delicate richness, unless the
jags are alternate, and the leaf-tissue continuous at the
stem; and the moment these conditions appear, so does
the raggedness.

§ 14. It is yet more worthy of note that the proper duty
of these leaves, which catch the eye so clearly and power-
fully, would appear to be to draw the attention of man to
spots where his work is needed, for they nearly all habitually
grow on ruins or neglected ground: not noble ruins, or on
wild ground, but on heaps of rubbish, or pieces of land
which have been indolently cultivated or much disturbed.
The leaf on the right of the three in the Plate, which is the
most characteristic of the class, is that of the Sisymbrium
Irio, which grows, by choice, always on ruins left by fire.
The plant, which, as far as I have observed, grows first
on earth that has been moved, is the coltsfoot: its broad
covering leaf is much jagged, but only irregular, not alternate in the rent; but the weeds that mark habitual neglect,
such as the thistle, give clear alternation.

§ 15. The aspects of complexity and carelessness of
injury are farther increased in the herb of the field, because
it is "herb yielding seed;" that is to say, a seed different
in character from that which trees form in their fruit.

I am somewhat alarmed in reading over the above
sentence, lest a botanist, or other scientific person, should
open the book at it. For of course the essential character
of either fruit or seed being only that in the smallest compass, the vital principle of the plant is rendered portable,

and for some time preservable, we ought to call every such vegetable dormitory a "fruit" or a "seed" indifferently. But with respect to man there is a notable difference between them.

A seed is what we "sow."

A fruit, what we "enjoy."

Fruit is seed prepared especially for the sight and taste of man and animals; and in this sense we have true fruit and traitorous fruit (poisonous); but it is perhaps the best available distinction,[1] that, seed being the part necessary for the renewed birth of the plant, a fruit is such seed enclosed or sustained by some extraneous substance, which is soft and juicy, and beautifully coloured, pleasing and useful to animals and men.

§ 16. I find it convenient in this volume, and wish I had thought of the expedient before, whenever I get into a difficulty, to leave the reader to work it out. He will perhaps, therefore, be so good as to define fruit for himself. Having defined it, he will find that the sentence about which I was alarmed above is, in the main, true, and that tented plants principally are herbs yielding seed, while building plants give fruit. The berried shrubs of rock and wood, however dwarfed in stature, are true builders. The strawberry-plant is the only important exception—a tender Bedouin.

§ 17. Of course the principal reason for this is the plain, practical one, that fruit should not be trampled on, and had better perhaps be put a little out of easy reach than too near the hand, so that it may not be gathered wantonly

---

[1] I say the "best available distinction." It is, of course, no real distinction. A pea-pod is a kind of central type of seed and seed-vessel, and it is difficult so to define fruit as to keep clear of it. Pea-shells are boiled and eaten in some countries rather than pease. It does not sound like a scientific distinction to say that fruit is a "shell which is good without being boiled." Nay, even if we humiliate ourselves into this practical reference to the kitchen, we are still far from success. For the pulp of a strawberry is not a "shell," the seeds being on the outside of it. The available part of a pomegranate or orange, though a seed envelope, is itself shut within a less useful rind. While in an almond the shell becomes less profitable still, and all goodness retires into the seed itself, as in a grain of corn.

or without some little trouble, and may be waited for until it is properly ripe; while the plants meant to be trampled on have small and multitudinous seed, hard and wooden, which may be shaken and scattered about without harm.

Also, fine fruit is often only to be brought forth with patience: not by young and hurried trees—but in due time, after much suffering; and the best fruit is often to be an adornment of old age, so as to supply the want of other grace. While the plants which will not work, but only bloom and wander, do not (except the grasses) bring forth fruit of high service, but only the seed that prolongs their race, the grasses alone having great honour put on them for their humility, as we saw in our first account of them.

§ 18. This being so, we find another element of very complex effect added to the others which exist in tented plants, namely, that of minute, granular, feathery, or downy seed-vessels, mingling quaint brown punctuation, and dusty tremors of dancing grain, with the bloom of the nearer fields; and casting a gossamered grayness and softness of plumy mist along their surfaces far away; mysterious evermore, not only with dew in the morning or mirage at noon, but with the shaking threads of fine arborescence, each a little belfry of grain-bells, all a-chime.

§ 19. I feel sorely tempted to draw one of these same spires of the fine grasses, with its sweet changing proportions of pendent grain, but it would be a useless piece of finesse, as such form, of course, never enters into general foreground effect.[1] I have, however, engraved at the top

---

[1] For the same reason, I enter into no consideration respecting the geometrical forms of flowers, though they are deeply interesting, and perhaps some day I may give a few studies of them separately. The reader should note, however, that beauty of form in flowers is chiefly dependent on a more accurately finished or more studiously varied development of the tre-foil, quatre-foil, and cinq-foil structures which we have seen irregularly approached by leaf-buds. The most beautiful six-foiled flowers (like the rhododendron-shoot) are composed of two triangular groups, one superimposed on the other, as in the narcissus; and the most interesting types both of six-foils and cinq-foils are unequally leaved, symmetrical on opposite sides, as the iris and violet.

of the group of woodcuts opposite (Fig. 74), a single leaf
cluster of Dürer's foreground in the St. Hubert, which is
interesting in several ways; as an example of modern work,
no less than old; for it is a facsimile twice removed; being
first drawn from the plate with the pen, by Mr. Allen, and
then facsimiled on wood by Miss Byfield; and if the reader
can compare it with the original, he will find it still come
tolerably close in most parts (though the nearest large leaf
has got spoiled), and of course some of the finest and most
precious qualities of Dürer's work are lost.   Still, it gives
a fair idea of his perfectness of conception, every leaf being
thoroughly set in perspective, and drawn with unerring
decision.   On each side of it (Figs. 75, 76) are two pieces
from a fairly good modern etching, which I oppose to the
Dürer in order to show the difference between true work
and that which pretends to give detail, but is without feeling
or knowledge.   There are a great many leaves in the piece
on the left, but they are all set the same way; the draughts-
man has not conceived their real positions, but draws one
after another as he would deliver a tale of bricks.   The
grasses on the right look delicate, but are a mere series
of inorganic lines.   Look how Dürer's grass-blades cross
each other.   If you take a pen and copy a little piece of
each example, you will soon feel the difference.   Underneath (Fig. 77) is a piece of grass out of Landseer's
etching of the "Ladies' Pets," more massive and effective
than the two lateral fragments, but still loose and uncom-
posed.   Then overleaf (Fig. 78) is a piece of firm and
good work again, which will stand with Dürer's; it is the
outline only of a group of leaves out of Turner's foreground
in the Richmond from the Moors, of which I give a reduced
etching, Plate 61, for the sake of the foreground principally,
and in Plate 62, the group of leaves in question, in their
light and shade, with the bridge beyond.   What I have chiefly
to say of them belongs to our section on composition; but
this mere fragment of a Turner foreground may perhaps
lead the reader to take note in his great pictures of the
almost inconceivable labour with which he has sought to
express the redundance and delicacy of ground leafage.

§ 20. By comparing the etching in Plate 61 with the

J. M. W. Turner

J. C. Armytage

61. Richmond from the Moors

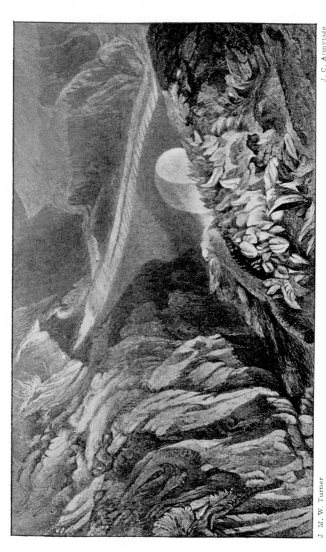

J. M. W. Turner

J. C. Armytage

62 By the Brookside

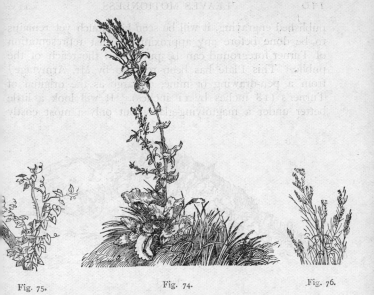

Fig. 75.   Fig. 74.   Fig. 76.

Fig. 77.

published engraving, it will be seen how much yet remains to be done before any approximately just representation of Turner foreground can be put within the reach of the public. This Plate has been reduced by Mr. Armytage [1] from a pen-drawing of mine, as large as the original of Turner's (18 inches by 11 inches). It will look a little better under a magnifying-glass; but only a most costly

Fig. 78.

engraving of the real size could give any idea of the richness of mossy and ferny leafage included in the real design. And if this be so on one of the ordinary England drawings of a barren Yorkshire moor, it may be imagined what the task would be of engraving truly such a foreground as that of the "Bay of Baiæ" or "Daphne and Leucippus," in which Turner's aim has been luxuriance.

§ 21. His mind recurred, in all these classical foregrounds, to strong impressions made upon him during his studies at Rome, by the masses of vegetation which enrich its heaps of ruin with their embroidery and bloom. I have always partly regretted these Roman studies, thinking that they led him into too great fondness of wandering luxuriance in vegetation, associated with decay; and prevented his giving affection enough to the more solemn and more sacred infinity with which, among the mightier ruins of the Alpine Rome, glow the pure and motionless splendours of the gentian and the rose.

§ 22. Leaves motionless. The strong pines wave above

[1] [Reproduced in photogravure for this edition.]

them, and the weak grasses tremble beside them ; but the blue stars rest upon the earth with a peace as of heaven ; and far along the ridges of iron rock, moveless as they, the rubied crests of Alpine rose flush in the low rays of morning. Nor these yet the stillest leaves. Others there are subdued to a deeper quietness, the mute slaves of the earth, to whom we owe, perhaps, thanks, and tenderness, the most profound of all we have to render for the leaf ministries.

§ 23. It is strange to think of the gradually diminished power and withdrawn freedom among the orders of leaves —from the sweep of the chestnut and gadding of the vine, down to the close shrinking trefoil, and contented daisy, pressed on earth ; and, at last, to the leaves that are not merely close to earth, but themselves a part of it ; fastened down to it by their sides, here and there only a wrinkled edge rising from the granite crystals. We have found beauty in the tree yielding fruit, and in the herb yielding seed. How of the herb yielding *no* seed,[1] the fruitless, flowerless lichen of the rock ?

§ 24. Lichen, and mosses (though these last in their luxuriance are deep and rich as herbage, yet both for the most part humblest of the green things that live),—how of these ? Meek creatures ! the first mercy of the earth, veiling with hushed softness its dintless rocks ; creatures full of pity, covering with strange and tender honour the scarred disgrace of ruin,—laying quiet finger on the trembling stones, to teach them rest. No words, that I know of, will say what these mosses are. None are delicate enough, none perfect enough, none rich enough. How is one to tell of the rounded bosses of furred and beaming green,—the starred divisions of rubied bloom, fine-filmed, as if the Rock Spirits could spin porphyry as we do glass, —the traceries of intricate silver, and fringes of amber, lustrous, arborescent, burnished through every fibre into fitful brightness and glossy traverses of silken change, yet all subdued and pensive, and framed for simplest, sweetest offices of grace ? They will not be gathered, like the

---

[1] The reader must remember always that my work is concerning the *aspects* of things only. Of course, a lichen has seeds, just as other plants have, but not effectually or visibly for man.

flowers, for chaplet or love-token ; but of these the wild
bird will make its nest, and the wearied child his pillow.

And, as the earth's first mercy, so they are its last gift
to us. When all other service is vain, from plant and tree,
the soft mosses and gray lichen take up their watch by the
head-stone. The woods, the blossoms, the gift-bearing
grasses, have done their parts for a time, but these do
service for ever. Trees for the builder's yard, flowers for
the bride's chamber, corn for the granary, moss for the
grave.

§ 25. Yet as in one sense the humblest, in another they
are the most honoured of the earth-children. Unfading,
as motionless, the worm frets them not, and the autumn
wastes not. Strong in lowliness, they neither blanch in
heat nor pine in frost. To them, slow-fingered, constant-
hearted, is entrusted the weaving of the dark, eternal
tapestries of the hills ; to them, slow-pencilled, iris-dyed,
the tender framing of their endless imagery. Sharing the
stillness of the unimpassioned rock, they share also its endurance; and while the winds of departing spring scatter the
white hawthorn blossom like drifted snow, and summer dims
on the parched meadow the drooping of its cowslip-gold,
—far above, among the mountains, the silver lichen-spots
rest, star-like, on the stone ; and the gathering orange stain
upon the edge of yonder western peak reflects the sunsets
of a thousand years.

PART VII

OF CLOUD BEAUTY

CHAPTER I

THE CLOUD-BALANCINGS

§ 1. WE have seen that when the earth had to be prepared for the habitation of man, a veil, as it were, of intermediate being was spread between him and its darkness, in which were joined, in a subdued measure, the stability and insensibility of the earth, and the passion and perishing of mankind.

But the heavens, also, had to be prepared for his habitation.

Between their burning light,— their deep vacuity, and man, as between the earth's gloom of iron substance, and man, a veil had to be spread of intermediate being;— which should appease the unendurable glory to the level of human feebleness, and sign the changeless motion of the heavens with a semblance of human vicissitude.

Between the earth and man arose the leaf. Between the heaven and man came the cloud. His life being partly as the falling leaf, and partly as the flying vapour.

§ 2. Has the reader any distinct idea of what clouds are? We had some talk about them long ago, and perhaps thought their nature, though at that time not clear to us, would be easily enough understandable when we put ourselves seriously to make it out. Shall we begin with one or two easiest questions?

That mist which lies in the morning so softly in the valley, level and white, through which the tops of the trees rise as if through an inundation—why is *it* so heavy? and why does it lie so low, being yet so thin and frail that it will melt away utterly into splendour of morning, when the sun has shone on it but a few moments more? Those colossal pyramids, huge and firm, with outlines as of rocks, and strength to bear the beating of the high sun full on their fiery flanks—why are *they* so light,—their bases high over our heads, high over the heads of Alps? why will these melt away, not as the sun rises, but as he descends, and leave the stars of twilight clear, while the valley vapour gains again upon the earth like a shroud?

Or that ghost of a cloud, which steals by yonder clump of pines: nay, which does *not* steal by them, but haunts them, wreathing yet round them, and yet—and yet, slowly: now falling in a fair waved line like a woman's veil; now fading, now gone: we look away for an instant, and look back, and it is again there. What has it to do with that clump of pines, that it broods by them and weaves itself among their branches, to and fro? Has it hidden a cloudy treasure among the moss at their roots, which it watches thus? Or has some strong enchanter charmed it into fond returning, or bound it fast within those bars of bough? And yonder filmy crescent, bent like an archer's bow above the snowy summit, the highest of all the hill,—that white arch which never forms but over the supreme crest,—how is it stayed there, repelled apparently from the snow—nowhere touching it, the clear sky seen between it and the mountain edge, yet never leaving it—poised as a white bird hovers over its nest?

Or those war-clouds that gather on the horizon, dragon-crested, tongued with fire;—how is their barbed strength bridled? what bits are these they are champing with their vaporous lips; flinging off flakes of black foam? Leagued leviathans of the Sea of Heaven, out of their nostrils goeth smoke, and their eyes are like the eyelids of the morning. The sword of him that layeth at them cannot hold; the spear, the dart, nor the habergeon. Where ride the captains of their armies? Where are set the measures of their march? Fierce murmurers, answering each other from morning until evening—what rebuke is this which has awed them into peace? what hand has reined them back by the way by which they came?

§ 3. I know not if the reader will think at first that questions like these are easily answered. So far from it, I rather believe that some of the mysteries of the clouds never will be understood by us at all. "Knowest thou the balancings of the clouds?" Is the answer ever to be one of pride? "The wondrous works of Him which is *perfect* in knowledge?" Is *our* knowledge ever to be so?

It is one of the most discouraging consequences of the varied character of this work of mine, that I am wholly unable to take note of the advance of modern science. What has conclusively been discovered or observed about clouds, I know not; but by the chance inquiry possible to me I find no book which fairly states the difficulties of accounting for even the ordinary aspects of the sky. I shall, therefore, be able in this section to do little more than suggest inquiries to the reader, putting the subject in a clear form for him. All men accustomed to investigation will confirm me in saying that it is a great step when we are personally quite certain what we do *not* know.

§ 4. First, then, I believe we do not know what makes clouds float. Clouds are water, in some fine form or another; but water is heavier than air, and the finest form you can give a heavy thing will not make it float in a light thing. *On* it, yes; as a boat; but *in* it, no. Clouds are not boats, nor boat-shaped; and they float in the air, not on the top of it. "Nay, but though unlike boats, may they not be like feathers? If out of quill substance there may be constructed eider-down, and out of vegetable tissue, thistle-down, both buoyant enough for a time, surely of water-tissue may be constructed also water-down, which will be buoyant enough for all cloudy purposes." Not so. Throw out your eider plumage in a calm day, and it will all come settling to the ground: slowly indeed, to aspect; but practically so fast that all our finest clouds would be here in a heap about our ears in an hour or two, if they were only made of water-feathers.

"But may they not be quill feathers, and have air inside them? May not all their particles be minute little balloons?"

A balloon only floats when the air inside it is either specifically, or by heating, lighter than the air it floats in. If the cloud-feathers had warm air inside their quills, a cloud would be warmer than the air about it, which it is not (I believe). And if the cloud-feathers had hydrogen inside their quills, a cloud would be unwholesome for breathing, which it is not—at least so it seems to me.

"But may they not have nothing inside their quills?" Then they would rise, as bubbles do through water, just as certainly as, if they were solid feathers, they would fall. All our clouds would go up to the top of the air, and swim in eddies of cloud-foam.

"But is not that just what they do?" No. They float at different heights, and with definite forms, in the body of the air itself. If they rose like foam, the sky on a cloudy day would look like a very large flat glass of champagne seen from below, with a stream of bubbles (or clouds) going up as fast as they could to a flat foam-ceiling.

"But may they not be just so nicely mixed out of something and nothing, as to float where they are wanted?"

Yes; that is just what they not only may, but must be: only this way of mixing something and nothing is the very thing I want to explain or have explained, and cannot do it, nor get it done.

§ 5. Except thus far. It is conceivable that minute hollow spherical globules might be formed of water, in which the enclosed vacuity just balanced the weight of the enclosing water, and that the arched sphere formed by the watery film was strong enough to prevent the pressure of the atmosphere from breaking it in. Such a globule would float like a balloon at the height in the atmosphere where the equipoise between the vacuum it enclosed, and its own excess of weight above that of the air, was exact. It would, probably, approach its companion globules by reciprocal attraction, and form aggregations which might be visible.

This is, I believe, the view usually taken by meteorologists.

I state it as a possibility, to be taken into account in examining the question—a possibility confirmed by the Scriptural words which I have taken for the title of this chapter.

§ 6. Nevertheless, I state it as a possibility only, not seeing how any known operation of physical law could explain the formation of such molecules. This, however, is not the only difficulty. Whatever shape the water is thrown into, it seems at first improbable that it should lose its property of wetness. Minute division of rain, as in "Scotch mist," makes it capable of floating farther,[1] or floating up and down a little, just as dust will float, though pebbles will not; or gold-leaf, though a sovereign will not; but minutely divided rain wets as much as any other kind, whereas a cloud, partially always, sometimes entirely, loses its power of moistening. Some low clouds look, when you are in them, as if they were made of specks of dust, like short hairs; and these clouds are

---

[1] The buoyancy of solid bodies of a given specific gravity, in a given fluid, depends, first on their size, then on their forms.

First, on their size; that is to say, on the proportion of the magnitude of the object (irrespective of the distribution of its particles) to the magnitude of the particles of the air.

Thus, a grain of sand is buoyant in wind, but a large stone is not; and pebbles and sand are buoyant in water in proportion to their smallness, fine dust taking long to sink, while a large stone sinks at once. Thus we see that water may be arranged in drops of any magnitude, from the largest rain-drop, about the size of a large pea, to an atom so small as not to be separately visible, the smallest rain passing gradually into mist. Of these drops of different sizes (supposing the strength of the wind the same), the largest fall fastest, the smaller drops are more buoyant, and the small misty rain floats about like a cloud, as often up as down, so that an umbrella is useless in it; though in a heavy thunderstorm, if there is no wind, one may stand gathered up under an umbrella without a drop touching the feet.

Secondly, buoyancy depends on the amount of surface which a given weight of the substance exposes to the resistance of the substance it floats in. Thus, gold-leaf is in a high degree buoyant, while the same quantity of gold in a compact grain would fall like a shot; and a feather is buoyant, though the same quantity of animal matter in a compact form would be as heavy as a little stone. A slate blows far from a house-top, while a brick falls vertically, or nearly so.

entirely dry. And also many clouds will wet some substances, but not others. So that we must grant farther,
if we are to be happy in our theory, that the spherical
molecules are held together by an attraction which prevents their adhering to any foreign body, or perhaps ceases
only under some peculiar electric conditions.

§ 7. The question remains, even supposing their pro-
duction accounted for,—What intermediate states of water
may exist between these spherical hollow molecules and
pure vapour?

Has the reader ever considered the relations of commonest
forms of volatile substance? The invisible particles which
cause the scent of the rose-leaf, how minute, how multitudinous, passing richly away into the air continually! The
visible cloud of frankincense—why visible? Is it in consequence of the greater quantity, or larger size of the
particles, and how does the heat act in throwing them off
in this quantity, or of this size?

Ask the same questions respecting water. It dries, that
is, becomes volatile, invisibly, at (any?) temperature. Snow
dries, as water does. Under increase of heat, it volatilizes
faster, so as to become dimly visible in large mass, as a
heat-haze. It reaches boiling point, then becomes entirely
visible. But compress it, so that no air shall get between
the watery particles—it is invisible again. At the first
issuing from the steam-pipe the steam is transparent; but
opaque, or visible, as it diffuses itself. The water is indeed
closer, because cooler, in that diffusion; but more air is
between its particles. Then this very question of visibility
is an endless one, wavering between form of substance
and action of light. The clearest (or least visible) stream
becomes brightly opaque by more minute division in its
foam, and the clearest dew in hoar-frost. Dust, unperceived
in shade, becomes constantly visible in sunbeam; and watery
vapour in the atmosphere, which is itself opaque, when
there is promise of fine weather, becomes exquisitely transparent; and (questionably) blue when it is going to rain.

§ 8. Questionably blue: for besides knowing very little
about water, we know what, except by courtesy, must, I
think, be called nothing—about air. Is it the watery

vapour, or the air itself, which is blue ? Is neither blue,
but only white, producing blue when seen over dark
spaces ? If either blue, or white, why, when crimson is
their commanded dress, are the most distant clouds
crimsonest ? Clouds close to us may be blue, but far
off golden—a strange result, if the air is blue. And again,
if blue, why are rays that come through large spaces of it
red ; and that Alp, or anything else that catches far away
light, why coloured red, at dawn and sunset ? No one
knows, I believe. It is true that many substances, as
opal, are blue, or green, by reflected light, yellow by
transmitted ; but air, if blue at all, is blue always by
transmitted light. I hear of a wonderful solution of
nettles, or other unlovely herb, which is green when
shallow,—red when deep. Perhaps some day, as the
motion of the heavenly bodies by help of an apple, their
light by help of a nettle, may be explained to mankind.

§ 9. But farther : these questions of volatility, and visibility, and hue, are all complicated with those of shape.
How is a cloud outlined ? Granted whatever you choose
to ask, concerning its material, or its aspect, its loftiness
and luminousness,—how of its limitation ? What hews
it into a heap, or spins it into a web ? Cold is usually
shapeless, I suppose, extending over large spaces equally,
or with gradual diminution. You cannot have, in the open
air, angles, and wedges, and coils, and cliffs of cold. Yet
the vapour stops suddenly, sharp and steep as a rock, or
thrusts itself across the gates of heaven in likeness of a
brazen bar ; or braids itself in and out, and across and
across, like a tissue of tapestry ; or falls into ripples like
sand ; or into waving shreds and tongues, as fire. On
what anvils and wheels is the vapour pointed, twisted,
hammered, whirled, as the potter's clay ? By what hands
is the incense of the sea built up into domes of marble ?

And, lastly, all these questions respecting substance, and
aspect, and shape, and line, and division, are involved with
others as inscrutable, concerning action. The curves in
which clouds move are unknown ;—nay, the very method
of their motion, or apparent motion, how far it is by
change of place, how far by appearance in one place and

vanishing from another. And these questions about movement lead partly far away into high mathematics, where I
cannot follow them, and partly into theories concerning
electricity and infinite space, where I suppose at present
no one can follow them.

What, then, is the use of asking the questions?

For my own part, I enjoy the mystery, and perhaps the
reader may. I think he ought. He should not be less
grateful for summer rain, or see less beauty in the clouds
of morning, because they come to prove him with hard
questions; to which, perhaps, if we look close at the
heavenly scroll,[1] we may find also a syllable or two of
answer illuminated here and there.

---

[1] There is a beautiful passage in *Sartor Resartus* concerning this old
Hebrew scroll, in its deeper meanings, and the child's watching it,
though long illegible for him, yet "with an eye to the gilding." It
signifies in a word or two nearly all that is to be said about clouds.
(Not quite.—J. R., 1884.)

CHAPTER II

THE CLOUD-FLOCKS

§ 1. FROM the tenor of the foregoing chapter, the reader will, I hope, be prepared to find me, though dogmatic (it is said) upon some occasions, anything rather than dogmatic respecting clouds. I will assume nothing concerning them, beyond the simple fact, that as a floating sediment forms in a saturated liquid, vapour forms in the body of the air; and all that I want the reader to be clear about, in the outset, is that this vapour floats in and with the wind (as, if you throw any thick colouring-matter into a river, it floats with the stream), and that it is not blown before a denser volume of the wind, as a fleece of wool would be.

§ 2. At whatever height they form, clouds may be broadly considered as of two species only, massive and striated. I cannot find a better word than massive, though it is not a good one, for I mean it only to signify a fleecy arrangement in which no *lines* are visible. The fleece may be so bright as to look like flying thistle-down, or so diffused as to show no visible outline at all. Still if it is all of one common texture, like a handful of wool, or a wreath of smoke, I call it massive.

On the other hand, if divided by parallel lines, so as to look more or less like spun-glass, I call it striated. In Plate 69, Fig. 4, the top of the Aiguille Dru (Chamouni) is seen emergent above low striated clouds, with heaped massive cloud beyond. I do not know in the least what causes this striation, except that it depends on the nature of the cloud, not on the wind. The strongest wind will not throw a cloud, massive by nature, into the linear form.

It will toss it about, and tear it to pieces, but not spin it into threads. On the other hand, often without any wind at all, the cloud will spin itself into threads fine as gossamer. These threads are often said to be a prognostic of storm; but they are not produced by storm.

§ 3. In the first volume, we considered all clouds as belonging to three regions, that of the cirrus, the central cloud, and the rain-cloud. It is of course an arrangement more of convenience than of true description, for cirrus clouds sometimes form low as well as high; and rain sometimes falls high as well as low. I will, nevertheless, retain this old arrangement, which is practically as serviceable as any.

Allowing, also, for various exceptions and modifications, these three bodies of cloud may be generally distinguished in our minds thus. The clouds of upper region are for the most part quiet, or seem to be so, owing to their distance. They are formed now of striated, now of massive substance; but always finely divided. The central clouds are entirely of massive substance, but divided into large ragged flakes or ponderous heaps. These heaps (cumuli) and flakes, or drifts, present different phenomena, but must be joined in our minds under the head of central cloud. The lower clouds, bearing rain abundantly, are composed partly of striated, partly of massive substance; but may generally be comprehended under the term rain-cloud.

Our business in this chapter then is with the upper clouds, which, owing to their quietness and multitude, we may perhaps conveniently think of as the " cloud-flocks." And we have to discover if any laws of beauty attach to them, such as we have seen in mountains or tree-branches.

§ 4. On one of the few mornings of this winter, when the sky was clear, and one of the far fewer, on which its clearness was visible from the neighbourhood of London,— which now entirely loses at least two out of three sunrises, owing to the environing smoke,—the dawn broke beneath a broad field of level purple cloud, under which floated ranks of divided cirri, composed of finely striated vapour. It was not a sky containing any extraordinary number

63. The Cloud-Flocks

of these minor clouds; but each was more than usually
distinct in separation from its neighbour, and as they
showed in nearly pure pale scarlet on the dark purple
ground, they were easily to be counted.

§ 5. There were five or six ranks, from the zenith to
the horizon; that is to say, three distinct ones, and then
two or three more running to-
gether, and losing themselves
in distance, in the manner
roughly shown in Fig. 79. The
nearest rank was composed of
more than 150 rows of cloud,
set obliquely, as in the figure.
I counted 150, which was near

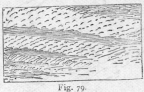

Fig. 79.

the mark, and then stopped, lest the light should fail, to
count the separate clouds in some of the rows. The average
number was 60 in each row, rather more than less.

There were therefore 150 × 60, that is, 9,000, separate
clouds in this one rank, or about 50,000 in the field of
sight.   Flocks of Admetus under Apollo's keeping.   Who
else could shepherd such?   He by day, dog Sirius by
night; or huntress Diana herself—her bright arrows driving
away the clouds of prey that would ravage her fair flocks.
We must leave fancies, however; these wonderful clouds
need close looking at.   I will try to draw one or two of
them before they fade.

§ 6. On doing which we find, after all, they are not
much more like sheep than Canis Major is like a dog.
They resemble more some of our old friends, the pine
branches, covered with snow.   The three, forming the
uppermost figure, in the Plate opposite, are as like three
of the fifty thousand as I could get them; complex enough
in structure, even this single group.   Busy workers they
must be, that twine the braiding of them all to the horizon,
and down beyond it.

And who are these workers?   You have two questions
here, both difficult.   What separates these thousands of
clouds each from the other, and each about equally from
the other?   How can they be drawn asunder, yet not
allowed to part?   Looped lace as it were, richest point—

invisible threads fastening embroidered cloud to cloud—the " plighted clouds " of Milton,—creatures of the element—

> " That in the colours of the rainbow live,
> And play in the plighted clouds."

Fig. 80.

Compare Geraldine dressing :—

> " Puts on her silken vestments white,
> And tricks her hair in lovely plight."

And Britomart's—

> " Her well-plighted frock
> She low let fall, that flowed from her lanck side,
> Down to her foot with careless modesty."

And, secondly, what bends each of them into these flame-like curves, tender and various, as motions of a bird, hither

and thither ?   Perhaps you may hardly see the curves well
in the softly finished forms ; here they are plainer in rude
outline, Fig. 80.[1]

§ 7. What is it that throws them into these lines ?

Eddies of wind ?

Nay, an eddy of wind will not stay quiet for three
minutes, as that cloud did to be drawn ; as all the others
did, each in his place.   You see there is perfect harmony
among the curves.   They all flow into each other as the
currents of a stream do.   If you throw dust that will float
on the surface of a slow river, it will arrange itself in lines
somewhat like these.   To a certain extent, indeed, it is

---

[1] Before going farther, I must say a word or two respecting method
of drawing clouds.

Absolutely well no cloud *can* be drawn with the point ; nothing but
the most delicate management of the brush will express its variety of
edge and texture.   By laborious and tender engraving, a close approximation may be obtained either to nature or to good painting ; and the
engravings of sky by our modern line engravers are often admirable ;—
in many respects as good as can be, and to my mind the best part of
their work.   There still exist some early proofs of Miller's plate of the
Grand Canal, Venice, in which the sky is the likest thing to Turner's
work I have ever seen in large engravings.   The plate was spoiled
after a few impressions were taken off by desire of the publisher.   The
sky was so exactly like Turner's that he thought it would not please
the public, and had all the fine cloud-drawing rubbed away to make it
soft.

The Plate opposite page 132, by Mr. Armytage, is also, I think, a
superb specimen of engraving, though, in result, not so good as the
one just spoken of, because this was done from my copy of Turner's
sky, not from the picture itself.

But engraving of this finished kind cannot, by reason of its costliness,
be given for every illustration of cloud form.   Nor, if it could, can skies
be sketched with the completion which would bear it.   It is sometimes
possible to draw one cloud out of fifty thousand with something like
fidelity before it fades.   But if we want the arrangement of the fifty
thousand, they can only be indicated with the rudest lines, and finished
from memory.   It was, as we shall see presently, only by his gigantic
powers of memory that Turner was enabled to draw skies as he did.

Now, I look upon my own memory of clouds, or of anything else, as
of no value whatever.   All the drawings on which I have ever rested
an assertion have been made without stirring from the spot ; and in
sketching clouds from nature, it is very seldom desirable to use the

true that there are gentle currents of change in the atmosphere, which move slowly enough to permit in the clouds
that follow them some appearance of stability.   But how
to obtain change so complex in an infinite number of consecutive spaces ;—fifty thousand separate groups of current
in half of a morning sky, with quiet invisible vapour between,
or none ;—and yet all obedient to one ruling law, gone
forth through their companies ;—each marshalled to their
white standards, in great unity of warlike march, unarrested,
unconfused ?   " One shall not trust another, they shall walk
every one in his own path."

§ 8.   These questions occur, at first sight, respecting
every group of cirrus cloud.   Whatever the form may be,
whether branched, as in this instance, or merely rippled, or
thrown into shield-like segments, as in Fig. 81—a frequent
arrangement—there is still the same difficulty in accounting
satisfactorily for the individual forces which regulate the
similar shape of each mass, while all are moved by a general

brush.   For broad effects and notes of colour (though these, hastily
made, are always inaccurate, and letters indicating the colour do nearly
as well) the brush may be sometimes useful ; but, in most cases, a dark
pencil, which will lay shade with its side and draw lines with its point,
is the best instrument.   Turner almost always outlined merely with the
point, being able to remember the relations of shade without the
slightest chance of error.   The point, at all events, is needful, however
much stump work may be added to it.

Now, in translating sketches made with the pencil point into engraving, we must either engrave delicately and expensively, or be
content to substitute for the soft varied pencil lines the finer and
uncloudlike touches of the pen.   It is best to do this boldly, if at all,
and without the least aim at fineness of effect, to lay down a vigorous
black line as the limit of the cloud-form or action.   The more subtle a
painter's finished work, the more fearless he is in using the vigorous
black line when he is making memoranda, or treating his subject
conventionally.   At page 230, Vol. IV., the reader may see the
kind of outline which Titian uses for clouds in his pen work.
Usually he is even bolder and coarser.   And in the rude woodcuts I
am going to employ here, I believe the reader will find ultimately that,
with whatever ill success used by me, the means of expression are the
fullest and most convenient that can be adopted, short of finished
engraving, while there are some conditions of cloud-action which I
satisfy myself better in expressing by these coarse lines than in any
other way.

force that has apparently no influence on the divided structure. Thus the mass of clouds disposed as in Fig. 81 will probably move, mutually, in the direction of the

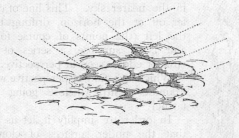

Fig. 81.

arrow; that is to say, sideways, as far as their separate curvature is concerned. I suppose it probable that as the science of electricity is more perfectly systematized, the explanation of many circumstances of cloud-form will be rendered by it. At present I see no use in troubling the reader or myself with conjectures which a year's progress in science might either effectively contradict or supersede. All that I want is, that we should have our questions ready to put clearly to the electricians when the electricians are ready to answer us.

§ 9. It is possible that some of the loveliest conditions of these parallel clouds may be owing to a structure which I forgot to explain, when it occurred in rocks, in the course of the last volume.

When they are finely stratified, and their surfaces abraded by broad, shallow furrows, the edges of the beds, of course, are thrown into undulations, and at some distance, where the furrows disappear, the surface looks as if the rock had flowed over it in successive waves. Such a condition is seen on the left at the top in Fig. 17 in Vol. IV. (p. 161). Supposing a series of beds of vapour cut across by a straight sloping current of air, and so placed as to catch the light on their edges, we should have a series of curved lights, looking like independent clouds.

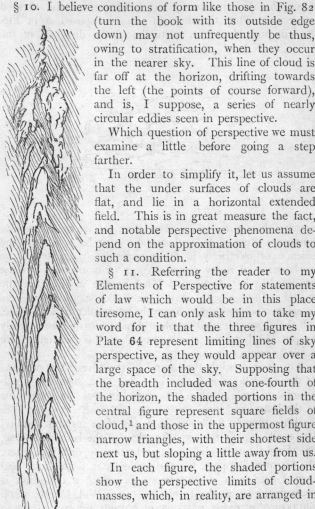

§ 10. I believe conditions of form like those in Fig. 82 (turn the book with its outside edge down) may not unfrequently be thus, owing to stratification, when they occur in the nearer sky. This line of cloud is far off at the horizon, drifting towards the left (the points of course forward), and is, I suppose, a series of nearly circular eddies seen in perspective.

Which question of perspective we must examine a little before going a step farther.

In order to simplify it, let us assume that the under surfaces of clouds are flat, and lie in a horizontal extended field. This is in great measure the fact, and notable perspective phenomena depend on the approximation of clouds to such a condition.

§ 11. Referring the reader to my Elements of Perspective for statements of law which would be in this place tiresome, I can only ask him to take my word for it that the three figures in Plate 64 represent limiting lines of sky perspective, as they would appear over a large space of the sky. Supposing that the breadth included was one-fourth of the horizon, the shaded portions in the central figure represent square fields of cloud,[1] and those in the uppermost figure narrow triangles, with their shortest side next us, but sloping a little away from us.

In each figure, the shaded portions show the perspective limits of cloud-masses, which, in reality, are arranged in

Fig. 82.

[1] If the figures are supposed to include less than one-fourth of the horizon, the shaded figures represent diamond-shaped clouds ; but the reader cannot understand this without studying perspective laws accurately.

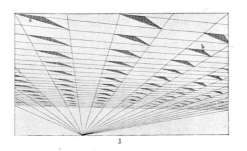

1

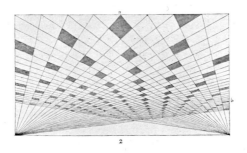

2

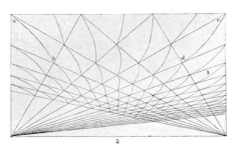

3

J Ruskin   J Emslie

64 Cloud Perspective (Rectilinear)

perfectly straight lines, are all similar, and are equidistant from each other. Their exact relative positions are marked by the lines connecting them, and may be determined by the reader if he knows perspective. If he does not, he may be surprised at first to be told that the stubborn and blunt little triangle, b, Fig. 1, Plate 64, represents a cloud precisely similar, and similarly situated, to that represented by the thin triangle, a; and, in like manner, the stout diamond, a, Fig. 2, represents precisely the same form and size of cloud as the thin strip at b. He may perhaps think it still more curious that the retiring perspective which causes stoutness in the triangle, causes leanness in the diamond.[1]

§ 12. Still greater confusion in aspect is induced by the apparent change caused by perspective in the direction of the wind. If Fig. 3 be supposed to include a quarter of the horizon, the spaces, into which its straight lines divide it, represent squares of sky. The curved lines, which cross these spaces from corner to corner, are precisely parallel throughout; and, therefore, two clouds moving, one on the curved line from a to b, and the other on the other side, from c to d, would, in reality, be moving with the same wind, in parallel lines. In Plate 66, which is a sketch of an actual sunset behind Beauvais cathedral (the point of the roof of the apse, a little to the left of the centre, shows it to be a summer sunset), the white cirri in the high light are all moving eastward, away from the sun, in perfectly parallel lines, curving a little round to the south. Underneath, are two straight ranks of rainy cirri, crossing each other; one directed south-east; the other, north-west. The meeting perspective of these, in extreme distance, determines the shape of the angular light which opens above the cathedral. Underneath all, fragments of true rain-cloud are floating between us and the sun, governed by curves of their own. They are, nevertheless, connected with the straight cirri

---

[1] In reality, the retiring ranks of cloud, if long enough, would, of course, go on converging to the horizon. I do not continue them, because the figures would become too compressed.

by the dark semi-cumulus in the middle of the shade above the cathedral.

§ 13. Sky perspective, however, remains perfectly simple, so long as it can be reduced to any rectilinear arrangement; but when nearly the whole system is curved, which nine times out of ten is the case, it becomes embarrassing. The central figure in Plate 65 represents the simplest possible combination of perspective of straight lines with that of curves, a group of concentric circles of small clouds being supposed to cast shadows from the sun near the horizon. Such shadows are often cast in misty air; the aspect of rays about the sun being, in fact, only caused by spaces between them. They are carried out formally and far in the Plate, to show how curiously they may modify the arrangement of light in a sky. The woodcut, Fig. 83, gives roughly the arrangement of the clouds in

Fig. 83.

Turner's Pools of Solomon, in which he has employed a concentric system of circles of this kind, and thus lighted. In the perspective figure the clouds are represented as small square masses, for the sake of greater simplicity, and are so beaded or strung as it were on the curves in which they move, as to keep their distances precisely equal, and their sides parallel. This is the usual condition of cloud: for though arranged in curved ranks, each

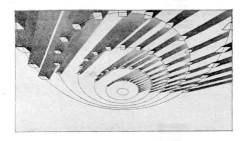

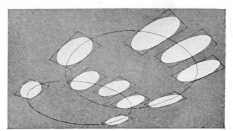

J Ruskin   J. Emslie

65. Cloud Perspective (Curvilinear)

cloud has its face to the front, or, at all events, acts in
some parallel line—generally another curve—with those
next to it : being rarely, except in the form of fine radiating striæ, arranged on the curves as at *a*, Fig. 84; but

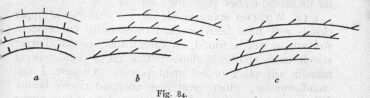

a   *b*   *c*

Fig. 84.

as at *b*, or *c*. It would make the diagram too complex
if I gave one of intersecting curves; but the lowest
figure in Plate **65** represents, in perspective, two groups
of ellipses arranged in equidistant straight and parallel
lines, and following each other on two circular curves.
Their exact relative position is shown in Fig. **2**, Plate **56**.
While the uppermost figure in Plate **65** represents, in
parallel perspective, a series of ellipses arranged in radiation on a circle, their exact relative size and position
are shown in Fig. **3**, Plate **56**, and the lines of such a
sky as would be produced by them, roughly, in Fig. 90,
page 145.[1]

§ 14. And in these figures, which, if we look up the
subject rightly, would be but the first and simplest of the
series necessary to illustrate the action of the upper cirri,
the reader may see, at once, how necessarily painters,
untrained in observance of proportion, and ignorant of
perspective, must lose in every touch the expression of
buoyancy and space in sky.   The absolute forms of each
cloud are, indeed, not alike, as the ellipses in the engraving;
but assuredly, when moving in groups of this kind, there
are among them the same proportioned inequalities of
relative distance, the same gradated changes from ponderous

[1] I use ellipses in order to make these figures easily intelligible;
the curves actually *are* variable curves, of the nature of the cycloid,
or other curves of continuous motion; probably produced by a current
moving in some such direction as that indicated by the dotted line
in Fig. 3, Plate **56**.

to elongated form, the same exquisite suggestions of including curve; and a common painter, dotting his clouds
down at random, or in more or less equal masses, can
no more paint a sky, than he could, by random dashes
for its ruined arches, paint the Coliseum.

§ 15. Whatever approximation to the character of upper
clouds may have been reached by some of our modern
students, it will be found, on careful analysis, that Turner
stands more absolutely alone in this gift of cloud-drawing
than in any other of his great powers. Observe, I say,
cloud-*drawing;* other great men coloured clouds beautifully; none but he ever drew them truly: this power
coming from his constant habit of drawing skies, like
everything else, with the pencil point. It is quite impossible to engrave any of his large finished skies on a
small scale; but the woodcut, Fig. 85, will give some idea
of the forms of cloud involved in one of his small drawings.
It is only half of the sky in question, that of Rouen from
St. Catherine's Hill, in the Rivers of France. Its clouds
are arranged on two systems of intersecting circles, crossed
beneath by long bars very slightly bent. The form of
every separate cloud is completely studied; the manner
of drawing them will be understood better by help of the
Plate opposite, which is a piece of the sky above the
"Campo Santo,"[1] at Venice, exhibited in 1842. It is
exquisite in rounding of the separate fragments and
buoyancy of the rising central group, as well as in its
expression of the wayward influence of curved lines of
breeze on a generally rectilinear system of cloud.

§ 16. To follow the subject farther would, however,
lead us into doctrine of circular storms, and all kinds of
pleasant, but infinite, difficulty, from which temptation I
keep clear, believing that enough is now stated to enable
the reader to understand what he is to look for in Turner's
skies; and what kind of power, thought, and science are
involved continually in the little white or purple dashes of
cloud-spray, which, in such pictures as the San Benedetto,

---

[1] Now in the possession of E. Bicknell, Esq., who kindly lent me
the picture, that I might make this drawing from it carefully.

J. M. W. Turner

67. Clouds

J. C. Armytage

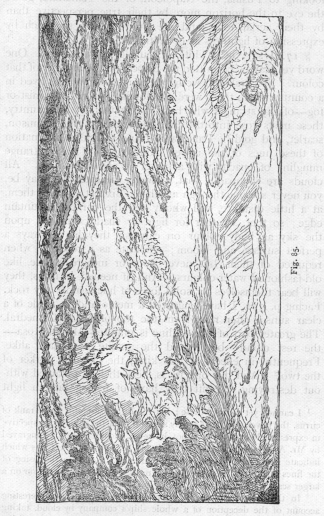

Fig. 85.

looking to Fusina, the Napoleon, or the Temeraire, guide the eye to the horizon more by their true perspective than by their aerial tone, and are buoyant, not so much by expression of lightness as of motion.[1]

§ 17. I say the "white or purple" cloud-spray. One word yet may be permitted me respecting the mystery of that colour. What should we have thought—if we had lived in a country where there were no clouds, but only low mist or fog—of any stranger who had told us that, in his country, these mists rose into the air and became purple, crimson, scarlet, and gold? I am aware of no sufficient explanation of these hues of the upper clouds, nor of their strange mingling of opacity with a power of absorbing light. All clouds are so opaque that, however delicate they may be, you never see one through another. Six feet depth of them, at a little distance, will wholly veil the darkest mountain edge; so that, whether for light or shade, they tell upon the sky as body colour on canvas; they have always a perfect surface and bloom;—delicate as a rose-leaf, when required of them, but never poor or meagre in hue, like old-fashioned water-colours. And, if needed, in mass, they will bear themselves for solid force of hue against any rock. Facing p. 372, I have engraved a memorandum made of a clear sunset after rain, from the top of Milan Cathedral. The greater part of the outline is granite—Monte Rosa— the rest cloud: but it and the granite were dark alike. Frequently, in effects of this kind, the cloud is darker of the two.[2] And this opacity is, nevertheless, obtained without destroying the gift they have of letting broken light

---

[1] I cannot yet engrave these; but the little study of a single rank of cirrus, the lowest in Plate 63, may serve to show the value of perspective in expressing buoyancy. It is not, however, though beautifully engraved by Mr. Armytage, as delicate as it should be, in the finer threads which indicate increasing distance at the extremity. Compare the rising of the lines of curve at the edges of this mass, with the similar action on a larger scale, of Turner's cloud, facing p. 132.

[2] In the Autobiography of John Newton there is an interesting account of the deception of a whole ship's company by cloud, taking the aspect and outline of mountainous land. They ate the last provision in the ship, so sure were they of its being land, and were nearly starved to death in consequence.

through them, so that, between us and the sun, they may become golden fleeces, and float as fields of light.

Now their distant colours depend on these two properties together; partly on the opacity, which enables them to reflect light strongly; partly on a spongelike power of gathering light into their bodies.

§ 18. Long ago it was noted by Aristotle, and again by Leonardo, that vaporous bodies looked russet, or even red, when warm light was seen through them, and blue, when deep shade was seen through them. Both colours may, generally, be seen on any wreath of cottage smoke.

Whereon, easy conclusion has been sometimes founded by modern reasoners. All red in sky is caused by light seen through vapour, and all blue by shade seen through vapour.

Easy, indeed, but not sure, even in cloud-colour only. It is true that the smoke of a town may be of a rich brick red against golden twilight; and of a very lovely, though not bright, blue against shade. But I never saw crimson or scarlet smoke, nor ultramarine smoke.

Even granting that watery vapour in its purity may give the colours more clearly, the red colours are by no means always relieved against light. The finest scarlets are constantly seen in broken flakes on a deep purple ground of heavier cloud beyond, and some of the loveliest rose-colours on clouds in the east, opposite the sunset, or in the west in the morning. Nor are blues always attainable by throwing vapour over shade. Especially, you cannot get them by putting it over blue itself. A thin vapour on dark blue sky is of a warm gray, not blue. A thunder-cloud, deep enough to conceal everything behind it, is often dark lead colour, or sulphurous blue; but the thin vapours crossing it, milky white. The vividest hues are connected also with another attribute of clouds, their lustre—metallic in effect, watery in reality. They not only reflect colour as dust or wool would, but, when far off, as water would; sometimes even giving a distinct image of the sun underneath the orb itself; in all cases becoming dazzling in lustre, when at a low angle, capable of strong reflection. Practically, this low angle is only obtained when the cloud seems near the sun, and hence we get into the careless

habit of looking at the golden reflected light, as if it were
actually caused by nearness to the fiery ball.

§ 19. Without, however, troubling ourselves at all about
laws, or causes of colour, the visible consequences of their
operation are notably these—that when near us, clouds
present only subdued and uncertain colours ; but when far
from us, and struck by the sun on their under surfaces—
so that the greater part of the light they receive is reflected
—they may become golden, purple, scarlet, and intense
fiery white, mingled in all kinds of gradations, such as I
tried to describe in the chapter on the upper clouds in the
first volume, in hope of being able to return to them " when
we knew what was beautiful."

The question before us now is, therefore, What value
ought this attribute of clouds to possess in the human
mind ? Ought we to admire their colours, or despise them ?
Is it well to watch them as Turner does, and strive to paint
them through all deficiency and darkness of inadequate
material ? Or, is it wiser and nobler—like Claude, Salvator, Ruysdael, Wouvermans—never to look for them—
never to pourtray ? We must yet have patience a little
before deciding this, because we have to ascertain some
facts respecting the typical meaning of colour itself ; which
reserving for another place, let us proceed here to learn
the forms of the inferior clouds.

J. Ruskin

J. C. Armytage

66. Light in the West, Beauvais

CHAPTER III

THE CLOUD CHARIOTS

§ 1. BETWEEN the flocks of small countless clouds which occupy the highest heavens, and the gray undivided film of the true rain-cloud, form the fixed masses or torn fleeces, sometimes collected and calm, sometimes fiercely drifting, which are, nevertheless, known under one general name of cumulus, or heaped cloud.

The true cumulus, the most majestic of clouds, and almost the only one which attracts the notice of ordinary observers, is for the most part windless; the movements of its masses being solemn, continuous, inexplicable, a steady advance or retiring, as if they were animated by an inner will, or compelled by an unseen power. They appear to be peculiarly connected with heat, forming perfectly only in the afternoon, and melting away in the evening. Their noblest conditions are strongly electric, and connect themselves with storm-cloud and true thunder-cloud. When there is thunder in the air, they will form in cold weather, or early in the day.

§ 2. I have never succeeded in drawing a cumulus. Its divisions of surface are grotesque and endless, as those of a mountain; perfectly defined, brilliant beyond all power of colour, and transitory as a dream. Even Turner never attempted to paint them, any more than he did the snows of the high Alps.

Nor can I explain them any more than I can draw them. The ordinary account given of their structure is, I believe, that the moisture raised from the earth by the sun's heat becomes visible by condensation at a certain height in the colder air, that the level of the condensing point is that of the cloud's base, and that above it, the heaps are pushed up higher and higher as more vapour accumulates, till, towards evening, the supply beneath ceases ; and at sunset, the fall of dew enables the surrounding atmosphere to absorb and melt them away. Very plausible. But it seems to me herein unexplained how the vapour is held together in those heaps. If the clear air about and above it has no aqueous vapour in it, or at least a much less quantity, why does not the clear air keep pulling the cloud to pieces, eating it away, as steam is consumed in open air ? Or, if any cause prevents such rapid devouring of it, why does not the aqueous vapour diffuse itself softly in the air like smoke, so that one would not know where the cloud ended ? What should make it bind itself in those solid mounds, and stay so :—positive, fantastic, defiant, determined ?

§ 3. If ever I am able to understand the process of the cumulus formation,[1] it will become to me one of the most interesting of all subjects of study to trace the connection of the threatening and terrible outlines of thunder-cloud with the increased action of the electric power. I am for the present utterly unable to speak respecting this matter, and must pass it by, in all humility, to say what little I have ascertained respecting the more broken and rapidly moving forms of the central clouds, which connect themselves with mountains, and may, therefore, among mountains, be seen close and truly.

§ 4. Yet even of these, I can only reason with great doubt and continual pause. This last volume ought certainly to be better than the first of the series, for two reasons. I have learned during the sixteen years to say little where I said much, and to see difficulties where I saw none. And I am in a great state of marvel in looking back to my first account of clouds, not only at myself, but even at my dear master, M. de Saussure. To think that both of us should have looked at drifting mountain clouds, for years together, and been content with the theory which

---

[1] One of the great difficulties in doing this is to distinguish the portions of cloud outline which really slope upwards from those which only appear to do so, being in reality horizontal, and thrown into apparent inclination by perspective.

you will find set forth in § 4, of the chapter on the central
cloud region (Vol. I.), respecting the action of the snowy
summits on watery vapour passing them. It is quite true
that this action takes place, and that the said fourth paragraph is right, as far as it reaches. But both Saussure
and I ought to have known—we both did know, but did
not think of it,—that the covering or cap-cloud forms on
hot summits as well as cold ones ;—that the red and bare
rocks of Mont Pilate, hotter, certainly, after a day's sunshine than the cold storm-wind which sweeps to them from
the Alps, nevertheless have been renowned for their helmet
of cloud, ever since the Romans watched the cloven summit,
gray against the south, from the ramparts of Vindonissa,
giving it the name from which the good Catholics of Lucerne
have warped out their favourite piece of terrific sacred bio-
graphy.[1] And both my master and I should also have
reflected that if our theory about its formation had been
generally true, the helmet cloud ought to form on every
cold summit, at the approach of rain, in approximating
proportions to the bulk of the glaciers ; which is so far
from being the case that not only (A) the cap-cloud may
often be seen on lower summits of grass or rock, while the
higher ones are splendidly clear (which may be accounted
for by supposing the wind containing the moisture not to
have risen so high) ; but (B) the cap-cloud always shows a
preference for hills of a conical form, such as the Mole or
Niesen, which can have very little power in chilling the air,
even supposing they were cold themselves, while it will
entirely refuse to form round huge masses of mountain,
which, supposing them of chilly temperament, must have
discomforted the atmosphere in their neighbourhood for
leagues. And finally (C) reversing the principle under
letter A, the cap-cloud constantly forms on the summit
of Mont Blanc, while it will obstinately refuse to appear on
the Dome du Goûté or Aiguille Sans-nom, where the snow-
fields are of greater extent, and the air must be moister,
because lower.

---

[1] *Pileatus*, capped (strictly speaking, with the cap of liberty ; stormy
cloud enough sometimes on men's brows as well as on mountains'),
corrupted into Pilatus, and Pilate.

§ 5. The fact is, that the explanation given in that fourth paragraph can, in reality, account only for what may properly be termed "leeside cloud," slightly noticed in the continuation of the same chapter, but deserving most attentive illustration, as one of the most beautiful phenomena of the Alps. When a moist wind blows in clear weather over a cold summit, it has not time to get chilled as it approaches the rock, and therefore the air remains clear, and the sky bright on the windward side; but under the lee of the peak, there is partly a back eddy, and partly still air; and in that lull and eddy the wind gets time to be chilled by the rock, and the cloud appears,

Fig. 86.

as a boiling mass of white vapour, rising continually with the return current to the upper edge of the mountain, where it is caught by the straight wind and partly torn, partly melted away in broken fragments. In Fig. 86 the dark mass represents the mountain peak, the arrow the main direction of the wind, the curved lines show the directions of such current and its concentration, and the dotted line encloses the space in which cloud forms densely, floating away beyond and above in irregular tongues and flakes. The third figure from the top in Plate 69 represents the actual aspect of it when in full development, with a strong south wind, in a clear day, on the Aiguille Dru, the sky being perfectly blue and lovely around.

So far all is satisfactory. But the true helmet cloud will not allow itself to be thus explained away. The uppermost figure in Plate 69 represents the loveliest form of it, seen in that perfect arch, so far as I know, only over the highest piece of earth in Europe.

§ 6. Respecting which there are two mysteries :—First, why it should form only at a certain distance above the snow, showing blue sky between it and the summit.

J. Ruskin   J. C. Armytage

69 Aiguilles and their Friends

Secondly, why, so forming, it should always show as an arch, not as a concave cup. This last question puzzles me especially. For, if it be a true arch, and not a cup, it ought to show itself in certain positions of the spectator, or directions of the wind, like the ring of Saturn, as a mere line, or as a spot of cloud pausing over the hill-top. But I never saw it so. While, as above noticed, the lowest form of the helmet cloud is not white as of silver, but like Dolon's helmet of wolf-skin,—it is a gray, flaky veil, lapping itself over the shoulders of a more or less conical peak ; and of this, also, I have no word to utter but the old one, " Electricity," and I might as well say nothing.

§ 7. Neither the helmet cloud, nor the lee-side cloud, however, though most interesting and beautiful, is of much importance in picturesque effect. They are too isolated and strange. But the great mountain cloud, which seems to be a blending of the two with independent forms of vapour (that is to say, a greater development, in consequence of the mountain's action, of clouds which would in some way or other have formed anywhere), requires prolonged attention, as the principal element of the sky in noblest landscape.

§ 8. For which purpose, first, it may be well to clear a few clouds out of the way. I believe the true cumulus is never seen in a great mountain region, at least never associated with hills. It is always broken up and modified by them. Boiling and rounded masses of vapour occur continually, as behind the Aiguille Dru (lowest figure in Plate 69) ; but the quiet, thoroughly defined, infinitely divided and modelled pyramid never develops itself. It would be very grand if one ever saw a great mountain peak breaking through the domed shoulders of a true cumulus ; but this I have never seen.

§ 9. Again, the true high cirri never cross a mountain in Europe. How often have I hoped to see an Alp rising through and above their level-laid and rippled fields ! but those white harvest-fields are heaven's own. And, finally, even the low, level cirrus (used so largely in Martin's pictures) rarely crosses a mountain. If it does, it usually becomes slightly waved or broken, so as to destroy its character. Sometimes, however, at great distances, a very level bar of cloud will strike across a peak; but nearer, too much of the under surface of the field is seen, so that a well-defined bar across a peak seen at a high angle, is of the greatest rarity.

§ 10. The ordinary mountain cloud, therefore, if well defined, divides itself into two kinds : a broken condition of cumulus, grand in proportion as it is solid and quiet,— and a strange modification of drift-cloud, midway, as I said, between the helmet and the lee-side forms. The broken, quiet cumulus impressed Turner exceedingly when he first saw it on hills. He uses it, slightly exaggerating its definiteness, in all his early studies among the mountains of the Chartreuse, and very beautifully in the vignette of St. Maurice in Rogers's Italy. There is nothing, however, to be specially observed of it, as it only differs from the cumulus of the plains, by being smaller and more broken.

§ 11. Not so the mountain drift-cloud, which is as peculiar as it is majestic. The Plates 70 and 71 show, as well as I can express, two successive phases of it on a mountain crest; (in this instance the great limestone ridge above St. Michel, in Savoy.) But what colossal proportions this noble cloud assumes may be best gathered from the rude sketch, Fig. 87, in which I have simply put firm black ink over the actual pencil-lines made at the moment, giving the form of a single wreath of the drift-cloud, stretching about five miles in a direct line from the summit of one of the Alps of the Val d'Aosta, as seen from the plain of Turin. It has a grand volcanic look, but I believe its aspect of rising from the peak to be almost, if not altogether, deceptive; and that the apparently gigantic column is a nearly horizontal stream of lee-side cloud, tapered into the distance by perspective, and thus rising at its apparently lowest, but in reality most distant point, from the mountain summit whose shade calls it into being out of the clear winds.

Whether this be so or not, the apparent origin of the cloud on the peak, and radiation from it, distinguish it from the drift-cloud of level country, which arranges itself at the horizon in broken masses, such as Fig. 89, showing

J. Ruskin

70. The Graize

J. C Armytage

J. Ruskin   J. C. Armytage

71. "Venga Medusa"

Fig. 87.

no point of origin; and I do not know how far they are
vertical cliffs or horizontally extended fields. They are apt
to be very precipitous in aspect, breaking into fragments
with an apparently concentric motion, as in the figure; but
of this motion also—whether vertical or horizontal—I can
say nothing positive.

§ 12. The absolute scale of such clouds may be seen,
or at least demonstrated, more clearly in Fig. 88, which is
a rough note of an effect of sky behind the tower of Berne
Cathedral. It was made from the mound beside the railroad bridge. The Cathedral tower is half-a-mile distant.
The great Eiger of Grindelwald is seen just on the right of
it. This mountain is distant from the tower thirty-four
miles as the crow flies, and ten thousand feet above it in
height. The drift-cloud behind it, therefore, being in full
light, and showing no overhanging surfaces, must rise at
least twenty thousand feet into the air.

§ 13. The extreme whiteness of the volume of vapour
in this case (not, I fear, very intelligible in the woodcut [1])
may be partly owing to recent rain, which, by its evaporation, gives a peculiar density and brightness to some forms
of clearing cloud. In order to understand this, we must
consider another set of facts. When weather is thoroughly
wet among hills, we ought no more to accuse the mountains
of forming the clouds, than we do the plains in similar
circumstances. The unbroken mist buries the mountains
to their bases; but that is not their fault. It may be just
as wet and just as cloudy elsewhere. (This is not true of
Scottish mountain, by the way.) But when the wet weather
is breaking, and the clouds pass, perhaps, in great measure,
away from the plains, leaving large spaces of blue sky, the

---

[1] I could not properly illustrate the subject of clouds without numbers
of these rude drawings, which would probably offend the general reader
by their coarseness, while the cost of engraving them in facsimile is
considerable, and would much add to the price of the book. If I find
people at all interested in the subject, I may, perhaps, some day sys-
tematize and publish my studies of cloud separately. I am sorry not to
have given in this volume a careful study of a rich cirrus sky, but no
wood-engraving that I can employ on this scale will express the finer
threads and waves.

Fig. 88.

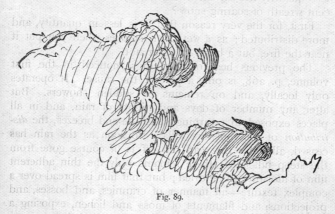

Fig. 89.

Fig. 90.

mountains begin to shape clouds for themselves. The fallen moisture evaporates from the plain invisibly; but not so from the hill-side. There, what quantity of rain has not gone down in the torrents, ascends again to heaven instantly in white clouds. The storm passes as if it had tormented the crags, and the strong mountains smoke like tired horses.

§ 14. Here is another question for us of some interest. Why does the much greater quantity of moisture lying on the horizontal fields send up no visible vapour, and the less quantity left on the rocks glorify itself into a magnificent wreath of soaring snow?

First, for the very reason that it is less in quantity, and more distributed; as a wet cloth smokes when you put it near the fire, but a basin of water not.

The previous heat of the crags, noticed in the first volume, p. 268, is only a part of the cause. It operates only locally, and on remains of sudden showers. But after any number of days and nights of rain, and in all places exposed to returning sunshine and breezes, the *distribution* of the moisture tells. So soon as the rain has ceased, all water that can run off is of course gone from the steep hill-sides; there remains only the thin adherent film of moisture to be dried; but that film is spread over a complex texture—all manner of crannies, and bosses, and projections, and filaments of moss and lichen, exposing a vast extent of drying surface to the air. And the evaporation is rapid in proportion.

§ 15. Its rapidity, however, observe, does not account for its visibility, and this is one of the questions I cannot clearly solve, unless I were sure of the nature of the vesicular vapour. When our breath becomes visible on a frosty day, it is easily enough understood that the moisture which was invisible, carried by the warm air from the lungs, becomes visible when condensed or precipitated by the surrounding chill; but one does not see why air passing over a moist surface quite as cold as itself should take up one particle of water more than it can conveniently—that is to say, invisibly—carry. Whenever you *see* vapour, you may not inaccurately consider the air as having got more than it can properly hold, and dropping some. Now it is easily understood how it should take up much in the lungs, and let some of it fall when it is pinched by the frost outside; but why should it overload itself there on the hills, when it is at perfect liberty to fly away as soon as it likes, and come back for more? I do not see my way well in this. I do not see it clearly, even through the wet cloth. I shall leave all the embarrassment of the matter, however, to my reader, contenting myself, as usual, with the actual fact, that the hill-side air does behave in this covetous and unreasonable manner; and that, in consequence, when the weather is breaking (and sometimes, provokingly, when it is not), phantom clouds form and rise in sudden crowds of wild and spectral imagery along all the far succession of the hill slopes and ravines.

§ 16. There is this distinction, however, between the clouds that form during the rain and after it. In the worst weather, the rain-cloud keeps rather high, and is unbroken; but when there is a disposition in the rain to relax, every now and then a sudden company of white clouds will form quite low down (in Chamouni or Grindelwald, and such high districts, even down to the bottom of the valley), which will remain, perhaps, for ten minutes, filling all the air, then disappear as suddenly as they came, leaving the gray upper cloud and steady rain to their work. These "clouds of relaxation," if we may so call them, are usually flaky and horizontal, sometimes tending to the silky cirrus, yet showing no fine forms of drift; but when the rain has passed, and the air is getting warm, forms the true clearing cloud, in wreaths that ascend continually, with a slow circling motion, melting as they rise. The woodcut, Fig. 91, is a rude note of it floating more quietly from the hill of the Superga, the church (nearly as large as St. Paul's) appearing above, and thus showing the scale of the wreath.

§ 17. This cloud of evaporation, however, does not always rise. It sometimes rests in absolute stillness, low laid in the hollows of the hills, their peaks emergent from it. Fig. 92 shows this condition of it, seen from a

Fig. 91c.

distance, among the Cenis hills. I do not know what
gives it this disposition to rest in the ravines, nor whether
there is a greater chill in the hollows, or a real action of
gravity on the particles of cloud. In general, the position
seems to depend on the temperature. Thus, in Chamouni,
the crests of La Côte and Taconay continually appear in
stormy weather as in Plate 36, Vol. IV., in which I intended
to represent rising drift-cloud, made dense between the
crests by the chill from the glaciers. But in the condition
shown in Fig. 92, on a comparatively open sweep of hill-
side, the thermometer would certainly indicate a higher
temperature in the sheltered valley than on the exposed

Fig. 92.

peaks ; yet the cloud still subsides into the valleys like
folds of a garment ; and, more than this, sometimes conditions of morning cloud, dependent, I believe, chiefly on
dew evaporation, form first on the *tops* of the soft hills of
wooded Switzerland, and droop down in rent fringes, and
separate tongues, clinging close to all the hill-sides, and
giving them exactly the appearance of being covered with
white fringed cloth, falling over them in torn or divided
folds. It always looks like a true action of gravity. How
far it is, in reality, the indication of the power of the
rising sun causing evaporation, first on the hill-top, and
then in separate streams, by its divided light on the ravines,

I cannot tell. The subject is, as the reader perceives, always inextricably complicated by these three necessities —that to get a cloud in any given spot, you must have moisture to form the material of it, heat to develop it, and cold[1] to show it; and the adverse causes inducing the moisture, the evaporation, and the visibility are continually interchanged in presence and in power. And thus, also, the phenomena which properly belong to a certain elevation are confused, among hills at least, with those which in plains would have been lower or higher.

I have been led unavoidably in this chapter to speak of some conditions of the rain-cloud; nor can we finally understand the forms even of the cumulus, without considering those into which it descends or diffuses itself. Which, however, being, I think, a little more interesting than our work hitherto, we will leave this chapter to its dulness, and begin another.

[1] We might say light, as well as cold; for it wholly depends on the degree of light in the sky how far delicate cloud is seen.

The second figure from the top in Plate 69 shows an effect of morning light on the range of the Aiguille Bouchard (Chamouni). Every crag casts its shadow up into apparently clear sky. The shadow is, in such cases, a bluish grey, the colour of clear sky; and the defining light is caused by the sunbeams showing mist which otherwise would have been unperceived. The shadows are not irregular enough in outline—the sketch was made for their colour and sharpness, not their shape,—and I cannot now put them right, so I leave them as they were drawn at the moment.

CHAPTER IV

THE ANGEL OF THE SEA

§ 1. PERHAPS the best and truest piece of work done in the first volume of this book, was the account given in it of the rain-cloud; to which I have here little, descriptively, to add. But the question before us now is, not who has drawn the rain-cloud best, but if it were worth drawing at all. Our English artists naturally painted it often and rightly; but are their pictures the better for it? We have seen how mountains are beautiful; how trees are beautiful; how sun-lighted clouds are beautiful; but can rain be beautiful?

I spoke roughly of the Italian painters in that chapter, because they could only draw distinct clouds, or violent storms, "massive concretions," while our northern painters could represent every phase of mist and fall of shower.

But is this indeed so delightful? Is English wet weather, indeed, one of the things which we should desire to see Art give perpetuity to?

Yes, assuredly. I have given some reasons for this answer in the fifth chapter of last volume; one or two, yet unnoticed, belong to the present division of our subject.

§ 2. The climates or lands into which our globe is divided may, with respect to their fitness for Art, be perhaps conveniently ranged under five heads:—

1. Forest - lands, sustaining the great mass of the magnificent vegetation of the tropics, for the most part characterized by moist and unhealthy heat, and watered by enormous rivers, or periodical rains. This country cannot, I believe, develop the mind or art of man. He

may reach great subtlety of intellect, as the Indian, but not become learned, nor produce any noble art, only a savage or grotesque form of it. Even supposing the evil influences of climate could be vanquished, the scenery is on too large a scale. It would be difficult to conceive of groves less fit for academic purposes than those mentioned by Humboldt, into which no one can enter except under a stout wooden shield, to avoid the chance of being killed by the fall of a nut.

2. Sand-lands, including the desert and dry rock-plains of the earth, inhabited generally by a nomad population, capable of high mental cultivation and of solemn monumental or religious art, but not of art in which pleasureableness forms a large element, their life being essentially one of hardship.

3. Grape and wheat lands, namely, rocks and hills, such as are good for the vine, associated with arable ground, forming the noblest and best ground given to man. In these districts only art of the highest kind seems possible, the religious art of the sand-lands being here joined with that of pleasure or sense.

4. Meadow - lands, including the great pastoral and agricultural districts of the north, capable only of an inferior art : apt to lose its spirituality and become wholly material.

5. Moss-lands, including the rude forest and mountain ground of the North, inhabited by a healthy race, capable of high mental cultivation and moral energy, but wholly incapable of art, except savage, like that of the forest-lands, or as in Scandinavia.

We might carry out these divisions into others, but these are, I think, essential, and easily remembered in a tabular form ; saying " wood " instead of " forest," and " field " for " meadow," we can get such a form shortly worded :—

Wood-lands	Shrewd intellect	No art.
Sand-lands	High intellect	Religious art.
Vine-lands	Highest intellect	Perfect Art.
Field-lands	High intellect	Material Art.
Moss-lands	Shrewd intellect	No Art.

§ 3. In this table the moss-lands appear symmetrically

opposed to the wood-lands, which in a sort they are; the too diminutive vegetation under bleakest heaven, opposed to the too colossal under sultriest heaven, while the perfect ministry of the elements, represented by bread and wine, produces the perfect soul of man.

But this is not altogether so. The moss-lands have one great advantage over the forest-lands, namely, sight of the sky.

And not only sight of it, but continual and beneficent help from it. What they have to separate them from barren rock, namely, their moss and streams, being dependent on its direct help, not on great rivers coming from distant mountain chains, nor on vast tracts of ocean-mist, coming up at evening, but on the continual play and change of sun and cloud.

§ 4. Note this word "change." The moss-lands have an infinite advantage, not only in sight, but in liberty; they are the freest ground in all the world. You can only traverse the great woods by crawling like a lizard, or climbing like a monkey—the great sands with slow steps and veiled head. But bare-headed, and open-eyed, and free-limbed, commanding all the horizon's space of changeful light, and all the horizon's compass of tossing ground, you traverse the moss-land. In discipline it is severe as the desert, but it is a discipline compelling to action; and the moss-lands seem, therefore, the rough schools of the world, in which its strongest human frames are knit and tried, and so sent down, like the northern winds, to brace and brighten the languor into which the repose of more favoured districts may degenerate.

§ 5. It would be strange, indeed, if there were no beauty in the phenomena by which this great renovating and purifying work is done. And it is done almost entirely by the great Angel of the Sea—rain;—the Angel, observe, the messenger sent to a special place on a special errand. Not the diffused perpetual presence of the burden of mist, but the going and returning of intermittent cloud. All turns upon that intermittence. Soft moss on stone and rock;—cave fern of tangled glen;—wayside well—perennial, patient, silent, clear; stealing through its square font of

rough-hewn stone; ever thus deep, no more; which the
winter wreck sullies not, the summer thirst wastes not,
incapable of stain as of decline;—where the fallen leaf
floats undecayed, and the insect darts undefiling: cressed
brook and ever-eddying river, lifted even in flood scarcely
over its stepping-stones,—but through all sweet summer
keeping tremulous music with harp-strings of dark water
among the silver fingering of the pebbles. Far away in
the south the strong river Gods have all hasted, and gone
down to the sea. Wasted and burning, white furnaces of
blasting sand, their broad beds lie ghastly and bare; but
here in the moss-lands, the soft wings of the Sea Angel
droop still with dew, and the shadows of their plumes
falter on the hills: strange laughings and glitterings of
silver streamlets, born suddenly, and twined about the
mossy heights in trickling tinsel, answering to them as
they wave.[1]

§ 6. Nor are those wings colourless. We habitually
think of the rain-cloud only as dark and gray; not knowing that we owe to it perhaps the fairest, though not the
most dazzling of the hues of heaven. Often in our English
mornings, the rain-clouds in the dawn form soft, level
fields, which melt imperceptibly into the blue; or, when of
less extent, gather into apparent bars, crossing the sheets
of broader cloud above; and all these bathed throughout
in an unspeakable light of pure rose-colour, and purple, and
amber, and blue; not shining, but misty-soft; the barred
masses, when seen nearer, composed of clusters or tresses
of cloud, like floss silk; looking as if each knot were a
little swathe or sheaf of lighted rain. No clouds form
such skies, none are so tender, various, inimitable. Turner
himself never caught them. Correggio, putting out his
whole strength, could have painted them, no other man.[2]

[1] Compare the beautiful stanza beginning the epilogue of the " Golden
Legend."
[2] I do not mean that Correggio is greater than Turner, but that only
his way of work, the touch which he has used for the golden hair of
Antiope, for instance, could have painted these clouds. In open lowland country I have never been able to come to any satisfactory conclusion about their height, so strangely do they blend with each

§ 7. For these are the robes of love of the Angel of the Sea. To these that name is chiefly given, the "spreadings of the clouds," from their extent, their gentleness, their fulness of rain. Note how they are spoken of in Job, xxxvi. 31–33. "By them judgeth He the people; He giveth meat in abundance. With clouds He covereth the light.[1] He hath hidden the light in His hands, and commanded

other. Here, for instance, is the arrangement of an actual group of them. The space at A was deep, purest ultramarine blue, traversed by streaks of absolutely pure and perfect rose-colour. The blue passed downwards imperceptibly into gray at G, and then into amber, and at the white edge below into gold. On this amber ground the streaks P were

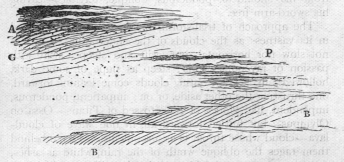

dark purple, and, finally, the spaces at B B, again clearest and most precious blue, paler than that at A. The *two* levels of these clouds are always very notable. After a continuance of fine weather among the Alps, the determined approach of rain is usually announced by a soft, unbroken film of level cloud, white and thin at the approaching edge, gray at the horizon, covering the whole sky from side to side, and advancing steadily from the south-west. Under its gray veil, as it approaches, are formed detached bars, darker or lighter than the field above, according to the position of the sun. These bars are usually of a very sharply elongated oval shape, something like fish. I habitually call them "fish-clouds," and look upon them with much discomfort, if any excursions of interest have been planned within the next three days. Their oval shape is a perspective deception dependent on their flatness; they are probably thin, extended fields, irregularly circular.

[1] I do not copy the interpolated words which follow, "and commandeth it *not to shine*." The closing verse of the chapter, as we have it, is unintelligible; not so in the Vulgate, the reading of which I give.

it that it should return. He speaks of it to His friend ; that it is his possession, and that he may ascend thereto."

That, then, is the Sea Angel's message to God's friends ; *that*, the meaning of those strange golden lights and purple flushes before the morning rain. The rain is sent to judge, and feed us ; but the light is the possession of the friends of God, and they may ascend thereto,—where the tabernacle veil will cross and part its rays no more.

§ 8. But the Angel of the Sea has also another message, —in the " great rain of his strength," rain of trial, sweeping away ill-set foundations. Then his robe is not spread softly over the whole heaven, as a veil, but sweeps back from his shoulders, ponderous, oblique, terrible—leaving his sword-arm free.

The approach of trial-storm, hurricane-storm, is indeed in its vastness as the clouds of the softer rain. But it is not slow nor horizontal, but swift and steep : swift with passion of ravenous winds ; steep as slope of some dark, hollowed hill. The fronting clouds come leaning forward, one thrusting the other aside, or on ; impatient, ponderous, impendent, like globes of rock tossed of Titans—Ossa on Olympus—but hurled forward all, in one wave of cloud-lava—cloud whose throat is as a sepulchre. Fierce behind them rages the oblique wrath of the rain, white as ashes, dense as showers of driven steel ; the pillars of it full of ghastly life ; Rain-Furies, shrieking as they fly ;—scourging, as with whips of scorpions;—the earth ringing and trembling under them, heaven wailing wildly, the trees stooped blindly down, covering their faces, quivering in every leaf with horror, ruin of their branches flying by them like black stubble.

§ 9. I wrote Furies. I ought to have written Gorgons. Perhaps the reader does not know that the Gorgons are not dead, are ever undying. We shall have to take our chance of being turned into stones by looking them in the face, presently. Meantime, I gather what part of the great Greek story of the Sea Angels has meaning for us here.

Nereus, the God of the Sea, who dwells in it always (Neptune being the God who rules it from Olympus), has

children by the Earth; namely, Thaumas, the father of
Iris; that is, the "wonderful" or miracle-working angel
of the sea; Phorcys, the malignant angel of it (you will find
him degraded through many forms, at last, in the story
of Sinbad, into the old man of the sea); Ceto, the deep
places of the sea, meaning its bays among rocks, therefore
called by Hesiod "Fair-cheeked" Ceto; and Eurybia, the
tidal force or sway of the sea, of whom more hereafter.

§ 10. Phorcys and Ceto, the malignant angel of the
sea, and the spirit of its deep rocky places, have children,
namely, first, Graiæ, the soft rain-clouds. The Greeks
had a greater dislike of storm than we have, and therefore
whatever violence is in the action of rain, they represented
by harsher types than we should—types given in one
group by Aristophanes (speaking in mockery of the poets):
"This was the reason, then, that they made so much talk
about the fierce rushing of the moist clouds, coiled in
glittering; and the locks of the hundred-headed Typhon;
and the blowing storms: and the bent-clawed birds drifted
on the breeze, fresh, and aerial." Note the expression
"bent-clawed birds." It illustrates two characters of these
clouds; partly their coiling form; but more directly the
way they tear down the earth from the hill-sides; especially
those twisted storm-clouds which in violent action become
the waterspout. These always strike at a narrow point,
often opening the earth on a hill-side into a trench as a
great pickaxe would (whence the Graiæ are said to have
only one beak between them). Nevertheless, the rain-
cloud was, on the whole, looked upon by the Greeks as
beneficent, so that it is boasted of in the Œdipus Coloneus
for its perpetual feeding of the springs of Cephisus,[1] and
elsewhere often; and the opening song of the rain-clouds
in Aristophanes is entirely beautiful:—

"O eternal Clouds! let us raise into open sight our
dewy existence, from the deep-sounding Sea, our Father,
up to the crests of the wooded hills, whence we look down
over the sacred land, nourishing its fruits, and over the

[1] I assume the ἄϋπνοι κρῆναι νομάδες to mean clouds, not springs;
but this does not matter, the whole passage being one of rejoicing in
moisture and dew of heaven.

rippling of the divine rivers, and over the low murmuring bays of the deep." I cannot satisfy myself about the meaning of the names of the Graiæ—Pephredo and Enuo —but the epithets which Hesiod gives them are interesting; "Pephredo, the well-robed; Enuo, the crocus-robed;" probably, it seems to me, from their beautiful colours in morning.

§ 11. Next to the Graiæ, Phorcys and Ceto begat the Gorgons, which are the true storm-clouds. The Graiæ have only one beak or tooth, but all the Gorgons have tusks like boars; brazen hands (brass being the word used for the metal of which the Greeks made their spears), and golden wings.

Their names are "Steino" (straitened), of storms compressed into narrow compass; "Euryale" (having wide threshing-floor), of storms spread over great space; "Medusa" (the dominant), the most terrible. She is essentially the highest storm-cloud; therefore the hail-cloud or cloud of cold, her countenance turning all who behold it to stone. ("He casteth forth His ice like morsels. Who can stand before His cold?") The serpents about her head are the fringes of the hail, the idea of coldness being connected by the Greeks with the bite of the serpent, as with the hemlock.

§ 12. On Minerva's shield, her head signifies, I believe, the cloudy coldness of knowledge, and its venomous character ("Knowledge puffeth up," compare Bacon in Advancement of Learning). But the idea of serpents rose essentially from the change of form in the cloud as it broke; the cumulus cloud not breaking into full storm till it is cloven by the cirrus; which is twice hinted at in the story of Perseus; only we must go back a little to gather it together.

Perseus was the son of Jupiter by Danaë, who being shut in a brazen tower, Jupiter came to her in a shower of gold: the brazen tower being, I think, only another expression for the cumulus or Medusa cloud; and the golden rain for the rays of the sun striking it; but we have not only this rain of Danaë's to remember in connection with the Gorgon, but that also of the sieves of the

Danaïdes, said to represent the provision of Argos with
water by their father Danaüs, who dug wells about the
Acropolis; nor only wells, but opened, I doubt not,
channels of irrigation for the fields, because the Danaïdes
are said to have brought the mysteries of Ceres from Egypt.
And though I cannot trace the root of the names Danaüs
and Danaë, there is assuredly some farther link of connection
in the deaths of the lovers of the Danaïdes, whom they slew,
as Perseus Medusa. And again note, that when the father
of Danaë, Acrisius, is detained in Seriphos by storms, a
disk thrown by Perseus is carried *by the wind against his
head*, and kills him; and lastly, when Perseus cuts off the
head of Medusa, from her blood springs Chrysaor, "wielder
of the golden sword," the Angel of the Lightning, and
Pegasus, the Angel of the "Wild Fountains," that is to
say, the fastest flying or lower rain-cloud; winged, but
racing as upon the earth.

§ 13. I say, "wild" fountains; because the kind of
fountain from which Pegasus is named is especially the
"fountain of the great deep" of Genesis; sudden and
furious, (cataracts of heaven, not windows, in the Septuagint);—the mountain torrent caused by thunderous storm,
or as our "fountain"—a Geyser-like leaping forth of water.
Therefore, it is the deep and full source of streams, and so
used typically of the source of evils, or of passions; whereas
the word "spring" with the Greeks is like our "well-head"
—a gentle issuing forth of water continually. But, because
both the lightning-fire and the gushing forth, as of a fountain, are the signs of the poet's true power, together with
perpetuity, it is Pegasus who strikes the earth with his foot,
on Helicon,[1] and causes Hippocrene to spring forth—"the
horse's well-head." It is perpetual; but has, nevertheless,
the Pegasean storm-power.

§ 14. Wherein we may find, I think, sufficient cause for
putting honour upon the rain-cloud. Few of us, perhaps,

---

[1] I believe, however, that when Pegasus strikes forth this fountain,
he is to be regarded, not as springing from Medusa's blood, but as born
of Medusa by Neptune; the true horse was given by Neptune striking
the earth with his trident; the divine horse is born to Neptune and the
storm-cloud.

have thought, in watching its career across our own mossy hills, or listening to the murmur of the springs amidst the mountain quietness, that the chief masters of the human imagination owed, and confessed that they owed, the force of their noblest thoughts, not to the flowers of the valley, nor the majesty of the hill, but to the flying cloud.

Yet they never saw it fly, as we may in our own England. So far, at least, as I know the clouds of the south, they are often more terrible than ours, but the English Pegasus is swifter. On the Yorkshire and Derbyshire hills, when the rain-cloud is low and much broken, and the steady west wind fills all space with its strength,[1] the sun-gleams fly like golden vultures : they are flashes rather than shinings ; the dark spaces and the dazzling race and skim along the acclivities, and dart and dip from crag to dell, swallow-like ;—no Graiæ these,—gray and withered : Grey Hounds rather, following the Cerinthian stag with the golden antlers.

§ 15. There is one character about these lower rain-clouds, partly affecting all their connection with the upper sky, which I have never been able to account for ; that which, as before noticed, Aristophanes fastened on at once for their distinctive character—their obliquity. They always fly in an oblique position, as in the Plate opposite, which is a careful facsimile of the first advancing mass of the rain-cloud in Turner's Slave Ship. When the head of the cloud is foremost, as in this instance, and rain falling beneath, it is easy to imagine that its drops, increasing in size as they fall, may exercise some retarding action on the wind. But the head of the cloud is not always first, the base of it is

---

[1] I have been often at great heights on the Alps in rough weather, and have seen strong gusts of storm in the plains of the south. But, to get full expression of the very heart and meaning of wind, there is no place like a Yorkshire moor. I think Scottish breezes are thinner, very bleak and piercing, but not substantial. If you lean on them they will let you fall, but one may rest against a Yorkshire breeze as one would on a quickset hedge. I shall not soon forget,—having had the good fortune to meet a vigorous one on an April morning, between Hawes and Settle, just on the flat under Whernside,—the vague sense of wonder with which I watched Ingleborough stand without rocking.

J. M. W. Turner   72. The Locks of Typhon   J C Armytage

sometimes advanced.[1] The only certainty is, that it will not shape itself horizontally, its thin-drawn lines and main contours will always be oblique, though its motion is horizontal ; and, which is still more curious, their sloping lines are hardly ever modified in their descent by any distinct retiring tendency or perspective convergence. A troop of leaning clouds will follow one another, each stooping forward at the same apparent slope, round a fourth of the horizon.

§ 16. Another circumstance which the reader should note in this cloud of Turner's, is the witch-like look of drifted or erected locks of hair at its left side. We have just read the words of the old Greek poet, "Locks of the hundred-headed Typhon ; " and must remember that Turner's account of this picture, in the Academy catalogue, was "Slaver throwing overboard the Dead and Dying. *Typhoon* coming on." The resemblance to wildly drifted hair is stronger in the picture than in the engraving ; the gray and purple tints of torn cloud being relieved against golden sky beyond.

§ 17. It was not, however, as we saw, merely to locks of hair, but to serpents, that the Greeks likened the dissolving of the Medusa cloud in blood. Of that sanguine rain, or of its meaning, I cannot yet speak. It is connected with other and higher types, which must be traced in another place.[2]

But the likeness to serpents we may illustrate here. The two Plates already given, **70** and **71** (at page 142), represent successive conditions of the Medusa cloud on one of the Cenis hills (the great limestone precipice above St. Michel, between Lanslebourg and St. Jean de Maurienne).[3] In the first, the cloud is approaching, with the lee-side cloud forming beyond it ; in the second, it has

---

[1] When there is a violent current of wind near the ground, the rain columns slope *forward* at the foot. See the Entrance to Fowey Harbour, of the England Series.

[2] See Part IX. chap. 2, "The Hesperid Ægle."

[3] The reader must remember that sketches made as these are, on the instant, cannot be far carried, and would lose all their use if they were finished at home. These were both made in pencil, and merely washed with gray on returning to the inn, enough to secure the main forms.

approached, increased, and broken, the Medusa serpents writhing about the central peak, the rounded tops of the broken cumulus showing above. In this instance, they take nearly the forms of flame; but when the storm is more violent, they are torn into fragments, and magnificent revolving wheels of vapour are formed, broken, and tossed into the air, as the grass is tossed in the hayfield from the toothed wheels of the raking-machine; (perhaps, in common with all other inventions of the kind, likely to bring more evil upon men than ever the Medusa cloud did, and turn them more effectually into stone.[1])

§ 18. I have named in the first volume the principal works of Turner representing these clouds; and until I am able to draw them better, it is useless to say more of them; but in connection with the subject we have been examining, I should be glad if the reader could turn to the engravings of the England drawings of Salisbury and Stonehenge. What opportunities Turner had of acquainting himself with classical literature, and how he used them, we shall see presently. In the meantime, let me simply assure the reader that, in various byways, he had gained a knowledge of most of the great Greek traditions, and that he felt them more than he knew them; his mind being affected, up to a certain point, precisely as an ancient painter's would have been, by external phenomena of nature. To him, as to the Greek, the storm-clouds seemed messengers of fate. He feared them, while he reverenced; nor does he ever introduce them without some hidden purpose, bearing upon the expression of the scene he is painting.

§ 19. On that plain of Salisbury, he had been struck first by its widely-spacious pastoral life; and secondly, by its monuments of the two great religions of England— Druidical and Christian.

He was not a man to miss the possible connection of these impressions. He treats the shepherd life as a type

---

[1] I do not say this carelessly, nor because machines throw the labouring man " out of work." The labouring man will always have more work than he wants. I speak thus because the use of such machinery involves the destruction of all pleasures in rural labour; and I doubt not, in that destruction, the essential deterioration of the national mind.

of the ecclesiastical; and composes his two drawings so as to illustrate both.

In the drawing of Salisbury, the plain is swept by rapid but not distressful rain. The cathedral occupies the centre of the picture, towering high over the city, of which the houses (made on purpose smaller than they really are) are scattered about it like a flock of sheep. The cathedral is surrounded by a great light. The storm gives way at first in a subdued gleam over a distant parish church, then bursts down again, breaks away into full light about the cathedral, and passes over the city, in various sun and shade. In the foreground stands a shepherd leaning on his staff, watching his flock;—bareheaded: he has given his cloak to a group of children, who have covered themselves up with it, and are shrinking from the rain; his dog crouches under a bank; his sheep, for the most part, are resting quietly, some coming up the slope of the bank towards him.[1]

§ 20. The rain-clouds in this picture are wrought with a care which I have never seen equalled in any other sky of the same kind. It is the rain of blessing—abundant, but full of brightness; golden gleams are flying across the wet grass, and fall softly on the lines of willows in the valley—willows by the watercourses; the little brooks flash out here and there between them and the fields. Turn now to the Stonehenge. That, also, stands in great light; but it is the Gorgon light—the sword of Chrysaor is bared against it. The cloud of judgment hangs above. The rock pillars seem to reel before its slope, pale beneath the lightning. And nearer, in the darkness, the shepherd lies dead, his flock scattered.

I alluded, in speaking before of this Stonehenge, to Turner's use of the same symbol in the drawing of Pæstum for Rogers's Italy; but a more striking instance of its employment occurs in a Study of Pæstum, which he engraved himself before undertaking the Liber Studiorum, and another in his drawing of the Temple of Minerva, on

---

[1] You may see the arrangement of subject in the published engraving, but nothing more; it is among the worst engravings in the England Series.

Cape Colonna; and observe farther that he rarely introduces lightning, if the ruined building has not been devoted
to religion. The wrath of man may destroy the fortress,
but only the wrath of heaven can destroy the temple.

§ 21. Of these secret meanings of Turner's, we shall
see enough in the course of the inquiry we have to undertake, lastly, respecting ideas of relation; but one more
instance of his opposed use of the lightning symbol, and
of the rain of blessing, I name here, to confirm what has
been noted above. For, in this last instance, he was
questioned respecting his meaning, and explained it. I
refer to the drawings of Sinai and Lebanon, made for
Finden's Bible. The sketches from which Turner prepared that series were, I believe, careful and accurate;
but the treatment of the subjects was left wholly to him.
He took the Sinai and Lebanon to show the opposite
influences of the Law and the Gospel. The rock of Moses
is shown in the burning of the desert, among fallen stones,
forked lightning cleaving the blue mist which veils the
summit of Sinai. Armed Arabs pause at the foot of the
rock. No human habitation is seen, nor any herb or tree,
nor any brook, and the lightning strikes without rain.[1]
Over the Mount Lebanon an intensely soft gray-blue sky
is melting into dewy rain. Every ravine is filled, every
promontory crowned, by tenderest foliage, golden in
slanting sunshine.[2] The white convent nestles into the
hollow of the rock; and a little brook runs under the
shadow of the nearer trees, beside which two monks sit
reading.

§ 22. It was a beautiful thought, yet an erring one, as
all thoughts are which oppose the Law to the Gospel.
When people read, "The law came by Moses, but grace
and truth by Christ," do they suppose it means that the
law was ungracious and untrue? The law was given for a
foundation; the grace (or mercy) and truth for fulfilment;
—the whole forming one glorious Trinity of judgment,
mercy, and truth. And if people would but read the text
of their Bibles with heartier purpose of understanding it,

[1] Hosea xiii. 5 & 15.
[2] Hosea xiv. 4, 5, 6. Compare Psalm lxxii. 6–16.

instead of superstitiously, they would see that throughout the parts, which they are intended to make most personally their own (the Psalms), it is always the Law which is spoken of with chief joy. The Psalms respecting mercy are often sorrowful, as in thought of what it cost; but those respecting the law are always full of delight. David cannot contain himself for joy in thinking of it,—he is never weary of its praise :—" How love I thy law! it is my meditation all the day. Thy testimonies are my delight and my counsellors; sweeter, also, than honey and the honeycomb."

§ 23. And I desire, especially, that the reader should note this, in now closing the work through which we have passed together in the investigation of the beauty of the visible world. For perhaps he expected more pleasure and freedom in that work; he thought that it would lead him at once into fields of fond imagination, and may have been surprised to find that the following of beauty brought him always under a sterner dominion of mysterious law; that brightness was continually based upon obedience, and all majesty only another form of submission. But this is indeed so. I have been perpetually hindered in this inquiry into the sources of beauty by fear of wearying the reader with their severities. It was always accuracy I had to ask of him, not sympathy; patience, not zeal; apprehension, not sensation. The thing to be shown him was not a pleasure to be snatched, but a law to be learned.

§ 24. It is in this character, however, that the beauty of the natural world completes its message. We saw long ago, how its various *powers* of appeal to the mind of men might be traced to some typical expression of Divine attributes. We have seen since how its *modes* of appeal present constant types of human obedience to the Divine law, and constant proofs that this law, instead of being contrary to mercy, is the foundation of all delight, and the guide of all fair and fortunate existence.

§ 25. Which understanding, let us receive our last message from the Angel of the Sea.

Take up the 19th Psalm and look at it verse by verse.

Perhaps to my younger readers, one word may be permitted respecting their Bible-reading in general.[1] The Bible is, indeed, a deep book, when depth is required, that is to say, for deep people. But it is not intended, particularly, for profound persons; on the contrary, much more for shallow and simple persons. And therefore the first, and generally the main and leading idea of the Bible, is on its surface, written in plainest possible Greek, Hebrew, or English, needing no penetration, nor amplification, needing nothing but what we all might give—attention.

But this, which is in every one's power, and is the only thing that God wants, is just the last thing any one will give Him. We are delighted to ramble away into daydreams, to repeat pet verses from other places, suggested by chance words; to snap at an expression which suits our own particular views, or to dig up a meaning from under a verse, which we should be amiably grieved to think any human being had been so happy as to find before. But the plain, intended, immediate, fruitful meaning, which every one ought to find always, and especially that which depends on our seeing the relation of the verse to those near it, and getting the force of the whole passage, in due relation—this sort of significance we do not look for; it being, truly, not to be discovered, unless we really attend to what is said, instead of to our own feelings.

§ 26. It is unfortunate, also, but very certain, that in

---

[1] I believe few sermons are more false or dangerous than those in which the teacher proposes to impress his audience by showing "how much there is in a verse." If he examined his own heart closely before beginning, he would often find that his real desire was to show how much he, the expounder, could make out of the verse. But entirely honest and earnest men often fall into the same error. They have been taught that they should always look deep, and that Scripture is full of hidden meanings; and they easily yield to the flattering conviction that every chance idea which comes into their heads in looking at a word, is put there by Divine agency. Hence they wander away into what they believe to be an inspired meditation, but which is, in reality, a meaningless jumble of ideas; perhaps, very proper ideas, but with which the text in question has nothing whatever to do.

order to attend to what is said, we must go through the irksomeness of knowing the meaning of the words. And the first thing that children should be taught about their Bibles is, to distinguish clearly between words that they understand and words that they do not; and to put aside the words they do not understand, and verses connected with them, to be asked about, or for a future time; and never to think they are reading the Bible when they are merely repeating phrases of an unknown tongue.

§ 27. Let us try, by way of example, this 19th Psalm, and see what plain meaning is uppermost in it.

"The heavens declare the glory of God."

What are the heavens?

The word occurring in the Lord's Prayer, and the thing expressed being what a child may, with some advantage, be led to look at, it might be supposed among a schoolmaster's first duties to explain this word clearly.

Now there can be no question that in the minds of the sacred writers, it stood naturally for the entire system of cloud, and of space beyond it, conceived by them as a vault set with stars. But there can, also, be no question, as we saw in previous inquiry, that the firmament, which is said to have been "called" heaven, at the creation, expresses, in all definite use of the word, the system of clouds, as spreading the power of the water over the earth; hence the constant expressions dew of heaven, rain of heaven, etc., where heaven is used in the singular; while "the heavens," when used plurally, and especially when in distinction, as here, from the word "firmament," remained expressive of the starry space beyond.

§ 28. A child might therefore be told (surely, with advantage), that our beautiful word Heaven may possibly have been formed from a Hebrew word, meaning "the high place;" that the great warrior Roman nation, camping much out at night, generally overtired and not in moods for thinking, are believed by many people to have seen in the stars only the likeness of the glittering studs of their armour, and to have called the sky "The bossed, or studded;" but that others think those Roman soldiers on their night-watches had rather been impressed by the great emptiness and void of night, and by the far-coming of sounds through its darkness, and had called the heaven, " The Hollow place." Finally, I should tell the children, showing them first the setting of a star, how the great Greeks had found out the truest power of the heavens, and had called them, " The Rolling." But whatever different nations had called them, at least I would make it clear to the child's mind that in this 19th Psalm, their whole power being intended, the two words are used which express it; the Heavens, for the great vault or void, with all its planets, and stars, and ceaseless march of orbs innumerable; and the Firmament, for the ordinance of the clouds.

These heavens, then, " declare the *glory* of God;" that is, the light of God, the eternal glory, stable and changeless. As their orbs fail not—but pursue their course for ever, to give light upon the earth—so God's glory surrounds man for ever—changeless, in its fulness insupportable—infinite.

" And the firmament sheweth His *handywork*."

§ 29. The clouds, prepared by the hands of God for the help of man, varied in their ministration—veiling the inner splendour—show, not His eternal glory, but his daily handiwork. So He dealt with Moses. I will cover thee " with my hand" as I pass by. Compare Job xxxvi. 24 : " Remember that thou magnify His work, which men behold. Every man may see it." Not so the glory—that only in part; the courses of these stars are to be seen imperfectly, and but by few. But this firmament, " every man may see it, man may behold it afar off." " Behold, God is great, and we know Him not. For He maketh small the drops of water : they pour down rain according to the vapour thereof."

§ 30. " Day unto day uttereth speech, and night unto night sheweth knowledge. They have no speech nor language, yet without these their voice is heard. Their rule is gone out throughout the earth, and their words to the end of the world."

Note that. Their rule throughout the earth, whether inhabited or not—their law of light is thereon ; but their words, spoken to human souls, to the end of the inhabited world.

"In them hath He set a tabernacle for the sun," etc. Literally, a tabernacle, or curtained tent, with its veil and its hangings ; also of the colours of His desert tabernacle —blue, and purple, and scarlet.

Thus far the psalm describes the manner of this great heaven's message.

Thenceforward it comes to the matter of it.

§ 31. Observe, you have the two divisions of the declaration. The heavens (compare Psalm viii.) declare the eternal glory of God before men, and the firmament the daily mercy of God towards men. And the eternal glory is in this—that the law of the Lord is perfect, and His testimony sure, and His statutes right.

And the daily mercy in this—that the commandment of the Lord is pure, and His fear is clean, and His judgments true and righteous.

There are three oppositions :—

Between law and commandment.

Between testimony and fear.

Between statute and judgment.

§ 32. I. Between law and commandment.

The law is fixed and everlasting ; uttered once, abiding for ever, as the sun, it may not be moved. It is " perfect, converting the soul : " the whole question about the soul being, whether it has been turned from darkness to light, acknowledged this law or not,—whether it is godly or ungodly ? But the commandment is given momentarily to each man, according to the need. It does not convert : it guides. It does not concern the entire purpose of the soul : but it enlightens the eyes, respecting a special act. The law is, " Do this always ; " the commandment, " Do *thou* this *now* : " often mysterious enough, and through the cloud ; chilling, and with strange rain of tears ; yet always pure (the law converting, but the commandment cleansing) : a rod not for guiding merely, but for strengthening, and tasting honey with. " Look how mine eyes have been enlightened, because I tasted a little of this honey."

§ 33. II. Between testimony and fear.

The testimony is everlasting : the true promise of salvation. Bright as the sun beyond all the earth-cloud, it makes

wise the simple; all wisdom being assured in perceiving it
and trusting it; all wisdom brought to nothing which does
not perceive it.

But the fear of God is taught through special encouragement and special withdrawal of it, according to each man's
need—by the earth-cloud—smile and frown alternately: it
also, as the commandment, is clean, purging, and casting
out all other fear, it only remaining for ever.

§ 34. III. Between statute and judgment.

The statutes are the appointments of the Eternal justice;
fixed and bright, and constant as the stars; equal and
balanced as their courses. They "are right, rejoicing the
heart." But the judgments are special judgments of given
acts of men. "True," that is to say, fulfilling the warning
or promise given to each man; "righteous altogether,"
that is, done or executed in truth and righteousness. The
statute is right, in appointment. The judgment righteous
altogether, in appointment and fulfilment;—yet not always
rejoicing the heart.

Then, respecting all these, comes the expression of
passionate desire, and of joy; that also divided with
respect to each. The glory of God, eternal in the
Heavens, is future, "to be *desired* more than gold, than
much fine gold"—treasure in the heavens that faileth
not. But the present guidance and teaching of God are
on earth; they are now possessed, sweeter than all earthly
food—"sweeter than honey and the honeycomb. Moreover by them" (the law and the testimony) "is Thy
servant warned"—warned of the ways of death and life.

"And in keeping them" (the commandments and the
judgments) "there is great reward:" pain now, and bitterness of tears, but reward unspeakable.

§ 35. Thus far the psalm has been descriptive and interpreting. It ends in prayer.

"Who can understand his errors?" (wanderings from
the perfect law). "Cleanse Thou me from secret faults;"
from all that I have done against Thy will, and far from
Thy way, in the darkness. "Keep back thy servant from
presumptuous sins" (sins against the commandment) against
Thy will when it is seen and direct, pleading with heart

and conscience. "So shall I be undefiled, and innocent from the great transgression" — the transgression that crucifies afresh.

"Let the words of my mouth (for I have set them to declare Thy law), and the meditation of my heart (for I have set it to keep Thy commandments), be acceptable in Thy sight," whose glory is my strength, and whose work, my redemption; "my Strength, and my Redeemer."

PART VIII

OF IDEAS OF RELATION:—FIRST, OF INVENTION FORMAL

CHAPTER I

THE LAW OF HELP

§ 1. WE have now reached the last and the most important part of our subject. We have seen in the first division of this book, how far art may be, and has been, consistent with physical or material facts. In its second division, we examined how far it may be and has been obedient to the laws of physical beauty. In this last division we have to consider the relations of art to God and man : its work in the help of human beings, and service of their Creator.

We have to inquire into the various Powers, Conditions, and Aims of mind involved in the conception or creation of pictures ; in the choice of subject, and the mode and order of its history ;—the choice of forms, and the modes of their arrangement.

And these phases of mind being concerned, partly with choice and arrangement of incidents, partly with choice and arrangement of forms and colours, the whole subject will fall into two main divisions, namely, expressional or spiritual invention ; and material or formal invention.

They are of course connected ;—all good formal invention being expressional also ; but as a matter of convenience it is best to say what may be ascertained of the nature of formal invention, before attempting to illustrate the faculty in its higher field.

§ 2. First, then, of INVENTION FORMAL, otherwise and

Drawn by J. M. W. Turner   Etched by J. Ruskin   Engraved by T. Lupton

85. Château de Blois

most commonly called technical composition ; that is to say, the arrangement of lines, forms, or colours, so as to produce the best possible effect.

I have often been accused of slighting this quality in pictures ; the fact being that I have avoided it only because I considered it too great and wonderful for me to deal with. The longer I thought, the more wonderful it always seemed : and it is, to myself personally, the quality, above all others, which gives me delight in pictures. Many others I admire, or respect ; but this one I rejoice in. Expression, sentiment, truth to nature, are essential : but all these are not enough. I never care to look at a picture again, if it be ill composed ; and if well composed I can hardly leave off looking at it.

"Well composed." Does that mean according to rule ?

No. Precisely the contrary. Composed as only the man who did it could have done it ; composed as no other picture is, or was, or ever can be again. Every great work stands alone.

§ 3. Yet there are certain elementary laws of arrangement traceable a little way; a few of these only I shall note, not caring to pursue the subject far in this work, so intricate it becomes even in its first elements : nor could it be treated with any approach to completeness, unless I were to give many and elaborate outlines of large pictures. I have a vague hope of entering on such a task, some future day. Meantime I shall only indicate the place which technical composition [1] should hold in our scheme.

---

[1] The word composition has been so much abused, and is in itself so inexpressive, that when I wrote the first part of this work I intended always to use, in this final section of it, the word "invention," and to reserve the term "composition" for that false composition which can be taught on principles ; as I have already so employed the term in the chapter on "Imagination Associative," in the second volume. But, in arranging this section, I find it is not conveniently possible to avoid the ordinary modes of parlance ; I therefore only head the section as I intended (and as is, indeed, best), using in the text the ordinarily accepted term ; only the reader must be careful to note that what I spoke of shortly as "composition" in the chapters on "Imagination," I here always call, distinctly, "false composition ;" using here, as I find most convenient, the words "invention" or "composition" indifferently, for the true faculty.

And, first, let us understand what composition is, and how far it is required.

§ 4. Composition may be best defined as the help of everything in the picture by everything else.

I wish the reader to dwell a little on this word "Help." It is a grave one.

In substance which we call "inanimate," as of clouds, or stones, their atoms may cohere to each other, or consist with each other, but they do not help each other. The removal of one part does not injure the rest.

But in a plant, the taking away of any one part does injure the rest. Hurt or remove any portion of the sap, bark, or pith, the rest is injured. If any part enters into a state in which it no more assists the rest, and has thus become "helpless," we call it also "dead."

The power which causes the several portions of the plant to help each other, we call life. Much more is this so in an animal. We may take away the branch of a tree without much harm to it; but not the animal's limb. Thus, intensity of life is also intensity of helpfulness—completeness of depending of each part on all the rest. The ceasing of this help is what we call corruption; and in proportion to the perfectness of the help, is the dreadfulness of the loss. The more intense the life has been, the more terrible is its corruption.

The decomposition of a crystal is not necessarily impure at all. The fermentation of a wholesome liquid begins to admit the idea slightly; the decay of leaves yet more; of flowers, more; of animals, with greater painfulness and terribleness in exact proportion to their original vitality; and the foulest of all corruption is that of the body of man; and, in his body, that which is occasioned by disease, more than that of natural death.

§ 5. I said just now, that though atoms of inanimate substance could not help each other, they could "consist" with each other. "Consistence" is their virtue. Thus the parts of a crystal are consistent, but of dust, inconsistent. Orderly adherence, the best help its atoms can give, constitutes the nobleness of such substance.

When matter is either consistent, or living, we call it

pure, or clean; when inconsistent or corrupting (unhelpful), we call it impure, or unclean. The greatest uncleanliness being that which is essentially most opposite to life.

Life and consistency, then, both expressing one character (namely, helpfulness of a higher or lower order), the Maker of all creatures and things, "by whom all creatures live, and all things consist," is essentially and for ever the Helpful One, or in softer Saxon, the "Holy" One.

The word has no other ultimate meaning: Helpful, harmless, undefiled: "living" or "Lord of life."

The idea is clear and mighty in the cherubim's cry: "Helpful, helpful, helpful, Lord God of Hosts;" *i.e.* of all the hosts, armies, and creatures of the earth.[1]

§ 6. A pure or holy state of anything, therefore, is that in which all its parts are helpful or consistent. They may or may not be homogeneous. The highest or organic purities are composed of many elements in an entirely helpful state. The highest and first law of the universe—and the other name of life is, therefore, "help." The other name of death is "separation." Government and co-operation are in all things and eternally the laws of life. Anarchy and competition, eternally, and in all things, the laws of death.

§ 7. Perhaps the best, though the most familiar example we could take of the nature and power of consistence, will be that of the possible changes in the dust we tread on.

Exclusive of animal decay, we can hardly arrive at a more absolute type of impurity than the mud or slime of a damp, over-trodden path, in the outskirts of a manufacturing town. I do not say mud of the road, because that is mixed with animal refuse; but take merely an ounce or two of the blackest slime of a beaten footpath on a rainy day, near a large manufacturing town.

---

[1] "The cries of them which have reaped have entered into the ears of the Lord of Sabaoth (of all the creatures of the earth)." You will find a wonderful clearness come into many texts by reading, habitually, "helpful" and "helpfulness" for "holy" and "holiness" or else "living," as in Rom. xi. 16. The sense "dedicated" (the Latin *sanctus*), being, of course, inapplicable to the Supreme Being, is an entirely secondary and accidental one.

§ 8. That slime we shall find in most cases composed of clay (or brickdust, which is burnt clay) mixed with soot, a little sand, and water. All these elements are at helpless war with each other, and destroy reciprocally each other's nature and power, competing and fighting for place at every tread of your foot;—sand squeezing out clay, and clay squeezing out water, and soot meddling everywhere and defiling the whole. Let us suppose that this ounce of mud is left in perfect rest, and that its elements gather together, like to like, so that their atoms may get into the closest relations possible.

§ 9. Let the clay begin. Ridding itself of all foreign substance, it gradually becomes a white earth, already very beautiful; and fit, with help of congealing fire, to be made into finest porcelain, and painted on, and be kept in king's palaces. But such artificial consistence is not its best. Leave it still quiet to follow its own instinct of unity, and it becomes not only white, but clear; not only clear, but hard; nor only clear and hard, but so set that it can deal with light in a wonderful way, and gather out of it the loveliest blue rays only, refusing the rest. We call it then a sapphire.

Such being the consummation of the clay, we give similiar permission of quiet to the sand. It also becomes, first, a white earth, then proceeds to grow clear and hard, and at last arranges itself in mysterious, infinitely fine, parallel lines, which have the power of reflecting not merely the blue rays, but the blue, green, purple, and red rays in the greatest beauty in which they can be seen through any hard material whatsoever. We call it then an opal.

In next order the soot sets to work; it cannot make itself white at first, but instead of being discouraged, tries harder and harder, and comes out clear at last, and the hardest thing in the world; and for the blackness that it had, obtains in exchange the power of reflecting all the rays of the sun at once in the vividest blaze that any solid thing can shoot. We call it then a diamond.

Last of all the water purifies or unites itself, contented enough if it only reach the form of a dew-drop; but if we insist on its proceeding to a more perfect consistence, it crystallizes into the shape of a star.

And for the ounce of slime which we had by political economy of competition, we have by political economy of co-operation, a sapphire, an opal, and a diamond, set in the midst of a star of snow.

§ 10. Now invention in art signifies an arrangement, in which everything in the work is thus consistent with all things else, and helpful to all else.

It is the greatest and rarest of all the qualities of art. The power by which it is effected is absolutely inexplicable and incommunicable; but exercised with entire facility by those who possess it, in many cases even unconsciously.[1]

In work which is not composed, there may be many beautiful things, but they do not help each other. They at the best only stand beside, and more usually compete with and destroy, each other. They may be connected artificially in many ways, but the test of there being no invention is, that if one of them be taken away, the others are no worse than before. But in true composition, if one be taken away, all the rest are helpless and valueless. Generally, in falsely composed work, if anything be taken away, the rest will look better; because the attention is less distracted. Hence the pleasure of inferior artists in sketching, and their inability to finish: all that they add destroys.

§ 11. Also in true composition, everything not only helps everything else a *little*, but helps with its utmost power. Every atom is in full energy; and *all* that energy is kind. Not a line, nor spark of colour, but is doing its very best, and that best is aid. The extent to which this law is carried in truly right and noble work is wholly inconceivable to the

---

[1] By diligent study of good compositions, it is possible to put work together, so that the parts shall help each other a little, or at all events do no harm; and when some tact and taste are associated with this diligence, semblances of real invention are often produced, which, being the results of great labour, the artist is always proud of; and which, being capable of learned explanation and imitation, the spectator naturally takes interest in. The common precepts about composition all produce and teach this false kind, which, as true composition is the noblest, being the corruption of it, is the ignoblest condition of art.

ordinary observer, and no true account of it would be believed.

§ 12. True composition being entirely easy to the man who can compose, he is seldom proud of it, though he clearly recognizes it. Also, true composition is inexplicable. No one can explain how the notes of a Mozart melody, or the folds of a piece of Titian's drapery, produce their essential effects on each other. If you do not feel it, no one can by reasoning make you feel it. And, the highest composition is so subtle, that it is apt to become unpopular, and sometimes seem insipid.

§ 13. The reader may be surprised at my giving so high a place to invention. But if he ever come to know true invention from false, he will find that it is not only the highest quality of art, but is simply the most wonderful act or power of humanity. It is pre-eminently the deed of human creation ; ποίησις, otherwise, poetry.

If the reader will look back to my definition of poetry, he will find it is "the suggestion by the imagination of noble grounds for noble emotion" (Vol. III. p. 11), amplified below (§ 14) into "assembling by help of the imagination ;" that is to say, imagination associative, described at length in Vol. II., in the chapter just referred to. The mystery of the power is sufficiently set forth in that place. Of its dignity I have a word or two to say here.

§ 14. Men in their several professed employments, looked at broadly, may be properly arranged under five classes :—

1. Persons who see. These in modern language are sometimes called sight-seers, that being an occupation coming more and more into vogue every day. Anciently they used to be called, simply, seers.

2. Persons who talk. These, in modern language, are usually called talkers, or speakers, as in the House of Commons, and elsewhere. They used to be called prophets.

3. Persons who make. These, in modern language, are usually called manufacturers. Anciently they were called poets.

4. Persons who think. There seems to be no very distinct modern title for this kind of person, anciently called philosophers, nevertheless we have a few of them among us.

5. Persons who do : in modern language, called practical persons ; anciently, believers.

Of the first two classes I have only this to note—that we ought neither to say that a person sees, if he sees falsely, nor speaks, if he speaks falsely. For seeing falsely is worse than blindness, and speaking falsely, than silence. A man who is too dim-sighted to discern the road from the ditch, may feel which is which ;—but if the ditch appears manifestly to him to be the road, and the road to be the ditch, what shall become of him ? False seeing is unseeing, on the negative side of blindness ; and false speaking, unspeaking,—on the negative side of silence.

To the persons who think, also, the same test applies very shrewdly. Theirs is a dangerous profession ; and from the time of the Aristophanes thought-shop to the great German establishment, or thought-manufactory, whose productions have, unhappily, taken in part the place of the older and more serviceable commodities of Nuremberg toys and Berlin wool, it has been often harmful enough to mankind. It should not be so, for a false thought is more distinctly and visibly no thought, than a false saying is no saying. But it is touching the two great productive classes of the doers and makers, that we have one or two important points to note here.

§ 15. Has the reader ever considered, carefully, what is the meaning of " doing " a thing ?

Suppose a rock falls from a hill-side, crushes a group of cottages, and kills a number of people. The stone has produced a great effect in the world. If any one asks, respecting the broken roofs, " What did it ? " you say the stone did it. Yet you don't talk of the deed of the stone. If you enquire farther, and find that a goat had been feeding beside the rock, and had loosened it by gnawing the roots of the grasses beneath, you find the goat to be the active cause of the calamity, and you say the goat did it. Yet you don't call the goat the doer, nor talk of its evil deed.

But if you find any one went up to the rock, in the night, and with deliberate purpose loosened it, that it might fall on the cottages, you say in quite a different sense, " It is his deed ; he is the doer of it."

§ 16. It appears, then, that deliberate purpose and resolve are needed to constitute a deed or doing, in the true sense of the word ; and that when, accidentally or mechanically, events take place without such purpose, we have indeed effects or results, and agents or causes, but neither deeds nor doers.

Now it so happens, as we all well know, that by far the largest part of things happening in practical life *are* brought about with no deliberate purpose. There are always a number of people who have the nature of stones ; they fall on other persons and crush them. Some again have the nature of weeds, and twist about other people's feet and entangle them. More have the nature of logs, and lie in the way, so that every one falls over them. And most of all have the nature of thorns, and set themselves by waysides, so that every passer-by must be torn, and all good seed choked ; or perhaps make wonderful crackling under various pots, even to the extent of practically boiling water and working pistons. All these people produce immense and sorrowful effect in the world. Yet none of them are doers ; it is their nature to crush, impede, and prick : but deed is not in them.[1]

§ 17. And farther, observe, that even when some effect is finally intended, you cannot call it the person's deed, unless it is *what* he intended.

If an ignorant person, purposing evil, accidentally does good, (as if a thief's disturbing a family should lead them to discover in time that their house was on fire) ; or, *vice versâ*, if an ignorant person intending good accidentally does evil (as if a child should give hemlock to his

---

[1] We may, perhaps, expediently recollect as much of our botany as to teach us that there may be sharp and rough persons, like spines, who yet have good in them, and are essentially branches, and can bud. But the true thorny person is no spine, only an excrescence ; rootless evermore, leafless evermore. No crown made of such can ever meet glory of Angel's hand. (In Memoriam, lxviii.)

companions for celery), in neither case do you call them
the doers of what may result. So that in order to a true
deed, it is necessary that the effect of it should be fore-
seen. Which, ultimately, it cannot be, but by a person
who knows, and in his deed obeys, the laws of the universe,
and of its Maker. And this knowledge is in its highest
form, respecting the will of the Ruling Spirit, called
Trust. For it is not the knowledge that a thing is, but
that, according to the promise and nature of the Ruling
Spirit, a thing will be. Also obedience in its highest
form is not obedience to a constant and compulsory law,
but a persuaded or voluntarily yielded obedience to an
issued command; and so far as it was a *persuaded* submission to command, it was anciently called, in a passive
sense, "persuasion," or πίστις, and in so far as it alone
assuredly did, and it alone *could* do, what it meant to do,
and was therefore the root and essence of all human deed,
it was called by the Latins the "doing," or *fides*, which
has passed into the French *foi* and the English *faith*.
And therefore because in His doing always certain, and
in His speaking always true, His name who leads the
armies of Heaven is "Faithful and true,"[1] and all deeds
which are done in alliance with those armies, be they
small or great, are essentially deeds of faith, which therefore, and in this one stern, eternal sense, subdues all
kingdoms, and turns to flight the armies of the aliens,
and is at once the source and the substance of all human
deed, rightly so called.

§ 18. Thus far then of practical persons, once called
believers, as set forth in the last word of the noblest
group of words ever, so far as I know, uttered by simple
man concerning his practice, being the final testimony of
the leaders of a great practical nation, whose deed thenceforward became an example of deed to mankind:

    Ὦ ξεῖν', ἀγγέλλειν Λακεδαιμονίοις, ὅτι τῇδε
    κείμεθα, τοῖς κείνων ῥήμασι πειθόμενοι.

---

[1] "True," means, etymologically, not "consistent with fact," but
"which may be trusted." "This is a true saying, and worthy of all
acceptation," etc., meaning a trusty saying,—a saying to be rested on,
leant upon.

"O stranger! (we pray thee), tell the Lacedæmonians that we are lying here, having *obeyed* their words."

§ 19. "What, let us ask next, is the ruling character of the person who produces — the creator or maker, anciently called the poet?"

We have seen what a deed is. What then is a "creation"? Nay, it may be replied, to "create" cannot be said of man's labour.

On the contrary, it not only can be said, but is and must be said continually. You certainly do not talk of creating a watch, or creating a shoe; nevertheless you *do* talk of creating a feeling. Why is this?

Look back to the greatest of all creation, that of the world. Suppose the trees had been ever so well or so ingeniously put together, stem and leaf, yet if they had not been able to grow, would they have been well created? Or suppose the fish had been cut and stitched finely out of skin and whalebone; yet, cast upon the waters, had not been able to swim? Or suppose Adam and Eve had been made in the softest clay, ever so neatly, and set at the foot of the tree of knowledge, fastened up to it, quite unable to fall, or do anything else, would they have been well created, or in any true sense created at all?

§ 20. It will, perhaps, appear to you, after a little farther thought, that to create anything in reality is to put life into it.

A poet, or creator, is therefore a person who puts things together, not as a watchmaker steel, or a shoemaker leather, but who puts life into them.

His work is essentially this: it is the gathering and arranging of material by imagination, so as to have in it at last the harmony or helpfulness of life, and the passion or emotion of life. Mere fitting and adjustment of material is nothing; that is watchmaking. But helpful and passionate harmony, essentially choral harmony, so called from the Greek word "rejoicing,"[1] is the harmony of Apollo and the Muses; the word Muse and Mother being derived from the same root, meaning "passionate seeking," or love, of which the issue is passionate finding, or sacred

[1] χορούς τε ὠνομακέναι παρὰ τῆς χαρᾶς ἔμφυτον ὄνομα. (De leg. II. 1.)

THE LAW OF HELP

INVENTION. For which reason I could not bear to use
any baser word than this of invention. And if the reader
will think over all these things, and follow them out, as I
think he may easily with this much of clue given him, he
will not any more think it wrong in me to place invention
so high among the powers of man.[1] Nor any more think
it strange that the last act of the life of Socrates[2] should
have been to purify himself from the sin of having negli-
gently listened to the voice within him, which, through all
his past life, had bid him " labour, and make harmony."

[1] This being, indeed, among the visiblest signs of the Divine or
immortal life. We have got a base habit of opposing the word
"mortal" or "deathful" merely to " *im*-mortal ;" whereas it is essentially
contrary to "divine" (to θεῖος, not to ἀθάνατος, Phaedo, 66), that which
is deathful being anarchic or disobedient, and that which is divine
ruling and obedient ; this being the true distinction between flesh and
spirit.

[2] πολλάκις μοι φοιτῶν τὸ αὐτὸ ἐνύπνιον ἐν τῷ παρελθόντι βίῳ, ἄλλοτ'
ἐν ἄλλῃ ὄψει φαινόμενον, τὰ αὐτὰ δὲ λέγον, Ὦ Σώκρατες, ἔφη, μουσικὴν
ποίει καὶ ἐργάζου. (Phaedo, 11.)

CHAPTER II

THE TASK OF THE LEAST

§ 1. THE reader has probably been surprised at my assertions made often before now, and reiterated here, that the *minutest* portion of a great composition is helpful to the whole. It certainly does not seem easily conceivable that this should be so. I will go farther, and say that it is inconceivable. But it is the fact.

We shall discern it to be so by taking one or two compositions to pieces, and examining the fragments. In doing which, we must remember that a great composition always has a leading emotional purpose, technically called its motive, to which all its lines and forms have some relation. Undulating lines, for instance, are expressive of action; and would be false in effect if the motive of the picture was one of repose. Horizontal and angular lines are expressive of rest and strength; and would destroy a design whose purpose was to express disquiet and feebleness. It is therefore necessary to ascertain the motive before descending to the detail.

§ 2. One of the simplest subjects, in the series of the Rivers of France, is " Rietz, near Saumur." The published Plate gives a better rendering than usual of its tone of light; and my rough etching, Plate 73, sufficiently shows the arrangement of its lines. What is their motive?

To get at it completely, we must know something of the Loire.

The district through which it here flows is, for the most part, a low place, yet not altogether at the level of the stream, but cut into steep banks of chalk or gravel, thirty

J. M. W. Turner

J. Ruskin

73. Loire-side

or forty feet high, running for miles at about an equal height above the water.

These banks are excavated by the peasantry, partly for houses, partly for cellars, so economizing vineyard space above; and thus a kind of continuous village runs along the river-side, composed half of caves, half of rude buildings, backed by the cliff, propped against it, therefore always leaning away from the river; mingled with overlappings of vineyard trellis from above, and little towers or summer-houses for outlook, when the grapes are ripe, or for gossip over the garden wall.

§ 3. It is an autumnal evening, then, by this Loire side. The day has been hot, and the air is heavy and misty still; the sunlight warm, but dim; the brown vine-leaves motion-less: all else quiet. Not a sail in sight on the river,[1] its strong noiseless current lengthening the stream of low sunlight.

The motive of the picture, therefore, is the expression of rude but perfect peace, slightly mingled with an indolent languor and despondency; the space between intervals of enforced labour; happy, but listless, and having little care or hope about the future; cutting its home out of this gravel bank, and letting the vine and the river twine and undermine as they will; careless to mend or build, so long as the walls hold together, and the black fruit swells in the sunshine.

§ 4. To get this repose, together with rude stability, we have therefore horizontal lines and bold angles. The grand horizontal space and sweep of Turner's distant river show perhaps better in the etching than in the Plate; but de-pend wholly for value on the piece of near wall. It is the vertical line of its dark side which drives the eye up into the distance, right against the horizontal, and so makes it felt, while the flatness of the stone prepares the eye to understand the flatness of the river. Farther: hide with your finger the little ring on that stone, and you will find the river has stopped flowing. That ring is to repeat the curved lines of the river bank, which express its line of

---

[1] The sails in the engraving were put in to catch the public eye. There are none in the drawing.

current, and to bring the feeling of them down near us. On the other side of the road the horizontal lines are taken up again by the dark pieces of wood, without which we should still lose half our space.

Next: The repose is to be not only perfect, but indolent: the repose of out-wearied people; not caring much what becomes of them.

You see the road is covered with litter. Even the crockery is left outside the cottage to dry in the sun, after being washed up. The steps of the cottage door have been too high for comfort originally, only it was less trouble to cut three large stones than four or five small. They are now all aslope and broken, not repaired for years. Their weighty forms increase the sense of languor throughout the scene, and of stability also, because we feel how difficult it would be to stir them. The crockery has its work to do also ;—the arched door on the left being necessary to show the great thickness of walls and the strength they require to prevent falling in of the cliff above ;—as the horizontal lines must be diffused on the right, so this arch must be diffused on the left; and the large round plate on one side of the steps, with the two small ones on the other, are to carry down the element of circular curvature. Hide them, and see the result.

As they carry the arched group of forms down, the arched window-shutter diffuses it upwards, where all the lines of the distant buildings suggest one and the same idea of disorderly and careless strength, mingling masonry with rock.

§ 5. So far of the horizontal and curved lines. How of the radiating ones? What has the black vine trellis got to do?

Lay a pencil or ruler parallel with its lines. You will find that they point to the massive building in the distance. To which, as nearly as is possible without at once showing the artifice, every other radiating line points also; almost ludicrously when it is once pointed out; even the curved line of the top of the terrace runs into it, and the last sweep of the river evidently leads to its base. And so nearly is it in the exact centre of the picture, that one diagonal from corner to corner passes through it, and the other only misses the base by the twentieth of an inch.

If you are accustomed to France, you will know in a moment by its outline that this massive building is an old church.

Without it, the repose would not have been essentially the labourer's rest—rest as of the Sabbath. Among all the groups of lines that point to it, two are principal : the first, those of the vine trellis : the second, those of the handles of the saw left in the beam : the blessing of human life, and its labour.

Whenever Turner wishes to express profound repose, he puts in the foreground some instrument of labour cast aside. See, in Rogers's Poems, the last vignette, " Datur hora quieti," with the plough in the furrow : and in the first vignette of the same book, the scythe on the shoulder of the peasant going home. (There is nothing about the scythe in the passage of the poem which this vignette illustrates.)

§ 6. Observe, farther, the outline of the church itself. As our habitations are, so is our church, evidently a heap of old, but massive walls, patched, and repaired, and roofed in, and over and over, until its original shape is hardly recognizable. I know the kind of church well—can tell even here, two miles off, that I shall find some Norman arches in the apse, and a flamboyant porch, rich and dark, with every statue broken out of it ; and a rude wooden belfry above all ; and a quantity of miserable shops built in among the buttresses ; and that I may walk in and out as much as I please, but that how often soever, I shall always find some one praying at the Holy Sepulchre, in the darkest aisle, and my going in and out will not disturb them. For they *are* praying, which in many a handsomer and highlier-furbished edifice might, perhaps, not be so assuredly the case.

§ 7. Lastly : What kind of people have we on this winding road ? Three indolent ones, leaning on the wall to look over into the gliding water ; and a matron with her market panniers ; by her figure, not a fast rider. The road, besides, is bad, and seems unsafe for trotting, and she has passed without disturbing the cat, who sits comfortably on the block of wood in the middle of it.

§ 8. Next to this piece of quietness, let us glance at a composition in which the motive is one of tumult : that of the Fall of Schaffhausen. It is engraved in the Keepsake. I have etched in Plate 74, at the top, the chief lines of its composition,[1] in which the first great purpose is to give swing enough to the water. The line of fall is straight and monotonous in reality. Turner wants to get the great concave sweep and rush of the river well felt, in spite of the unbroken form. The column of spray, rocks, mills, and bank, all radiate like a plume, sweeping round together in grand curves to the left, where the group of figures, hurried about the ferry boat, rises like a dash of spray ; they also radiating : so as to form one perfectly connected cluster, with the two gens-d'armes and the millstones ; the millstones at the bottom being the root of it ; the two soldiers laid right and left to sustain the branch of figures beyond, balanced just as a tree bough would be.

§ 9. One of the gens-d'armes is flirting with a young lady in a round cap and full sleeves, under pretence of wanting her to show him what she has in her bandbox. The motive of which flirtation is, so far as Turner is concerned in it, primarily the bandbox : this and the millstones below, give him a series of concave lines, which, concentrated by the recumbent soldiers, intensify the hollow sweep of the fall, precisely as the ring on the stone does the Loire eddies. These curves are carried out on the right by the small plate of eggs, laid to be washed at the spring ; and, all these concave lines being a little too quiet and recumbent, the staggering casks are set on the left, and the ill-balanced milk-pail on the right, to give a

---

[1] These etchings of compositions are all reversed, for they are merely sketches on the steel, and I cannot sketch easily except straight from the drawing, and without reversing. The looking-glass plagues me with cross lights. As examples of composition, it does not the least matter which way they are turned ; and the reader may see this Schaffhausen subject from the right side of the Rhine, by holding the book before a glass. The rude indications of the figures in the Loire subject are nearly facsimiles of Turner's.

J. M. W. Turner   J. Ruskin

74. The Millstream

general feeling of things being rolled over and over. The things which are to give this sense of rolling are dark, in order to hint at the way in which the cataract rolls boulders of rock ; while the forms which are to give the sense of its sweeping force are white. The little spring, splashing out of its pine-trough, is to give contrast with the power of the fall,—while it carries out the general sense of splashing water.

§ 10. This spring exists on the spot, and so does everything else in the picture; but the combinations are wholly arbitrary ; it being Turner's fixed principle to collect out of any scene, whatever was characteristic, and put it together just as he liked. The changes made in this instance are highly curious. The mills have no resemblance whatever to the real group as seen from this spot; for there is a vulgar and formal dwelling-house in front of them. But if you climb the rock behind them, you find they form on that side a towering cluster, which Turner has put with little modification into the drawing. What he has done to the mills, he has done with still greater audacity to the central rock. Seen from this spot, it shows, in reality, its greatest breadth, and is heavy and uninteresting ; but on the Lauffen side, exposes its consumed base, worn away by the rush of water, which Turner resolving to show, serenely draws the rock as it appears from the other side of the Rhine, and brings that view of it over to this side. I have etched the bit with the rock a little larger below ; and if the reader knows the spot, he will see that this piece of the drawing, reversed in the etching, is almost a bonâ fide unreversed study of the fall from the Lauffen side.[1]

Finally, the castle of Lauffen itself, being, when seen from this spot, too much foreshortened to show its extent, Turner walks a quarter of a mile lower down the river, draws the castle accurately there, brings it back with him,

---

[1] With the exception of the jagged ledge rising out of the foam below, which comes from the north side, and is admirable in its expression of the position of the limestone-beds, which, rising from below the drift gravel of Constance, are the real cause of the fall of Schaffhausen.

and puts it in all its extent, where he chooses to have it, beyond the rocks.

I tried to copy and engrave this piece of the drawing of its real size, merely to show the forms of the trees, drifted back by the breeze from the fall, and wet with its spray; but in the endeavour to facsimile the touches, great part of their grace and ease has been lost; still, Plate 75 may, if compared with the same piece in the Keepsake engraving, at least show that the original drawing has not yet been rendered with completeness.

§ 11. These two examples may sufficiently serve to show the mode in which minor details, both in form and spirit, are used by Turner to aid his main motives; of course I cannot, in the space of this volume, go on examining subjects at this length, even if I had time to etch them; but every design of Turner's would be equally instructive, examined in a similar manner. Thus far, however, we have only seen the help of the parts to the whole; we must give yet a little attention to the mode of combining the smallest details.

I am always led away, in spite of myself, from my proper subject here, invention formal, or the merely pleasant placing of lines and masses, into the emotional results of such arrangement. The chief reason of this is that the emotional power can be explained; but the perfection of formative arrangement, as I said, cannot be explained, any more than that of melody in music. An instance or two of it, however, may be given.

§ 12. Much fine formative arrangement depends on a more or less elliptical or pear-shaped balance of the group, obtained by arranging the principal members of it on two opposite curves, and either centralizing it by some powerful feature at the base, centre, or summit; or else clasping it together by some conspicuous point or knot. A very small object will often do this satisfactorily.

If you can get the complete series of Lefèbre's engravings from Titian and Veronese, they will be quite enough to teach you, in their dumb way, everything that is teachable of composition; at all events, try to get the Madonna, with St. Peter and St. George under the two great pillars;

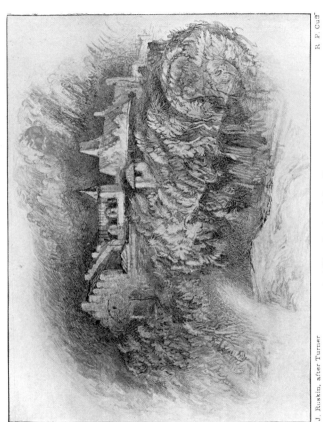

J. Ruskin, after Turner

R. P. Cuff

75. The Castle of Laufen

the Madonna and Child, with mitred bishop on her left, and St. Andrew on her right; and Veronese's Triumph of Venice. The first of these Plates unites two formative symmetries: that of the two pillars, clasped by the square altar-cloth below and cloud above, catches the eye first; but the main group is the fivefold one rising to the left, crowned by the Madonna. St. Francis and St. Peter form its two wings, and the kneeling portrait figures, its base. It is clasped at the bottom by the key of St. Peter, which points straight at the Madonna's head, and is laid on the steps solely for this purpose; the curved lines, which enclose the group, meet also in her face; and the straight line of light, on the cloak of the nearest senator, points at her also. If you have Turner's Liber Studiorum, turn to the Lauffenburg, and compare the figure group there: a fivefold chain, one standing figure, central; two recumbent, for wings; two half-recumbent, for bases; and a cluster of weeds to clasp. Then turn to Lefèbre's Europa (there are two in the series—I mean the one with the two tree trunks over her head). It is a wonderful ninefold group. Europa central; two stooping figures, each surmounted by a standing one, for wings; a cupid on one side, and dog on the other, for bases: a cupid and trunk of tree, on each side, to terminate above; and a garland for clasp.

§ 13. Fig. 94, p. 192, will serve to show the mode in which similar arrangements are carried into the smallest detail. It is magnified four times[1] from a cluster of leaves in the foreground of the "Isis" (Liber Studiorum). Figs. 95 and 96, page 193, show the arrangement of the two groups composing it; the lower is purely symmetrical, with trefoiled centre and broad masses for wings; the uppermost is a sweeping continuous curve, symmetrical, but foreshortened. Both are clasped by arrow-shaped leaves. The two whole groups themselves are, in turn, members of another larger group, composing the entire foreground, and consisting of broad dock-leaves, with minor clusters on the right and left, of which these form the chief portion on the right side.

§ 14. Unless every leaf, and every visible point or object, however small, forms a part of some harmony of this kind

[1] [Reduced for this edition.]

(these symmetrical conditions being only the most simple and obvious), it has no business in the picture. It is the necessary connection of all the forms and colours, down to the last touch, which constitutes great or inventive work, separated from all common work by an impassable gulf.

By diligently copying the etchings of the Liber Studiorum,

Fig. 94.

the reader may, however, easily attain the perception of the existence of these relations, and be prepared to understand Turner's more elaborate composition. It would take many figures to disentangle and explain the arrangements merely of the leaf cluster, Fig. 78, page 110; but that there *is* a system, and that every leaf has a fixed value and place in it, can hardly but be felt at a glance.

It is curious that, in spite of all the constant talking of " composition " which goes on among art students, true

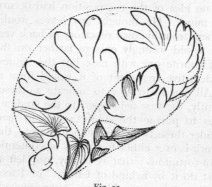

Fig. 95.

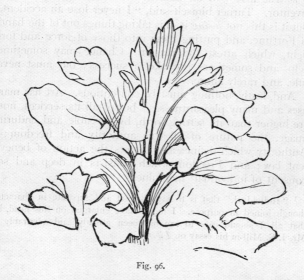

Fig. 96.

composition is just the last thing which appears to be per-ceived. One would have thought that in this group, at least the value of the central black leaf would have been seen, of which the principal function is to point towards, and continue, the line of bank above. See Plate 62. But a glance at the published Plate in the England series will show that no idea of the composition had occurred to the engraver's mind. He thought any leaves would do, and supplied them from his own repertory of hack vegetation.

§ 15. I would willingly enlarge farther on this subject—it is a favourite one with me; but the figures required for any exhaustive treatment of it would form a separate volume. All that I can do is to indicate, as these examples do sufficiently, the vast field open to the student's analysis if he cares to pursue the subject; and to mark for the general reader these two strong conclusions :—that nothing in great work is ever either fortuitous or contentious.

It is not fortuitous; that is to say, not left to fortune. The "must do it by a kind of felicity" of Bacon is true; it is true also that an accident is often suggestive to an inventor. Turner himself said, "I never lose an accident." But it is this not *losing* it, this taking things out of the hands of Fortune, and putting them into those of force and fore-sight, which attest the master. Chance may sometimes help, and sometimes provoke, a success; but must never rule, and rarely allure.

And, lastly, nothing must be contentious. Art has many uses and many pleasantnesses; but of all its services, none are higher than its setting forth, by a visible and enduring image, the nature of all true authority and freedom;— Authority which defines and directs the action of benevolent law; and Freedom which consists in deep and soft consent of individual[1] helpfulness.

---

[1] "Individual," that is to say, distinct and separate in character, though joined in purpose. I might have enlarged on this head, but that all I should care to say has been already said admirably by Mr. J. S. Mill in his essay on *Liberty*.

CHAPTER III

THE RULE OF THE GREATEST

§ 1. In the entire range of art principles, none perhaps present a difficulty so great to the student, or require from the teacher expression so cautious, and yet so strong, as those which concern the nature and influence of magnitude.

In one sense, and that deep, there is no such thing as magnitude. The least thing is as the greatest, and one day as a thousand years, in the eyes of the Maker of great and small things. In another sense, and that close to us and necessary, there exist both magnitude and value. Though not a sparrow falls to the ground unnoted, there are yet creatures who are of more value than many; and the same Spirit which weighs the dust of the earth in a balance, counts the isles as a little thing.

§ 2. The just temper of human mind in this matter may, nevertheless, be told shortly. Greatness can only be rightly estimated when minuteness is justly reverenced. Greatness is the aggregation of minuteness; nor can its sublimity be felt truthfully by any mind unaccustomed to the affectionate watching of what is least.

But if this affection for the least be unaccompanied by the powers of comparison and reflection; if it be intemperate in its thirst, restless in curiosity, and incapable of the patient and self-commandant pause which is wise to arrange, and submissive to refuse, it will close the paths of noble art to the student as effectually, and hopelessly, as even the blindness of pride, or impatience of ambition.

§ 3. I say the paths of noble art, not of useful art. All accurate investigation will have its reward; the morbid curiosity will at least slake the thirst of others, if not its own; and the diffused and petty affections will distribute, in serviceable measure, their minute delights and narrow discoveries. The opposite error, the desire of greatness as such, or rather of what appears great to indolence and vanity;—the instinct which I have described in the "Seven Lamps," noting it, among the Renaissance builders, to be an especial and unfailing sign of baseness of mind, is as fruitless as it is vile; no way profitable—every way harmful; the widest and most corrupting expression of vulgarity. The microscopic drawing of an insect may be precious; but nothing except disgrace and misguidance will ever be gathered from such work as that of Haydon or Barry.

§ 4. The work I have mostly had to do, since this essay was begun, has been that of contention against such debased issues of swollen insolence and windy conceit; but I have noticed lately, that some lightly-budding philosophers have depreciated true greatness; confusing the relations of scale, as they bear upon human instinct and morality; reasoning as if a mountain were no nobler than a grain of sand, or as if many souls were not of mightier interest than one. To whom it must be shortly answered that the Lord of power and life knew which were His noblest works, when He bade His servant watch the play of the Leviathan, rather than dissect the spawn of the minnow; and that when it comes to practical question whether a single soul is to be jeoparded for many, and this Leonidas, or Curtius, or Winkelried shall abolish—so far as abolishable—his own spirit, that he may save more numerous spirits, such question is to be solved by the simple human instinct respecting number and magnitude, not by reasoning on infinity:—

"Le navigateur, qui, la nuit, voit l'océan étinceler de lumière, danser en guirlandes de feu, s'égaye d'abord de ce spectacle. Il fait dix lieues; la guirlande s'allonge indéfiniment, elle s'agite, se tord, se noue, aux mouvements de la lame; c'est un serpent monstrueux qui va toujours s'allongeant, jusqu'à trente lieues, quarante lieues. Et tout cela n'est qu'une danse d'animalcules imperceptibles. En quel nombre? À cette question l'imagination s'effraye; elle sent la une nature de puissance immense, de richesse épouvantable. . . . . Que sont ces petits des petits? Rien moins que les constructeurs du globe où nous sommes. De leurs corps, de leurs débris, ils ont

préparé le sol qui est sous nos pas. . . . . Et ce sont les plus
petits qui ont fait les plus grandes choses. L'imperceptible rhizopode
s'est bâti un monument bien autre que les pyramides, pas moins que
l'Italie centrale, une notable partie de la chaîne des Apennins. Mais
c'était trop peu encore ; les masses énormes du Chili, les prodigieuses
Cordillères, qui regardent le monde à leurs pieds, sont le monument
funéraire où cet être insaisissable, et pour ainsi dire, invisible, a
enseveli les débris de son espèce disparue."—(Michelet : *L'Insecte*.)

§ 5. In these passages, and those connected with them
in the chapter from which they are taken, itself so vast in
scope, and therefore so sublime, we may perhaps find the
true relations of minuteness, multitude, and magnitude.
We shall not feel that there is no such thing as littleness,
or no such thing as magnitude. Nor shall we be disposed
to confuse a Volvox with the Cordilleras ; but we may learn
that they both are bound together by links of eternal life
and toil ; we shall see the vastest thing noble, chiefly for
what it includes ; and the meanest for what it accomplishes.
Thence we might gather—and the conclusion will be found
in experience true—that the sense of largeness would be
most grateful to minds capable of comprehending, balancing, and comparing ; but capable also of great patience
and expectation ; while the sense of minute wonderfulness
would be attractive to minds acted upon by sharp, small,
penetrative sympathies, and apt to be impatient, irregular,
and partial. This fact is curiously shown in the relations
between the temper of the great composers and the modern
pathetic school. I was surprised at the first rise of that
school, now some years ago, by observing how they restrained themselves to subjects which in other hands would
have been wholly uninteresting (compare Vol. IV., p. 19) :
and in their succeeding efforts, I saw with increasing wonder,
that they were almost destitute of the power of feeling vastness, or enjoying the forms which expressed it. A mountain
or great building only appeared to them as a piece of colour
of a certain shape. The powers it represented, or included,
were invisible to them. In general they avoided subjects expressing space or mass, and fastened on confined,
broken, and sharp forms ; liking furze, fern, reeds, straw,
stubble, dead leaves, and such like, better than strong stones,

broad-flowing leaves, or rounded hills; in all such greater things, when forced to paint them, they missed the main and mighty lines; and this no less in what they loved than in what they disliked; for though fond of foliage, their trees always had a tendency to congeal into little acicular thorn-hedges, and never tossed free. Which modes of choice proceed naturally from a petulant sympathy with local and immediately visible interests or sorrows, not regarding their large consequences, nor capable of understanding more massive view or more deeply deliberate mercifulness;—but peevish and horror-struck, and often incapable of self-control, though not of self-sacrifice. There are more people who can forget themselves than govern themselves.

This narrowly pungent and bitter virtue has, however, its beautiful uses, and is of special value in the present day, when surface-work, shallow generalization, and cold arithmetical estimates of things, are among the chief dangers and causes of misery, which men have to deal with.

§ 6. On the other hand, and in clear distinction from all such workers, it is to be remembered that the great composers, not less deep in feeling, are in the fixed habit of regarding as much the relations and positions, as the separate nature, of things; that they reap and thresh in the sheaf, never pluck ears to rub in the hand; fish with net, not line, and sweep their prey together within great cords of errorless curve;—that nothing ever bears to them a separate or isolated aspect, but leads or links a chain of aspects—that to them it is not merely the surface, nor the substance, of anything that is of import; but its circumference and continence; that they are pre-eminently patient and reserved; observant, not curious;—comprehensive, not conjectural; calm exceedingly; unerring, constant, terrible in stedfastness of intent; unconquerable; incomprehensible; always suggesting, implying, including, more than can be told.

§ 7. And this may be seen down to their treatment of the smallest things.

For there is nothing so small but we may, as we choose, see it in the whole, or in part, and in subdued connection with other things, or in individual and petty prominence.

The greatest treatment is always that which gives conception the widest range, and most harmonious guidance;—it being permitted us to employ a certain quantity of time, and certain number of touches of pencil—he who with these embraces the largest sphere of thought, and suggests within that sphere the most perfect order of thought, has wrought the most wisely, and therefore most nobly.

§ 8. I do not, however, purpose here to examine or illustrate the nature of great treatment—to do so effectually would need many examples from the figure composers; and it will be better (if I have time to work out the subject carefully) that I should do so in a form which may be easily accessible to young students. Here I will only state in conclusion what it is chiefly important for all students to be convinced of, that all the technical qualities by which greatness of treatment is known, such as reserve in colour, tranquillity and largeness of line, and refusal of unnecessary objects of interest are, when they are real, the exponents of an habitually noble temper of mind, never the observances of a precept supposed to be useful. The refusal or reserve of a mighty painter cannot be imitated; it is only by reaching the same intellectual strength that you will be able to give an equal dignity to your self-denial. No one can tell you beforehand what to accept, or what to ignore; only remember always, in painting as in eloquence, the greater your strength, the quieter will be your manner, and the fewer your words; and in painting, as in all the arts and acts of life, the secret of high success will be found, not in a fretful and various excellence, but in a quiet singleness of justly chosen aim.

CHAPTER IV

THE LAW OF PERFECTNESS

§ 1. AMONG the several characteristics of great treatment which in the last chapter were alluded to without being enlarged upon, one will be found several times named ;—reserve.

It is necessary for our present purpose that we should understand this quality more distinctly. I mean by it the power which a great painter exercises over himself in fixing certain limits, either of force, of colour, or of quantity of work ;—limits which he will not transgress in any part of his picture, even though here and there a painful sense of incompletion may exist, under the fixed conditions, and might tempt an inferior workman to infringe them. The nature of this reserve we must understand in order that we may also determine the nature of true completion or perfectness, which is the end of composition.

§ 2. For perfectness, properly so called, means harmony. The word signifies literally the doing our work *thoroughly*. It does not mean carrying it up to any constant and established degree of finish, but carrying the whole of it up to a degree determined upon. In a chalk or pencil sketch by a great master, it will often be found that the deepest shades are feeble tints of pale gray ; the outlines nearly invisible, and the forms brought out by a ghostly delicacy of touch, which, on looking close to the paper, will be indistinguishable from its general texture. A single line of ink, occurring anywhere in such a drawing, would of course destroy it ; placed in the darkness of a mouth or nostril, it would turn the expression into a caricature ; on a cheek or brow it would be simply a blot. Yet let the blot remain, and let the master work up to it with lines of similar force; and the drawing which was before perfect, in terms of pencil, will become, under his hand, perfect in terms of ink; and what was before a scratch on the cheek will become a necessary and beautiful part of its gradation.

All great work is thus reduced under certain conditions, and its right to be called complete depends on its fulfilment of them, not on the nature of the conditions chosen. Habitually, indeed, we call a coloured work which is satisfactory to us, finished, and a chalk drawing unfinished; but in the mind of the master, all his work is, according to the sense in which you use the word, equally perfect or imperfect. Perfect, if you regard its purpose and limitation; imperfect, if you compare it with the natural standard. In what appears to you consummate, the master has assigned to himself terms of shortcoming, and marked with a sad severity the point up to which he will permit himself to contend with nature. Were it not for his acceptance of such restraint, he could neither quit his work, nor endure it. He could not quit it, for he would always perceive more that might be done; he could not endure it, because all doing ended only in more elaborate deficiency.

§ 3. But we are apt to forget in modern days, that the reserve of a man who is not putting forth half his strength is different in manner and dignity from the effort of one who can do no more. Charmed, and justly charmed, by the harmonious sketches of great painters, and by the grandeur of their acquiescence in the point of pause, we have put ourselves to produce sketches as an end instead of a means, and thought to imitate the painter's scornful restraint of his own power, by a scornful rejection of the things beyond ours. For many reasons, therefore, it becomes desirable to understand precisely and finally what a good painter means by completion.

§ 4. The sketches of true painters may be classed under the following heads:—

I. *Experimental.*—In which they are assisting an imperfect conception of a subject by trying the look of it on paper in different ways.

By the greatest men this kind of sketch is hardly ever made; they conceive their subjects distinctly at once, and their sketch is not to try them, but to fasten them down. Raphael's form the only important exception—and the numerous examples of experimental work by him are evidence of his composition being technical rather than imaginative. I have never seen a drawing of the kind by any great Venetian. Among the nineteen thousand sketches by Turner—which I arranged in the National Gallery—there was, to the best of my recollection, *not one*. In several instances the work, after being carried forward a certain length, had been abandoned and begun again with another view; sometimes also two or more modes of treatment had been set side by side with a view to choice. But there were always two distinct imaginations contending for realization—not experimental modifications of one.

§ 5. II. *Determinant.*—The fastening down of an idea in the simplest terms, in order that it may not be disturbed or confused by after work. Nearly all the great composers do this, methodically, before beginning a painting. Such sketches are usually in a high degree resolute and compressive; the best of them outlined or marked calmly with the pen, and deliberately washed with colour, indicating the places of the principal lights.

Fine drawings of this class never show any hurry or confusion. They are the expression of concluded operations of mind, are drawn slowly, and are not so much sketches, as maps.

§ 6. III. *Commemorative.*—Containing records of facts which the master required. These in their most elaborate form are "studies," or drawings from Nature, or parts needed in the composition, often highly finished in the part which is to be introduced. In this form, however, they never occur by the greatest imaginative masters. For by a truly great inventor everything is invented; no atom of the work is unmodified by his mind; and no study from Nature, however beautiful, could be introduced by him into his design without change; it would not fit with the rest. Finished studies for introduction are therefore chiefly by Leonardo and Raphael, both technical designers rather than imaginative ones

Commemorative sketches by great masters are generally hasty, merely to put them in mind of motives of invention, or they are shorthand memoranda of things with which they do not care to trouble their memory ; or, finally, accurate notes of things which they must *not* modify by invention, as local detail, costume, and such like. You may find perfectly accurate drawings of coats of arms, portions of dresses, pieces of architecture, and so on, by all the great men ; but you will not find elaborate studies of bits of their pictures.

§ 7. When the sketch is made merely as a memorandum, it is impossible to say how little, or what kind of drawing, may be sufficient for the purpose. It is of course likely to be hasty from its very nature, and unless the exact purpose be understood, it may be as unintelligible as a piece of shorthand writing. For instance, in the corner of a sheet of sketches made at sea, among those of Turner, at the National Gallery, occurs this one, Fig. 97 (see next page). I suppose most persons would not see much use in it. It nevertheless was probably one of the most important sketches made in Turner's life, fixing for ever in his mind certain facts respecting the sunrise from a clear sea-horizon. Having myself watched such sunrise occasionally, I perceive this sketch to mean as follows :

(Half circle at the top.) When the sun was only half out of the sea, the horizon was sharply traced across its disk, and red streaks of vapour crossed the lower part of it.

(Horseshoe underneath.) When the sun had risen so far as to show three-quarters of its diameter, its light became so great as to conceal the sea-horizon, consuming it away in descending rays.

(Smaller horseshoe below.) When on the point of detaching itself from the horizon, the sun still consumed away the line of the sea, and looked as if pulled down by it.

(Broken oval.) Having risen about a fourth of its

diameter above the horizon, the sea-line reappeared; but the risen orb was flattened by refraction into an oval.

(Broken circle.) Having risen a little farther above the sea-line, the sun, at last, got itself round, and all

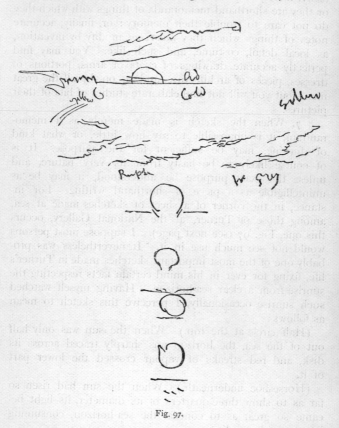

Fig. 97.

right, with sparkling reflection on the waves just below the sea-line.

This memorandum is for its purpose entirely perfect and efficient, though the sun is not drawn carefully round, but with a dash of the pencil; but there is no affected or

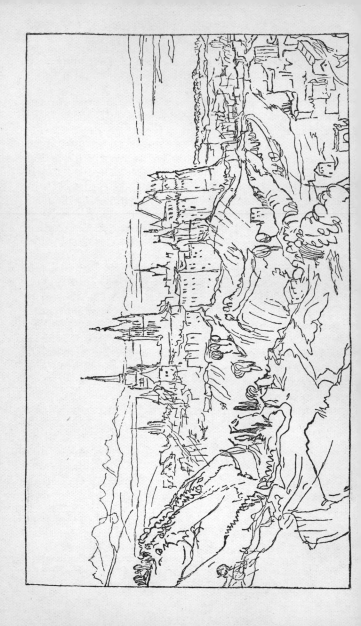

desired slightness. Could it have been drawn round as
instantaneously, it would have been. The purpose is
throughout determined; there is no scrawling, as in vulgar
sketching.[1]

§ 8. Again, Fig. 98 is a facsimile of one of Turner's
"memoranda," of a complete subject,[2] Lausanne, from
the road to Fribourg.

This example is entirely characteristic of his usual drawings from nature, which unite two characters, being *both*
commemorative and determinant :—Commemorative, in so
far as they note certain facts about the place : determinant,
in that they record an impression received from the place
there and then, together with the principal arrangement of
the composition in which it was afterwards to be recorded.
In this mode of sketching, Turner differs from all other
men whose work I have studied. He never draws accurately
on the spot, with the intention of modifying or composing afterwards from the materials ; but instantly modifies
as he draws, placing his memoranda where they are to be
ultimately used, and taking exactly what he wants, not a
fragment or line more.

§ 9. This sketch has been made in the afternoon. He
had been impressed, as he walked up the hill, by the
vanishing of the lake in the golden horizon, without end
of waters, and by the opposition of the pinnacled castle
and cathedral to its level breadth. That must be drawn !
and from this spot, where all the buildings are set well
together. But it lucklessly happens that, though the
buildings come just where he wants them in situation,
they don't in height. For the castle (the square mass
on the right) is in reality higher than the cathedral, and

[1] The word in the uppermost note, to the right of the sun, is "red ;"
the others, "yellow," "purple," "cold," "light grey." He always
noted the colours of skies in this way.

[2] It is not so good a facsimile as those I have given from Dürer,
for the original sketch is in light pencil ; and the thickening and
delicate emphasis of the lines, on which nearly all the beauty of the
drawing depended, cannot be expressed in the woodcut, though marked
by a double line as well as I could. But the figure will answer its
purpose well enough in showing Turner's mode of sketching. [Reduced
for this edition.]

would block out the end of the lake. Down it goes instantly a hundred feet, that we may see the lake over it; without the smallest regard for the military position of Lausanne.

§ 10. Next: The last low spire on the left is in truth concealed behind the nearer bank, the town running far down the hill (and climbing another hill) in that direction. But the group of spires, without it, would not be rich enough to give a proper impression of Lausanne, as a spiry place. Turner quietly sends to fetch the church from round the corner, places it where he likes, and indicates its distance only by aerial perspective (much greater in the pencil drawing than in the woodcut).

§ 11. But again : Not only the spire of the lower church, but the peak of the Rochers d'Enfer (that highest in the distance) would in reality be out of sight; it is much farther round to the left. This would never do either; for without it, we should have no idea that Lausanne was opposite the mountains, nor should we have a nice sloping line to lead us into the distance.

With the same unblushing tranquillity of mind in which he had ordered up the church, Turner sends also to fetch the Rochers d'Enfer; and puts *them* also where he chooses, to crown the slope of distant hill, which, as every traveller knows, in its decline to the west, is one of the most notable features of the view from Lausanne.

§ 12. These modifications, easily traceable in the large features of the design, are carried out with equal audacity and precision in every part of it. Every one of those confused lines on the right indicates something that is really there, only everything is shifted and sorted into the exact places that Turner chose. The group of dark objects near us at the foot of the bank is a cluster of mills, which, when the picture was completed, were to be the blackest things in it, and to throw back the castle, and the golden horizon ; while the rounded touches at the bottom, under the castle, indicate a row of trees, which follow a brook coming out of the ravine behind us ; and were going to be made very round indeed in the picture, (to oppose the spiky and angular masses of castle), and very consecutive, in order to form another conducting line into the distance.

§ 13. These motives, or motives like them, might perhaps be guessed on looking at the sketch. But no one without going to the spot would understand the meaning of the vertical lines in the left-hand lowest corner.

They are a "memorandum" of the artificial verticalness of a low sandstone cliff, which has been cut down there to give space for a bit of garden belonging to a public-house beneath, from which garden a path leads along the ravine to the Lausanne rifle-ground. The value of these vertical lines in repeating those of the cathedral, is very great; it would be greater still in the completed picture, increasing the sense of looking down from a height, and giving grasp of, and power over, the whole scene.

§ 14. Throughout the sketch, as in all that Turner made, the observing and combining intellect acts in the same manner. Not a line is lost, nor a moment of time; and though the pencil flies, and the whole thing is literally done as fast as a piece of shorthand writing, it is to the full as purposeful and compressed, so that while there are indeed dashes of the pencil which are unintentional, they are only unintentional as the form of a letter is, in fast writing, not from want of intention, but from the accident of haste.

§ 15. I know not if the reader can understand,—I myself cannot, though I see it to be demonstrable,—the simultaneous occurrence of idea which produces such a drawing as this: the grasp of the whole, from the laying of the first line, which induces continual modifications of all that is done, out of respect to parts not done yet. No line is ever changed or effaced: no experiment made; but every touch is placed with reference to all that are to succeed, as to all that have gone before; every addition takes its part, as the stones in an arch of a bridge; the last touch locks the arch. Remove that keystone, or remove any other of the stones of the vault, and the whole will fall.

§ 16. I repeat—the power of mind which accomplishes this, is yet wholly inexplicable to me, as it was when first I defined it in the chapter on imagination associative, in the second volume. But the grandeur of the power impresses me daily more and more; and, in quitting the subject of invention, let me assert finally, in clearest and strongest terms, that no painting is of any true imaginative perfectness at all, unless it has been thus conceived.

One sign of its being thus conceived may be always found in the straightforwardness of its work. There are continual disputes among artists as to the best way of doing things, which may nearly all be resolved into confessions of indetermination. If you know precisely what you want, you will not feel much hesitation in setting about it; and a picture may be painted almost any way, so only that it be a straight way. Give a true painter a ground of black, white, scarlet, or green, and out of it he will bring what you choose. From the black, brightness; from the white, sadness; from the scarlet, coolness; from the green, glow; he will make anything out of anything, but in each case his method will be pure, direct, perfect, the shortest and simplest possible. You will find him, moreover, indifferent as to succession of process. Ask him to begin at the bottom of the picture instead of the top,—to finish two square inches of it without touching the rest, or to lay a separate ground for every part before finishing any;—it is all the same to him! What he will do, if left to himself, depends on mechanical convenience, and on the time at his disposal. If he has a large brush in his hand, and plenty of one colour ground, he may lay as much as is wanted of that colour, at once, in every part of the picture where it is to occur; and if any is left, perhaps walk to another canvas, and lay the rest of it where it will be wanted on that. If, on the contrary, he has a small brush in his hand, and is interested in a particular spot of the picture, he will, perhaps, not stir from it till that bit is finished. But the absolutely best, or centrally, and entirely *right* way of painting is as follows:—

§ 17. A light ground, white, red, yellow, or gray, not brown, or black. On that an entirely accurate, and firm black outline of the whole picture, in its principal masses. The outline to be exquisitely correct as far as it reaches, but not to include small details; the use of it being to limit the masses of first colour. The ground-colours then to be laid firmly, each on its own proper part of the picture, as inlaid work in a mosaic table, meeting each other truly at the edges : as much of each being laid as will get itself into the state which the artist requires it to be in for his second painting, by the time he comes to it. On this first colour, the second colours and subordinate masses laid in due order, now, of course, necessarily without previous outline, and all small detail reserved to the last, the bracelet being not touched, nor indicated in the least, till the arm is finished.[1]

§ 18. This is, as far as it can be expressed in a few words, the right, or Venetian way of painting ; but it is incapable of absolute definition, for it depends on the scale, the material, and the nature of the object represented, *how much* a great painter will do with his first colour ; or how many after processes he will use. Very often the first colour, richly blended and worked into, is also the last ; sometimes it wants a glaze only to modify it ; sometimes an entirely different colour above it. Turner's storm-blues, for instance, were produced by a black ground with opaque blue, mixed with white, struck over it.[2] The amount of detail given in the first colour will also depend on convenience. For instance, if a jewel *fastens* a fold of dress, a Venetian will lay probably a piece of the jewel colour in its place at the time he draws the fold ; but if the jewel *falls upon* the dress, he will paint the folds only in the ground colour, and the jewel afterwards. For in the first case his hand must pause, at any rate, where the fold is

---

[1] Thus, in the Holy Family of Titian, lately purchased for the National Gallery, the piece of St. Catherine's dress over her shoulders is painted on the under dress, after that was dry. All its value would have been lost, had the slightest tint or trace of it been given previously. This picture, I think, and certainly many of Tintoret's, are painted on dark grounds ; but this is to save time, and with some loss to the future brightness of the colour.

[2] In cleaning the "Hero and Leander," now in the National collection, these upper glazes were taken off, and only the black ground left. I remember the picture when its distance was of the most exquisite blue. I have no doubt the "Fire at Sea" has had its distance destroyed in the same manner.

fastened; so that he may as well mark the colour of the gem : but he would have to check his hand in the sweep with which he drew the drapery, if he painted a jewel that fell upon it with the first colour. So far, however, as he can possibly use the under colour, he will, in whatever he has to superimpose. There is a pretty little instance of such economical work in the painting of the pearls on the breast of the elder princess, in our best Paul Veronese (Family of Darius). The lowest is about the size of a small hazel-nut, and falls on her rose-red dress. Any other but a Venetian would have put a complete piece of white paint over the dress, for the whole pearl, and painted into that the colours of the stone. But Veronese knows beforehand that all the dark side of the pearl will reflect the red of the dress. He will not put white over the red, only to put red over the white again. He leaves the actual dress for the dark side of the pearl, and with two small separate touches, one white, another brown, places its high light and shadow. This he does with perfect care and calm ; but in two decisive seconds. There is no dash, nor display, nor hurry, nor error. The exactly right thing is done in the exactly right place, and not one atom of colour, nor moment of time spent vainly. Look close at the two touches,—you wonder what they mean. Retire six feet from the picture—the pearl is there !

§ 19. The degree in which the ground colours are extended over his picture, as he works, is to a great painter absolutely indifferent. It is all the same to him whether he grounds a head, and finishes it at once to the shoulders, leaving all round it white ; or whether he grounds the whole picture. His harmony, paint as he will, never can be complete till the last touch is given ; so long as it remains incomplete, he does not care how little of it is suggested, or how many notes are missing. All is wrong, till all is right ; and he must be able to bear the all-wrongness till his work is done, or he cannot paint at all. His mode of treatment will, therefore, depend on the nature of his subject, as is beautifully shown in the water-colour sketches by Turner in the National Gallery. His general system was to complete inch by inch ; leaving the paper quite white all round, especially if the work was to be delicate. The most exquisite drawings left unfinished in the collection—those at Rome and Naples—are thus outlined accurately on pure white paper, begun in the middle of the sheet, and worked out to the side, finishing as he proceeds. If, however, any united effect of light or colour is to embrace a large part of the subject, he will lay it in with a broad wash over the whole paper at once; then paint into it, using it as a ground, and modifying it in the pure Venetian manner. His oil pictures were laid roughly with ground colours, and painted into with such rapid skill, that the artists who used to see him finishing at the Academy sometimes suspected him of having the picture finished underneath the colours he showed, and removing, instead of adding, as they watched.

§ 20. But, whatever the means used may be, the certainty and directness of them imply absolute grasp of the whole subject, and without this grasp there is no good painting. This, finally, let me declare, without qualification —that partial conception is no conception. The whole picture must be imagined, or none of it is. And this grasp of the whole implies very strange and sublime qualities of mind. It is not possible, unless the feelings are completely under control; the least excitement or passion will disturb the measured equity of power; a painter needs to be as cool as a general; and as little moved or subdued by his sense of pleasure, as a soldier by the sense of pain. Nothing good can be done without intense feeling; but it must be feeling so crushed, that the work is set about with mechanical steadiness, absolutely untroubled, as a surgeon—not without pity, but conquering it and putting it aside—begins an operation. Until the feelings can give strength enough to the will to enable it to conquer them, they are not strong enough. If you cannot leave your picture at any moment;—cannot turn from it, and go on with another, while the colour is drying;—cannot work at any part of it you choose with equal contentment—you have not firm enough grasp of it.

§ 21. It follows, also, that no vain or selfish person can possibly paint, in the noble sense of the word. Vanity and selfishness are troublous, eager, anxious, petulant :—painting can only be done in calm of mind. Resolution is not enough to secure this; it must be secured by disposition as well. You may resolve to think of your picture only; but, if you have been fretted before beginning, no manly or clear grasp of it will be possible for you. No forced calm is calm enough. Only honest calm,—natural calm. You might as well try by external pressure to smooth a lake till it could reflect the sky, as by violence of effort to secure the peace through which only you can reach imagination. That peace must come in its own time; as the waters settle themselves into clearness as well as quietness; you can no more filter your mind into purity than you can compress it into calmness; you must keep it pure, if you would have it pure; and throw no stones into it, if you would have it quiet. Great courage and self-command may, to a certain extent, give power of painting without the true calmness underneath; but never of doing first-rate work. There is sufficient evidence of this, in even what we know of great men, though of the greatest, we nearly always know the least (and that necessarily; they being very silent, and not much given to setting themselves forth to questioners; apt to be contemptuously reserved, no less than unselfishly). But in such writings and sayings as we possess of theirs, we may trace a quite curious gentleness and serene courtesy. Rubens' letters are almost ludicrous in their unhurried politeness. Reynolds, swiftest of painters, was gentlest of companions; so also Velasquez, Titian, and Veronese.

§ 22. It is gratuitous to add that no shallow or petty person can paint. Mere cleverness or special gift never made an artist. It is only perfectness of mind, unity, depth, decision,—the highest qualities, in fine, of the intellect, which will form the imagination.

§ 23. And, lastly, no false person can paint. A person false at heart may, when it suits his purposes, seize a stray truth here or there; but the relations of truth,—its perfectness,—that which makes it wholesome truth, he can never perceive. As wholeness and wholesomeness go together, so also sight with sincerity; it is only the constant desire of and submissiveness to truth, which can measure its strange angles and mark its infinite aspects; and fit them and knit them into the strength of sacred invention.

Sacred, I call it deliberately; for it is thus, in the most accurate senses, humble as well as helpful; meek in its receiving, as magnificent in its disposing; the name it bears being rightly given even to invention formal, not because it forms, but because it finds. For you cannot find a lie; you must make it for yourself. False things may be imagined, and false things composed; but only truth can be invented.

PART IX

OF IDEAS OF RELATION:—SECOND, OF INVENTION SPIRITUAL

CHAPTER I

THE DARK MIRROR

§ 1. IN the course of our inquiry into the moral of landscape (Vol. III., Chap. XVII.), we promised at the close of our work to seek for some better, or at least clearer, conclusions than were then possible to us. We confined ourselves in that chapter to the vindication of the probable utility of the *love* of natural scenery. We made no assertion of the usefulness of *painting* such scenery. It might be well to delight in the real country, or admire the real flowers and true mountains. But it did not follow that it was advisable to paint them.

Far from it. Many reasons might be given why we should not paint them. All the purposes of good which we saw that the beauty of Nature could accomplish, may be better fulfilled by the meanest of her realities, than by the brightest of imitations. For prolonged entertainment, no picture can be compared with the wealth of interest which may be found in the herbage of the poorest field, or blossoms of the narrowest copse. As suggestive of supernatual power, the passing away of a fitful raincloud, or opening of dawn, are in their change and mystery more pregnant than any pictures. A child would, I suppose, receive a religious lesson from a flower more willingly than from a print of one; and might be taught to understand

the nineteenth Psalm, on a starry night, better than by
diagrams of the constellations.

Whence it might seem a waste of time to draw landscape at all.

I believe it is ;—to draw landscape mere and solitary,
however beautiful (unless it be for the sake of geographi-
cal or other science, or of historical record). But there *is*
a kind of landscape which it is not inexpedient to draw.
What kind, we may probably discover by considering that
which mankind has hitherto contented itself with painting.

§ 2. We may arrange nearly all existing landscape under
the following heads :—

I. HEROIC.—Representing an imaginary world, inhabited
by men not perhaps perfectly civilized, but noble, and
usually subjected to severe trials, and by spiritual powers
of the highest order. It is frequently without architecture ;
never without figure-action, or emotion. Its principal
master is Titian.

II. CLASSICAL.—Representing an imaginary world, inhabited by perfectly civilized men, and by spiritual powers
of an inferior order.

It generally assumes this condition of things to have
existed among the Greek and Roman nations. It contains usually architecture of an elevated character, and
always incidents of figure-action, or emotion. Its principal
master is Nicolo Poussin.

III. PASTORAL.—Representing peasant life and its daily
work, or such scenery as may naturally be suggestive of
it, consisting usually of simple landscape, in part subjected
to agriculture, with figures, cattle, and domestic buildings.
No supernatural being is ever visibly present. It does
not in ordinary cases admit architecture of an elevated
character nor exciting incident. Its principal master is
Cuyp.

IV. CONTEMPLATIVE.—Directed principally to the observance of the powers of Nature, and record of the
historical associations connected with landscape, illustrated
by, or contrasted with, existing states of human life. No
supernatural being is visibly present. It admits every
variety of subject, and requires, in general, figure incident,

but not of an exciting character. It was not developed completely until recent times. Its principal master is Turner.[1]

§ 3. These are the four true orders of landscape, not of course distinctly separated from each other in all cases, but very distinctly in typical examples. Two spurious forms require separate note.

(A) PICTURESQUE.—This is indeed rather the degradation (or sometimes the undeveloped state) of the contemplative, than a distinct class; but it may be considered generally as including pictures meant to display the skill of the artist, and his powers of composition; or to give agreeable forms and colours, irrespective of sentiment. It will include much modern art, with the street views and church interiors of the Dutch, and the works of Canaletto, Guardi, Tempesta, and the like.

(B) HYBRID.—Landscape in which the painter endeavours to unite the irreconcilable sentiment of two or more of the above-named classes. Its principal masters are Berghem and Wouvermans.

§ 4. Passing for the present by these inferior schools, we find that all true landscape, whether simple or exalted, depends primarily for its interest on connection with humanity, or with spiritual powers. Banish your heroes and nymphs from the classical landscape—its laurel shades will move you no more. Show that the dark clefts of the most romantic mountain are uninhabited and untraversed; it will cease to be romantic. Fields without shepherds and without fairies will have no gaiety in their green, nor will the noblest masses of ground or colours of cloud arrest or raise your thoughts, if the earth has no life to sustain, and the heaven none to refresh.

[1] I have been embarrassed in assigning the names to these orders of art, the term "Contemplative" belonging in justice nearly as much to the romantic and pastoral conception as to the modern landscape. I intended, originally, to call the four schools—Romantic, Classic, Georgic, and Theoretic—which would have been more accurate; and more consistent with the nomenclature of the second volume; but would not have been pleasant in sound, nor, to the general reader, very clear in sense.

§ 5. It might perhaps be thought that, since from scenes in which the figure was principal, and landscape symbolical and subordinate (as in the art of Egypt), the process of ages had led us to scenes in which landscape was principal and the figure subordinate,—a continuance in the same current of feeling might bring forth at last an art from which humanity and its interests should wholly vanish, leaving us to the passionless admiration of herbage and stone. But this will not, and cannot be. For observe the parallel instance in the gradually increasing importance of dress. From the simplicity of Greek design, concentrating, I suppose, its skill chiefly on the naked form, the course of time developed conditions of Venetian imagination which found nearly as much interest, and expressed nearly as much dignity, in folds of dress and fancies of decoration as in the faces of the figures themselves : so that if from Veronese's Marriage in Cana we remove the architecture and the gay dresses, we shall not in the faces and hands remaining, find a satisfactory abstract of the picture. But try it the other way. Take out the faces ; leave the draperies, and how then ? Put the fine dresses and jewelled girdles into the best group you can ; paint them with all Veronese's skill : will they satisfy you ?

§ 6. Not so. As long as they are in their due service and subjection—while their folds are formed by the motion of men, and their lustre adorns the nobleness of men—so long the lustre and the folds are lovely. But cast them from the human limbs ;—golden circlet and silken tissue are withered ; the dead leaves of autumn are more precious than they.

This is just as true, but in a far deeper sense, of the weaving of the natural robe of man's soul. Fragrant tissue of flowers, golden circlets of clouds, are only fair when they meet the fondness of human thoughts, and glorify human visions of heaven.

§ 7. It is the leaning on this truth which, more than any other, has been the distinctive character of all my own past work. And in closing a series of Art-studies, prolonged during so many years, it may be perhaps permitted me to point out this specialty—the rather that it has been, of all their characters, the one most denied. I constantly see that the same thing takes place in the estimation formed by the modern public of the work of almost any true person, living or dead. It is not needful to state here the causes of such error; but the fact is indeed so, that precisely the distinctive root and leading force of any true man's work and way are the things denied concerning him.

And in these books of mine, their distinctive character, as essays on art, is their bringing everything to a root in human passion or human hope. Arising first not in any desire to explain the principles of art, but in the endeavour to defend an individual painter from injustice, they have been coloured throughout,—nay, continually altered in shape, and even warped and broken, by digressions respecting social questions, which had for me an interest tenfold greater than the work I had been forced into undertaking. Every principle of painting which I have stated is traced to some vital or spiritual fact; and in my works on architecture the preference accorded finally to one school over another, is founded on a comparison of their influences on the life of the workman—a question by all other writers on the subject of architecture wholly forgotten or despised.

§ 8. The essential connection of the power of landscape with human emotion is not less certain, because in many impressive pictures the link is slight or local. That the connection should exist at a single point is all that we need. The comparison with the dress of the body may be carried out into the extremest parallelism. It may often happen that no part of the figure wearing the dress is discernible, nevertheless, the perceivable fact that the drapery is worn by a figure makes all the difference. In one of the most sublime figures in the world this is actually so: one of the fainting Maries in Tintoret's Crucifixion has cast her mantle over her head, and her face is lost in its shade, and her whole figure veiled in folds of gray. But what the difference is between that gray woof, that gathers round her as she falls, and the same folds cast in a heap upon the ground, that difference, and more, exists between the power of Nature through which humanity is seen, and her power in the desert. Desert—whether of leaf or sand—true desertness is not in the want of leaves, but of life. Where humanity is not, and was not, the best natural beauty is more than vain. It is even terrible ; not as the dress cast aside from the body ; but as an embroidered shroud hiding a skeleton.

§ 9. And on each side of a right feeling in this matter there lie, as usual, two opposite errors.

The first, that of caring for man only ; and for the rest of the universe, little, or not at all, which, in a measure, was the error of the Greeks and Florentines ; the other, that of caring for the universe only ;—for man, not at all —which, in a measure, is the error of modern science, and of the Art connecting itself with such science.

The degree of power which any man may ultimately possess in landscape-painting will depend finally on his perception of this influence. If he has to paint the desert, its awfulness—if the garden, its gladsomeness—will arise simply and only from his sensibility to the story of life. Without this he is nothing but a scientific mechanist ; this, though it cannot make him yet a painter, raises him to the sphere in which he may become one. Nay, the mere shadow and semblance of this have given dangerous power to works in all other respects unnoticeable ; and the least degree of its true presence has given value to work in all other respects vain.

The true presence, observe, of sympathy with the spirit of man. Where this is not, sympathy with any higher spirit is impossible.

For the directest manifestation of Deity to man is in His own image, that is, in man.

§ 10. "In His own image. After His likeness." *Ad imaginem et Similitudinem Suam.* I do not know what people in general understand by those words. I suppose they ought to be understood. The truth they contain seems to lie at the foundation of our knowledge both of God and man ; yet do we not usually pass the sentence by, in dull reverence, attaching no definite sense to it at all ? For all practical purpose, might it not as well be out of the text ?

I have no time, nor much desire, to examine the

vague expressions of belief with which the verse has been encumbered. Let us try to find its only possible plain significance.

§ 11. It cannot be supposed that the bodily shape of man resembles, or resembled, any bodily shape in Deity. The likeness must therefore be, or have been, in the soul. Had it wholly passed away, and the divine soul been altered into a soul brutal or diabolic, I suppose we should have been told of the change. But we are told nothing of the kind. The verse still stands as if for our use and trust. It was only death which was to be our punishment. Not *change*. So far as we live, the image is still there; defiled, if you will; broken, if you will; all but effaced, if you will, by death and the shadow of it. But not changed. We are not made now in any other image than God's. There are, indeed, the two states of this image—the earthly and heavenly, but both Adamite, both human, both the same likeness; only one defiled, and one pure. So that the soul of man is still a mirror, wherein may be seen, darkly, the image of the mind of God.

These may seem daring words. I am sorry that they do; but I am helpless to soften them. Discover any other meaning of the text if you are able ;—but be sure that it *is* a meaning—a meaning in your head and heart ;— not a subtle gloss, nor a shifting of one verbal expression into another, both idealess. I repeat that, to me, the verse has, and can have, no other signification than this— that the soul of man is a mirror of the mind of God. A mirror, dark, distorted, broken, use what blameful words you please of its state; yet in the main, a true mirror, out of which alone, and by which alone, we can know anything of God at all.

" How ? " the reader, perhaps, answers indignantly. " I know the nature of God by revelation, not by looking into myself."

Revelation to what? To a nature incapable of receiving truth ? That cannot be; for only to a nature capable of truth, desirous of it, distinguishing it, feeding upon it, revelation is possible. To a being undesirous of it, and

hating it, revelation is impossible.   There can be none
to a brute, or fiend.   In so far, therefore, as you love
truth, and live therein, in so far revelation can exist for
you ;—and in so far, your mind is the image of God's.

§ 12. But consider, farther, not only *to* what, but *by*
what, is the revelation.   By sight ? or word ?   If by sight,
then to eyes which see justly.   Otherwise, no sight would
be revelation.   So far, then, as your sight is just, it is the
image of God's sight.

If by words, — how do you know their meanings ?
Here is a short piece of precious word revelation, for
instance.   "God is love."

Love ! yes.   But what is *that ?*   The revelation does
not tell you that, I think.   Look into the mirror, and
you will see.   Out of your own heart, you may know
what love is.   In no other possible way,—by no other
help or sign.   All the words and sounds ever uttered, all
the revelations of cloud, or flame, or crystal, are utterly
powerless.   They cannot tell you, in the smallest point,
what love means.   Only the broken mirror can.

§ 13. Here is more revelation.   "God is just !"   Just !
What is that ?   The revelation cannot help you to discover.
You say it is dealing equitably or equally.   But how do
you discern the equality ?   Not by inequality of mind ; not
by a mind incapable of weighing, judging, or distributing.
If the lengths seem unequal in the broken mirror, for you
they are unequal ; but if they seem equal, then the mirror
is true.   So far as you recognize equality, and your conscience tells you what is just, so far your mind is the
image of God's ; and so far as you do *not* discern this
nature of justice or equality, the words "God is just"
bring no revelation to you.

§ 14. "But His thoughts are not as our thoughts."
No ; the sea is not as the standing pool by the wayside.
Yet when the breeze crisps the pool, you may see the
image of the breakers, and a likeness of the foam.   Nay,
in some sort, the same foam.   If the sea is for ever invisible to you, something you may learn of it from the
pool.   Nothing, assuredly, any otherwise.

"But this poor miserable Me !   Is *this*, then, all the

book I have got to read about God in?" Yes, truly so.
No other book, nor fragment of book, than that, will you
ever find; no velvet-bound missal, nor frankincensed manu-
script;—nothing hieroglyphic nor cuneiform; papyrus and
pyramid are alike silent on this matter;—nothing in the
clouds above, nor in the earth beneath. That flesh-bound
volume is the only revelation that is, that was, or that can
be. In that is the image of God painted; in that is the
law of God written; in that is the promise of God revealed.
Know thyself; for through thyself only thou canst know God.

§ 15. Through the glass, darkly. But, except through
the glass, in nowise.

A tremulous crystal, waved as water, poured out upon
the ground;—you may defile it, despise it, pollute it, at
your pleasure and at your peril; for on the peace of those
weak waves must all the heaven you shall ever gain be first
seen; and through such purity as you can win for those
dark waves, must all the light of the risen Sun of righteousness be bent down, by faint refraction. Cleanse them, and
calm them, as you love your life.

Therefore it is that all the power of nature depends on
subjection to the human soul. Man is the sun of the
world; more than the real sun. The fire of his wonderful
heart is the only light and heat worth gauge or measure.
Where he is, are the tropics; where he is not, the
ice-world.

CHAPTER II

THE LANCE OF PALLAS

§ 1. It might be thought that the tenor of the preceding chapter was in some sort adverse to my repeated statement that all great art is the expression of man's delight in God's work, not in *his own*. But observe, he is not himself his own work : he is himself precisely the most wonderful piece of God's workmanship extant. In this best piece not only he is bound to take delight, but cannot, in a right state of thought, take delight in anything else, otherwise than through himself. Through himself, however, as the sun of creation, not as *the* creation. In himself, as the light of the world.[1] Not as being the world. Let him stand in his due relation to other creatures, and to inanimate things—know them all and love them, as made for him, and he for them ;—and he becomes himself the greatest and holiest of them. But let him cast off this relation, despise and forget the less creation round him, and instead of being the light of the world, he is a sun in space—a fiery ball, spotted with storm.

§ 2. All the diseases of mind leading to fatalest ruin consist primarily in this isolation. They are the concentration of man upon himself, whether his heavenly interests or his worldly interests, matters not ; it is the being *his own* interests which makes the regard of them so mortal. Every form of asceticism on one side, of sensualism on the other, is an isolation of his soul or of his body ; the fixing his thoughts upon them alone ; while every healthy state of nations and of individual minds consists in the unselfish

[1] Matt. v. 14.

presence of the human spirit everywhere, energizing over all things; speaking and living through all things.

§ 3. Man being thus the crowning and ruling work of God, it will follow that all his best art must have something to tell about himself, as the soul of things, and ruler of creatures. It must also make this reference to himself under a true conception of his own nature. Therefore all art which involves no reference to man is inferior or nugatory. And all art which involves misconception of man, or base thought of him, is in that degree false and base.

Now the basest thought possible concerning him is, that he has no spiritual nature; and the foolishest misunderstanding of him possible is, that he has or should have, no animal nature. For his nature is nobly animal, nobly spiritual—coherently and irrevocably so; neither part of it may, but at its peril, expel, despise, or defy the other. All great art confesses and worships both.

§ 4. The art which, since the writings of Rio and Lord Lindsay, is specially known as "Christian," erred by pride in its denial of the animal nature of man;—and, in connection with all monkish and fanatical forms of religion, by looking always to another world instead of this. It wasted its strength in visions, and was therefore swept away, notwithstanding all its good and glory, by the strong truth of the naturalist art of the sixteenth century. But that naturalist art erred on the other side; denied at last the spiritual nature of man, and perished in corruption.

A contemplative reaction is taking place in modern times, out of which it may be hoped a new spiritual art may be developed. The first school of landscape, named, in the foregoing chapter, the Heroic, is that of the noble naturalists. The second (Classical), and third (Pastoral), belong to the time of sensual decline. The fourth (Contemplative) is that of modern revival.

§ 5. But why, the reader will ask, is no place given in this scheme to the "Christian" or spiritual art which preceded the naturalists? Because all landscape belonging to that art is subordinate, and in one essential principle false. It is subordinate, because intended only to exalt the conception of saintly or Divine presence : — rather therefore to be considered as a landscape decoration or type, than an effort to paint nature. If I included it in my list of schools, I should have to go still farther back, and include with it the conventional and illustrative landscape of the Greeks and Egyptians.

§ 6. But also it cannot constitute a real school, because its first assumption is false, namely, that the natural world can be represented without the element of death.

The real schools of landscape are primarily distinguished from the preceding unreal ones by their introduction of this element. They are not at first in any sort the worthier for it. But they are more true, and capable, therefore, in the issue, of becoming worthier.

It will be a hard piece of work for us to think this rightly out, but it must be done.

§ 7. Perhaps an accurate analysis of the schools of art of all time might show us that when the immortality of the soul was practically and completely believed, the elements of decay, danger, and grief in visible things were always disregarded. However this may be, it is assuredly so in the early Christian schools. The ideas of danger or decay seem not merely repugnant, but inconceivable to them; the expression of immortality and perpetuity is alone possible. I do not mean that they take no note of the absolute fact of corruption. This fact the early painters often compel themselves to look fuller in the front than any other men: as in the way they usually paint the Deluge (the raven feeding on the bodies), and in all the various triumphs and processions of the power of Death, which formed one great chapter of religious teaching and painting, from Orcagna's time to the close of the Purist epoch. But I mean that this external fact of corruption is separated in their minds from the main conditions of their work; and its horror enters no more into their general treatment of landscape than the fear of murder or martyrdom, both of which they had nevertheless continually to represent. None of these things appeared to them as affecting the general dealings of the Deity with His world. Death, pain, and decay were simply momentary accidents in the course of immortality, which never ought to exercise any depressing

influence over the hearts of men, or in the life of Nature.
God, in intense life, peace, and helping power, was always
and everywhere. Human bodies, at one time or another,
had indeed to be made dust of, and raised from it ; and
this becoming dust was hurtful and humiliating, but not
in the least melancholy, nor, in any very high degree, important ; except to thoughtless persons who needed sometimes to be reminded of it, and whom, not at all fearing
the things much himself, the painter accordingly did remind
of it, somewhat sharply.

§ 8. A similar condition of mind seems to have been
attained, not unfrequently, in modern times, by persons
whom either narrowness of circumstance or education, or
vigorous moral efforts, have guarded from the troubling
of the world, so as to give them firm and childlike trust
in the power and presence of God, together with peace
of conscience, and a belief in the passing of all evil into
some form of good. It is impossible that a person thus
disciplined should feel, in any of its more acute phases,
the sorrow for any of the phenomena of nature, or terror
in any material danger which would occur to another.
The absence of personal fear, the consciousness of security
as great in the midst of pestilence and storm, as amidst
beds of flowers on a summer's morning, and the certainty
that whatever appeared evil, or was assuredly painful, must
eventually issue in a far greater and enduring good—this
general feeling and conviction, I say, would gradually lull,
and at last put to entire rest, the physical sensations of
grief and fear ; so that the man would look upon danger
without dread,—expect pain without lamentation.

§ 9. It may perhaps be thought that this is a very high
and right state of mind.

Unfortunately, it appears that the attainment of it is
never possible without inducing some form of intellectual
weakness.

No painter belonging to the purest religious schools
ever mastered his art. Perugino nearly did so ; but it was
because he was more rational—more a man of the world
—than the rest. No literature exists of a high class produced by minds in the pure religious temper. On the

contrary, a great deal of literature exists, produced by persons in that temper, which is markedly, and very far, below average literary work.

§ 10. The reason of this I believe to be, that the right faith of man is not intended to give him repose, but to enable him to do his work. It is not intended that he should look away from the place he lives in now, and cheer himself with thoughts of the place he is to live in next, but that he should look stoutly into this world, in faith that if he does his work thoroughly here, some good to others or himself, with which however he is not at present concerned, will come of it hereafter. And this kind of brave, but not very hopeful or cheerful faith, I perceive to be always rewarded by clear practical success and splendid intellectual power; while the faith which dwells on the future fades away into rosy mist, and emptiness of musical air. That result indeed follows naturally enough on its habit of assuming that things must be right, or must come right, when, probably, the fact is, that so far as we are concerned, they are entirely wrong; and going wrong: and also on its weak and false way of looking on what these religious persons call " the bright side of things," that is to say, on one side of them only, when God has given them two sides, and intended us to see both.

§ 11. I was reading but the other day, in a book by a zealous, useful, and able Scotch clergyman, one of these rhapsodies, in which he described a scene in the Highlands to show (he said) the goodness of God. In this Highland scene there was nothing but sunshine, and fresh breezes, and bleating lambs, and clean tartans, and all manner of pleasantness. Now a Highland scene is, beyond dispute, pleasant enough in its own way; but, looked close at, has its shadows. Here, for instance, is the very fact of one, as pretty as I can remember—having seen many. It is a little valley of soft turf, enclosed in its narrow oval by jutting rocks and broad flakes of nodding fern. From one side of it to the other winds, serpentine, a clear brown stream, drooping into quicker ripple as it reaches the end of the oval field, and then, first islanding a purple and white rock with an amber pool, it dashes away into a narrow fall of foam under a thicket of mountain-ash and alder. The autumn sun, low but clear, shines on the scarlet ash-berries and on the golden birch-leaves, which, fallen here and there, when the breeze has not caught them, rest quiet in the crannies of the purple rock. Beside the rock, in the hollow under the thicket, the carcase of a ewe, drowned in the last flood, lies nearly bare to the bone, its white ribs protruding through the skin, raven-torn; and the rags of its wool still flickering from the branches that first stayed it as the stream swept it down. A little lower, the current plunges, roaring, into a circular chasm like a well, surrounded on three sides by a chimney-like hollowness of polished rock, down which the foam slips in detached snow-flakes. Round the edges of the pool beneath, the water circles slowly, like black oil; a little butterfly lies on its back, its wings glued to one of the eddies, its limbs feebly quivering; a fish rises, and it is gone. Lower down the stream, I can just see over a knoll, the green and damp turf roofs of four or five hovels, built at the edge of a morass, which is trodden by the cattle into a black Slough of Despond at their doors, and traversed by a few ill-set stepping-stones, with here and there a flat slab on the tops, where they have sunk out of sight, and at the turn of the brook I see a man fishing, with a boy and a dog—a picturesque and pretty group enough certainly, if they had not been there all day starving. I know them, and I know the dog's ribs also, which are nearly as bare as the dead ewe's; and the child's wasted shoulders, cutting his old tartan jacket through, so sharp are they. We will go down and talk with the man.

§ 12. Or, that I may not piece pure truth with fancy, for I have none of his words set down, let us hear a word or two from another such, a Scotchman also, and as true-hearted, and in just as fair a scene. I write out the passage, in which I have kept his few sentences, word for word, as it stands in my private diary :—" 22nd April (1851). Yesterday I had a long walk up the Via Gellia, at Matlock, coming down upon it from the hills above,

all sown with anemones and violets, and murmuring with
sweet springs. Above all the mills in the valley, the brook,
in its first purity, forms a small shallow pool, with a sandy
bottom covered with cresses and other water plants. A
man was wading in it for cresses as I passed up the valley,
and bade me good-day. I did not go much farther; he
was there when I returned. I passed him again, about
one hundred yards, when it struck me I might as well
learn all I could about watercresses : so I turned back.
I asked the man, among other questions, what he called
the common weed, something like watercress, but with a
serrated leaf, which grows at the edge of nearly all such
pools. 'We calls that brooklime, hereabouts,' said a voice
behind me. I turned, and saw three men, miners or manufacturers—two evidently Derbyshire men, and respectable-
looking in their way; the third, thin, poor, old, and
harder-featured, and utterly in rags. 'Brooklime?' I said.
'What do you call it lime for ?' The man said he did
not know; it was called that. 'You'll find that in the
British 'Erba,' said the weak, calm voice of the old man.
I turned to him in much surprise; but he went on saying
something drily (I hardly understood what) to the cress-
gatherer; who contradicting him, the old man said he
'didn't know fresh water,' he 'knew enough of sa't.'
'Have you been a sailor ?' I asked. 'I was a sailor
for eleven years and ten months of my life,' he said, in
the same strangely quiet manner. 'And what are you
now ?' 'I lived for ten years after my wife's death by
picking up rags and bones; I hadn't much occasion afore.'
'And now how do you live ?' 'Why, I lives hard and
honest, and haven't got to live long,' or something to that
effect. He then went on, in a kind of maundering way,
about his wife. 'She had rheumatism and fever very bad;
and her second rib growed over her hench-bone. A' was
a clever woman, but a' grow'd to be a very little one'
(this, with an expression of deep melancholy). 'Eighteen
years after her first lad she was in the family-way again,
and they had doctors up from Lunnon about it. They
wanted to rip her open, and take the child out of her
side. But I never would give my consent.' (Then, after

a pause:) 'She died twenty-six hours and ten minutes after it. I never cared much what come of me since; but I know that I shall soon reach her; that's a knowledge I would na gie for the king's crown.' 'You are a Scotchman, are not you?' I asked. 'I'm from the Isle of Skye, sir; I'm a McGregor.' I said something about his religious faith. 'Ye'll know I was bred in the Church of Scotland, sir,' he said, 'and I love it as I love my own soul: but I think thae Wesleyan Methodists ha' got salvation among them too.'"

Truly, this Highland and English hill-scenery is fair enough; but has its shadows; and deeper colouring, here and there, than that of heath and rose.

§ 13. Now, as far as I have watched the main powers of human mind, they have risen first from the resolution to see fearlessly, pitifully, and to its very worst, what these deep colours mean, wheresoever they fall; not by any means to pass on the other side, looking pleasantly up to the sky, but to stoop to the horror, and let the sky, for the present, take care of its own clouds. However this may be in moral matters, with which I have nothing here to do, in my own field of inquiry the fact is so; and all great and beautiful work has come of first gazing without shrinking into the darkness. If, having done so, the human spirit can, by its courage and faith, conquer the evil, it rises into conceptions of victorious and consummated beauty. It is then the spirit of the highest Greek and Venetian Art. If unable to conquer the evil, but remaining in strong though melancholy war with it, not rising into supreme beauty, it is the spirit of the best northern art, typically represented by that of Holbein and Dürer. If, itself conquered by the evil, infected by the dragon breath of it, and at last brought into captivity, so as to take delight in evil for ever, it becomes the spirit of the dark, but still powerful sensualistic art, represented typically by that of Salvator. We must trace this fact briefly through Greek, Venetian, and Düreresque art; we shall then see how the art of decline came of avoiding the evil, and seeking pleasure only; and thus obtain, at last, some power of judging whether the tendency of our own contemplative art be right or ignoble.

§ 14. The ruling purpose of Greek poetry is the assertion of victory, by heroism, over fate, sin, and death. The
terror of these great enemies is dwelt upon chiefly by the
tragedians. The victory over them, by Homer.

The adversary chiefly contemplated by the tragedians is
Fate, or predestinate misfortune. And that under three
principal forms.

(A) Blindness or ignorance ; not in itself guilty, but inducing acts which otherwise would have been guilty ; and
leading, no less than guilt, to destruction.[1]

(B) Visitation upon one person of the sin of another.

(C) Repression by brutal, or tyrannous strength, of a
benevolent will.

§ 15. In all these cases sorrow is much more definitely
connected with sin by the Greek tragedians than by Shakspere. The "fate" of Shakspere is, indeed, a form of
blindness, but it issues in little more than haste or in-
discretion. It is, in the literal sense, "fatal," but hardly
criminal.

The "I am fortune's fool" of Romeo, expresses Shakspere's primary idea of tragic circumstance. Often his
victims are entirely innocent, swept away by mere current
of strong encompassing calamity (Ophelia, Cordelia, Arthur,
Queen Katherine). This is rarely so with the Greeks. The
victim may indeed be innocent, as Antigone, but is in some
way resolutely entangled with crime, and destroyed by it,
as if it struck by pollution, no less than participation.

The victory over sin and death is therefore also with
the Greek tragedians more complete than with Shakspere.
As the enemy has more direct moral personality,—as it
is sinfulness more than mischance, it is met by a higher

---

[1] The speech of Achilles to Priam expresses this idea of fatality and
submission clearly, there being two vessels—one full of sorrow, the
other of great and noble gifts (a sense of disgrace mixing with that of
sorrow, and of honour with that of joy), from which Jupiter pours forth
the destinies of men ; the idea partly corresponding to the scriptural—
"In the hand of the Lord there is a cup, and the wine is red ; it is full
mixed, and He poureth out of the same." But the title of the gods,
nevertheless, both with Homer and Hesiod, is given not from the cup
of sorrow, but of good : "givers of good" (δωτῆρες ἐάων).—*Hes. Theog.*
664 ; *Odyss.* viii. 325.

moral resolve, a greater preparation of heart, a more solemn patience and purposed self-sacrifice. At the close of a Shakspere tragedy, nothing remains but dead march and clothes of burial. At the close of a Greek tragedy there are far-off sounds of a divine triumph, and a glory as of resurrection.[1]

§ 16. The Homeric temper is wholly different. Far more tender, more practical, more cheerful; bent chiefly on present things and giving victory now, and here, rather than in hope, and hereafter. The enemies of mankind, in Homer's conception, are more distinctly conquerable; they are ungoverned passions, especially anger, and unreasonable impulse generally (ἀτή). Hence the anger of Achilles. misdirected by pride, but rightly directed by friendship, is the subject of the *Iliad*. The anger of Ulysses ('Οδυσσεὺς, "the angry"), misdirected at first into idle and irregular hostilities, directed at last to execution of sternest justice, is the subject of the *Odyssey*.

Though this is the central idea of the two poems, it is connected with general display of the evil of all unbridled passions, pride, sensuality, indolence, or curiosity. The pride of Atrides, the passion of Paris, the sluggishness of Elpenor, the curiosity of Ulysses himself about the Cyclops, the impatience of his sailors in untying the winds, and all other faults or follies down to that—(evidently no small one in Homer's mind)—of domestic disorderliness, are throughout shown in contrast with conditions of patient affection and household peace.

Also, the wild powers and mysteries of Nature are in the Homeric mind among the enemies of man; so that all the labours of Ulysses are an expression of the contest of manhood, not only with its own passions or with the folly of others, but with the merciless and mysterious powers of the natural world.

§ 17. This is perhaps the chief signification of the seven years' stay with Calypso, "the concealer." Not, as vulgarly thought, the concealer of Ulysses, but the great concealer—the hidden power of natural things. She

[1] The Alcestis is perhaps the central example of the *idea* of all Greek drama.

is the daughter of Atlas and the Sea, (Atlas, the sustainer of heaven, and the Sea, the disturber of the Earth). She dwells in the island of Ogygia (" the ancient or venerable "). (Whenever Athens, or any other Greek city, is spoken of with any peculiar reverence, it is called " Ogygian.") Escaping from this goddess of secrets, and from other spirits, some of destructive natural force (Scylla), others signifying the enchantment of mere natural beauty (Circe, daughter of the Sun and Sea), he arrives at last at the Phæacian land, whose king is "strength with intellect," and whose queen, "virtue." These restore him to his country.

§ 18. Now observe that in their dealing with all these subjects the Greeks never shrink from horror; down to its uttermost depth, to its most appalling physical detail, they strive to sound the secrets of sorrow. For them there is no passing by on the other side, no turning away the eyes to vanity from pain. Literally, they have not "lifted up their souls unto vanity." Whether there be consolation for them or not, neither apathy nor blindness shall be their saviour; if, for them, thus knowing the facts of the grief of earth, any hope, relief, or triumph may hereafter seem possible,—well; but if not, still hopeless, reliefless, eternal, the sorrow shall be met face to face. This Hector, so righteous, so merciful, so brave, has, nevertheless, to look upon his dearest brother in miserablest death. His own soul passes away in hopeless sobs through the throat-wound of the Grecian spear. That is one aspect of things in this world, a fair world truly, but having, among its other aspects, this one, highly ambiguous.

§ 19. Meeting it boldly as they may, gazing right into the skeleton face of it, the ambiguity remains; nay, in some sort gains upon them. We trusted in the gods;— we thought that wisdom and courage would save us. Our wisdom and courage themselves deceive us to our death. Athena had the aspect of Deiphobus—terror of the enemy. She has not terrified him, but left us, in our mortal need.

And beyond that mortality, what hope have we? Nothing is clear to us on that horizon, nor comforting. Funeral honours; perhaps also rest; perhaps a shadowy

life—artless, joyless, loveless. No devices in that darkness of the grave, nor daring, nor delight. Neither
marrying nor giving in marriage, nor casting of spears,
nor rolling of chariots, nor voice of fame. Lapped in
pale Elysian mist, chilling the forgetful heart and feeble
frame, shall we waste on for ever? Can the dust of earth
claim more of immortality than this? Or shall we have
even so much as rest? May we, indeed, lie down again
in the dust: or have not our sins hidden from us even
the things that belong to that peace? May not chance
and the whirl of passion govern us there: when there
shall be no thought, nor work, nor wisdom, nor breathing
of the soul?[1]

Be it so. With no better reward, no brighter hope,
we will be men while we may: men, just, and strong,
and fearless, and up to our power, perfect. Athena
herself, our wisdom and our strength, may betray us:—
Phœbus, our sun, smite us with plague, or hide his face
from us helpless;—Jove and all the powers of fate oppress
us, or give us up to destruction. While we live, we will
hold fast our integrity; no weak tears shall blind us, no
untimely tremors abate our strength of arm nor swift-
ness of limb. The gods have given us at least this glorious
body and this righteous conscience; these will we keep
bright and pure to the end. So may we fall to misery,
but not to baseness; so may we sink to sleep, but not
to shame.

§ 20. And herein was conquest. So defied, the betray-
ing and accusing shadows shrank back; the mysterious
horror subdued itself to majestic sorrow. Death was
swallowed up in victory. Their blood, which seemed to
be poured out upon the ground, rose into hyacinthine
flowers. All the beauty of earth opened to them; they
had ploughed into its darkness, and they reaped its
gold; the gods, in whom they had trusted through all
semblance of oppression, came down to love them and
be their helpmates. All nature round them became

---

[1] τῷ καὶ τεθνειῶτι νόον πόρε Περσεφόνεια,
οἴῳ πεπνῦσθαι· τοὶ δὲ σκιαὶ ἀΐσσουσιν.
                                        Od. x. 495.

divine,—one harmony of power and peace.   The sun hurt
them not by day, nor the moon by night; the earth
opened no more her jaws into the pit: the sea whitened
no more against them the teeth of his devouring waves.
Sun, and moon, and earth, and sea,—all melted into grace
and love; the fatal arrows rang not now at the shoulders
of Apollo, the healer; lord of life, and of the three great
spirits of life—Care, Memory, and Melody.   Great Artemis
guarded their flocks by night; Selene kissed in love the
eyes of those who slept.   And from all came the help
of heaven to body and soul; a strange spirit lifting the
lovely limbs; strange light glowing on the golden hair;
and strangest comfort filling the trustful heart, so that
they could put off their armour, and lie down to sleep,—
their work well done, whether at the gates of their temples[1]
or of their mountains;[2] accepting the death they once
thought terrible, as the gift of Him who knew and granted
what was best.

[1] οὐκέτι ἀνέστησαν, ἀλλ᾽ ἐν τέλει τούτῳ ἔσχοντο.   Herod. i. 31.
[2] ὁ δὲ ἀποπεμπόμενος, αὐτὸς μὲν οὐκ ἀπελίπετο· τὸν δὲ παῖδα συστρα-
τευόμενον ἐόντα οἱ μουνογενέα, ἀπέπεμψε.   Herod. vii. 221.

CHAPTER III

THE WINGS OF THE LION

§ 1. SUCH being the heroic spirit of Greek religion and art, we may now with ease trace the relations between it and that which animated the Italian, and chiefly the Venetian, schools.

Observe, all the nobleness, as well as the faults, of the Greek art were dependent on its making the most of this present life. It might do so in the Anacreontic temper —Τί Πλειάδεσσι, κἀμοί; "What have I to do with the Pleiads?" or in the defiant or the trustful endurance of fate;—but its dominion was in this world.

Florentine art was essentially Christian, ascetic, expectant of a better world, and antagonistic, therefore, to the Greek temper. So that the Greek element, once forced upon it, destroyed it. There was absolute imcompatibility between them. Florentine art, also, could not produce landscape. It despised the rock, the tree, the vital air itself, aspiring to breathe empyreal air.

Venetian art began with the same aim and under the same restrictions. Both are healthy in the youth of art. Heavenly aim and severe law for boyhood; earthly work and fair freedom for manhood.

§ 2. The Venetians began, I repeat, with asceticism; always, however, delighting in more massive and deep colour than other religious painters. They are especially fond of saints who have been cardinals, because of their red hats, and they sunburn all their hermits into splendid russet brown.

They differed from the Pisans in having no Maremma between them and the sea; from the Romans in continually quarrelling with the Pope; and from the Florentines in having no gardens.

They had another kind of garden, deep furrowed, with blossom in white wreaths—fruitless. Perpetual May therein, and singing of wild, nestless birds. And they had no Maremma to separate them from this garden of theirs. The destiny of Pisa was changed, in all probability, by the ten miles of marsh-land and poisonous air between it and the beach. The Genoese energy was feverish; too much heat reflected from their torrid Apennine. But the Venetian had his free horizon, his salt breeze, and sandy Lido-shore; sloped far and flat,—ridged sometimes under the Tramontane winds with half a mile's breadth of rollers;—sea and sand shrivelled up together in one yellow careering field of fall and roar.

§ 3. They were, also, we said, always quarrelling with the Pope. Their religious liberty came, like their bodily health, from that wave training; for it is one notable effect of a life passed on ship-board to destroy weak beliefs in appointed forms of religion. A sailor may be grossly superstitious, but his superstitions will be connected with amulets and omens, not cast in systems. He must accustom himself, if he prays at all, to pray anywhere and anyhow. Candlesticks and incense not being portable into the maintop, he perceives those decorations to be, on the whole, inessential to a maintop mass. Sails must be set and cables bent, be it never so strict a saint's day, and it is found that no harm comes of it. Absolution on a lee-shore must be had of the breakers, it appears, if at all, and they give it plenary and brief, without listening to confession.

Whereupon our religious opinions become vague, but our religious confidences strong; and the end of it all is that we perceive the Pope to be on the other side of the Apennines, and able, indeed, to sell indulgences, but not winds, for any money. Whereas, God and the sea are with us, and we must even trust them both, and take what they shall send.

§ 4. Then, farther. This ocean-work is wholly adverse to any morbid conditions of sentiment. Reverie, above all things, is forbidden by Scylla and Charybdis. By the dogs and the depths, no dreaming! The first thing required of us is presence of mind. Neither love, nor poetry, nor piety, must ever so take up our thoughts as to make us slow or unready. In sweet Val d'Arno it is permissible enough to dream among the orange blossoms, and forget the day in twilight of ilex. But along the avenues of the Adrian waves there can be no careless walking. Vigilance, night and day, required of us, besides learning of many practical lessons in severe and humble dexterities. It is enough for the Florentine to know how to use his sword and to ride. We Venetians, also, must be able to use our swords, and on ground which is none of the steadiest; but, besides, we must be able to do nearly everything that hands can turn to—rudders, and yards, and cables, all needing workmanly handling and workmanly knowledge, from captain as well as from men. To drive a nail, lash a spar, reef a sail—rude work this for noble hands; but to be done sometimes, and done well on pain of death. All which not only takes mean pride out of us, and puts nobler pride of power in its stead; but it tends partly to soothe, partly to chasten, partly to employ and direct, the hot Italian temper, and make us every way greater, calmer, and happier.

§ 5. Moreover, it tends to induce in us great respect for the whole human body; for its limbs, as much as for its tongue or its wit. Policy and eloquence are well; and, indeed, we Venetians can be politic enough, and can speak melodiously when we choose; but to put the helm up at the right moment is the beginning of all cunning—and for that we need arm and eye;—not tongue. And with this respect for the body as such, comes also the sailor's preference of massive beauty in bodily form. The landsmen, among their roses and orange-blossoms, and chequered shadows of twisted vine, may well please themselves with pale faces, and finely drawn eyebrows, and fantastic braiding of hair. But from the sweeping glory of the sea we learn to love another kind of beauty; broad-breasted, level-browed, like the horizon;—thighed and shouldered like the billows; footed like their stealing foam;—bathed in cloud of golden hair like their sunsets.

§ 6. Such were the physical influences constantly in operation on the Venetians; their painters, however, were partly prepared for their work by others in their infancy. Associations connected with early life among mountains softened and deepened the teaching of the sea; and the wildness of form of the Tyrolese Alps gave greater strength and grotesqueness to their imaginations than the Greek painters could have found among the cliffs of the Ægean. Thus far, however, the influences on both are nearly similar. The Greek Sea was indeed less bleak, and the Greek hills were less grand; but the difference was in degree rather than in the nature of their power. The moral influences at work on the two races were far more sharply opposed.

§ 7. Evil, as we saw, had been fronted by the Greek, and thrust out of his path. Once conquered, if he thought of it more, it was involuntarily, as we remember a painful dream, yet with a secret dread that the dream might return and continue for ever. But the teaching of the Church in the middle ages had made the contemplation of evil one of the duties of men. As sin, it was to be duly thought upon, that it might be confessed. As suffering, endured joyfully, in hope of future reward. Hence conditions of bodily distemper which an Athenian would have looked upon with the severest contempt and aversion, were in the Christian Church regarded always with pity, and often with respect: while the partial practice of celibacy by the clergy, and by those over whom they had influence,—together with the whole system of conventual penance and pathetic ritual (with the vicious reactionary tendencies necessarily following), introduced calamitous conditions both of body and soul, which added largely to the pagan's simple list of elements of evil, and introduced the most complicated states of mental suffering and decrepitude.

§ 8. Therefore the Christian painters differed from the Greek in two main points. They had been taught a faith which put an end to restless questioning and discouragement. All was at last to be well—and their best genius might be peacefully given to imagining the glories of heaven and the happiness of its redeemed. But on the

other hand, though suffering was to cease in heaven, it
was to be not only endured, but honoured upon earth.
And from the Crucifixion, down to a beggar's lameness,
all the tortures and maladies of men were to be made,
at least in part, the subjects of art. The Venetian was,
therefore, in his inner mind, less serious than the Greek :
in his superficial temper, sadder. In his heart there was
none of the deep horror which vexed the soul of Æschylus
or Homer. His Pallas-shield was the shield of Faith, not
the shield of the Gorgon. All was at last to issue happily ;
in sweetest harpings and seven-fold circles of light. But
for the present he had to dwell with the maimed and the
blind, and to revere Lazarus more than Achilles.

§ 9. This reference to a future world has a morbid
influence on all their conclusions. For the earth and all
its natural elements are despised. They are to pass away
like a scroll. Man, the immortal, is alone revered ; his
work and presence are all that can be noble or desirable.
Men, and fair architecture, temples and courts such as
may be in a celestial city, or the clouds and angels of
Paradise ; these are what we must paint when we want
beautiful things. But the sea, the mountains, the forests,
are all adverse to us,—a desolation. The ground that
was cursed for our sake ;—the sea that executed judgment
on all our race, and rages against us still, though bridled ;
storm-demons churning it into foam in nightly glare on
Lido, and hissing from it against our palaces. Nature is
but a terror, or a temptation. She is for hermits, martyrs,
murderers,—for St. Jerome, and St. Mary of Egypt, and
the Magdalen in the desert, and monk Peter, falling before
the sword.

§ 10. But the worst point we have to note respecting
the spirit of Venetian landscape is its pride.

It was observed in the course of the third volume how
the mediæval temper had rejected agricultural pursuits,
and whatever pleasures could come of them.

At Venice this negation had reached its extreme.
Though the Florentines and Romans had no delight in
farming, they had in gardening. The Venetian possessed,
and cared for, neither fields nor pastures. Being delivered,

to his loss, from all the wholesome labours of tillage, he was also shut out from the sweet wonders and charities of the earth, and from the pleasant natural history of the year. Birds and beasts, and times and seasons, all unknown to him. No swallow chattered at his window,[1] nor, nested under his golden roofs, claimed the sacredness of his mercy;[2] no Pythagorean fowl taught him the blessings of the poor,[3] nor did the grave spirit of poverty rise at his side to set forth the delicate grace and honour of lowly life.[4] No humble thoughts of grasshopper sire had he, like the Athenian; no gratitude for gifts of olive; no childish care for figs, any more than thistles. The rich Venetian feast had no need of the figtree spoon.[5] Dramas about birds, and wasps and frogs, would have passed unheeded by his proud fancy; carol or murmur of them had fallen unrecognized on ears accustomed only to grave syllables of war-tried men, and wash of songless wave.

§ 11. No simple joy was possible to him. Only stateliness and power; high intercourse with kingly and beautiful humanity, proud thoughts, or splendid pleasures; throned sensualities, and ennobled appetites. But of innocent, childish, helpful, holy pleasures, he had none. As in the classical landscape, nearly all rural labour is banished from the Titianesque: there is one bold etching of a landscape, with grand ploughing in the foreground, but this is only a caprice; the customary Venetian background is without sign of laborious rural life. We find, indeed, often a shepherd with his flock, sometimes a woman spinning, but no division of fields, no growing crops, nor nestling villages. In the numerous drawings and woodcuts variously connected with or representative of Venetian work, a watermill is a frequent object, a river constant, generally the sea. But the prevailing idea in all the great pictures I have seen is that of mountainous land with wild but graceful forest, and rolling or horizontal clouds. The mountains are dark blue; the clouds glowing or soft gray, always massive; the light, deep, clear, melancholy; the foliage, neither intricate

---

[1] Anacreon, Ode 12th.   [2] Herod. i. 59.   [3] Lucian (Micyllus).
[4] Aristophanes, Plutus.   [5] Hippias Major, 208.

nor graceful, but compact and sweeping (with undulated trunks), dividing much into horizontal flakes, like the clouds; the ground rocky and broken somewhat monotonously, but richly green with wild herbage; here and there a flower, by preference white or blue, rarely yellow, still more rarely red.

§ 12. It was stated that this heroic landscape of theirs was peopled by spiritual beings of the highest order. And in this rested the dominion of the Venetians over all later schools. They were the *last believing* school of Italy. Although, as I said above, always quarrelling with the Pope, there is all the more evidence of an earnest faith in their religion. People who trusted the Madonna less, flattered the Pope more. But down to Tintoret's time, the Roman Catholic religion was still real and sincere at Venice; and though faith in it was compatible with much which to us appears criminal or absurd, the religion itself was entirely sincere.

§ 13. Perhaps when you see one of Titian's splendidly passionate subjects, or find Veronese making the Marriage in Cana one blaze of worldly pomp, you imagine that Titian must have been a sensualist, and Veronese an unbeliever.

Put the idea from you at once, and be assured of this for ever; it will guide you through many a labyrinth of life, as well as of painting,—that of an evil tree, men never gather good fruit—good of any sort or kind; even good sensualism.

Let us look to this calmly. We have seen what physical advantage the Venetian had, in his sea and sky: also what moral disadvantage he had, in scorn of the poor; now finally, let us see with what power he was invested, which men since his time have never recovered more.

§ 14. "Neither of a bramble bush gather they grapes." The great saying has twofold help for us. Be assured, first, that if it were bramble from which you gathered them, these are not grapes in your hand, though they look like grapes. Or if these are indeed grapes, it was no bramble you gathered them from, though it looked like one.

It is difficult for persons, accustomed to receive, without

questioning, the modern English idea of religion, to understand the temper of the Venetian Catholics. I do not
enter into examination of our own feelings ; but I have to
note this one significant point of difference between us.

§ 15. An English gentleman, desiring his portrait, gives
probably to the painter a choice of several actions, in any
of which he is willing to be represented. As for instance,
riding his best horse, shooting with his favourite pointer,
manifesting himself in his robes of state on some great
public occasion, meditating in his study, playing with his
children, or visiting his tenants ; in any of these or other
such circumstances, he will give the artist free leave to paint
him. But in one important action he would shrink even
from the suggestion of being drawn. He will assuredly
not let himself be painted praying.

Strangely, this is the action which, of all others, a
Venetian desires to be painted in. If they want a noble
and complete portrait, they nearly all choose to be painted
on their knees.

§ 16. " Hypocrisy," you say ; and " that they might
be seen of men." If we examine ourselves, or any one
else, who will give trustworthy answer on this point, so
as to ascertain, to the best of our judgment, what the
feeling *is*, which would make a modern English person
dislike to be painted praying, we shall not find it, I believe,
to be excess of sincerity. Whatever we find it to be, the
opposite Venetian feeling is certainly not hypocrisy. It is
often conventionalism, implying as little devotion in the
person represented, as regular attendance at church does
with us. But that it is not hypocrisy, you may ascertain
by one simple consideration (supposing you not to have
enough knowledge of the expression of sincere persons to
judge by the portraits themselves). The Venetians, when
they desired to deceive, were much too subtle to attempt
it clumsily. If they assumed the mask of religion, the
mask must have been of some use. The persons whom
it deceived must, therefore, have been religious, and, being
so, have believed in the Venetians' sincerity. If, therefore,
among other contemporary nations with whom they had
intercourse, we can find any, more religious than they,

who were duped, or even influenced, by their external religiousness, we might have some ground for suspecting that religiousness to be assumed. But if we can find no one likely to have been deceived, we must believe the Venetian to have been, in reality, what there was no advantage in seeming.

§ 17. I leave the matter to your examination, forewarning you, confidently, that you will discover by severest evidence, that the Venetian religion was true. Not only true, but one of the main motives of their lives. In the field of investigation to which we are here limited, I will collect some of the evidence of this.

For one profane picture by great Venetians, you will find ten of sacred subjects ; and those, also, including their grandest, most laboured, and most beloved works. Tintoret's power culminates in two great religious pictures : the Crucifixion, and the Paradise. Titian's in the Assumption, the Peter Martyr, and Presentation of the Virgin. Veronese's in the Marriage in Cana. John Bellini and Basaiti never, so far as I remember, painted any other than sacred subjects. By the Palmas, Vincenzo Catena, and Bonifazio, I remember no profane subject of importance.

§ 18. There is, moreover, one distinction of the very highest import between the treatment of sacred subjects by Venetian painters and by all others.

Throughout the rest of Italy, piety had become abstract, and opposed theoretically to worldly life ; hence the Florentine and Umbrian painters generally separated their saints from living men. They delighted in imagining scenes of spiritual perfectness ;—Paradises, and companies of the redeemed at the judgment ;—glorified meetings of martyrs ; —madonnas surrounded by circles of angels. If, which was rare, definite portraitures of living men were introduced, these real characters formed a kind of chorus or attendant company, taking no part in the action. At Venice all this was reversed, and so boldly as at first to shock, with its seeming irreverence, a spectator accustomed to the formalities and abstractions of the so-called sacred schools. The madonnas are no more seated apart on their thrones, the saints no more breathe celestial air. They are on our own plain ground—nay, here in our houses with us. All kind of worldly business going on in their presence, fearlessly; our own friends and respected acquaintances, with all their mortal faults, and in their mortal flesh, looking at them face to face unalarmed : nay, our dearest children playing with their pet dogs at Christ's very feet.

I once myself thought this irreverent. How foolishly! As if children whom He loved *could* play anywhere else.

§ 19. The picture most illustrative of this feeling is perhaps that at Dresden, of Veronese's family, painted by himself.

He wishes to represent them as happy and honoured. The best happiness and highest honour he can imagine for them is that they should be presented to the Madonna, to whom, therefore, they are being brought by the three virtues—Faith, Hope, and Charity.

The Virgin stands in a recess behind two marble shafts, such as may be seen in any house belonging to an old family in Venice. She places the boy Christ on the edge of a balustrade before her. At her side are St. John the Baptist, and St. Jerome. This group occupies the left side of the picture. The pillars, seen sideways, divide it from the group formed by the Virtues, with the wife and children of Veronese. He himself stands a little behind, his hands clasped in prayer.

§ 20. His wife kneels full in front, a strong Venetian woman, well advanced in years. She has brought up her children in fear of God, and is not afraid to meet the Virgin's eyes. She gazes steadfastly on them ; her proud head and gentle, self-possessed face are relieved in one broad mass of shadow against a space of light, formed by the white robes of Faith, who stands beside her—guardian, and companion. Perhaps a somewhat disappointing Faith at the first sight, for her face is not in any special way exalted or refined. Veronese knew that Faith had to companion simple and slow-hearted people, perhaps oftener than able or refined people—does not therefore insist on her being severely intellectual, or looking as if she were always in the best company. So she is only distinguished

by her pure white (not bright white) dress, her delicate
hand, her golden hair drifted in light ripples across her
breast, from which the white robes fall nearly in the shape
of a shield—the shield of Faith. A little behind her stands
Hope; she also, at first, not to most people a recognizable
Hope. We usually paint Hope as young, and joyous.
Veronese knows better. That young hope is vain hope—
passing away in rain of tears; but the Hope of Veronese
is aged, assured, remaining when all else has been taken
away. " For tribulation worketh patience, and patience
experience, and experience hope;" and *that* hope maketh
not ashamed.

She has a black veil on her head.

Then again, in the front, is Charity, red-robed; stout in
the arms,—a servant of all work, she; but small-headed,
not being specially given to thinking; soft-eyed, her hair
braided brightly; her lips rich red, sweet-blossoming. She
has got some work to do even now, for a nephew of
Veronese's is doubtful about coming forward, and looks
very humbly and penitently towards the Virgin—his life
perhaps not having been quite so exemplary as might at
present be wished. Faith reaches her small white hand
lightly back to him, lays the tips of her fingers on his; but
Charity takes firm hold of him by the wrist from behind,
and will push him on presently, if he still hangs back.

§ 21. In front of the mother kneel her two eldest children, a girl of about sixteen, and a boy a year or two
younger. They are both rapt in adoration—the boy's being
the deepest. Nearer us, at their left side, is a younger
boy, about nine years old—a black-eyed fellow, full of life
—and evidently his father's darling (for Veronese has put
him full in light in the front; and given him a beautiful
white silken jacket, barred with black, that nobody may
ever miss seeing him to the end of time). He is a little
shy about being presented to the Madonna, and for the
present has got behind the pillar, blushing, but opening
his black eyes wide; he is just summoning courage to
peep round and see if she looks kind. A still younger
child, about six years old, is really frightened, and has run
back to his mother, catching hold of her dress at the

waist.   She throws her right arm round him and over him, with exquisite instinctive action, not moving her eyes from the Madonna's face.   Last of all, the youngest child, perhaps about three years old, is neither frightened nor interested, but finds the ceremony tedious, and is trying to coax the dog to play with him; but the dog, which is one of the little curly, short-nosed, fringy-pawed things, which all Venetian ladies petted, will not now be coaxed.   For the dog is the last link in the chain of lowering feeling, and takes his doggish views of the matter.   He cannot understand, first, how the Madonna got into the house; nor, secondly, why she is allowed to stay, disturbing the family, and taking all their attention from his dogship.   And he is walking away, much offended.

§ 22.   The dog is thus constantly introduced by the Venetians in order to give the fullest contrast to the highest tones of human thought and feeling.   I shall examine this point presently farther, in speaking of pastoral landscape and animal painting; but at present we will merely compare the use of the same mode of expression in Veronese's Presentation of the Queen of Sheba.

§ 23.   This picture is at Turin, and is of quite inestimable value.   It is hung high; and the really principal figure, the Solomon, being in the shade, can hardly be seen, but is painted with Veronese's utmost tenderness, in the bloom of perfect youth, his hair golden, short, crisply curled.   He is seated high on his lion throne: two elders on each side beneath him, the whole group forming a tower of solemn shade.   I have alluded, elsewhere, to the principle on which all the best composers act, of supporting these lofty groups by some vigorous mass of foundation.   This column of noble shade is curiously sustained.   A falconer leans forward from the left-hand side, bearing on his wrist a snow-white falcon, its wings spread, and brilliantly relieved against the purple robe of one of the elders.   It touches with its wings one of the golden lions of the throne, on which the light also flashes strongly; thus forming, together with it, the lion and eagle symbol, which is the type of Christ throughout mediæval work.   In order to show the meaning of this symbol, and that Solomon is typically invested with the Christian royalty, one of the elders, by a bold ana-chronism, holds a jewel in his hand of the shape of a cross, with which he (by accident of gesture) points to Solomon; his other hand is laid on an open book.

§ 24. The group opposite, of which the Queen forms the centre, is also painted with Veronese's highest skill; but contains no point of interest bearing on our present subject, except its connection by a chain of descending emotion. The Queen is wholly oppressed and subdued; kneeling, and nearly fainting, she looks up to Solomon with tears in her eyes; he, startled by fear for her, stoops forward from the throne, opening his right hand, as if to support her, so as almost to drop the sceptre. At her side her first maid of honour is kneeling also, but does not care about Solomon; and is gathering up her dress that it may not be crushed; and looking back to encourage a negro-girl, who, carrying two toy-birds, made of enamel and jewels, for presentation to the King, is frightened at seeing her Queen fainting, and does not know what she ought to do; while, lastly, the Queen's dog, another of the little fringy-paws, is wholly unabashed by Solomon's presence, or anybody else's; and stands with his forelegs well apart, right in front of his mistress, thinking everybody has lost their wits; and barking violently at one of the attendants, who has set down a golden vase disrespectfully near him.

§ 25. Throughout these designs I want the reader to notice the purpose of representing things as they were likely to have occurred, down to trivial, or even ludicrous detail—the nobleness of all that was intended to be noble being so great that nothing could detract from it. A farther instance, however, and a prettier one, of this familiar realization, occurs in a Holy Family, by Veronese, at Brussels. The Madonna has laid the infant Christ on a projecting base of pillar, and stands behind, looking down on Him. St. Catherine, having knelt down in front, the child turns round to receive her—so suddenly, and so far, that any other child must have fallen over the edge of the stone. St. Catherine, terrified, thinking He is really going to fall, stretches out her arms to catch Him. But the Madonna, looking down, only smiles, "He will not fall."

§ 26. A more touching instance of this realization occurs, however, in the treatment of the Saint Veronica (in the Ascent to Calvary), at Dresden. Most painters merely represent her as one of the gentle, weeping, attendant women; and show her giving the handkerchief as though these women had been allowed to approach Christ without any difficulty. But in Veronese's conception, she has to break through the executioners to Him. She is not weeping; and the expression of pity, though intense, is overborne by that of resolution. She is determined to reach Christ; has set her teeth close, and thrusts aside one of the executioners, who strikes fiercely at her with a heavy doubled cord.

§ 27. These instances are enough to explain the general character of the mind of Veronese, capable of tragic power to the utmost, if he chooses to exert it in that direction, but, by habitual preference, exquisitely graceful and playful; religious, without severity, and winningly noble; delighting in slight, sweet, every-day incident, but hiding deep meanings underneath it; rarely painting a gloomy subject, and never a base one.

§ 28. I have, in other places, entered enough into the examination of the great religious mind of Tintoret; supposing then, that he was distinguished from Titian chiefly by this character. But in this I was mistaken;—the religion of Titian is like that of Shakspere—occult behind his magnificent equity. It is not possible, however, within the limits of this work, to give any just account of the mind of Titian: nor shall I attempt it; but will only explain some of those more strange and apparently inconsistent attributes of it, which might otherwise prevent the reader from getting clue to its real tone. The first of these is its occasional coarseness in choice of type of feature.

§ 29. In the second volume (p. 133) I had to speak of Titian's Magdalen, in the Pitti Palace, as treated basely, and that in strong terms, "the disgusting Magdalen of the Pitti."

Truly she is so, as compared with the received types of the Magdalen. A stout, red-faced woman, dull, and coarse of feature, with much of the animal in even her expression of repentance——her eyes strained, and inflamed with weeping. I ought, however, to have remembered another picture of the Magdalen by Titian (Mr. Rogers's, now in the National Gallery), in which she is just as refined, as in the Pitti Palace she is gross ; and had I done so, I should have seen Titian's meaning. It had been the fashion before his time to make the Magdalen always young and beautiful ; her, if no one else, even the rudest painters flattered ; her repentance was not thought perfect unless she had lustrous hair and lovely lips. Titian first dared to doubt the romantic fable, and reject the narrowness of sentimental faith. He saw that it was possible for plain women to love no less vividly than beautiful ones ; and for stout persons to repent, as well as those more delicately made. It seemed to him that the Magdalen would have received her pardon not the less quickly because her wit was none of the readiest ; and would not have been regarded with less compassion by her Master because her eyes were swollen, or her dress disordered. It is just because he has set himself sternly to enforce this lesson that the picture is so painful : the only instance, so far as I remember, of Titian's painting a woman markedly and entirely belonging to the lowest class.

§ 30. It may perhaps appear more difficult to account for the alternation of Titian's great religious pictures with others devoted wholly to the expression of sensual qualities, or to exulting and bright representation of heathen deities.

The Venetian mind, we have said, and Titian's especially, as the central type of it, was wholly realist, universal, and manly.

In this breadth and realism, the painter saw that sensual passion in man was, not only a fact, but a Divine fact ; the human creature, though the highest of the animals, was, nevertheless, a perfect animal, and his happiness, health, and nobleness, depended on the due power of every animal passion, as well as the cultivation of every spiritual tendency.

He thought that every feeling of the mind and heart, as well as every form of the body, deserved painting. Also to a painter's true and highly trained instinct, the human body is the loveliest of all objects. I do not stay to trace the reasons why, at Venice, the female body could be found in more perfect beauty than the male ; but so it was, and it becomes the principal subject, therefore, both with Giorgione and Titian. They painted it fearlessly, with all right and natural qualities ; never, however, representing it as exercising any overpowering attractive influence on man ; but only on the Faun or Satyr.

Yet they did this so majestically that I am perfectly certain no untouched Venetian picture ever yet excited one base thought (otherwise than in base persons anything may do so) ; while in the greatest studies of the female body by the Venetians, all other characters are overborne by majesty, and the form becomes as pure as that of a Greek statue.

§ 31. There is no need, I should think, to point out how this contemplation of the entire personal nature was reconcilable with the severest conceptions of religious duty and faith.

But the fond introduction of heathen gods may appear less explicable.

On examination, however, it will be found, that these deities are never painted with any heart-reverence or affection. They are introduced for the most part symbolically (Bacchus and Venus oftenest, as incarnations of the spirit of revelry and beauty), of course always conceived with deep imaginative truth, much resembling the mode of Keats's conception ; but never so as to withdraw any of the deep devotion rendered to the objects of Christian faith.

In all its roots of power, and modes of work ;—in its belief, its breadth, and its judgment, I find the Venetian mind perfect.

How, then, did its art so swiftly pass away ? How become, what it became unquestionably, one of the chief causes of the corruption of the mind of Italy, and of her subsequent decline in moral and political power ?

§ 32. By reason of one great, one fatal fault ;—recklessness in aim. Wholly noble in its sources, it was wholly unworthy in its purposes.

Separate and strong, like Samson, chosen from its youth,

and with the spirit of God visibly resting on it,—like him, it warred in careless strength, and wantoned in untimely pleasure. No Venetian painter ever worked with any aim beyond that of delighting the eye, or expressing fancies agreeable to himself or flattering to his nation. They could not be either, unless they were religious. But he did not desire the religion. He desired the delight.

The Assumption is a noble picture, because Titian believed in the Madonna. But he did not paint it to make any one else believe in her. He painted it, because he enjoyed rich masses of red and blue, and faces flushed with sunlight.

Tintoret's Paradise is a noble picture, because he believed in Paradise. But he did not paint it to make any one think of heaven; but to form a beautiful termination for the hall of the Greater Council.

Other men used their effete faiths and mean faculties with a high moral purpose. The Venetian gave the most earnest faith, and the lordliest faculty, to gild the shadows of an antechamber, or heighten the splendours of a holiday.

§ 33. Strange and lamentable as this carelessness may appear, I find it to be almost the law with the great workers. Weak and vain men have acute consciences, and labour under a profound sense of responsibility. The strong men, sternly disdainful of themselves, do what they can, too often merely as it pleases them at the moment, reckless what comes of it.

I know not how far in humility, or how far in bitter and hopeless levity, the great Venetians gave their art to be blasted by the sea-winds or wasted by the worm. I know not whether in sorrowful obedience, or in wanton compliance, they fostered the folly, and enriched the luxury of their age. This only I know, that in proportion to the greatness of their power was the shame of its desecration and the suddenness of its fall. The enchanters' spell, woven by centuries of toil, was broken in the weakness of a moment; and swiftly, and utterly, as a rainbow vanishes, the radiance and the strength faded from the wings of the Lion.

CHAPTER IV

DÜRER AND SALVATOR

"EMIGRAVIT"

§ 1. By referring to the first analysis of our subject, it will be seen we have next to examine the art which cannot conquer the evil, but remains at war with, or in captivity to it.

Up to the time of the Reformation, it was possible for men even of the highest powers of intellect, to obtain a tranquillity of faith, in the highest degree favourable to the pursuit of any particular art. Possible, at least, we see it to have been; there is no need—nor, so far as I see, any ground for argument about it. I am myself unable to understand how it was so, but the fact is unquestionable. It is not that I wonder at men's trust in the Pope's infallibility, or in his virtue; nor at their surrendering their private judgment; nor at their being easily cheated by imitations of miracles; nor at their thinking indulgences could be purchased with money. But I wonder at this one thing only; the acceptance of the doctrine of eternal punishment as dependent on accident of birth, or momentary excitement of devotional feeling. I marvel at the acceptance of the system (as stated in its fulness by Dante) which condemned guiltless persons to the loss of heaven because they had lived before Christ, and which made the obtaining of Paradise turn frequently on a passing thought or a momentary invocation. How this came to pass, it is no part of our work here to determine. That in this faith, it was possible to attain entire peace of mind, to live calmly, and die hopefully, is indisputable.

§ 2. But this possibility ceased at the Reformation. Thenceforward human life became a school of debate, troubled and fearful. Fifteen hundred years of spiritual teaching were called into fearful question, whether indeed it had been teaching by angels or devils? Whatever it had been, there was no longer any way of trusting it peacefully.

A dark time for all men. We cannot now conceive it. The great horror of it lay in this :—that, as in the trial-hour of the Greek, the heavens themselves seemed to have deceived those who had trusted in them.

"We had prayed with tears; we had loved with our hearts. There was no choice of way open to us. No guidance, from God or man, other than this, and behold, it was a lie. 'When He, the Spirit of Truth, is come, He shall guide you into all truth.' And he has guided us into *no* truth. There can be no such Spirit. There is no Advocate, no Comforter. Has there been no Resurrection?"

§ 3. Then came the Resurrection of Death. Never since man first saw him face to face, had his terror been so great. "Swallowed up in victory:" alas! no; but king over all the earth. All faith, hope, and fond belief were betrayed. Nothing of futurity was now sure but the grave.

For the Pan-Athenaic Triumph, and the Feast of Jubilee, there came up, through fields of spring, the Dance of Death.

The brood of weak men fled from the face of him. A new Bacchus and his crew this, with worm for snake and gall for wine. They recoiled to such pleasure as yet remained possible to them—feeble infidelities, and luxurious sciences, and so went their way.

§ 4. At least, of the men with whom we are concerned—the artists—this was almost the universal fate. They gave themselves to the following of pleasure only; and, as a religious school, after a few pale rays of fading sanctity from Guido, and brown gleams of gipsy Madonnahood from Murillo, came utterly to an end.

Three men only stood firm, facing the new Dionysiac revel, to see what would come of it.

Two in the north, Holbein and Dürer; and, later, one in the south, Salvator.

But the ground on which they stood differed strangely; Dürer and Holbein, amidst the formal delights, the tender religions, and practical science, of domestic life and honest commerce. Salvator, amidst the pride of lascivious wealth, and the outlawed distress of impious poverty.

§ 5. It would be impossible to imagine any two phases of scenery or society more contrary in character, more opposite in teaching, than those surrounding Nuremberg and Naples, in the sixteenth and seventeenth centuries. What they were then, both districts still to all general intents remain. The cities have in each case lost their splendour and power, but not their character. The surrounding scenery remains wholly unchanged. It is still in our power, from the actual aspect of the places, to conceive their effect on the youth of the two painters.

§ 6. Nuremberg is gathered at the base of a sandstone rock, rising in the midst of a dry but fertile plain. The rock forms a prolonged and curved ridge, of which the concave side, at the highest point, is precipitous; the other slopes gradually to the plain. Fortified with wall and tower along its whole crest, and crowned with a stately castle, it defends the city—not with its precipitous side—but with its slope. The precipice is turned to the town. It wears no aspect of hostility towards the surrounding fields; the roads lead down into them by gentle descents from the gates. To the south and east the walls are on the level of the plain; within them, the city itself stands on two swells of hill, divided by a winding river. Its architecture has, however, been much overrated. The effect of the streets, so delightful to the eye of the passing traveller, depends chiefly on one appendage of the roof, namely, its warehouse windows. Every house, almost without exception, has at least one boldly opening dormer window, the roof of which sustains a pulley for raising goods; and the under part of this strong overhanging roof is always carved with a rich pattern, not of refined

design, but effective.[1]   Among these comparatively modern
structures are mingled, however, not unfrequently, others,
turreted at the angles, which are true Gothic of the
fifteenth, some of the fourteenth, century; and the principal churches remain nearly as in Dürer's time.   Their
Gothic is none of it good, nor even rich (though the
façades have their ornament so distributed as to give them
a sufficiently elaborate effect at a distance); their size is
diminutive; their interiors mean, rude, and ill-propor-
tioned, wholly dependent for their interest on ingenious
stone-cutting in corners, and finely-twisted ironwork;
of these the mason's exercises are in the worst possible
taste, possessing not even the merit of delicate execution;
but the designs in metal are usually meritorious, and
Fischer's shrine of St. Sebald is good, and may rank with
Italian work.[2]

§ 7.   Though, however, not comparable for an instant
to any great Italian or French city, Nuremberg possesses
one character peculiar to itself, that of a self-restrained,
contented, quaint domesticity.   It would have been vain
to expect any first-rate painting, sculpture, or poetry,
from the well-regulated community of merchants of small
ware.   But it is evident they were affectionate and trustworthy — that they had playful fancy and honourable

---

[1] To obtain room for the goods, the roofs slope steeply, and their
other dormer windows are richly carved—but all are of wood; and,
for the most part, I think, some hundred years later than Dürer's
time.   A large number of the oriel and bow windows on the façades
are wooden also, and of recent date.

[2] His piece in the cathedral of Magdeburg is strangely inferior,
wanting both the grace of composition and bold handling of the
St. Sebald's.   The bronze fountains at Nuremberg (three, of fame,
in as many squares) are highly wrought, and have considerable merit;
the ordinary ironwork of the houses, with less pretension, is, perhaps,
more truly artistic.   In Plate 52 (p. 28), the right-hand figure is a
characteristic example of the bell-handle at the door of a private
house, composed of a wreath of flowers and leafage twisted in a spiral
round an upright rod, the spiral terminating below in a delicate
tendril; the whole of wrought-iron.   It is longer than represented,
some of the leaf links of the chain being omitted in the dotted spaces,
as well as the handle, which though often itself of leafage, is always
convenient for the hand.

J. Ruskin

76. The Moat of Nuremberg

J. H. Le Keux

pride. There is no exalted grandeur in their city, nor any deep beauty; but an imaginative homeliness, mingled with some elements of melancholy and power, and a few even of grace.

This homeliness, among many other causes, arises out of one in chief. The richness of the houses depends, as I just said, on the dormer windows; but their deeper character on the pitch and space of roofs. I had to notice long ago how much our English cottage depended for expression on its steep roof. The German house does so in far greater degree. Plate 76 is engraved [1] from a slight pen-and-ink sketch of mine on the ramparts of Nuremberg, showing a piece of its moat and wall, and a little corner of the city beneath the castle; of which the tower on the extreme right rises just in front of Dürer's house. The character of this scene approaches more nearly that which Dürer would see in his daily walks, than most of the modernized inner streets. In Dürer's own engraving, "The Cannon," the distance (of which the most important passage is facsimiled in my Elements of Drawing, p. 111) is an actual portrait of part of the landscape seen from those castle ramparts, looking towards Franconian Switzerland.

§ 8. If the reader will be at the pains to turn to it, he will see at a glance the elements of the Nuremberg country, as they still exist. Wooden cottages, thickly grouped, enormously high in the roofs; the sharp church spire, small and slightly grotesque, surmounting them; beyond, a richly cultivated, healthy plain, bounded by woody hills. By a strange coincidence the very plant which constitutes the staple produce of those fields, is in almost ludicrous harmony with the grotesqueness and neatness of the architecture around; and one may almost fancy that the builders of the little knotted spires and turrets of the town, and workers of its dark iron flowers, are in spiritual presence, watching and guiding the produce of the field,—when one finds the footpaths bordered, everywhere, by the bossy spires and lustrous jetty flowers of the black hollyhock.

§ 9. Lastly, when Dürer penetrated among those hills

[1] By Mr. Le Keux, very admirably.

of Franconia he would find himself in a pastoral country, much resembling the Gruyère districts of Switzerland, but less thickly inhabited, and giving in its steep, though not lofty, rocks,—its scattered pines,—and its fortresses and chapels, the motives of all the wilder landscape introduced by the painter in such pieces as his St. Jerome, or St. Hubert. His continual and forced introduction of sea in almost every scene, much as it seems to me to be regretted, is possibly owing to his happy recollections of the sea-city where he received the rarest of all rewards granted to a good workman ; and, for once in his life, was understood.

§ 10. Among this pastoral simplicity and formal sweetness of domestic peace, Dürer had to work out his question concerning the grave. It haunted him long; he learnt to engrave death's heads well before he had done with it ; looked deeper than any other man into those strange rings, their jewels lost; and gave answer at last conclusively in his great Knight and Death—of which more presently. But while the Nuremberg landscape is still fresh in our minds, we had better turn south quickly, and compare the elements of education which formed, and of creation which companioned, Salvator.

§ 11. Born with a wild and coarse nature (how coarse I will show you soon), but nevertheless an honest one, he set himself in youth hotly to the war, and cast himself carelessly on the current, of life. No rectitude of ledger-lines stood in his way ; no tender precision of household customs ; no calm successions of rural labour. But past his half-starved lips rolled profusion of pitiless wealth ; before him glared and swept the troops of shameless pleasure. Above him muttered Vesuvius ; beneath his feet shook the Solfatara.

In heart disdainful, in temper adventurous ; conscious of power, impatient of labour, and yet more of the pride of the patrons of his youth, he fled to the Calabrian hills, seeking, not knowledge, but freedom. If he was to be surrounded by cruelty and deceit, let them at least be those of brave men or savage beasts, not of the timorous and the contemptible. Better the wrath of the robber, than enmity of the priest; and the cunning of the wolf than of the hypocrite.

§ 12. We are accustomed to hear the south of Italy spoken of as a beautiful country. Its mountain forms are graceful above others, its sea bays exquisite in outline and hue; but it is only beautiful in superficial aspect. In closer detail it is wild and melancholy. Its forests are sombre-leaved, labyrinth-stemmed; the carubbe, the olive, laurel, and ilex, are alike in that strange feverish twisting of their branches, as if in spasms of half human pain:— Avernus forests; one fears to break their boughs, lest they should cry to us from the rents; the rocks they shade are of ashes, or thrice-molten lava; iron sponge whose every pore has been filled with fire. Silent villages, earthquake shaken, without commerce, without industry, without knowledge, without hope, gleam in white ruin from hillside to hillside; far-winding wrecks of immemorial walls surround the dust of cities long forsaken: the mountain streams moan through the cold arches of their foundations, green with weed, and rage over the heaps of their fallen towers. Far above, in thunder-blue serration, stand the eternal edges of the angry Apennine, dark with rolling impendence of volcanic cloud.

§ 13. Yet even among such scenes as these, Salvator might have been calmed and exalted, had he been, indeed, capable of exaltation. But he was not of high temper enough to perceive beauty. He had not the sacred sense —the sense of colour; all the loveliest hues of the Calabrian air were invisible to him; the sorrowful desolation of the Calabrian villages unfelt. He saw only what was gross and terrible,—the jagged peak, the splintered tree, the flowerless bank of grass, and wandering weed, prickly and pale. His temper confirmed itself in evil, and became more and more fierce and morose; though not, I believe, cruel, ungenerous, or lascivious. I should not suspect Salvator of wantonly inflicting pain. His constantly painting it does not prove he delighted in it; he felt the horror of it, and in that horror, fascination. Also, he desired fame, and saw that here was an untried field rich enough in morbid excitement to catch the humour of his indolent patrons. But the gloom gained upon him, and grasped him. He could jest, indeed, as men jest in prison-yards (he became afterwards a renowned mime in Florence); his satires are full of good mocking, but his own doom to sadness is never repealed.

§ 14. Of all men whose work I have ever studied, he gives me most distinctly the idea of a lost spirit. Michelet calls him, " Ce damné Salvator," perhaps in a sense merely harsh and violent; the epithet to me seems true in a more literal, more merciful sense,—" That condemned Salvator." I see in him, notwithstanding all his baseness, the last traces of spiritual life in the art of Europe. He was the last man to whom the thought of a spiritual existence presented itself as a conceivable reality. All succeeding men, however powerful—Rembrandt, Rubens, Vandyck, Reynolds—would have mocked at the idea of a spirit. They were men of the world; they are never in earnest, and they are never appalled. But Salvator was capable of pensiveness, of faith, and of fear. The misery of the earth is a marvel to him; he cannot leave off gazing at it. The religion of the earth is a horror to him. He gnashes his teeth at it, rages at it, mocks and gibes at it. He would have acknowledged religion, had he seen any that was true. Anything rather than that baseness which he did see. " If there is no other religion than this of pope and cardinals, let us to the robber's ambush and the dragon's den." He was capable of fear also. The gray spectre, horse-headed, striding across the sky—(in the Pitti Palace)—its bat wings spread, green bars of the twilight seen between its bones; it was no play to him—the painting of it. Helpless Salvator! A little early sympathy, a word of true guidance, perhaps, had saved him. What says he of himself? " Despiser of wealth and of death." Two grand scorns; but, oh, condemned Salvator! the question is not for man what he can scorn, but what he can love.

§ 15. I do not care to trace the various hold which Hades takes on this fallen soul. It is no part of my work here to analyze his art, nor even that of Dürer; all that we need to note is the opposite answer they gave to the question about death.

To Salvator it came in narrow terms. Desolation, without

hope, throughout the fields of nature he had to explore; hypocrisy and sensuality, triumphant and shameless, in the cities from which he derived his support. His life, so far as any nobility remained in it, could only pass in horror, disdain, or despair. It is difficult to say which of the three prevails most in his common work; but his answer to the great question was of despair only. He represents " Umana Fragilita " by the type of a skeleton with plumy wings, leaning over a woman and child; the earth covered with ruin round them —a thistle, casting its seed, the only fruit of it. " Thorns, also, and thistles shall it bring forth to thee." The same tone of thought marks all Salvator's more earnest work.

§ 16. On the contrary, in the sight of Dürer, things were for the most part as they ought to be. Men did their work in his city and in the fields round it. The clergy were sincere. Great social questions unagitated; great social evils either non-existent, or seemingly a part of the nature of things, and inevitable. His answer was that of patient hope; and twofold, consisting of one design in praise of Fortitude, and another in praise of Labour. The Fortitude, commonly known as the " Knight and Death," represents a knight riding through a dark valley overhung by leafless trees, and with a great castle on a hill beyond. Beside him, but a little in advance, rides Death on a pale horse. Death is gray-haired and crowned;— serpents wreathed about his crown; (the sting of Death involved in the kingly power). He holds up the hour-glass, and looks earnestly into the knight's face. Behind him follows Sin; but Sin powerless; he has been conquered and passed by, but follows yet, watching if any way of assault remains. On his forehead are two horns—I think of sea-shell—to indicate his insatiableness and instability. He has also the twisted horns of the ram, for stubbornness, the ears of an ass, the snout of a swine, the hoofs of a goat. Torn wings hang useless from his shoulders, and he carries a spear with two hooks, for catching as well as wounding. The knight does not heed him, nor even Death, though he is conscious of the presence of the last.

He rides quietly, his bridle firm in his hand, and his lips set close in a slight sorrowful smile, for he hears what

Death is saying; and hears it as the word of a messenger who brings pleasant tidings, thinking to bring evil ones. A little branch of delicate heath is twisted round his helmet. His horse trots proudly and straight; its head high, and with a cluster of oak on the brow where on the fiend's brow is the sea-shell horn. But the horse of Death stoops its head; and its rein catches the little bell which hangs from the knight's horse-bridle, making it toll as a passing-bell.[1]

§ 17. Dürer's second answer is the plate of " Melencholia," which is the history of the sorrowful toil of the earth, as the " Knight and Death " is of its sorrowful patience under temptation.

Salvator's answer, remember, is in both respects that of despair. Death as he reads, lord of temptation, is victor over the spirit of man; and lord of ruin, is victor over the work of man. Dürer declares the sad but unsullied conquest over Death the tempter; and the sad but enduring conquest over Death the destroyer.

§ 18. Though the general intent of the Melencholia is clear, and to be felt at a glance, I am in some doubt respecting its special symbolism. I do not know how far Dürer intended to show that labour, in many of its most earnest forms, is closely connected with the morbid sadness or " dark anger," of the northern nations. Truly some of the best work ever done for man, has been in that dark anger;[2] but I have not yet been able to determine for

[1] This was first pointed out to me by a friend—Mr. Robin Allen. It is a beautiful thought : yet, possibly, an after-thought. I have some suspicion that there is an alteration in the plate at that place, and that the rope to which the bell hangs was originally the line of the chest of the nearer horse, as the grass blades about the lifted hind leg conceal the lines which could not, in Dürer's way of work, be effaced, indicating its first intended position. What a proof of his general decision of handling is involved in this "repentir!"

[2] " Yet withal, you see that the Monarch is a great, valiant, cautious, melancholy, commanding man."—*Friends in Council*, last volume, p. 269 ; Milverton giving an account of Titian's picture of Charles the Fifth. (Compare Ellesmere's description of Milverton himself, p. 140.) Read carefully also what is said at p. 269 respecting Titian's freedom, and fearless withholding of flattery ; comparing it with the note on Giorgione and Titian, here, p. 370.

myself how far this is necessary, or how far great work may also be done with cheerfulness. If I knew what the truth was, I should be able to interpret Dürer better; meantime the design seems to me his answer to the complaint, " Yet is his strength labour and sorrow."

"Yes," he replies, "but labour and sorrow are his strength."

§ 19. The labour indicated is in the daily work of men. Not the inspired or gifted labour of the few (it is labour connected with the sciences, not with the arts), shown in its four chief functions: thoughtful, faithful, calculating, and executing.

Thoughtful, first; all true power coming of that resolved, resistless calm of melancholy thought. This is the first and last message of the whole design. Faithful, the right arm of the spirit resting on the book. Calculating (chiefly in the sense of self-command), the compasses in her right hand. Executive—roughest instruments of labour at her feet: a crucible, and geometrical solids, indicating her work in the sciences. Over her head the hour-glass and the bell, for their continual words, "Whatsoever thy hand findeth to do." Beside her, childish labour (lesson-learning?) sitting on an old millstone, with a tablet on its knees. I do not know what instrument it has in its hand. At her knees a wolf-hound asleep. In the distance a comet (the disorder and threatening of the universe) setting, the rainbow dominant over it. Her strong body is close girded for work; at her waist hang the keys of wealth; but the coin is cast aside contemptuously under her feet. She has eagle's wings, and is crowned with fair leafage of spring.

Yes, Albert of Nuremberg, it was a noble answer, yet an imperfect one. This is indeed the labour which is crowned with laurel and has the wings of the eagle. It was reserved for another country to prove, for another hand to pourtray, the labour which is crowned with fire, and has the wings of the bat.

CHAPTER V

CLAUDE AND POUSSIN

§ 1. It was stated in the last chapter that Salvator was the last painter of Italy on whom any fading trace of the old faithful spirit rested. Carrying some of its passion far into the seventeenth century, he deserved to be remembered together with the painters whom the questioning of the Reformation had exercised eighty years before. Not so his contemporaries. The whole body of painters around him, but chiefly those of landscape, had cast aside all regard for the faith of their fathers, or for any other ; and founded a school of art properly called "classical,"[1] of which the following are the chief characteristics.

§ 2. The belief in a supreme benevolent Being having ceased, and the sense of spiritual destitution fastening on the mind, together with the hopeless perception of ruin and decay in the existing world, the imagination sought to quit itself from the oppression of these ideas by realizing a perfect worldly felicity, in which the inevitable ruin should at least be lovely, and the necessarily short life entirely happy and refined. Labour must be banished, since it was to be unrewarded. Humiliation and degradation of body must be prevented, since there could be no compensation for them by preparation of the soul for another world. Let us eat and drink (refinedly), for to-morrow we die, and attain the highest possible dignity as men in this world, since we shall have none as spirits in the next.

[1] The word "classical" is carelessly used in the preceding volumes, to signify the characters of the Greek or Roman nations. Henceforward, it is used in a limited and accurate sense, as defined in the text.

§ 3. Observe, this is neither the Greek nor the Roman spirit. Neither Claude nor Poussin, nor any other painter or writer, properly termed "classical," ever could enter into the Greek or Roman heart, which was as full, in many cases fuller, of the hope of immortality than our own.

On the absence of belief in a good supreme Being, follows, necessarily, the habit of looking to ourselves for supreme judgment in all matters, and for supreme government. Hence, first, the irreverent habit of judgment instead of admiration. It is generally expressed under the justly degrading term "good taste."

§ 4. Hence, in the second place, the habit of restraint or self-government (instead of impulsive and limitless obedience), based upon pride, and involving, for the most part, scorn of the helpless and weak, and respect only for the orders of men who have been trained to this habit of self-government. Whence the title classical, from the Latin *classicus*.

§ 5. The school is, therefore, generally to be characterized as that of taste and restraint. As the school of taste, everything is, in its estimation, beneath it, so as to be tasted or tested; not above it, to be thankfully received. Nothing was to be fed upon as bread; but only palated as a dainty. This spirit has destroyed art since the close of the sixteenth century, and nearly destroyed French literature, our English literature being at the same time severely depressed, and our education (except in bodily strength) rendered nearly nugatory by it, so far as it affects common-place minds. It is not possible that the classical spirit should ever take possession of a mind of the highest order. Pope is, as far as I know, the greatest man who ever fell strongly under its influence; and though it spoiled half his work, he broke through it continually into true enthusiasm and tender thought.[1] Again, as the school of reserve, it refuses to allow itself in any violent or "spasmodic" passion; the schools of literature which have been in modern times called "spasmodic" being reactionary against it. The word,

[1] Cold-hearted, I have called him. He was so in writing the Pastorals, of which I then spoke; but in after life his errors were those of his time, his wisdom was his own; it would be well if we also made it ours.

though an ugly one, is quite accurate, the most spasmodic
books in the world being Solomon's Song, Job, and Isaiah.

§ 6. The classical landscape, properly so called, is therefore the representative of perfectly trained and civilized
human life, associated with perfect natural scenery and with
decorative spiritual powers.

I will expand this definition a little.

1. Perfectly civilized human life; that is, life freed from
the necessity of humiliating labour, from passions inducing
bodily disease, and from abasing misfortune. The personages of the classical landscape, therefore, must be virtuous
and amiable; if employed in labour, endowed with strength,
such as may make it not oppressive. (Considered as a
practical ideal, the classical life necessarily implies slavery,
and the command, therefore, of a higher order of men over
a lower, occupied in servile work.) Pastoral occupation is
allowable as a contrast with city life. War, if undertaken
by classical persons, must be a contest for honour, more
than for life, not at all for wealth,[1] and free from all fearful
or debasing passion. Classical persons must be trained
in all the polite arts, and, because their health is to be
perfect, chiefly in the open air. Hence, the architecture
around them must be of the most finished kind, the rough
country and ground being subdued by frequent and happy
humanity.

§ 7. 2. Such personages and buildings must be associated
with natural scenery, uninjured by storms or inclemency of
climate (such injury implying interruption of the open-air
life); and it must be scenery conducing to pleasure, not to
material service; all cornfields, orchards, olive-yards, and
such like, being under the management of slaves,[2] and the
superior beings having nothing to do with them; but passing their lives under avenues of scented and otherwise

---

[1] Because the pursuit of wealth is inconsistent at once with the peace
and dignity of perfect life.

[2] It is curious, as marking the peculiarity of the classical spirit in its
resolute degradation of the lower orders, that a sailing vessel is hardly
admissible in a classical landscape, because its management implies too
much elevation of the inferior life. But a galley, with oars, is admissible, because the rowers may be conceived as absolute slaves.

delightful trees,—under picturesque rocks, and by clear fountains.

§ 8. 3. The spiritual powers in classical scenery must be decorative; ornamental gods, not governing gods; otherwise they could not be subjected to the principles of taste, but would demand reverence. In order, therefore, as far as possible, without taking away their supernatural power, to destroy their dignity, they are made more criminal and capricious than men, and, for the most part, those only are introduced who are the lords of lascivious pleasures. For the appearance of any great god would at once destroy the whole theory of the classical life; therefore, Pan, Bacchus, and the Satyrs, with Venus and the Nymphs, are the principal spiritual powers of the classical landscape. Apollo with the Muses appear as the patrons of the liberal arts. Minerva rarely presents herself (except to be insulted by judgment of Paris); Juno seldom, except for some purpose of tyranny; Jupiter seldom, but for purpose of amour.

§ 9. Such being the general ideal of the classical landscape, it can hardly be necessary to show the reader how such charm as it possesses must in general be strong only over weak or second-rate orders of mind. It has, however, been often experimentally or playfully aimed at by great men; but I shall only take note of its two leading masters.

§ 10. I. Claude. As I shall have no farther occasion to refer to this painter, I will resume, shortly, what has been said of him throughout the work. He had a fine feeling for beauty of form, and considerable tenderness of perception. (Vol. I., p. 80; Vol. III., p. 337.) His aerial effects are unequalled. (Vol. III., p. 338.) Their character appears to me to arise rather from a delicacy of bodily constitution in Claude, than from any mental sensibility: such as they are, they give a kind of feminine charm to his work, which partly accounts for its wide influence. To whatever the character may be traced, it renders him incapable of enjoying or painting anything energetic or terrible. Hence the weakness of his conceptions of rough sea. (Vol. I., p. 81.)

II. He had sincerity of purpose. (Vol. III., p. 337.) But in common with other landscape painters of his day, neither earnestness, humility, nor love, such as would ever cause him to forget himself. (Vol. I., p. 82.)

That is to say, so far as he felt the truth, he tried to be true; but he never felt it enough to sacrifice supposed propriety or habitual method to it. Very few of his sketches, and none of his pictures, show evidence of interest in other natural phenomena than the quiet afternoon sunshine which would fall methodically into a composition. One would suppose he had never seen scarlet in a morning cloud, nor a storm burst on the Apennines. But he enjoys a quiet misty afternoon in a ruminant sort of way (Vol. III., p. 340), yet truly; and strives for the likeness of it, therein differing from Salvator, who never attempts to be truthful, but only to be impressive.

§ 11. III. His seas are the most beautiful in old art. (Vol. I., p. 366.) For he studied tame waves, as he did tame skies, with great sincerity, and some affection; and modelled them with more care not only than any other landscape painter of his day, but even than any of the great men; for they, seeing the perfect painting of sea to be impossible, gave up the attempt, and treated it conventionally. But Claude took so much pains about this, feeling it was one of his *fortes*, that I suppose no one can model a small wave better than he.

IV. He first set the pictorial sun in the pictorial heaven. (Vol. III., p. 337.) We will give him the credit of this, with no drawbacks.

V. He had hardly any knowledge of physical science (Vol. I., p. 80), and shows a peculiar incapacity of understanding the main point of a matter. (Vol. III., p. 341.) Connected with which incapacity is his want of harmony in expression. (Vol. II., p. 167.) (Compare, for illustration of this, the account of the picture of the Mill in the preface to Vol. I.)

§ 12. Such were the principal qualities of the leading painter of classical landscape, his effeminate softness, carrying him to dislike all evidences of toil, or distress, or terror, and to delight in the calm formalities which mark the school.

Although he often introduces romantic incidents and

mediæval as well as Greek or Roman personages, his
landscape is always in the true sense classic—everything
being "elegantly" (selectingly or tastefully), not passionately, treated. The absence of indications of rural labour,
of hedges, ditches, haystacks, ploughed fields, and the like :
the frequent occurrence of ruins of temples, or masses of
unruined palaces ; and the graceful wildness of growth in
his trees, are the principal sources of the "elevated" character which so many persons feel in his scenery.

There is no other sentiment traceable in his work than
this weak dislike to entertain the conception of toil or
suffering. Ideas of relation, in the true sense, he has
none ; nor ever makes an effort to conceive an event in
its probable circumstances, but fills his foregrounds with
decorative figures, using commonest conventionalism to
indicate the subject he intends. We may take two examples, merely to show the general character of such
designs of his.

§ 13. 1. St. George and the Dragon.

The scene is a beautiful opening in woods by a river
side, a pleasant fountain springs on the right, and the
usual rich vegetation covers the foreground. The dragon
is about the size of ten bramble leaves, and is being killed
by the remains of a lance, barely the thickness of a walking-
stick, in his throat, curling his tail in a highly offensive
and threatening manner. St. George, notwithstanding, on
a prancing horse, brandishes his sword, at about thirty
yards' distance from the offensive animal.

A semicircular shelf of rocks encircles the foreground,
by which the theatre of action is divided into pit and
boxes. Some women and children having descended
unadvisedly into the pit, are helping each other out of
it again, with marked precipitation. A prudent person
of rank has taken a front seat in the boxes,—crosses his
legs, leans his head on his hand, and contemplates the
proceedings with the air of a connoisseur. Two attendants
stand in graceful attitudes behind him, and two more walk
away under the trees, conversing on general subjects.

§ 14. 2. Worship of the Golden Calf.

The scene is nearly the same as that of the St. George ;

but in order better to express the desert of Sinai, the river is much larger, and the trees and vegetation softer. Two people, uninterested in the idolatrous ceremonies, are rowing in a pleasure boat on the river. The calf is about sixteen inches long (perhaps, we ought to give Claude credit for remembering that it was made of ear-rings, though he might as well have inquired how large Egyptian ear-rings were). Aaron has put it on a handsome pillar, under which five people are dancing, and twenty-eight, with several children, worshipping. Refreshments for the dancers are provided in four large vases under a tree on the left, presided over by a dignified person holding a dog in a leash. Under the distant group of trees appears Moses, conducted by some younger personage (Nadab or Abihu). This younger personage holds up his hands, and Moses, in the way usually expected of him, breaks the tables of the law, which are as large as an ordinary octavo volume.

§ 15. I need not proceed farther, for any reader of sense or ordinary powers of thought can thus examine the subjects of Claude, one by one, for himself. We may quit him with these few final statements concerning him.

The admiration of his works was legitimate, so far as it regarded their sunlight effects and their graceful details. It was base, in so far as it involved irreverence both for the deeper powers of nature, and carelessness as to conception of subject. Large admiration of Claude is wholly impossible in any period of national vigour in art. He may by such tenderness as he possesses, and by the very fact of his banishing painfulness, exercise considerable influence over certain classes of minds; but this influence is almost exclusively hurtful to them.

§ 16. Nevertheless, on account of such small sterling qualities as they possess, and of their general pleasantness, as well as their importance in the history of art, genuine Claudes must always possess a considerable value, either as drawing-room ornaments or museum relics. They may be ranked with fine pieces of china manufacture, and other agreeable curiosities, of which the price depends on the rarity rather than the merit, yet always on a merit of a certain low kind.

§ 17. The other characteristic master of classical landscape is Nicolo Poussin.

I named Claude first, because the forms of scenery he has represented are richer and more general than Poussin's; but Poussin has a far greater power, and his landscapes, though more limited in material, are incomparably nobler than Claude's. It would take considerable time to enter into accurate analysis of Poussin's strong but degraded mind; and bring us no reward, because whatever he has done has been done better by Titian. His peculiarities are, without exception, weaknesses, induced in a highly intellectual and inventive mind by being fed on medals, books, and bassi-relievi instead of nature, and by the want of any deep sensibility. His best works are his Bacchanalian revels, always brightly wanton and wild, full of frisk and fire; but they are coarser than Titian's, and infinitely less beautiful. In all minglings of the human and brutal character he leans on the bestial, yet with a sternly Greek severity of treatment. This restraint, peculiarly classical, is much too manifest in him; for, owing to his habit of never letting himself be free, he does nothing as well as it ought to be done, rarely even as well as he can himself do it; and his best beauty is poor, incomplete, and characterless, though refined. The Nymph pressing the honey in the "Nursing of Jupiter," and the Muse leaning against the tree, in the "Inspiration of Poet" (both in the Dulwich Gallery), appear to me examples of about his highest reach in this sphere.

§ 18. His want of sensibility permits him to paint frightful subjects, without feeling any true horror: his pictures of the Plague, the Death of Polydectes, etc., are thus ghastly in incident, sometimes disgusting, but never impressive. The prominence of the bleeding head in the Triumph of David marks the same temper. His battle pieces are cold and feeble; his religious subjects wholly nugatory, they do not excite him enough to develop even his ordinary powers of invention. Neither does he put much power into his landscape when it becomes principal;

the best pieces of it occur in fragments behind his figures. Beautiful vegetation, more or less ornamental in character, occurs in nearly all his mythological subjects, but his pure landscape is notable only for its dignified reserve; the great squareness and horizontality of its masses, with lowness of tone, giving it a deeply meditative character. His Deluge might be much depreciated, under this head of ideas of relation, but it is so uncharacteristic of him that I pass it by. Whatever power this lowness of tone, light in the distance, etc., give to his landscape, or to Gaspar's (compare Vol. II., Chapter on Infinity, § 12), is in both conventional and artificial.

I have nothing, therefore, to add farther, here, to what was said of him in Vol. I. (p. 95); and, as no other older masters of the classical landscape are worth any special note, we will pass on at once to a school of humbler but more vital power.

CHAPTER VI

RUBENS AND CUYP

§ 1. The examination of the causes which led to the final departure of the religious spirit from the hearts of painters, would involve discussion of the whole scope of the Reformation on the minds of persons unconcerned directly in its progress. This is of course impossible.

One or two broad facts only can be stated, which the reader may verify, if he pleases, by his own labour. I do not give them rashly.

§ 2. The strength of the Reformation lay entirely in its being a movement towards purity of practice.

The Catholic priesthood was hostile to it in proportion to the degree in which they had been false to their own principles of moral action, and had become corrupt or worldly in heart.

The Reformers indeed cast out many absurdities, and demonstrated many fallacies, in the teaching of the Roman Catholic Church. But they themselves introduced errors, which rent the ranks, and finally arrested the march of the Reformation, and which paralyze the Protestant Church to this day. Errors of which the fatality was increased by the controversial bent which lost accuracy of meaning in force of declamation, and turned expressions, which ought to be used only in retired depth of thought, into phrases of custom, or watchwords of attack. Owing to which habits of hot, ingenious, and unguarded controversy, the Reformed Churches themselves soon forgot the meaning of the word which, of all words, was oftenest in their mouths. They forgot that πίστις is a derivative of πείθομαι, not of πιστεύω, and that " fides," closely connected with " fio " on one side, and with "confido" on the other, is but distantly related to "credo." [1]

§ 3. By whatever means, however, the reader may himself be disposed to admit, the Reformation *was* arrested; and got itself shut up into chancels of cathedrals in England (even those, generally too large for it), and into conventicles everywhere else.   Then rising between the infancy of Reformation, and the palsy of Catholicism;—between a new shell of half-built religion on one side, daubed with untempered mortar, and a falling ruin of out-worn religion on the other, lizard-crannied, and ivy-grown;—rose, on its independent foundation, the faithless and materialized mind of modern Europe — ending in the rationalism of Germany, the polite formalism of England, the careless blasphemy of France, and the helpless sensualities of Italy; in the midst of which, steadily advancing science, and the charities of more and more widely extended peace, are preparing the way for a Christian Church, which shall depend neither on ignorance for its continuance, nor on controversy for its progress, but shall reign at once in light and love.

§ 4. The whole body of painters (such of them as were left,) necessarily fell into the rationalistic chasm.   The Evangelicals despised the arts, while the Roman Catholics were effete or insincere, and could not retain influence over men of strong reasoning power.

The painters could only associate frankly with men of the world, and themselves became men of the world.   Men, I mean, having no belief in spiritual existences, no interests or affections beyond the grave.

§ 5. Not but that they still painted scriptural subjects. Altar-pieces were wanted occasionally, and pious patrons sometimes commissioned a cabinet Madonna.   But there

---

[1] None of our present forms of opinion are more curious than those which have developed themselves from this verbal carelessness.   It never seems to strike any of our religious teachers, that if a child has a father living, it either *knows* it has a father, or does not : it does not "believe" it has a father.   We should be surprised to see an intelligent child standing at its garden gate, crying out to the passers-by : "I believe in my father, because he built this house;" as logical people proclaim that they believe in God, because He must have made the world.

is just this difference between the men of this modern period, and the Florentines or Venetians—that whereas the latter never exert themselves fully except on a sacred subject, the Flemish and Dutch masters are always languid unless they are profane. Leonardo is only to be seen in the Cena; Titian only in the Assumption; but Rubens only in the battle of the Amazons, and Vandyck only at court.

§ 6. Altar-pieces, when wanted, of course either of them will supply as readily as anything else. Virgins in blue,[1] or St. Johns in red,[2] as many as you please. Martyrdoms also, by all means : Rubens especially delights in these. St. Peter, head downwards,[3] is interesting anatomically ; writhings of impenitent thieves, and bishops having their tongues pulled out, display our powers to advantage, also.[4] Theological instruction, if required : "Christ armed with thunder, to destroy the world, spares it at the intercession of St. Francis." [5] Last Judgments even, quite Michael-Angelesque, rich in twistings of limbs, with spiteful biting, and scratching ; and fine aerial effects in smoke of the pit.[6]

§ 7. In all this, however, there is not a vestige of religious feeling or reverence. We have even some visible difficulty in meeting our patron's pious wishes. Daniel in the lion's den is indeed an available subject, but duller than a lion hunt ; and Mary of Nazareth must be painted if an order come for her ; but (says polite Sir Peter), Mary of Medicis, or Catherine, her bodice being fuller, and better embroidered, would, if we might offer a suggestion, probably give greater satisfaction.

§ 8. No phenomenon in human mind is more extra-ordinary than the junction of this cold and worldly temper with great rectitude of principle, and tranquil kindness of heart. Rubens was an honourable and entirely well-intentioned man, earnestly industrious, simple and temperate in habits of life, high-bred, learned and discreet. His affection for his mother was great ; his generosity to contemporary artists unfailing. He is a healthy, worthy, kind-hearted, courtly-phrased—Animal—without any clearly

---

[1] Düsseldorf.   [2] Antwerp.   [3] Cologne.   [4] Brussels.
[5] Brussels.   [6] Munich.

perceptible traces of a soul, except when he paints his
children. Few descriptions of pictures could be more
ludicrous in their pure animalism than those which he gives
of his own. " It is a subject," he writes to Sir D. Carleton,
" neither sacred nor profane, although taken from Holy
Writ, namely, Sarah in the act of scolding Hagar, who,
pregnant, is leaving the house in a feminine and graceful
manner, assisted by the Patriarch Abram." (What a graceful apology, by the way, instantly follows, for not having
finished the picture himself.) " I have engaged, as is my
custom, a very skilful man in his pursuit to finish the
landscapes, solely to augment the enjoyment of Y. E. ! "[1]

Again, in priced catalogue,—

" 50 florins each.—The Twelve Apostles, with a Christ.
Done by my scholars, from originals by my own hand,
each having to be retouched by my hand throughout.

" 600 florins.—A picture of Achilles clothed as a
woman ; done by the best of my scholars, and the whole
retouched by my hand : a most brilliant picture, and full
of many beautiful young girls."

§ 9. Observe, however, Rubens is always entirely honourable in his statements of what is done by himself and what
not. He is religious too, after his manner ; hears mass
every morning, and perpetually uses the phrase " by the
grace of God," or some other such, in writing of any
business he takes in hand ; but the tone of his religion
may be determined by one fact.

We saw how Veronese painted himself and his family,
as worshipping the Madonna.

Rubens has also painted himself and his family in an
equally elaborate piece. But they are not *worshipping* the
Madonna. They are *performing* the Madonna, and her
saintly entourage. His favourite wife " en Madonne ; "
his youngest boy " as Christ ; " his father-in-law (or father,
it matters not which) " as Simeon ; " another elderly relation, with a beard, " as St. Jerome ; " and he himself " as
St. George."

---

[1] Original Papers relating to Rubens ; edited by W. Sainsbury.
London, 1859 : page 39. Y. E. is the person who commissioned the
picture.

§ 10. Rembrandt has also painted (it is, on the whole, his greatest picture, so far as I have seen) himself and his wife in a state of ideal happiness. He sits at supper with his wife on his knee, flourishing a glass of champagne, with a roast peacock on the table.

The Rubens is in the Church of St. James at Antwerp; the Rembrandt at Dresden—marvellous pictures, both. No more precious works by either painter exist. Their hearts, such as they have, are entirely in them; and the two pictures, not inaptly, represent the Faith and Hope of the 17th century. We have to stoop somewhat lower, in order to comprehend the pastoral and rustic scenery of Cuyp and Teniers, which must yet be held as forming one group with the historical art of Rubens, being connected with it by Rubens' pastoral landscape. To these, I say, we must stoop lower; for they are destitute, not of spiritual character only, but of spiritual thought.

Rubens often gives instructive and magnificent allegory; Rembrandt, pathetic or powerful fancies, founded on real scripture reading, and on his interest in the picturesque character of the Jew. And Vandyck, a graceful dramatic rendering of received scriptural legends.

But in the pastoral landscape we lose, not only all faith in religion, but all remembrance of it. Absolutely now at last we find ourselves without sight of God in all the world.

§ 11. So far as I can hear or read, this is an entirely new and wonderful state of things achieved by the Hollanders. The human being never got wholly quit of the terror of spiritual being before. Persian, Egyptian, Assyrian, Hindoo, Chinese, all kept some dim, appalling record of what they called "gods." Farthest savages had—and still have—their Great Spirit, or, in extremity, their feather-idols, large-eyed; but here in Holland we have at last got utterly done with it all. Our only idol glitters dimly, in tangible shape of a pint pot, and all the incense offered thereto, comes out of a small censer or bowl at the end of a pipe. "Of deities or virtues, angels, principalities, or powers, in the name of our ditches, no more. Let us have cattle, and market vegetables."

This is the first and essential character of the Holland landscape art. Its second is a worthier one; respect for rural life.

§ 12. I should attach greater importance to this rural feeling, if there were any true humanity in it, or any feeling for beauty. But there is neither. No incidents of this lower life are painted for the sake of the incidents, but only for the effects of light. You will find that the best Dutch painters do not care about the people, but about the lustres on them. Paul Potter, their best herd and cattle painter, does not care even for sheep, but only for wool; regards not cows, but cowhide. He attains great dexterity in drawing tufts and locks, lingers in the little parallel ravines and furrows of fleece that open across sheep's backs as they turn; is unsurpassed in twisting a horn or pointing a nose; but he cannot paint eyes, nor perceive any condition of an animal's mind, except its desire of grazing. Cuyp can, indeed, paint sunlight, the best that Holland's sun can show; he is a man of large natural gift, and sees broadly, nay, even seriously; finds out—a wonderful thing for men to find out in those days —that there are reflections in water, and that boats require often to be painted upside down. A brewer by trade, he feels the quiet of a summer afternoon, and his work will make you marvellously drowsy. It is good for nothing else that I know of; strong; but unhelpful and unthoughtful. Nothing happens in his pictures, except some indifferent person's asking the way of somebody else, who, by his cast of countenance, seems not likely to know it. For farther entertainment perhaps a red cow and a white one; or puppies at play, not playfully; the man's heart not going even with the puppies. Essentially he sees nothing but the shine on the flaps of their ears.

§ 13. Observe always, the fault lies not in the thing's being little, or the incident being slight. Titian could have put issues of life and death into the face of a man asking the way; nay, into the back of him, if he had so chosen. He has put a whole scheme of dogmatic theology into a row of bishop's backs at the Louvre. And for dogs, Velasquez has made some of them nearly as grand as his surly kings.

Into the causes of which grandeur we must look a little, with respect not only to these puppies, and grey horses, and cattle of Cuyp, but to the hunting pieces of Rubens and Snyders. For closely connected with the Dutch rejection of motives of spiritual interest, is the increasing importance attached by them to animals, seen either in the chase or in agriculture; and to judge justly of the value of this animal painting, it will be necessary for us to glance at that of earlier times.

§ 14. And first of the animals which have had more influence over the human soul, in its modern life, than ever Apis or the crocodile had over Egyptian — the dog and horse. I stated, in speaking of Venetian religion, that the Venetians always introduced the dog as a contrast to the high aspects of humanity. They do this, not because they consider him the basest of animals, but the highest—the connecting link between men and animals; in whom the lower forms of really human feeling may be best exemplified, such as conceit, gluttony, indolence, petulance. But they saw the noble qualities of the dog, too;—all his patience, love, and faithfulness; therefore Veronese, hard as he is often on lap-dogs, has painted one great heroic poem on the dog.

§ 15. Two mighty brindled mastiffs, and beyond them, darkness. You scarcely see them at first, against the gloomy green. No other sky for them — poor things. They are gray themselves, spotted with black all over; their multitudinous doggish vices may not be washed out of them,—are in grain of nature. Strong thewed and sinewed, however, — no blame on them as far as bodily strength may reach; their heads coal-black, with drooping ears and fierce eyes, bloodshot a little. Wildest of beasts perhaps they would have been, by nature. But between them stands the spirit of their human love, dove-winged and beautiful, the resistless Greek boy, golden quivered; his glowing breast and limbs the only light upon the sky,— purple and pure. He has cast his chain about the dogs' necks, and holds it in his strong right hand, leaning proudly a little back from them. They will never break loose.

§ 16. This is Veronese's highest, or spiritual view of the

dog's nature. He can only give this when looking at the creature alone. When he sees it in company with men, he subdues it, like an inferior light in presence of the sky; and generally then gives it a merely brutal nature, not insisting even on its affection. It is thus used in the Marriage in Cana to symbolize gluttony. That great picture I have not yet had time to examine in all its bearings of thought; but the chief purpose of it is, I believe, to express the pomp and pleasure of the world, pursued without thought of the presence of Christ; therefore the Fool with the bells is put in the centre, immediately underneath the Christ; and in front are the couple of dogs in leash, one gnawing a bone. A cat lying on her back scratches at one of the vases which hold the wine of the miracle.

§ 17. In the picture of Susannah, her little pet dog is merely doing his duty, barking at the Elders. But in that of the Magdalen (at Turin) a noble piece of bye-meaning is brought out by a dog's help. On one side is the principal figure, the Mary washing Christ's feet; on the other, a dog has just come out from beneath the table (the dog under the table eating of the crumbs), and in doing so, has touched the robe of one of the Pharisees, thus making it unclean. The Pharisee gathers up his robe in a passion, and shows the hem of it to a bystander, pointing to the dog at the same time.

§ 18. In the Supper at Emmaus, the dog's affection is, however, fully dwelt upon. Veronese's own two little daughters are playing, on the hither side of the table, with a great wolf-hound, larger than either of them. One with her head down, nearly touching his nose, is talking to him—asking him questions it seems, nearly pushing him over at the same time:—the other raising her eyes, half archly, half dreamily,—some far-away thought coming over her,—leans against him on the other side, propping him with her little hand, laid slightly on his neck. He, all passive, and glad at heart, yielding himself to the pushing or sustaining hand, looks earnestly into the face of the child close to his; would answer her with the gravity of a senator, if so it might be:—can only look at her, and love her.

§ 19. To Velasquez and Titian dogs seem less interesting than to Veronese; they paint them simply as noble brown beasts, but without any special character; perhaps Velasquez' dogs are sterner and more threatening than the Venetian's, as are also his kings and admirals. This fierceness in the animal increases, as the spiritual power of the artist declines; and, with the fierceness, another character. One great and infallible sign of the absence of spiritual power is the presence of the slightest taint of obscenity. Dante marked this strongly in all his representations of demons, and as we pass from the Venetians and Florentines to the Dutch, the passing away of the soul-power is indicated by every animal becoming savage or foul. The dog is used by Teniers, and many other Hollanders, merely to obtain unclean jest; while by the more powerful men, Rubens, Snyders, Rembrandt, it is painted only in savage chase, or butchered agony. I know no pictures more shameful to humanity than the boar and lion hunts of Rubens and Snyders, signs of disgrace all the deeper, because the powers desecrated are so great. The painter of the village alehouse sign may, not dishonourably, paint the fox-hunt for the village squire; but the occupation of magnificent art-power in giving semblance of perpetuity to those bodily pangs which Nature has mercifully ordained to be transient, and in forcing us, by the fascination of its stormy skill, to dwell on that from which eyes of merciful men should instinctively turn away, and eyes of high-minded men scornfully, is dishonourable, alike in the power which it degrades, and the joy to which it betrays.

§ 20. In our modern treatment of the dog, of which the prevailing tendency is marked by Landseer, the interest taken in him is disproportionate to that taken in man, and leads to a somewhat trivial mingling of sentiment, or warping, by caricature; giving up the true nature of the animal for the sake of a pretty thought or pleasant jest. Neither Titian nor Velasquez ever jests; and though Veronese jests gracefully and tenderly, he never for an instant oversteps the absolute facts of nature. But the English painter looks for sentiment or jest primarily, and reaches both by a feebly romantic taint of fallacy, except in one or two simple and touching pictures, such as the Shepherd's Chief Mourner.

I was pleased by a little unpretending modern German picture at Düsseldorf, by E. Bosch, representing a boy carving a model of his sheep-dog in wood; the dog sitting on its haunches in front of him, watches the progress of the sculpture with a grave interest and curiosity, not in the least caricatured, but highly humorous. Another small picture, by the same artist, of a forester's boy being taught to shoot by his father,—the dog critically and eagerly watching the raising of the gun,—shows equally true sympathy.

§ 21. I wish I were able to trace any of the leading circumstances in the ancient treatment of the horse, but I have no sufficient data. Its function in the art of the Greeks is connected with all their beautiful fable philosophy; but I have not a tithe of the knowledge necessary to pursue the subject in this direction. It branches into questions relating to sacred animals, and Egyptian and Eastern mythology. I believe the Greek interest in *pure* animal character corresponded closely to our own, except that it is less sentimental, and either distinctly true or distinctly fabulous; not hesitating between truth and falsehood. Achilles' horses, like Anacreon's dove, and Aristophanes' frogs and birds, speak clearly out, if at all. They do not become feebly human by fallacies and exaggerations, but frankly and wholly.

Zeuxis' picture of the Centaur indicates, however, a more distinctly sentimental conception; and I suppose the Greek artists always to have fully appreciated the horse's fineness of temper and nervous constitution.[1] They seem, by the way, hardly to have done justice to the dog. My pleasure in the entire Odyssey is diminished because Ulysses gives not a word of kindness or of regret to Argus.

§ 22. I am still less able to speak of Roman treatment of the horse. It is very strange that in the chivalric ages he is despised; their greatest painter drawing him with ludicrous neglect. The Venetians, as was natural, painted

[1] "A single harsh word will raise a nervous horse's pulse ten beats a minute."—Mr. Rarey.

him little and ill; but he becomes important in the equestrian statues of the fifteenth and sixteenth centuries, chiefly,
I suppose, under the influence of Leonardo.

I am not qualified to judge of the merit of the equestrian
statues; but, in painting, I find that no real interest is
taken in the horse until Vandyck's time, he and Rubens
doing more for it than all previous painters put together.
Rubens was a good rider, and rode nearly every day, as I
doubt not, Vandyck also. Some notice of an interesting
equestrian picture of Vandyck's will be found in the next
chapter. The horse has never, I think, been painted
worthily again, since he died.[1] Of the influence of its
unworthy painting, and unworthy use, I do not at present
care to speak, noticing only that it brought about in England
the last degradations of feeling and of art. The Dutch,
indeed, banished all Deity from the earth; but I think
only in England has death-bed consolation been sought in
a fox's tail.[2]

I wish, however, the reader distinctly to understand that
the expressions of reprobation of field-sports which he will
find scattered through these volumes,—and which, in concluding them, I wish I had time to collect and farther
enforce,—refer only to the chase and the turf; that is to
say, to hunting, shooting, and horse-racing, but not to
athletic exercises. I have just as deep a respect for box-
ing, wrestling, cricketing, and rowing, as contempt of all
the various modes of wasting wealth, time, land, and energy
of soul, which have been invented by the pride and selfishness of men, in order to enable them to be healthy in
uselessness, and get quit of the burdens of their own lives,
without condescending to make them serviceable to others.

§ 23. Lastly, of cattle.

The period when the interest of men began to be
transferred from the ploughman to his oxen is very distinctly marked by Bassano. In him the descent is even

---

[1] John Lewis has made grand sketches of the horse, but has never,
so far as I know, completed any of them. Respecting his wonderful
engravings of wild animals, see my pamphlet on Pre-Raphaelitism
["On the Old Road," Vol. I., part i., p. 270].

[2] See "The Fox-hunter's Death-bed," a popular sporting print.

greater, being, accurately, from the Madonna to the Manger
—one of perhaps his best pictures (now, I believe, some-
where in the north of England), representing an adoration
of shepherds 'with nothing to adore, they and their herds
forming the subject, and the Christ " being supposed " at
the side. From that time cattle-pieces become frequent,
and gradually form a staple art commodity. Cuyp's are
the best; nevertheless, neither by him nor any one else
have I ever seen an entirely well-painted cow. All the
men who have skill enough to paint cattle nobly, disdain
them. The real influence of these Dutch cattle-pieces, in
subsequent art, is difficult to trace, and is not worth tracing.
They contain a certain healthy appreciation of simple
pleasure which I cannot look upon wholly without respect.
On the other hand, their cheap tricks of composition
degraded the entire technical system of landscape; and
their clownish and blunt vulgarities too long blinded us,
and continue, so far as in them lies, to blind us yet, to all
the true refinement and passion of rural life. There have
always been truth and depth of pastoral feeling in the works
of great poets and novelists; but never, I think, in painting,
until lately. The designs of J. C. Hook are, perhaps, the
only works of the kind in existence which deserve to be
mentioned in connection with the pastorals of Wordsworth
and Tennyson.

We must not, however, yet pass to the modern school,
having still to examine the last phase of Dutch design, in
which the vulgarities which might be forgiven to the truth
of Cuyp, and forgotten in the power of Rubens, became
unpardonable and dominant in the works of men who were
at once affected and feeble. But before doing this, we
must pause to settle a preliminary question, which is an
important and difficult one, and will need a separate
chapter;—namely, What is vulgarity itself?

CHAPTER VII

§ 1. Two great errors, colouring, or rather discolouring, severally, the minds of the higher and lower classes, have sown wide dissension, and wider misfortune, through the society of modern days. These errors are in our modes of interpreting the word "gentleman."

Its primal, literal, and perpetual meaning is "a man of pure race;" well bred, in the sense that a horse or dog is well bred.

The so-called higher classes, being generally of purer race than the lower, have retained the true idea, and the convictions associated with it; but are afraid to speak it out, and equivocate about it in public; this equivocation mainly proceeding from their desire to connect another meaning with it, and a false one;—that of "a man living in idleness on other people's labour;"—with which idea the term has nothing whatever to do.

The lower classes, denying vigorously, and with reason, the notion that a gentleman means an idler, and rightly feeling that the more any one works, the more of a gentleman he becomes, and is likely to become,—have nevertheless got little of the good they otherwise might, from the truth, because, with it, they wanted to hold a falsehood,—namely, that race was of no consequence. It being precisely of as much consequence in man as it is in any other animal.

§ 2. The nation cannot truly prosper till both these errors are finally got quit of. Gentlemen have to learn that it is no part of their duty or privilege to live on other people's toil. They have to learn that there is

no degradation in the hardest manual, or the humblest
servile, labour, when it is honest. But that there *is*
degradation, and that deep, in extravagance, in bribery, in
indolence, in pride, in taking places they are not fit for,
or in coining places for which there is no need. It does
not disgrace a gentleman to become an errand boy, or a day
labourer; but it disgraces him much to become a knave,
or a thief. And knavery is not the less knavery because it
involves large interests, nor theft the less theft because it
is countenanced by usage, or accompanied by failure in
undertaken duty. It is an incomparably less guilty form
of robbery to cut a purse out of a man's pocket, than to
take it out of his hand on the understanding that you are
to steer his ship up channel, when you do not know the
soundings.

§ 3. On the other hand, the lower orders, and all
orders, have to learn that every vicious habit and chronic
disease communicates itself by descent; and that by purity
of birth the entire system of the human body and soul
may be gradually elevated, or, by recklessness of birth,
degraded; until there shall be as much difference between
the well-bred and ill-bred human creature (whatever pains
be taken with their education) as between a wolf-hound
and the vilest mongrel cur. And the knowledge of this
great fact ought to regulate the education of our youth,
and the entire conduct of the nation.[1]

---

[1] We ought always in pure English to use the term " good breeding "
literally; and to say " good nurture " for what we usually mean by
good breeding. Given the race and make of the animal, you may
turn it to good or bad account; you may spoil your good dog or colt,
and make him as vicious as you choose, or break his back at once by
ill-usage; and you may, on the other hand, make something serviceable
and respectable out of your poor cur and colt if you educate them carefully; but ill-bred they will both of them be to their lives' end; and
the best you will ever be able to say of them is, that they are useful,
and decently behaved, ill-bred creatures. An error, which is associated
with the truth, and which makes it always look weak and disputable,
is the confusion of race with name; and the supposition that the blood
of a family must still be good, if its genealogy be unbroken and its
name not lost, though sire and son have been indulging age after age
in habits involving perpetual degeneracy of race. Of course it is equally
an error to suppose that, because a man's name is common, his blood

§ 4. Gentlemanliness, however, in ordinary parlance, must be taken to signify those qualities which are usually the evidence of high breeding, and which, so far as they can be acquired, it should be every man's effort to acquire ; or, if he has them by nature, to preserve and exalt. Vulgarity, on the other hand, will signify qualities usually characteristic of ill-breeding, which, according to his power, it becomes every person's duty to subdue. We have briefly to note what these are.

§ 5. A gentleman's first characteristic is that fineness of structure in the body, which renders it capable of the most delicate sensation ; and of structure in the mind which renders it capable of the most delicate sympathies —one may say, simply, "fineness of nature." This is, of course, compatible with heroic bodily strength and mental firmness ; in fact, heroic strength is not conceivable without such delicacy. Elephantine strength may drive its way through a forest and feel no touch of the boughs ; but the white skin of Homer's Atrides would have felt a bent rose-leaf, yet subdue its feeling in glow of battle, and behave itself like iron. I do not mean to call an elephant a vulgar animal ; but if you think about him carefully, you will find that his non-vulgarity consists in such gentleness as is possible to elephantine nature ; not in his insensitive hide, nor in his clumsy foot ; but in the way he will lift his foot if a child lies in his way ; and in his sensitive trunk, and still more sensitive mind, and capability of pique on points of honour.

§ 6. And, though rightness of moral conduct is ultimately the great purifier of race, the sign of nobleness is not in this rightness of moral conduct, but in sensitiveness. When the make of the creature is fine, its temptations are strong, as well as its perceptions ; it is liable to all kinds of impressions from without in their most violent

must be base ; since his family may have been ennobling it by pureness of moral habit for many generations, and yet may not have got any title, or other sign of nobleness, attached to their names. Nevertheless, the probability is always in favour of the race which has had acknowledged supremacy, and in which every motive leads to the endeavour to preserve its true nobility.

form; liable therefore to be abused and hurt by all kinds
of rough things which would do a coarser creature little
harm, and thus to fall into frightful wrong if its fate will have
it so. Thus David, coming of gentlest as well as royalist
race, of Ruth as well as of Judah, is sensitiveness through
all flesh and spirit; not that his compassion will restrain
him from murder when his terror urges him to it; nay, he
is driven to the murder all the more by his sensitiveness
to the shame which otherwise threatens him. But when
his own story is told under a disguise, though only a lamb
is now concerned, his passion about it leaves him no time
for thought. "The man shall die"—note the reason—
"because he had no pity." He is so eager and indignant
that it never occurs to him as strange that Nathan hides
the name. This is true gentleman. A vulgar man would
assuredly have been cautious, and asked who it was.

§ 7. Hence it will follow, that one of the probable signs
of high-breeding in men generally, will be their kindness and
mercifulness; these always indicating more or less fineness
of make in the mind; and miserliness and cruelty the contrary; hence that of Isaiah: "The vile person shall no
more be called liberal, nor the churl said to be bountiful."
But a thousand things may prevent this kindness from displaying or continuing itself; the mind of the man may be
warped so as to bear mainly on his own interests, and then
all his sensibilities will take the form of pride, or fastidious-
ness, or revengefulness; and other wicked, but not ungentle-
manly tempers; or, farther, they may run into utter
sensuality and covetousness, if he is bent on pleasure,
accompanied with quite infinite cruelty when the pride is
wounded or the passions are thwarted;—until your gentleman becomes Ezzelin, and your lady, the deadly Lucrece;
yet still gentleman and lady, quite incapable of making
anything else of themselves, being so born.

§ 8. A truer sign of breeding than mere kindness is
therefore sympathy;—a vulgar man may often be kind in a
hard way, on principle, and because he thinks he ought to
be; whereas, a highly-bred man, even when cruel, will be
cruel in a softer way, understanding and feeling what he
inflicts, and pitying his victim. Only we must carefully

remember that the quantity of sympathy a gentleman feels
can never be judged of by its outward expression, for
another of his chief characteristics is apparent reserve. I
say "apparent" reserve; for the sympathy is real, but the
reserve not: a perfect gentleman is never reserved, but
sweetly and entirely open, so far as it is good for others, or
possible, that he should be. In a great many respects it is
impossible that he should be open except to men of his own
kind. To them, he can open himself, by a word or syllable,
or a glance; but to men not of his kind he cannot open
himself, though he tried it through an eternity of clear
grammatical speech. By the very acuteness of his sympathy he knows how much of himself he can give to anybody; and he gives that much frankly;—would always be
glad to give more if he could, but is obliged, nevertheless,
in his general intercourse with the world, to be a somewhat
silent person; silence is to most people, he finds, less reserve than speech. Whatever he said, a vulgar man would
misinterpret: no words that he could use would bear the
same sense to the vulgar man that they do to him; if he
used any, the vulgar man would go away saying, "He had
said so and so, and meant so and so" (something assuredly
he never meant): but he keeps silence, and the vulgar man
goes away saying, "He didn't know what to make of him."
Which is precisely the fact, and the only fact which he is
anywise able to announce to the vulgar man concerning
himself.

§ 9. There is yet another quite as efficient cause of the
apparent reserve of a gentleman. His sensibility being
constant and intelligent, it will be seldom that a feeling
touches him, however acutely, but it has touched him in the
same way often before, and in some sort is touching him
always. It is not that he feels little, but that he feels
habitually; a vulgar man having some heart at the bottom
of him, if you can by talk or by sight fairly force the pathos
of anything down to his heart, will be excited about it and
demonstrative; the sensation of pity being strange to him
and wonderful. But your gentleman has walked in pity all
day long; the tears have never been out of his eyes; you
thought the eyes were bright only; but they were wet. You

tell him a sorrowful story, and his countenance does not
change; the eyes can but be wet still: he does not speak
neither, there being, in fact, nothing to be said, only something to be done; some vulgar person, beside you both,
goes away saying, "How hard he is!" Next day he hears
that the hard person has put good end to the sorrow he
said nothing about;—and then he changes his wonder, and
exclaims, "How reserved he is!"

§ 10. Self-command is often thought a characteristic of
high-breeding; and to a certain extent it is so, at least it is
one of the means of forming and strengthening character;
but it is rather a way of imitating a gentleman than a characteristic of him; a true gentleman has no need of self-
command; he simply feels rightly on all occasions; and
desiring to express only so much of his feeling as it is right
to express, does not need to command himself. Hence
perfect ease is indeed characteristic of him; but perfect ease
is inconsistent with self-restraint. Nevertheless gentlemen,
so far as they fail of their own ideal, need to command
themselves, and do so; while, on the contrary, to feel un-
wisely, and to be unable to restrain the expression of the
unwise feeling, is vulgarity; and yet even then, the vulgarity,
at its root, is not in the mistimed expression, but in the
unseemly feeling; and when we find fault with a vulgar
person for "exposing himself," it is not his openness, but
clumsiness; and yet more the want of sensibility to his own
failure, which we blame; so that still the vulgarity resolves
itself into want of sensibility. Also, it is to be noted that
great powers of self-restraint may be attained by very vulgar
persons when it suits their purposes.

§ 11. Closely, but strangely, connected with this openness
is that form of truthfulness which is opposed to cunning,
yet not opposed to falsity absolute. And herein is a distinction of great importance.

Cunning signifies especially a habit or gift of over-
reaching, accompanied with enjoyment and a sense of
superiority. It is associated with small and dull conceit,
and with an absolute want of sympathy or affection. Its essential connection with vulgarity may be at once exemplified
by the expression of the butcher's dog in Landseer's "Low

Life." Cruikshank's "Noah Claypole," in the illustrations to Oliver Twist, in the interview with the Jew, is, however, still more characteristic. It is the intensest rendering of vulgarity absolute and utter with which I am acquainted.[1]

The truthfulness which is opposed to cunning ought, perhaps, rather to be called the desire of truthfulness; it consists more in unwillingness to deceive than in not deceiving,—an unwillingness implying sympathy with and respect for the person deceived; and a fond observance of truth up to the possible point, as in a good soldier's mode of retaining his honour through a *ruse-de-guerre*. A cunning person seeks for opportunities to deceive; a gentleman shuns them. A cunning person triumphs in deceiving; a gentleman is humiliated by his success, or at least by so much of the success as is dependent merely on the falsehood, and not on his intellectual superiority.

§ 12. The absolute disdain of all lying belongs rather to Christian chivalry than to mere high-breeding; as connected merely with this latter, and with general refinement and courage, the exact relations of truthfulness may be best studied in the well-trained Greek mind. The Greeks believed that mercy and truth were co-relative virtues—cruelty and falsehood, co-relative vices. But they did not call necessary severity, cruelty; nor necessary deception, falsehood. It was needful sometimes to slay men, and sometimes to deceive them. When this had to be done, it should be done well and thoroughly; so that to direct a spear well to its mark, or a lie well to its end, was equally the accomplishment of a perfect gentleman. Hence, in the pretty diamond-cut-diamond scene between Pallas and Ulysses, when she receives him on the coast of Ithaca, the goddess laughs delightedly at her hero's good lying, and gives him her hand upon it;—showing herself then in her woman's form, as just a little more than his match.

[1] Among the reckless losses of the right service of intellectual power with which this century must be charged, very few are, to my mind, more to be regretted than that which is involved in its having turned to no higher purpose than the illustration of the career of Jack Sheppard, and of the Irish Rebellion, the great, grave (I use the words deliberately and with large meaning), and singular genius of Cruikshank.

" Subtle would he be, and stealthy, who should go beyond
thee in deceit, even were he a god, thou many-witted!
What! here in thine own land, too, wilt thou not cease
from cheating? Knowest thou not me, Pallas Athena,
maid of Jove, who am with thee in all thy labours, and
gave thee favour with the Phæacians, and keep thee, and
have come now to weave cunning with thee?" But how
completely this kind of cunning was looked upon as a part
of a man's power, and not as a diminution of faithfulness,
is perhaps best shown by the single line of praise in which
the high qualities of his servant are summed up by Chrem-
ulus in the Plutus—" Of all my house servants, I hold you
to be the faithfullest, and the greatest cheat (or thief)."

§ 13. Thus, the primal difference between honourable and
base lying in the Greek mind lay in honourable purpose.
A man who used his strength wantonly to hurt others was
a monster; so, also, a man who used his cunning wantonly
to hurt others. Strength and cunning were to be used
only in self-defence, or to save the weak, and then were
alike admirable. This was their first idea. Then the
second, and perhaps the more essential, difference between
noble and ignoble lying in the Greek mind, was that the
honourable lie—or, if we may use the strange, yet just,
expression, the true lie—knew and confessed itself for such
—was ready to take the full responsibility of what it did.
As the sword answered for its blow, so the lie for its snare.
But what the Greeks hated with all their heart was the false
lie;—the lie that did not know itself, feared to confess itself,
which slunk to its aim under a cloak of truth, and sought
to do liars' work, and yet not take liars' pay, excusing itself
to the conscience by quibble and quirk. Hence the great
expression of Jesuit principle by Euripides, " The tongue
has sworn, but not the heart," was a subject of execration
throughout Greece, and the satirists exhausted their arrows
on it—no audience was ever tired of hearing (τὸ Εὐριπίδειον
ἐκεῖνο) " that Euripidean thing " brought to shame.

§ 14. And this is especially to be insisted on in the
early education of young people. It should be pointed
out to them with continual earnestness that the essence
of lying is in deception, not in words: a lie may be told

by silence, by equivocation, by the accent on a syllable, by
a glance of the eye attaching a peculiar significance to a
sentence; and all these kinds of lies are worse and baser
by many degrees than a lie plainly worded; so that no
form of blinded conscience is so far sunk as that which
comforts itself for having deceived, because the deception
was by gesture or silence, instead of utterance; and, finally,
according to Tennyson's deep and trenchant line, "A lie
which is half a truth is ever the worst of lies."

§ 15. Although, however, ungenerous cunning is usually
so distinct an outward manifestation of vulgarity, that I
name it separately from insensibility, it is in truth only an
effect of insensibility, producing want of affection to others,
and blindness to the beauty of truth. The degree in which
political subtlety in men such as Richelieu, Machiavel, or
Metternich, will efface the gentleman, depends on the
selfishness of political purpose to which the cunning is
directed, and on the base delight taken in its use. The
command, "Be ye wise as serpents, harmless as doves,"
is the ultimate expression of this principle, misunderstood
usually because the word "wise" is referred to the intellectual power instead of the subtlety of the serpent. The
serpent has very little intellectual power, but according to
that which it has, it is yet, as of old, the subtlest of the
beasts of the field.

§ 16. Another great sign of vulgarity is also, when
traced to its root, another phase of insensibility, namely,
the undue regard to appearances and manners, as in the
households of vulgar persons, of all stations, and the
assumption of behaviour, language, or dress unsuited to
them, by persons in inferior stations of life. I say "undue" regard to appearances, because in the undueness
consists, of course, the vulgarity. It is due and wise in
some sort to care for appearances, in another sort undue
and unwise. Wherein lies the difference?

At first one is apt to answer quickly: the vulgarity is
simply in pretending to be what you are not. But that
answer will not stand. A queen may dress like a waiting-
maid,—perhaps succeed, if she chooses, in passing for one;
but she will not, therefore, be vulgar; nay, a waiting-maid

may dress like a queen, and pretend to be one, and yet need not be vulgar, unless there is inherent vulgarity in her. In Scribe's very absurd but very amusing *Reine d'un jour*, a milliner's girl sustains the part of a queen for a day. She several times amazes and disgusts her courtiers by her straightforwardness; and once or twice very nearly betrays herself to her maids of honour by an unqueenly knowledge of sewing; but she is not in the least vulgar, for she is sensitive, simple, and generous, and a queen could be no more.

§ 17. Is the vulgarity, then, only in trying to play a part you cannot play, so as to be continually detected? No; a bad amateur actor may be continually detected in his part, but yet continually detected to be a gentleman: a vulgar regard to appearances has nothing in it necessarily of hypocrisy. You shall know a man not to be a gentleman by the perfect and neat pronunciation of his words: but he does not pretend to pronounce accurately; he *does* pronounce accurately, the vulgarity is in the real (not assumed) scrupulousness.

§ 18. It will be found on farther thought, that a vulgar regard for appearances is, primarily, a selfish one, resulting not out of a wish to give pleasure (as a wife's wish to make herself beautiful for her husband), but out of an endeavour to mortify others, or attract for pride's sake;—the common "keeping up appearances" of society, being a mere selfish struggle of the vain with the vain. But the deepest stain of the vulgarity depends on this being done, not selfishly only, but stupidly, without understanding the impression which is really produced, nor the relations of importance between oneself and others, so as to suppose that their attention is fixed upon us, when we are in reality ciphers in their eyes—all which comes of insensibility. Hence pride simple is not vulgar (the looking down on others because of their true inferiority to us), nor vanity simple (the desire of praise), but conceit simple (the attribution to ourselves of qualities we have not) is always so. In cases of over-studied pronunciation, etc., there is insensibility, first, in the person's thinking more of himself than of what he is saying; and, secondly, in his not having

musical fineness of ear enough to feel that his talking is
uneasy and strained.

§ 19. Finally, vulgarity is indicated by coarseness of
language or manners, only so far as this coarseness has
been contracted under circumstances not necessarily producing it. The illiterateness of a Spanish or Calabrian
peasant is not vulgar, because they had never an opportunity of acquiring letters ; but the illiterateness of an
English school-boy is. So again, provincial dialect is not
vulgar ; but cockney dialect, the corruption, by blunted
sense, of a finer language continually heard, is so in a deep
degree ; and again, of this corrupted dialect, that is the
worst which consists, not in the direct or expressive alteration of the form of a word, but in an unmusical destruction
of it by dead utterance and bad or swollen formation of lip.
There is no vulgarity in—

> "Blythe, blythe, blythe was she,
>   Blythe was she, but and ben,
> And weel she liked a Hawick gill,
>   And leugh to see a tappit hen ;"

but much in Mrs. Gamp's inarticulate "bottle on the
chimley-piece, and let me put my lips to it when I am so
dispoged."

§ 20. So also of personal defects, those only are vulgar
which imply insensibility or dissipation.

There is no vulgarity in the emaciation of Don Quixote,
the deformity of the Black Dwarf, or the corpulence of
Falstaff ; but much in the same personal characters, as
they are seen in Uriah Heep, Quilp, and Chadband.

§ 21. One of the most curious minor questions in this
matter is respecting the vulgarity of excessive neatness,
complicating itself with inquiries into the distinction between base neatness, and the perfectness of good execution
in the fine arts. It will be found on final thought that
precision and exquisiteness of arrangement are always
noble ; but become vulgar only when they arise from an
equality (insensibility) of temperament, which is incapable
of fine passion, and is set ignobly, and with a dullard
mechanism, on accuracy in vile things. In the finest

Greek coins, the letters of the inscriptions are purposely
coarse and rude, while the relievi are wrought with inestimable care. But in an English coin, the letters are the
best done, and the whole is unredeemably vulgar. In a
picture of Titian's, an inserted inscription will be complete
in the lettering, as all the rest is ; because it costs Titian
very little more trouble to draw rightly than wrongly, and
in him, therefore, impatience with the letters would be
vulgar, as in the Greek sculptor of the coin, patience would
have been. For the engraving of a letter accurately[1] is
difficult work, and his time must have been unworthily
thrown away.

[1] There is this farther reason also : "Letters are always ugly things"
—(Seven Lamps, chap. iv. s. 9). Titian often wanted a certain quantity
of ugliness to oppose his beauty with, as a certain quantity of black to
oppose his colour. He could regulate the size and quantity of inscription as he liked ; and, therefore, made it as neat—that is, as effectively
ugly—as possible. But the Greek sculpture could not regulate either
size or quantity of inscription. Legible it must be, to common eyes,
and contain an assigned group of words. He had more ugliness than
he wanted, or could endure. There was nothing for it but to make
the letters themselves rugged and picturesque ; to give them, that is, a
certain quantity of organic variety.

I do not wonder at people sometimes thinking I contradict myself
when they come suddenly on any of the scattered passages, in which
I am forced to insist on the opposite practical applications of subtle
principles of this kind. It may amuse the reader, and be finally
serviceable to him in showing him how necessary it is to the right
handling of any subject, that these contrary statements should be
made, if I assemble here the principal ones I remember having brought
forward, bearing on this difficult point of precision in execution.

It would be well if you would first glance over the chapter on Finish
in the third volume ; and if, coming to the fourth paragraph, about
gentlemen's carriages, you have time to turn to Sydney Smith's Memoirs
and read his account of the construction of the "Immortal," it will
furnish you with an interesting illustration.

The general conclusion reached in that chapter being that finish, for
the sake of added truth, or utility, or beauty, is noble ; but finish, for
the sake of workmanship, neatness, or polish, ignoble,—turn to the
fourth chapter of the Seven Lamps, where you will find the Campanile
of Giotto given as the model and mirror of perfect architecture, just on
account of its exquisite completion. Also, in the next chapter, I ex-
pressly limit the delightfulness of rough and imperfect work to developing

§ 22. All the different impressions connected with neg-ligence or foulness depend, in like manner, on the degree of insensibility implied. Disorder in a drawing-room is vulgar, in an antiquary's study, not; the black battle-stain on a soldier's face is not vulgar, but the dirty face of a housemaid is.

And lastly, courage, so far as it is a sign of race, is peculiarly the mark of a gentleman or a lady: but it be-comes vulgar if rude or insensitive, while timidity is not vulgar, if it be a characteristic of race or fineness of make.

and unformed schools (p. 152, edition of 1880); then turn to the 170th page of the Stones of Venice, Vol. II., and you will find this directly contrary statement:—

"No good work whatever can be perfect, and the demand for per-fection is always a sign of a misunderstanding of the ends of art." . . . "The first cause of the fall of the arts in Europe was a relentless re-quirement of perfection" (p. 172). By reading the intermediate text, you will be put in possession of many good reasons for this opinion; and, comparing it with that just cited about the Campanile of Giotto, will be brought, I hope, into a wholesome state of not knowing what to think.

Then turn to p. 167, where the great law of finish is again maintained as strongly as ever: "Delicate finish (finish—that is to say, up to the point possible) is always desirable from the greatest masters, and is always given by them."—(Vol. II. chap. vi. § 19.)

And, lastly, if you look to § 19 of the chapter on the Early Renais-sance, Vol. III., you will find the profoundest respect paid to completion; and, at the close of that chapter, § 38, the principle is resumed very strongly. "As *ideals of executive perfection*, these palaces are most notable among the architecture of Europe, and the Rio façade of the Ducal palace, as an example of finished masonry in a vast building, is one of the finest things, not only in Venice, but in the world."

Now all these passages are perfectly true; and, as in much more serious matters, the essential thing for the reader is to receive their truth, however little he may be able to see their consistency. If truths of apparently contrary character are candidly and rightly received, they will fit themselves together in the mind without any trouble. But no truth maliciously received will nourish you, or fit with others. The clue of connection may in this case, however, be given in a word. Absolute finish is always right; finish, inconsistent with prudence and passion, wrong. The imperative demand for finish is ruinous, because it refuses better things than finish. The stopping short of the finish, which is honourably possible to human energy, is destructive on the other side, and not in less degree. Err, of the two, on the side of completion.

A fawn is not vulgar in being timid, nor a crocodile "gentle" because courageous.

§ 23. Without following the inquiry into farther detail,[1]

[1] In general illustration of the subject, the following extract from my private diary possesses some interest. It refers to two portraits which happened to be placed opposite to each other in the arrangement of a gallery; one, modern, of a (foreign) general on horseback at a review; the other, by Vandyck, also an equestrian portrait, of an ancestor of his family, whom I shall here simply call "the knight :"

"I have seldom seen so noble a Vandyck, chiefly because it is painted with less flightiness and flimsiness than usual, with a grand quietness and reserve—almost like Titian. The other is, on the contrary, as vulgar and base a picture as I have ever seen, and it becomes a matter of extreme interest to trace the cause of the difference.

"In the first place, everything the general and his horse wear is evidently just made. It has not only been cleaned that morning, but has been sent home from the tailor's in a hurry last night. Horse bridle, saddle housings, blue coat, stars and lace thereupon, cocked hat, and sword hilt—all look as if they had just been taken from a shopboard in Pall Mall; the irresistible sense of the coat having been brushed to perfection is the first sentiment which the picture summons. The horse has also been rubbed down all the morning, and shines from head to tail.

"The knight rides in a suit of rusty armour. It has evidently been polished also carefully, and gleams brightly here and there; but all the polishing in the world will never take the battle-dints and battle-darkness out of it. His horse is grey, not lustrous, but a dark, lurid grey. Its mane is deep and soft; part of it shaken in front over its forehead—the rest, in enormous masses of waving gold, six feet long, falls streaming on its neck, and rises in currents of softest light, rippled by the wind over the rider's armour. The saddle cloth is of a dim red, fading into leathern brown, gleaming with sparkles of obscure gold. When, after looking a little while at the soft mane of the Vandyck horse, we turn back to the general's, we are shocked by the evident coarseness of its hair, which hangs, indeed, in long locks over the bridle, but is stiff, crude, sharp pointed, coarsely coloured (a kind of buff); no fine drawing of nostril or neck can give any look of nobleness to the animal which carries such hair; it looks like a hobby horse with tow glued to it, which riotous children have half pulled or scratched out. The next point of difference is the isolation of Vandyck's figure, compared with the modern painter's endeavour to ennoble his by subduing others. The knight seems to be just going out of his castle gates; his horse rears as he passes their pillars; there is nothing behind, but the sky. But the general is reviewing a regiment; the ensign lowers his colours to him; he takes off his hat in

we may conclude that vulgarity consists in a deadness of the heart and body, resulting from prolonged, and especially from inherited conditions of "degeneracy," or literally return. All which reviewing and bowing is in its very nature ignoble, wholly unfit to be painted : a gentleman might as well be painted leaving his card on somebody. And, in the next place, the modern painter has thought to enhance his officer by putting the regiment some distance back and in the shade, so that the men look only about five feet high, being besides very ill painted to keep them in better subordination. One does not know whether most to despise the feebleness of the painter who must have recourse to such an artifice, or his vulgarity in being satisfied with it. I ought by the way, before leaving the point of dress, to have noted that the vulgarity of the painter is considerably assisted by the vulgarity of the costume itself. Not only is it base in being new, but base in that it cannot last to be old. If one wanted a lesson on the ugliness of modern costume, it could not be more sharply received than by turning from one to the other horseman. The knight wears steel plate armour, chased here and there with gold ; the delicate, rich, pointed lace collar falling on the embossed breastplate ; his dark hair flowing over his shoulders ; a crimson silk scarf fastened round his waist, and floating behind him ; buff boots, deep folded at the instep, set in silver stirrup. The general wears his hair cropped short ; blue coat, padded and buttoned ; blue trowsers and red stripe ; black shiny boots ; common saddler's stirrups ; cocked hat in hand, suggestive of absurd completion, when assumed.

"Another thing noticeable as giving nobleness to the Vandyck is its feminineness ; the rich, light silken scarf, the flowing hair, the delicate, sharp, though sunburnt features, and the lace collar, do not in the least diminish the manliness, but *add* feminineness. One sees that the knight is indeed a soldier, but not a soldier only ; that he is accomplished in all ways, and tender in all thoughts : while the general is represented as nothing but a soldier—and it is very doubtful if he is even that— one is sure, at a glance, that if he can do anything but put his hat off and on, and give words of command, the anything must, at all events, have something to do with the barracks ; that there is no grace, nor music, nor softness, nor learnedness, in the man's soul ; that he is made up of forms and accoutrements.

"Lastly, the modern picture is as bad painting as it is wretched conceiving ; and one is struck, in looking from it to Vandyck's, peculiarly by the fact that good work is always *enjoyed* work. There is not a touch of Vandyck's pencil but he seems to have revelled in— not grossly, but delicately—tasting the colour in every touch as an epicure would wine. While the other goes on daub, daub, daub, like a bricklayer spreading mortar—nay, with far less lightness of hand or lightness of spirit than a good bricklayer's—covering his canvas heavily

" un-racing ; "—gentlemanliness, being another word for an intense humanity. And vulgarity shows itself primarily in dulness of heart, not in rage or cruelty, but in inability to feel or conceive noble character or emotion. This is its essential, pure, and most fatal form. Dulness of bodily sense and general stupidity, with such forms of crime as peculiarly issue from stupidity, are its material manifestation.

§ 24. Two years ago, when I was first beginning to work out the subject, and chatting with one of my keenest-minded friends (Mr. Brett, the painter of the Val d'Aosta in the Exhibition of 1859), I casually asked him, "What is vulgarity?" merely to see what he would say, not supposing it possible to get a sudden answer. He thought for about a minute, then answered quietly, " It is merely one of the forms of Death." I did not see the meaning of the reply at the time ; but on testing it, found that it met every phase of the difficulties connected with the inquiry, and summed the true conclusion. Yet, in order to be complete, it ought to be made a distinctive as well as conclusive definition ; showing *what* form of death vulgarity is ; for death itself is not vulgar, but only death mingled with

and conceitedly at once, caring only but to catch the public eye with his coarse, presumptuous, ponderous, illiterate work."

Thus far my diary. In case it should be discovered by any one where these pictures are, it should be noted that the vulgarity of the modern one is wholly the painter's fault. It implies none in the general (except bad taste in pictures). The same painter would have made an equally vulgar portrait of Bayard. And as for taste in pictures, the general's was not singular. I used to spend much time before the Vandyck ; and among all the tourist visitors to the gallery, who were numerous, I never saw one look at it twice, but all paused in respectful admiration before the padded surtout. The reader will find, farther, many interesting and most valuable notes on the subject of nobleness and vulgarity in Emersons's Essays, and every phase of nobleness illustrated in Sir Kenelm Digby's " Broad Stone of Honour." The best help I have ever had—so far as help depended on the sympathy or praise of others in work which, year after year, it was necessary to pursue through the abuse of the brutal and the base—was given me, when this author, from whom I had first learned to love nobleness, introduced frequent reference to my own writings in his " Children's Bower."

life.   I cannot, however, construct a short-worded definition which will include all the minor conditions of bodily
degeneracy; but the term "deathful selfishness" will embrace all the most fatal and essential forms of mental
vulgarity.

vulgarity.

CHAPTER VIII

WOUVERMANS AND ANGELICO

§ 1. HAVING determined the general nature of vulgarity,
we are now able to close our view of the character of the
Dutch school.

It is a strangely mingled one, which I have the more
difficulty in investigating, because I have no power of
sympathy with it. However inferior in capacity, I can
enter measuredly into the feelings of Correggio or of
Titian; what they like, I like; what they disdain, I
disdain. Going lower down, I can still follow Salvator's
passion, or Albano's prettiness; and lower still, I can
measure modern German heroics, or French sensualities.
I see what the people mean,—know where they are, and
what they are. But no effort of fancy will enable me to lay
hold of the temper of Teniers, or Wouvermans, any more
than I can enter into the feelings of one of the lower
animals. I cannot see why they painted,—what they are
aiming at,—what they liked or disliked. All their life and
work is the same sort of mystery to me as the mind of my
dog when he rolls on carrion. He is a well enough conducted dog in other respects, and many of these Dutchmen
were doubtless very well-conducted persons: certainly they
learned their business well; both Teniers and Wouvermans
touch with a workmanly hand, such as we cannot see
rivalled now; and they seem never to have painted
indolently, but gave the purchaser his thorough money's
worth of mechanism, while the burgesses who bargained for
their cattle and card parties were probably more respectable
men than the princes who gave orders to Titian for nymphs,
and to Raphael for nativities. But whatever patient merit

or commercial value may be in Dutch labour, this at least is clear, that it is wholly insensitive.

The very mastery these men have of their business proceeds from their never really seeing the whole of anything, but only that part of it which they know how to do. Out of all nature they felt their function was to extract the grayness and shininess. Give them a golden sunset, a rosy dawn, a green waterfall, a scarlet autumn on the hills, and they merely look curiously into it to see if there is anything gray and glittering which can be painted on their common principles.

§ 2. If this, however, were their only fault, it would not prove absolute insensibility, any more than it could be declared of the makers of Florentine tables, that they were blind or vulgar, because they took out of nature only what could be represented in agate. A Dutch picture is, in fact, merely a Florentine table more finely touched; it has its regular ground of slate, and its mother-of-pearl and tinsel put in with equal precision; and perhaps the fairest view one can take of a Dutch painter, is that he is a respectable tradesman furnishing well-made articles in oil paint; but when we begin to examine the designs of these articles, we may see immediately that it is his inbred vulgarity, and not the chance of fortune, which has made him a tradesman, and kept him one;—which essential character of Dutch work, as distinguished from all other, may be best seen in that hybrid landscape, introduced by Wouvermans and Berghem. Of this landscape Wouvermans' is the most characteristic. It will be remembered that I called it "hybrid," because it strove to unite the attractiveness of every other school. We will examine the motives of one of the most elaborate Wouvermans existing—landscape with a hunting party, No. 208 in the Pinacothek of Munich.

§ 3. A large lake in the distance narrows into a river in the foreground; but the river has no current, nor has the lake either reflections or waves. It is a piece of gray slate table, painted with horizontal touches, and only explained to be water by boats upon it. Some of the figures in these are fishing (the corks of a net are drawn in bad perspective);

others are bathing, one man pulling his shirt over his ears, others are swimming. On the farther side of the river are some curious buildings, half villa, half ruin ; or rather ruin dressed. There are gardens at the top of them, with beautiful and graceful trellised architecture and wandering tendrils of vine. A gentleman is coming down from a door in the ruins to get into his pleasure-boat. His servant catches his dog.

§ 4. On the nearer side of the river, a bank of broken ground rises from the water's edge up to a group of very graceful and carefully studied trees, with a French-antique statue on a pedestal in the midst of them, at the foot of which are three musicians, and a well-dressed couple dancing ; their coach is in waiting behind. In the foreground are hunters. A richly and highly dressed woman with falcon on fist, the principal figure in the picture, is wrought with Wouvermans' best skill. A stouter lady rides into the water after a stag and hind, who gallop across the middle of the river without sinking. Two horsemen attend the two Amazons, of whom one pursues the game cautiously, but the other is thrown headforemost into the river, with a splash which shows it to be deep at the edge, though the hart and hind find bottom in the middle. Running footmen, with other dogs, are coming up, and children are sailing a toy-boat in the immediate foreground. The tone of the whole is dark and gray, throwing out the figures in spots of light, on Wouvermans' usual system. The sky is cloudy, and very cold.

§ 5. You observe that in this picture the painter has assembled all the elements which he supposes pleasurable. We have music, dancing, hunting, boating, fishing, bathing, and child-play, all at once. Water, wide and narrow ; architecture, rustic and classical ; trees also of the finest ; clouds, not ill-shaped. Nothing wanting to our Paradise : not even practical jest ; for to keep us always laughing, somebody shall be for ever falling with a splash into the Pison. Things proceed, nevertheless, with an oppressive quietude. The dancers are uninterested in the hunters, the hunters in the dancers ; the hirer of the pleasure-boat perceives neither hart nor hind ; the children are unconcerned at the hunter's fall; the bathers regard not the draught of fishes; the fishers fish among the bathers, without apparently anticipating any diminution in their haul.

§ 6. Let the reader ask himself, would it have been possible for the painter in any clearer way to show an absolute, clay-cold, ice-cold incapacity of understanding what a pleasure meant? Had he had as much heart as a minnow, he would have given some interest to the fishing; with the soul of a grasshopper, some spring to the dancing; had he half the will of a dog, he would have made some one turn to look at the hunt, or given a little fire to the dash down to the water's edge. If he had been capable of pensiveness, he would not have put the pleasure-boat under the ruin;—capable of cheerfulness, he would not have put the ruin above the pleasure-boat. Paralyzed in heart and brain, he delivers his inventoried articles of pleasure one by one to his ravenous customers; palate-less; gluttonous. "We cannot taste it. Hunting is not enough; let us have dancing. That's dull; now give us a jest, or what is life! The river is too narrow, let us have a lake; and, for mercy's sake, a pleasure-boat, or how can we spend another minute of this languid day! But what pleasure can be in a boat? let us swim; we see people always drest, let us see them naked."

§ 7. Such is the unredeemed, carnal appetite for mere sensual pleasure. I am aware of no other painter who consults it so exclusively, without one gleam of higher hope, thought, beauty, or passion.

As the pleasure of Wouvermans, so also is his war. That, however, is not hybrid, it is of one character only.

The best example I know is the great battle-piece with the bridge, in the gallery of Turin. It is said that when this picture, which had been taken to Paris, was sent back, the French offered twelve thousand pounds (300,000 francs) for permission to keep it. The report, true or not, shows the estimation in which the picture is held at Turin.

§ 8. There are some twenty figures in the mêlée whose faces can be seen (about sixty in the picture altogether), and of these twenty, there is not one whose face indicates courage or power; or anything but animal rage and cowardice; the latter prevailing always. Every one is fighting for his life, with the expression of a burglar defending himself at extremity against a party of policemen. There is the same terror, fury, and pain which a low thief would show on receiving a pistol-shot through his arm. Most of them appear to be fighting only to get away; the standard-bearer *is* retreating, but whether with the enemy's flag or his own I do not see; he slinks away with it, with reverted eye, as if he were stealing a pocket-handkerchief. The swordsmen cut at each other with clenched teeth and terrified eyes; they are too busy to curse each other; but one sees that the feelings they have could be expressed no otherwise than by low oaths. Far away, to the smallest figures in the smoke, and to one drowning under the distant arch of the bridge, all are wrought with a consummate skill in vulgar touch; there is no good painting, properly so called, anywhere, but of clever, dotty, sparkling, telling execution, as much as the canvas will hold, and much delicate gray and blue colour in the smoke and sky.

§ 9. Now, in order fully to feel the difference between this view of war, and a gentleman's, go, if possible, into our National Gallery, and look at the young Malatesta riding into the battle of Sant' Egidio (as he is painted by Paul Uccello). His uncle Carlo, the leader of the army, a grave man of about sixty, has just given orders for the knights to close: two have pushed forward with lowered lances, and the mêlée has begun only a few yards in front; but the young knight, riding at his uncle's side, has not yet put his helmet on, nor intends doing so yet. Erect he sits, and quiet, waiting for his captain's order to charge; calm as if he were at a hawking party, only more grave; his golden hair wreathed about his proud white brow, as about a statue's.

§ 10. "Yes," the thoughtful reader replies, "this may be pictorially very beautiful; but those Dutchmen were good fighters, and generally won the day; whereas, this very battle of Sant' Egidio, so calmly and bravely begun, was lost."

Indeed, it is very singular that unmitigated expressions of cowardice in battle should be given by the painters of so brave a nation as the Dutch. Not but that it is possible enough for a coward to be stubborn, and a brave man weak ; the one may win his battle by a blind persistence, and the other lose it by a thoughtful vacillation. Nevertheless, the want of all expression of resoluteness in Dutch battle-pieces remains, for the present, a mystery to me. In those of Wouvermans, it is only a natural development of his perfect vulgarity in all respects.

§ 11. I do not think it necessary to trace farther the evidences of insensitive conception in the Dutch school. I have associated the name of Teniers with that of Wouvermans in the beginning of this chapter, because Teniers is essentially the painter of the pleasures of the ale-house and card-table, as Wouvermans of those of the chase ; and the two are leading masters of the peculiar Dutch trick of white touch on gray or brown ground ; but Teniers is higher in reach and more honest in manner. Berghem is the real associate of Wouvermans in the hybrid school of landscape. But all three are alike insensitive ; that is to say, unspiritual or deathful, and that to the uttermost, in every thought,— producing, therefore, the lowest phase of possible art of a skilful kind. There are deeper elements in De Hooghe and Gerard Terburg ; sometimes expressed with superb quiet painting by the former ; but the whole school is inherently mortal to all its admirers ; having by its influence in England destroyed our perception of all purposes of painting, and throughout the north of the Continent effaced the sense of colour among artists of every rank.

We have, last, to consider what recovery has taken place from the paralysis to which the influence of this Dutch art had reduced us in England seventy years ago. But, in closing my review of older art, I will endeavour to illustrate, by four simple examples, the main directions of its spiritual power, and the cause of its decline.

§ 12. The frontispiece of this volume is engraved[1] from an old sketch of mine, a pencil outline of the little Madonna by Angelico, in the Annunciation preserved in the sacristy of Santa Maria Novella. This Madonna has not, so far as I know, been engraved before, and it is one of the most characteristic of the Purist school. I believe through all

---

[1] [Reduced for this edition.]

my late work I have sufficiently guarded my readers from
over-estimating this school; but it is well to turn back to it
now, from the wholly carnal work of Wouvermans, in order
to feel its purity: so that, if we err, it may be on this side.
The opposition is the most accurate which I can set before
the student, for the technical disposition of Wouvermans,
in his search after delicate form and minute grace, much
resembles that of Angelico. But the thoughts of Wouvermans are wholly of this world. For him there is no heroism,
awe or mercy, hope, or faith. Eating and drinking, and
sleeping; rage and lust; the pleasures and distresses of the
debased body—from these, his thoughts, if so we may call
them, never for an instant rise or range.

§ 13. The soul of Angelico is in all ways the precise
reverse of this; habitually as incognizant of any earthly
pleasure as Wouvermans of any heavenly one. Both are
exclusive with absolute exclusiveness; — neither desiring
nor conceiving anything beyond their respective spheres.
Wouvermans lives under gray clouds, his lights come out as
spots. Angelico lives in an unclouded light: his shadows
themselves are colour; his lights are not the spots, but his
darks. Wouvermans lives in perpetual tumult—tramp of
horse—clash of cup—ring of pistol-shot. Angelico in perpetual peace. Not seclusion from the world. No shutting
out of the world is needful for him. There is nothing to
shut out. Envy, lust, contention, discourtesy, are to him
as though they were not; and the cloister walk of Fiesole
no penitential solitude, barred from the stir and joy of life,
but a possessed land of tender blessing, guarded from the
entrance of all but holiest sorrow. The little cell was as
one of the houses of heaven prepared for him by his Master.
"What need had it to be elsewhere? Was not the Val
d'Arno, with its olive woods in white blossom, paradise
enough for a poor monk? or could Christ be indeed in
heaven more than here? Was He not always with him?
Could he breathe or see, but that Christ breathed beside
him, and looked into his eyes? Under every cypress
avenue the angels walked; he had seen their white robes,
whiter than the dawn, at his bed-side, as he awoke in early
summer. They had sung with him, one on each side,

when his voice failed for joy at sweet vesper and matin
time; his eyes were blinded by their wings in the sunset,
when it sank behind the hills of Luni."

There may be weakness in this, but there is no baseness;
and while I rejoice in all recovery from monasticism which
leads to practical and healthy action in the world, I must,
in closing this work, severely guard my pupils from the
thought that sacred rest may be honourably exchanged for
selfish and mindless activity.

§ 14. In order to mark the temper of Angelico, by a
contrast of another kind, I give in Fig. 99 a facsimile of
one of the heads in Salvator's
etching of the Academy of Plato.
It is accurately characteristic of
Salvator, showing, by quite a
central type, his indignant, desolate, and degraded power. I
could have taken unspeakably
baser examples from others of
his etchings, but they would have
polluted my book, and been in
some sort unjust, representing
only the worst part of his work.
This head, which is as elevated

Fig. 99.

a type as he ever reaches, is assuredly debased enough;
and a sufficient image of the mind of the painter of Catiline
and the Witch of Endor.

§ 15. Then, in Fig. 100 (overleaf), you have also a central
type of the mind of Dürer. Complete, yet quaint; severely
rational and practical, yet capable of the highest imaginative religious feeling, and as gentle as a child's, it seemed to
be well represented by this figure of the old bishop, with
all the infirmities, and all the victory, of his life, written
on his calm, kind, and worldly face. He has been no
dreamer, nor persecutor, but a helpful and undeceivable
man; and by careful comparison of this conception with
the common kinds of episcopal ideal in modern religious
art, you will gradually feel how the force of Dürer is joined
with an unapproachable refinement, so that he can give
the most practical view of whatever he treats, without

the slightest taint or shadow of vulgarity. Lastly, the fresco of Giorgione, Plate **79**, which is as fair a type as I am able to give in any single figure, of the central Venetian art, will complete for us a series, sufficiently symbolical of the several ranks of art, from lowest to highest.[1] In Wouvermans (of whose work I suppose no example is needed, it being so generally known), we have the entirely carnal mind, —wholly versed in the material world, and incapable of conceiving any goodness or greatness whatsoever.

In Angelico, you have the entirely spiritual mind, wholly versed in the heavenly world, and incapable of conceiving any wickedness or vileness whatsoever.

In Salvator, you have an awakened conscience, and some spiritual power, contending with evil, but conquered by it, and brought into captivity to it.

In Dürer, you have a far purer conscience and higher spiritual power, yet, with some defect still in intellect, contending with evil, and nobly prevailing over it; yet retaining the marks of the contest, and never so entirely victorious as to conquer sadness.

In Giorgione, you have the same high spiritual power and practical sense; but now, with entirely perfect intellect, contending with evil; conquering it utterly, casting it away for ever, and rising beyond it into magnificence of rest.

---

[1] As I was correcting these pages, there was put into my hand a little work by a very dear friend—*Travels and Study in Italy*, by Charles Eliot Norton;—I have not yet been able to do more than glance at it ; but my impression is, that by carefully reading it, together with the essay by the same writer on the Vita Nuova of Dante, a more just estimate may be formed of the religious art of Italy than by the study of any other books yet existing. At least, I have seen none in which the tone of thought was at once so tender and so just.

I had hoped, before concluding this book, to have given it higher value by extracts from the works which have chiefly helped or guided me, especially from the writings of Helps, Lowell, and the Rev. A. J. Scott. But if I were to begin making such extracts, I find that I should not know, either in justice or affection, how to end.

Fig. 100.

Fig. 183.

CHAPTER IX

THE TWO BOYHOODS

§ 1. BORN half-way between the mountains and the sea—that young George of Castelfranco—of the Brave Castle:—Stout George they called him, George of Georges, so goodly a boy he was—Giorgione.

Have you ever thought what a world his eyes opened on—fair, searching eyes of youth? What a world of mighty life, from those mountain roots to the shore;—of loveliest life, when he went down, yet so young, to the marble city—and became himself as a fiery heart to it?

A city of marble, did I say? nay, rather a golden city, paved with emerald. For truly, every pinnacle and turret glanced or glowed, overlaid with gold, or bossed with jasper. Beneath, the unsullied sea drew in deep breathing, to and fro, its eddies of green wave. Deep-hearted, majestic, terrible as the sea,—the men of Venice moved in sway of power and war; pure as her pillars of alabaster, stood her mothers and maidens; from foot to brow, all noble, walked her knights; the low bronzed gleaming of sea-rusted armour shot angrily under their blood-red mantle-folds. Fearless, faithful, patient, impenetrable, implacable,—every word a fate—sate her senate. In hope and honour, lulled by flowing of wave around their isles of sacred sand, each with his name written and the cross graved at his side, lay her dead. A wonderful piece of world. Rather, itself a world. It lay along the face of the waters, no larger, as its captains saw it from their masts at evening, than a bar of sunset that could not pass away; but for its power, it must have seemed to them as if they were sailing in the expanse of heaven, and this

a great planet, whose orient edge widened through ether.
A world from which all ignoble care and petty thoughts
were banished, with all the common and poor elements
of life. No foulness, nor tumult, in those tremulous streets,
that filled, or fell, beneath the moon; but rippled music
of majestic change, or thrilling silence. No weak walls
could rise above them; no low-roofed cottage, nor straw-
built shed. Only the strength as of rock, and the finished
setting of stones most precious. And around them, far as
the eye could reach, still the soft moving of stainless waters,
proudly pure; as not the flower, so neither the thorn nor
the thistle, could grow in the glancing fields. Ethereal
strength of Alps, dreamlike, vanishing in high procession
beyond the Torcellan shore; blue islands of Paduan hills,
poised in the golden west. Above, free winds and fiery
clouds ranging at their will;—brightness out of the north,
and balm from the south, and the stars of the evening and
morning clear in the limitless light of arched heaven and
circling sea.

Such was Giorgione's school—such Titian's home.

§ 2. Near the south-west corner of Covent Garden, a
square brick pit or well is formed by a close-set block of
houses, to the back windows of which it admits a few rays
of light. Access to the bottom of it is obtained out of
Maiden Lane, through a low archway and an iron gate;
and if you stand long enough under the archway to
accustom your eyes to the darkness you may see on the
left hand a narrow door, which formerly gave quiet access
to a respectable barber's shop, of which the front window,
looking into Maiden Lane, is still extant, filled, in this year
(1860), with a row of bottles, connected, in some defunct
manner, with a brewer's business. A more fashionable
neighbourhood, it is said, eighty years ago than now—
never certainly a cheerful one—wherein a boy being born
on St. George's day, 1775, began soon after to take interest in the world of Covent Garden, and put to service
such spectacles of life as it afforded.

§ 3. No knights to be seen there, nor, I imagine, many
beautiful ladies; their costume at least disadvantageous,
depending much on incumbency of hat and feather, and

short waists; the majesty of men founded similarly on shoebuckles and wigs;—impressive enough when Reynolds will do his best for it; but not suggestive of much ideal delight to a boy.

"Bello ovile dov' io dormii agnello;" of things beautiful, besides men and women, dusty sunbeams up or down the street on summer mornings; deep furrowed cabbage-leaves at the greengrocer's; magnificence of oranges in wheelbarrows round the corner; and Thames' shore within three minutes' race.

§ 4. None of these things very glorious; the best, however, that England, it seems, was then able to provide for a boy of gift: who, such as they are, loves them—never, indeed, forgets them. The short waists modify to the last his visions of Greek ideal. His foregrounds had always a succulent cluster or two of greengrocery at the corners. Enchanted oranges gleam in Covent Gardens of the Hesperides; and great ships go to pieces in order to scatter chests of them on the waves. That mist of early sunbeams in the London dawn crosses, many and many a time, the clearness of Italian air; and by Thames' shore, with its stranded barges and glidings of red sail, dearer to us than Lucerne lake or Venetian lagoon,—by Thames' shore we will die.

§ 5. With such circumstance round him in youth, let us note what necessary effects followed upon the boy. I assume him to have had Giorgione's sensibility (and more than Giorgione's, if that be possible) to colour and form. I tell you farther, and this fact you may receive trustfully, that his sensibility to human affection and distress was no less keen than even his sense for natural beauty—heartsight deep as eyesight.

Consequently, he attaches himself with the faithfullest child-love to everything that bears an image of the place he was born in. No matter how ugly it is,—has it anything about it like Maiden Lane, or like Thames' shore? If so, it shall be painted for their sake. Hence, to the very close of life, Turner could endure ugliness which no one else, of the same sensibility, would have borne with for an instant. Dead brick walls, blank square windows, old

clothes, market-womanly types of humanity—anything fishy
and muddy, like Billingsgate or Hungerford Market, had
great attraction for him; black barges, patched sails, and
every possible condition of fog.

§ 6. You will find these tolerations and affections guiding
or sustaining him to the last hour of his life; the notablest
of all such endurances being that of dirt. No Venetian
ever draws anything foul; but Turner devoted picture after
picture to the illustration of effects of dinginess, smoke,
soot, dust, and dusty texture; old sides of boats, weedy
roadside vegetation, dung-hills, straw-yards, and all the soil-
ings and stains of every common labour.

And more than this, he not only could endure, but
enjoyed and looked for *litter*, like Covent Garden wreck
after the market. His pictures are often full of it, from
side to side; their foregrounds differ from all others in the
natural way that things have of lying about in them. Even
his richest vegetation, in ideal work, is confused; and he
delights in shingle, débris, and heaps of fallen stones. The
last words he ever spoke to me about a picture were in
gentle exultation about his St. Gothard : " that *litter* of
stones which I endeavoured to represent."

§ 7. The second great result of this Covent Garden
training was, understanding of and regard for the poor,
whom the Venetians, we saw, depised; whom, contrarily,
Turner loved, and more than loved—understood. He got
no romantic sight of them, but an infallible one, as he
prowled about the end of his lane, watching night effects
in the wintry streets; nor sight of the poor alone, but of
the poor in direct relations with the rich. He knew, in
good and evil, what both classes thought of, and how they
dealt with, each other.

Reynolds and Gainsborough, bred in country villages,
learned there the country boy's reverential theory of " the
squire," and kept it. They painted the squire and the
squire's lady as centres of the movements of the universe,
to the end of their lives. But Turner perceived the
younger squire in other aspects about his lane, occurring
prominently in its night scenery, as a dark figure, or one
of two, against the moonlight. He saw also the working

of city commerce, from endless warehouse, towering over
Thames, to the back shop in the lane, with its stale
herrings—highly interesting these last; one of his father's
best friends, whom he often afterwards visited affection-
ately at Bristol, being a fishmonger and glue-boiler; which
gives us a friendly turn of mind towards herring-fishing,
whaling, Calais poissardes, and many other of our choicest
subjects in after-life; all this being connected with that
mysterious forest below London Bridge on one side; and,
on the other, with these masses of human power and
national wealth which weigh upon us, at Covent Garden
here, with strange compression, and crush us into narrow
Hand Court.

§ 8. "That mysterious forest below London Bridge "—
better for the boy than wood of pine, or grove of myrtle.
How he must have tormented the watermen, beseeching
them to let him crouch anywhere in the bows, quiet
as a log, so only that he might get floated down there
among the ships, and round and round the ships, and
with the ships, and by the ships, and under the ships,
staring, and clambering;—these the only quite beautiful
things he can see in all the world, except the sky; but
these, when the sun is on their sails, filling or falling,
endlessly disordered by sway of tide and stress of anchor-
age, beautiful unspeakably; which ships also are inhabited
by glorious creatures—red-faced sailors, with pipes, appearing over the gunwales, true knights, over their castle para-
pets—the most angelic beings in the whole compass of
London world.   And Trafalgar happening long before we
can draw ships, we, nevertheless, coax all current stories
out of the wounded sailors, do our best at present to show
Nelson's funeral streaming up the Thames; and vow that
Trafalgar shall have its tribute of memory some day. Which,
accordingly, is accomplished—once, with all our might, for
its death; twice, with all our might, for its victory; thrice,
in pensive farewell to the old Téméraire, and with it, to
that order of things.

§ 9. Now this fond companying with sailors must have
divided his time, it appears to me, pretty equally between
Covent Garden and Wapping (allowing for incidental

excursions to Chelsea on one side, and Greenwich on the other), which time he would spend pleasantly, but not magnificently, being limited in pocket-money, and leading a kind of " Poor-Jack " life on the river.

In some respects, no life could be better for a lad. But it was not calculated to make his ear fine to the niceties of language, nor form his moralities on an entirely regular standard. Picking up his first scraps of vigorous English chiefly at Deptford and in the markets, and his first ideas of female tenderness and beauty among nymphs of the barge and the barrow,—another boy might, perhaps, have become what people usually term " vulgar." But the original make and frame of Turner's mind being not vulgar, but as nearly as possible a combination of the minds of Keats and Dante, joining capricious waywardness, and intense openness to every fine pleasure of sense, and hot defiance of formal precedent, with a quite infinite tenderness, generosity, and desire of justice and truth—this kind of mind did not become vulgar, but very tolerant of vulgarity, even fond of it in some forms ; and on the outside, visibly infected by it, deeply enough ; the curious result, in its combination of elements, being to most people wholly incomprehensible. It was as if a cable had been woven of blood-crimson silk, and then tarred on the outside. People handled it, and the tar came off on their hands ; red gleams were seen through the black underneath, at the places where it had been strained. Was it ochre ?—said the world—or red lead ?

§ 10. Schooled thus in manners, literature, and general moral principles at Chelsea and Wapping, we have finally to inquire concerning the most important point of all. We have seen the principal differences between this boy and Giorgione, as respects sight of the beautiful, understanding of poverty, of commerce, and of order of battle ; then follows another cause of difference in our training— not slight,—the aspect of religion, namely, in the neighbourhood of Covent Garden. I say the aspect ; for that was all the lad could judge by. Disposed, for the most part, to learn chiefly by his eyes, in this special matter he finds there is really no other way of learning. His father taught him "to lay one penny upon another." Of mother's teaching, we hear of none; of parish pastoral teaching, the reader may guess how much.

§ 11. I chose Giorgione rather than Veronese to help me in carrying out this parallel; because I do not find in Giorgione's work any of the early Venetian monarchist element. He seems to me to have belonged more to an abstract contemplative school. I may be wrong in this; it is no matter;—suppose it were so, and that he came down to Venice somewhat recusant or insentient, concerning the usual priestly doctrines of his day, how would the Venetian religion, from an outer intellectual standing-point, have *looked* to him?

§ 12. He would have seen it to be a religion indisputably powerful in human affairs; often very harmfully so; sometimes devouring widows' houses, and consuming the strongest and fairest from among the young: freezing into merciless bigotry the policy of the old: also, on the other hand, animating national courage, and raising souls, otherwise sordid, into heroism: on the whole, always a real and great power; served with daily sacrifice of gold, time, and thought; putting forth its claims, if hypocritically, at least in bold hypocrisy, not waiving any atom of them in doubt or fear; and, assuredly, in large measure, sincere, believing in itself, and believed: a goodly system, moreover, in aspect; gorgeous, harmonious, mysterious;—a thing which had either to be obeyed or combated, but could not be scorned. A religion towering over all the city—many-buttressed—luminous in marble stateliness, as the dome of our Lady of Safety shines over the sea; many-voiced, also, giving, over all the eastern seas, to the sentinel his watchword, to the soldier his war-cry; and, on the lips of all who died for Venice, shaping the whisper of death.

§ 13. I suppose the boy Turner to have regarded the religion of his city also from an external intellectual standing-point.

What did he see in Maiden Lane?

Let not the reader be offended with me: I am willing to let him describe, at his own pleasure, what Turner saw there; but to me, it seems to have been this. A religion

maintained occasionally, even the whole length of the lane,
at point of constable's staff; but, at other times, placed
under the custody of the beadle, within certain black and
unstately iron railings of St. Paul's, Covent Garden.
Among the wheelbarrows and over the vegetables, no
perceptible dominance of religion; in the narrow, dis-
quieted streets, none; in the tongues, deeds, daily ways of
Maiden Lane, little. Some honesty, indeed, and English
industry, and kindness of heart, and general idea of justice;
but faith, of any national kind, shut up from one Sunday
to the next, not artistically beautiful even in those Sabbati-
cal exhibitions; its paraphernalia being chiefly of high pews,
heavy elocution, and cold grimness of behaviour.

What chiaroscuro belongs to it—(dependent mostly on
candlelight),—we will, however, draw, considerately; no
goodliness of escutcheon, nor other respectability being
omitted, and the best of their results confessed, a meek
old woman and a child being let into a pew, for whom
the reading by candlelight will be beneficial.[1]

§ 14. For the rest, this religion seems to him dis-
creditable—discredited—not believing in itself: putting
forth its authority in a cowardly way, watching how far
it might be tolerated, continually shrinking, disclaiming,
fencing, finessing; divided against itself, not by stormy
rents, but by thin fissures, and splittings of plaster from
the walls. Not to be either obeyed, or combated, by an
ignorant, yet clear-sighted youth! only to be scorned.
And scorned not one whit the less, though also the dome
dedicated to *it* looms high over distant winding of the
Thames; as St. Mark's campanile rose, for goodly land-
mark, over mirage of lagoon. For St. Mark ruled over
life; the Saint of London over death; St. Mark over St.
Mark's Place, but St. Paul over St. Paul's Churchyard.

§ 15. Under these influences pass away the first reflective hours of life, with such conclusion as they can

---

[1] Liber Studiorum. "Interior of a church." It is worthy of re-
mark that Giorgione and Titian are always delighted to have an
opportunity of drawing priests. The English Church may, perhaps,
accept it as matter of congratulation that this is the only instance in
which Turner drew a clergyman.

reach. In consequence of a fit of illness, he was taken
—I cannot ascertain in what year—to live with an aunt,
at Brentford; and here, I believe, received some school-
ing, which he seems to have snatched vigorously; getting
knowledge, at least by translation, of the more picturesque
classical authors, which he turned presently to use, as we
shall see. Hence also, walks about Putney and Twickenham in the summer time acquainted him with the look
of English meadow-ground in its restricted states of
paddock and park; and with some round-headed appearances of trees, and stately entrances to houses of mark:
the avenue at Bushey, and the iron gates and carved
pillars of Hampton, impressing him apparently with great
awe and admiration; so that in after-life his little country
house is,—of all places in the world,—at Twickenham! Of
swans and reedy shores he now learns the soft motion and
the green mystery, in a way not to be forgotten.

§ 16. And at last fortune wills that the lad's true life
shall begin; and one summer's evening, after various
wonderful stage-coach experiences on the north road,
which gave him a love of stage-coaches ever after, he finds
himself sitting alone among the Yorkshire hills.[1] For the
first time, the silence of Nature round him, her freedom
sealed to him, her glory opened to him. Peace at last;
no roll of cart-wheel, nor mutter of sullen voices in the
back shop; but curlew-cry in space of heaven, and welling
of bell-toned streamlet by its shadowy rock. Freedom at
last. Dead-wall, dark railing, fenced field, gated garden,
all passed away like the dream of a prisoner; and behold,
far as foot or eye can race or range, the moor, and cloud.
Loveliness at last. It is here then, among these deserted
vales! Not among men. Those pale, poverty-struck, or
cruel faces;—that multitudinous, marred humanity—are
not the only things that God has made. Here is something He has made which no one has marred. Pride of
purple rocks, and river pools of blue, and tender wilderness

---

[1] I do not mean that this is his first acquaintance with the country,
but the first impressive and touching one, after his mind was formed.
The earliest sketches I found in the National collection are at Clifton
and Bristol; the next, at Oxford.

of glittering trees, and misty lights of evening on immeasurable hills.

§ 17. Beauty, and freedom, and peace; and yet another teacher, graver than these. Sound preaching at last here, in Kirkstall crypt, concerning fate and life. Here, where the dark pool reflects the chancel pillars, and the cattle lie in unhindered rest, the soft sunshine on their dappled bodies, instead of priests' vestments; their white furry hair ruffled a little, fitfully, by the evening wind deep-scented from the meadow thyme.

§ 18. Consider deeply the import to him of this, his first sight of ruin, and compare it with the effect of the architecture that was around Giorgione. There were indeed aged buildings, at Venice, in his time, but none in decay. All ruin was removed, and its place filled as quickly as in our London; but filled always by architecture loftier and more wonderful than that whose place it took, the boy himself happy to work upon the walls of it; so that the idea of the passing away of the strength of men and beauty of their works never could occur to him sternly. Brighter and brighter the cities of Italy had been rising and broadening on hill and plain, for three hundred years. He saw only strength and immortality, could not but paint both; conceived the form of man as deathless, calm with power, and fiery with life.

§ 19. Turner saw the exact reverse of this. In the present work of men, meanness, aimlessness, unsightliness: thin-walled, lath-divided, narrow-garreted houses of clay; booths of a darksome Vanity Fair, busily base.

But on Whitby Hill, and by Bolton Brook, remained traces of other handiwork. Men who could build had been there; and who also had wrought, not merely for their own days. But to what purpose? Strong faith, and steady hands, and patient souls—can this, then, be all you have left! this the sum of your doing on the earth;—a nest whence the night-owl may whimper to the brook, and a ribbed skeleton of consumed arches, looming above the bleak banks of mist, from its cliff to the sea?

As the strength of men to Giorgione, to Turner their weakness and vileness, were alone visible. They themselves, unworthy or ephemeral; their work, despicable, or de-cayed. In the Venetian's eyes, all beauty depended on man's presence and pride; in Turner's, on the solitude he had left, and the humiliation he had suffered.

§ 20. And thus the fate and issue of all his work were determined at once. He must be a painter of the strength of nature, there was no beauty elsewhere than in that; he must paint also the labour and sorrow and passing away of men: this was the great human truth visible to him.

Their labour, their sorrow, and their death. Mark the three. Labour; by sea and land, in field and city, at forge and furnace, helm and plough. No pastoral in-dolence nor classic pride shall stand between him and the troubling of the world; still less between him and the toil of his country,—blind, tormented, unwearied, marvellous England.

§ 21. Also their Sorrow; Ruin of all their glorious work, passing away of their thoughts and their honour, mirage of pleasure, FALLACY OF HOPE; gathering of weed on temple step; gaining of wave on deserted strand; weep-ing of the mother for the children, desolate by her breath-less first-born in the streets of the city,[1] desolate by her last sons slain, among the beasts of the field.[2]

§ 22. And their Death. That old Greek question again;—yet unanswered. The unconquerable spectre still flitting among the forest trees at twilight; rising ribbed out of the sea-sand;—white, a strange Aphrodite,—out of the sea-foam; stretching its gray, cloven wings among the clouds; turning the light of their sunsets into blood. This has to be looked upon, and in a more terrible shape than ever Salvator or Dürer saw it. The wreck of one guilty country does not infer the ruin of all countries, and need not cause general terror respecting the laws of the universe. Neither did the orderly and narrow succession of domestic joy and sorrow in a small German community bring the question in its breadth, or in any unresolvable shape, before the mind of Dürer. But the English death

---

[1] "The Tenth Plague of Egypt."
[2] "Rizpah, the Daughter of Aiah."

—the European death of the nineteenth century—was of
another range and power; more terrible a thousand-fold
in its merely physical grasp and grief; more terrible,
incalculably, in its mystery and shame. What were the
robber's casual pang, or the range of the flying skirmish,
compared to the work of the axe, and the sword, and the
famine, which was done during this man's youth on all
the hills and plains of the Christian earth, from Moscow to
Gibraltar? He was eighteen years old when Napoleon came
down on Arcola. Look on the map of Europe and count
the blood-stains on it, between Arcola and Waterloo.

§ 23. Not alone those blood-stains on the Alpine snow,
and the blue of the Lombard plain. The English death
was before his eyes also. No decent, calculable, consoled
dying; no passing to rest like that of the aged burghers
of Nuremberg town. No gentle processions to church-
yards among the fields, the bronze crests bossed deep on
the memorial tablets, and the skylark singing above them
from among the corn. But the life trampled out in the
slime of the street, crushed to dust amidst the roaring of
the wheel, tossed countlessly away into howling winter
wind along five hundred leagues of rock-fanged shore.
Or, worst of all, rotted down to forgotten graves through
years of ignorant patience, and vain seeking for help
from man, for hope in God—infirm, imperfect yearning,
as of motherless infants starving at the dawn; oppressed
royalties of captive thought, vague ague-fits of bleak,
amazed despair.

§ 24. A goodly landscape this, for the lad to paint, and
under a goodly light. Wide enough the light was, and
clear; no more Salvator's lurid chasm on jagged horizon,
nor Dürer's spotted rest of sunny gleam on hedgerow and
field; but light over all the world. Full shone now its awful
globe, one pallid charnel-house,—a ball strewn bright with
human ashes, glaring in poised sway beneath the sun, all
blinding-white with death from pole to pole,—death, not
of myriads of poor bodies only, but of will, and mercy,
and conscience; death, not once inflicted on the flesh, but
daily fastening on the spirit; death, not silent or patient,
waiting his appointed hour, but voiceful, venomous; death

with the taunting word, and burning grasp, and infixed sting.

" Put ye in the sickle, for the harvest is ripe." The word is spoken in our ears continually to other reapers than the angels,—to the busy skeletons that never tire for stooping. When the measure of iniquity is full, and it seems that another day might bring repentance and redemption,— " Put ye in the sickle." When the young life has been wasted all away, and the eyes are just opening upon the tracks of ruin, and faint resolution rising in the heart for nobler things,—" Put ye in the sickle." When the roughest blows of fortune have been borne long and bravely, and the hand is just stretched to grasp its goal,—" Put ye in the sickle." And when there are but a few in the midst of a nation, to save it, or to teach, or to cherish ; and all its life is bound up in those few golden ears,—" Put ye in the sickle, pale reapers, and pour hemlock for your feast of harvest home."

This was the sight which opened on the young eyes, this the watchword sounding within the heart of Turner in his youth.

So taught, and prepared for his life's labour, sate the boy at last alone among his fair English hills ; and began to paint, with cautious toil, the rocks, and fields, and trickling brooks, and soft white clouds of heaven.

CHAPTER X

THE NEREID'S GUARD

§ 1. THE work of Turner, in its first period, is said in my
account of his drawings at the National Gallery to be
distinguished by "boldness of handling, generally gloomy
tendency of mind, subdued colour, and perpetual reference
to precedent in composition." I must refer the reader to
those two catalogues[1] for a more special account of his
early modes of technical study. Here we are concerned
only with the expression of that gloomy tendency of mind,
whose causes we are now better able to understand.

§ 2. It was prevented from overpowering him by his
labour. This, continual, and as tranquil in its course as
a ploughman's in the field, by demanding an admirable
humility and patience, averted the tragic passion of youth.
Full of stern sorrow and fixed purpose, the boy set himself to
his labour silently and meekly, like a workman's child on
its first day at the cotton-mill. Without haste, but without relaxation,—accepting all modes and means of progress,
however painful or humiliating, he took the burden on his
shoulder and began his march. There was nothing so
little, but he noticed it; nothing so great, but he began
preparations to cope with it. For some time his work is,
apparently, feelingless, so patient and mechanical are the
first essays. It gains gradually in power and grasp; there
is no perceptible *aim* at freedom, or at fineness, but the
force insensibly becomes swifter, and the touch finer. The
colour is always dark or subdued.

[1] Notes on the Turner Collection at Marlborough House. 1857.
Catalogue of the Sketches of J. M. W. Turner exhibited at Marlborough
House. 1858.

J. M. W. Turner

78 Quivi Trovammo

J. Ruskin

§ 3. Of the first forty subjects which he exhibited at the Royal Academy, thirty-one are architectural, and of these, twenty-one are of elaborate Gothic architecture (Peterborough Cathedral, Lincoln Cathedral, Malmesbury Abbey, Tintern Abbey, etc.).   I look upon the discipline given to his hand by these formal drawings as of the highest importance.   His mind was also gradually led by them into a calmer pensiveness.[1]   Education amidst country possessing architectural remains of some noble kind, I believe to be wholly essential to the progress of a landscape artist.   The first verses he ever attached to a picture were in 1798. They are from Paradise Lost, and refer to a picture of Morning, on the Coniston Fells :—

> " Ye mists and exhalations, that now rise
> From hill or steaming lake, dusky or gray,
> Till the sun paints your fleecy skirts with gold,
> In honour to the world's great Author rise."

By glancing over the verses, which in following years[2] he quotes from Milton, Thomson, and Mallet, it may be seen at once how his mind was set, so far as natural scenes were concerned, on rendering atmospheric effect ;—and so far as emotion was to be expressed, how consistently it was melancholy.

He paints, first of heroic or meditative subjects, the Fifth Plague of Egypt ; next, the Tenth Plague of Egypt. His first tribute to the Memory of Nelson is the " Battle of the Nile," 1799.   I presume an unimportant picture, as the power was not then availably developed.   His first classical subject is Narcissus and Echo, in 1805 :—

> " So melts the youth, and languishes away,
> His beauty withers, and his limbs decay."

---

[1] The regret I expressed in the third volume at Turner's not having been educated under the influence of Gothic art was, therefore, mistaken ; I had not then had access to his earliest studies.   He *was* educated under the influence of Gothic architecture ; but, in more advanced life, his mind was warped and weakened by classical architecture.   Why he left the one for the other, or how far good influences were mingled with evil in the result of the change, I have not yet been able to determine.

[2] They may be referred to with ease in Boone's Catalogue of Turner's Pictures.   1857.

The year following he summons his whole strength, and paints what we might suppose would be a happier subject, the Garden of the Hesperides. This being the most important picture of the first period, I will analyse it completely.

§ 4. The fable of the Hesperides had, it seems to me, in the Greek mind two distinct meanings; the first referring to natural phenomena, and the second to moral. The natural meaning of it I believe to have been this :—

The Garden of the Hesperides was supposed to exist in the westernmost part of the Cyrenaica; it was generally the expression for the beauty and luxuriant vegetation of the coast of Africa in that district. The centre of the Cyrenaica "is occupied by a moderately elevated table-land, whose edge runs parallel to the coast, to which it sinks down in a succession of terraces, clothed with verdure, intersected by mountain-streams running through ravines filled with the richest vegetation; well watered by frequent rains, exposed to the cool sea-breeze from the north, and sheltered by the mass of the mountain from the sands and hot winds of the Sahara." [1]

The Greek colony of Cyrene itself was founded ten miles from the sea-shore, "in a spot backed by the mountains on the south, and thus sheltered from the fiery blasts of the desert; while at the height of about 1,800 feet an inexhaustible spring bursts forth amidst luxuriant vegetation, and pours its waters down to the Mediterranean through a most beautiful ravine."

The nymphs of the west, or Hesperides, are, therefore, I believe, as natural types, the representatives of the soft western winds and sunshine, which were in this district most favourable to vegetation. In this sense they are called daughters of Atlas and Hesperis, the western winds being cooled by the snow of Atlas. The dragon, on the contrary, is the representative of the Sahara wind, or Simoom, which blew over the garden from above the hills on the south, and forbade all advance of cultivation beyond their ridge. Whether this was the physical meaning

[1] Smith's Dictionary of Greek and Roman Geography. Art. "Cyrenaica."

of the tradition in the Greek mind or not, there can be no doubt of its being Turner's first interpretation of it. A glance at the picture may determine this : a clear fountain being made the principal object in the foreground, —a bright and strong torrent in the distance,—while the dragon, wrapped in flame and whirlwind, watches from the top of the cliff.

§ 5. But, both in the Greek mind and in Turner's, this natural meaning of the legend was a completely subordinate one. The moral significance of it lay far deeper. In the second, but principal sense, the Hesperides were not daughters of Atlas, nor connected with the winds of the west, but with its splendour. They are properly the nymphs of the sunset, and are the daughters of night, having many brothers and sisters, of whom I shall take Hesiod's account.

§ 6. " And the Night begat Doom, and short-withering Fate, and Death.

" And begat Sleep, and the company of Dreams, and Censure, and Sorrow.

" And the Hesperides, who keep the golden fruit beyond the mighty Sea.

" And the Destinies, and the Spirits of merciless punishment.

" And Jealousy, and Deceit, and Wanton Love ; and Old Age, that fades away ; and Strife, whose will endures."

§ 7. We have not, I think, hitherto quite understood the Greek feeling about those nymphs and their golden apples, coming as a light in the midst of a cloud ;—between Censure, and Sorrow,—and the Destinies. We must look to the precise meaning of Hesiod's words, in order to get the force of the passage.

" The night begat Doom ; " that is to say, the doom of unforeseen accident—doom essentially of darkness.

" And short-withering Fate." Ill translated. I cannot do it better. It means especially the sudden fate which brings untimely end to all purpose, and cuts off youth and its promise : called, therefore (the epithet hardly ever leaving it), " black Fate."

" And Death." This is the universal, inevitable death,

opposed to the interfering, untimely death. These three are named as the elder children. Hesiod pauses, and repeats the word "begat" before going on to number the others.

"And begat Sleep, and the Company of Dreams."

"And *Censure*." "Momus," the Spirit of Blame—the spirit which desires to blame rather than to praise;—false, base, unhelpful, unholy judgment;—ignorant and blind, child of the Night.

"And Sorrow." Accurately, sorrow of mourning; the sorrow of the night when no man can work : of the night that falls when what was the light of the eyes is taken from us; lamenting, sightless sorrow, without hope,—child of Night.

"And the Hesperides." We will come back to these.

"And the Destinies, and the Spirits of Merciless Punishment." These are the great Fates which have rule over conduct; the first fate spoken of (short-withering) is that which has rule over occurrence. These great Fates are Clotho, Lachesis, Atropos. Their three powers are,— Clotho's over the clue, the thread, or connecting energy, —that is, the conduct of life; Lachesis' over the lot—that is to say, the chance which warps, entangles, or bends the course of life. Atropos, inflexible, cuts the thread for ever.

"And Jealousy," especially the jealousy of Fortune, in balancing all good by evil. The Greeks had a peculiar dread of this form of fate.

"And Deceit, and sensual Love. And Old Age that fades, and Strife that endures;" that is to say, old age, which, growing not in wisdom, is marked only by its failing power—by the gradual gaining of darkness on the faculties, and helplessness on the frame. Such age is the forerunner of true death—the child of Night. "And Strife," the last and the mightiest, the nearest to man of the Night-children —blind leader of the blind.

§ 8. Understanding thus whose sisters they are, let us consider of the Hesperides themselves—spoken of commonly as the "Singing Nymphs." They are four.

Their names are, Ægle,—Brightness; Erytheia,—Blushing; Hestia,—the (spirit of the) Hearth; Arethusa,—the Ministering.

O English reader! hast thou ever heard of these fair and true daughters of Sunset, beyond the mighty sea?

And was it not well to trust to such keepers the guarding of the golden fruit which the earth gave to Juno at her marriage? Not fruit only: fruit on the tree, given by the earth, the great mother, to Juno (female power), at her marriage with Jupiter, or *ruling* manly power (distinguished from the tried and *agonizing* strength of Hercules). I call Juno, briefly, female power. She is, especially, the goddess presiding over marriage, regarding the woman as the mistress of a household. Vesta (the goddess of the hearth [1]), with Ceres, and Venus, are variously dominant over marriage, as the fulfilment of love; but Juno is preeminently the housewives' goddess. She therefore represents, in her character, whatever good or evil may result from female ambition, or desire of power: and, as to a housewife, the earth presents its golden fruit to her, which she gives to two kinds of guardians. The wealth of the earth, as the source of household peace and plenty, is watched by the singing nymphs—the Hesperides. But, as the source of household sorrow and desolation, it is watched by the Dragon.

We must, therefore, see who the Dragon was, and what kind of dragon.

§ 9. The reader will, perhaps, remember that we traced in an earlier chapter, the birth of the Gorgons, through Phorcys and Ceto, from Nereus. The youngest child of Phorcys and Ceto is the Dragon of the Hesperides; but this latest descent is not, as in Northern traditions, a sign of fortunateness: on the contrary, the children of Nereus receive gradually more and more terror and power, as they

---

[1] Her name is also that of the Hesperid nymph; but I give the Hesperid her Greek form of name, to distinguish her from the goddess. The Hesperid Arethusa has the same subordinate relation to Ceres; and Erytheia, to Venus. Ægle signifies especially the spirit of brightness or cheerfulness; including even the subordinate idea of household neatness or cleanliness.

are later born, till this last of the Nereids unites horror and power at their utmost. Observe the gradual change. Nereus himself is said to have been perfectly *true*, and *gentle*.

This is Hesiod's account of him :—

"And Pontus begat Nereus, simple and true, the oldest of children; but they call him the aged man, in that he is errorless and kind; neither forgets he what is right; but knows all just and gentle counsel."

§ 10. Now the children of Nereus, like the Hesperides themselves, bear a twofold typical character; one physical, the other moral. In his physical symbolism, Nereus himself is the calm and gentle sea, from which rise, in gradual increase of terror, the clouds and storms. In his moral character, Nereus is the type of the deep, pure, rightly-tempered human mind, from which, in gradual degeneracy, spring the troubling passions.

Keeping this double meaning in view, observe the whole line of descent to the Hesperides' Dragon. Nereus, by the Earth, begets (1) Thaumas (the wonderful), physically, the father of the Rainbow; morally, the type of the enchantments and dangers of imagination. His grandchildren, besides the Rainbow, are the Harpies. (2) Phorcys (Orcus?), physically, the treachery or devouring spirit of the sea; morally, covetousness or malignity of heart. (3) Ceto, physically, the deep places of the sea; morally, secretness of heart, called "fair-cheeked," because tranquil in outward aspect. (4) Eurybia (wide strength), physically, the flowing, especially the tidal power of the sea (she, by one of the sons of Heaven, becomes the mother of three great Titans, one of whom, Astræus, and the Dawn, are the parents of the four Winds); morally, the healthy passion of the heart. Thus far the children of Nereus.

§ 11. Next, Phorcys and Ceto, in their physical characters (the grasping or devouring of the sea, reaching out over the land, and its depth), beget the Clouds and Storms—namely, first, the Graiæ, or soft rain-clouds; then the Gorgons, or storm-clouds; and youngest and last, the Hesperides' Dragon,—Volcanic or earth-storm, associated, in conception, with the Simoom and fiery African winds

But, in its moral significance, the descent is this. Covetousness, or malignity (Phorcys), and Secretness (Ceto), beget, first, the darkening passions, whose hair is always gray; then the stormy and merciless passions, brazen-winged (the Gorgons), of whom the dominant, Medusa, is ice-cold, turning all who look on her to stone. And, lastly, the consuming (poisonous and volcanic) passions—the "flame-backed dragon," uniting the powers of poison, and instant destruction. Now the reader may have heard, perhaps, in other books of Genesis than Hesiod's, of a dragon being busy about a tree which bore apples, and of crushing the head of that dragon; but seeing how, in the Greek mind, this serpent was descended from the sea, he may, perhaps, be surprised to remember another verse, bearing also on the matter:—"Thou brakest the heads of the dragons in the waters;" and yet more surprised, going on with the Septuagint version, to find where he is being led: "Thou brakest the head of the dragon, and gavest him to be meat to the Ethiopian people. Thou didst tear asunder the strong fountains and the storm-torrents; thou didst dry up the rivers of Etham," πηγὰς καὶ χειμάρρους, the Pegasus fountains—"Etham on the edge of the wilderness."

§ 12. Returning then to Hesiod, we find he tells us of the Dragon himself:—"He, in the secret places of the desert land, kept the all-golden apples in his great knots" (coils of rope, or extremities of anything). With which compare Euripides' report of him:—"And Hercules came to the Hesperian dome, to the singing maidens, plucking the apple-fruit from the golden petals; slaying the flame-backed dragon, who, twined round and round, kept guard in unapproachable spires" (spirals or whirls, as of a whirl-wind-vortex).

Farther, we hear from other scattered syllables of tradition, that this dragon was sleepless, and that he was able to take various tones of human voice.

And we find a later tradition than Hesiod's calling him a child of Typhon and Echidna. Now Typhon is volcanic storm, generally the evil spirit of tumult.

Echidna (the adder) is a descendant of Medusa. She is a daughter of Chrysaor (the lightning), by Callirhoë (the fair flowing), a daughter of Ocean ;—that is to say, she joins the intense fatality of the lightning with perfect gentleness. In form she is half-maiden, half-serpent ; therefore she is the spirit of all the fatallest evil, veiled in gentleness : or, in one word, treachery ;—having dominion over many gentle things ;—and chiefly over a kiss, given, indeed, in another garden than that of the Hesperides, yet in relation to keeping of treasure also.

§ 13. Having got this farther clue, let us look who it is whom Dante makes the typical Spirit of Treachery. The eighth or lowest pit of hell is given to its keeping ; at the edge of which pit, Virgil casts a *rope* down for a signal ; instantly there rises, as from the sea, " as one returns who hath been down to loose some anchor," " the fell monster with the deadly sting, who passes mountains, breaks through fenced walls, and firm embattled spears ; and with his filth taints all the world."

Think for an instant of another place :—" Sharp stones are under him, he laugheth at the shaking of a spear." We must yet keep to Dante, however. Echidna, remember, is half-maiden, half-serpent ;—hear what Dante's Fraud is like :—

> " Forthwith that image vile of Fraud appear'd,
> His head and upper part exposed on land,
> But laid not on the shore his bestial train.
> His face the semblance of a just man's wore,
> So kind and gracious was its outward cheer ;
> The rest was serpent all : two shaggy claws
> Reach'd to the armpits ; and the back and breast,
> And either side, were painted o'er with nodes
> And orbits. Colours variegated more
> Nor Turks nor Tartars e'er on cloth of state
> With interchangeable embroidery wove,
> Nor spread Arachne o'er her curious loom.
> As oft-times a light skiff moor'd to the shore,
> Stands part in water, part upon the land ;
> Or, as where dwells the greedy German boor,
> The beaver settles, watching for his prey ;
> So on the rim, that fenced the sand with rock,
> Sat perch'd the fiend of evil. In the void
> Glancing, his tail upturn'd, its venomous fork
> With sting like scorpion's arm'd."

§ 14. You observe throughout this description the leaning on the character of the *Sea* Dragon; a little farther on, his way of flying is told us :—

> " As a small vessel, backing out from land,
> Her station quits ; so thence the monster loos'd,
> And, when he felt himself at large, turn'd round
> There, where the breast had been, his forked tail.
> Thus, like an eel, outstretch'd, at length he steer'd,
> Gathering the air up with retractile claws."

And, lastly, his name is told us : Geryon. Whereupon, looking back to Hesiod, we find that Geryon is Echidna's brother. Man-serpent, therefore, in Dante, as Echidna is woman-serpent.

We find next that Geryon lived in the island of Erytheia (blushing), only another kind of blushing than that of the Hesperid Erytheia. But it is on, also, a western island, and Geryon kept red oxen in it (said to be near the red setting sun); and Hercules kills him, as he does the Hesperian dragon : but in order to be able to reach him, a golden boat is given to Hercules by the Sun, to cross the sea in.

§ 15. We will return to this part of the legend presently, having enough of it now collected to get at the complete idea of the Hesperian dragon, who is, in fine, the " Pluto il gran nemico " of Dante ; the demon of all evil passions connected with covetousness ; that is to say, essentially of fraud, rage, and gloom. Regarded as the demon of Fraud, he is said to be descended from the viper Echidna, full of deadly cunning, in whirl on whirl ; as the demon of con-suming Rage from Phorcys ; as the demon of Gloom, from Ceto ;—in his watching and melancholy, he is sleepless (compare the Micyllus dialogue of Lucian); breathing whirl-wind and fire, he is the destroyer, descended from Typhon as well as Phorcys ; having, moreover, with all these, the irresistible strength of his ancestral sea.

§ 16. Now, look at him, as Turner has drawn him (p. 328.) I cannot reduce the creature to this scale with-out losing half his power ; his length, especially, seems to diminish more than it should in proportion to his bulk. In the picture he is far in the distance, cresting the mountain; and may be, perhaps, three-quarters of a mile long. The actual length on the canvas is a foot and eight inches; so that it may be judged how much he loses by the reduction, not to speak of my imperfect etching,[1] and of the loss which, however well he might have been engraved, he would still have sustained, in the impossibility of expressing the lurid colour of his armour, alternate bronze and blue.

§ 17. Still, the main points of him are discernible enough: and among all the wonderful things that Turner did in his day, I think this nearly the most wonderful. How far he had really found out for himself the collateral bearings of the Hesperid tradition I know not; but that he had got the main clue of it, and knew who the Dragon was, there can be no doubt; the strange thing is, that his conception of it throughout, down to the minutest detail, fits every one of the circumstances of the Greek traditions. There is, first, the Dragon's descent from Medusa and Typhon, indicated in the serpent-clouds floating from his head (compare my sketch of the Medusa-cloud, Plate 71); then note the grovelling and ponderous body, ending in a serpent, of which we do not see the end. He drags the weight of it forward by his claws, not being able to lift himself from the ground ("Mammon, the least erected spirit that fell"); then the grip of the claws themselves as if they would clutch (rather than tear) the rock itself into pieces; but chiefly, the designing of the body. Remember, one of the essential characters of the creature, as descended from Medusa, is its coldness and petrifying power; this, in the demon of covetousness, must exist to the utmost; breathing fire, he is yet himself of ice. Now, if I were merely to draw this dragon as white, instead of dark, and take his claws away, his body would become a representation of a great glacier, so nearly perfect, that I know no published engraving of glacier breaking over a rocky brow so like the truth as this dragon's shoulders would be, if they were thrown out in light; there being only this difference,

[1] It is merely a sketch on the steel, like the illustrations before given of composition; but it marks the points needing note. Perhaps some day I may be able to engrave it of the full size. [Etching reduced for this edition.]

that they have the form, but not the fragility of the ice; they are at once ice and iron. "His bones are like solid pieces of brass; his bones are like bars of iron; by his neesings a light doth shine."

§ 18. The strange unity of vertebrated action, and of a true bony contour, infinitely varied in every vertebra, with this glacial outline;—together with the adoption of the head of the Ganges crocodile, the fish-eater, to show his sea descent (and this in the year 1806, when hardly a single fossil saurian skeleton existed within Turner's reach), renders the whole conception one of the most curious exertions of the imaginative intellect with which I am acquainted in the arts.

§ 19. Thus far then, of the dragon; next, we have to examine the conception of the Goddess of Discord. We must return, for a moment, to the tradition about Geryon. I cannot yet decipher the meaning of his oxen, said to be fed together with those of Hades; nor of the journey of Hercules, in which, after slaying Geryon, he returns through Europe like a border forager, driving these herds, and led into farther battle in protection or recovery of them. But it seems to me the main drift of the legend cannot be mistaken; viz., that Geryon is the evil spirit of wealth, as arising from commerce; hence, placed as a guardian of isles in the most distant sea, and reached in a golden boat; while the Hesperian dragon is the evil spirit of wealth, as possessed in households; and associated, therefore, with the true household guardians, or singing nymphs. Hercules (manly labour), slaying both Geryon and Ladon, presents oxen and apples to Juno, who is their proper mistress; but the Goddess of Discord, contriving that one portion of this household wealth shall be ill bestowed by Paris, he, according to Coleridge's interpretation, choosing pleasure instead of wisdom or power;— there issue from this evil choice the catastrophe of the Trojan war, and the wanderings of Ulysses, which are essentially, both in the Iliad and Odyssey, the troubling of household peace; terminating with the restoration of this peace by repentance and patience; Helen and Penelope seen at last sitting upon their household thrones, in the Hesperian light of age.

§ 20. We have, therefore, to regard Discord, in the
Hesperides garden, eminently as the disturber of households, assuming a different aspect from Homer's wild and
fierce discord of war.   They are, nevertheless, one and the
same power; for she changes her aspect at will.   I cannot
get at the root of her name, Eris.   It seems to me as if it
ought to have one in common with Erinnys (Fury); but it
means always contention, emulation, or competition, either
in mind or in words;—the final work of Eris is essentially
"division," and she is herself always double-minded;
shouts two ways at once (in Iliad, xi. 6), and wears a
mantle rent in half (Æneid, viii. 702).   Homer makes her
loud-voiced, and insatiably covetous.   This last attribute is,
with him, the source of her usual title.   She is little when
she first is seen, then rises till her head touches heaven.
By Virgil she is called mad; and her hair is of serpents,
bound with bloody garlands.

§ 21. This is the conception first adopted by Turner,
but combined with another which he found in Spenser;
only note that there is some confusion in the minds of
English poets between Eris (Discord) and Até (Error),
who is a daughter of Discord, according to Hesiod.   She
is properly—mischievous error, tender-footed; for she does
not walk on the earth, but on heads of men (Iliad, xix.
92); i.e., not on the solid ground, but on human vain
thoughts; therefore, her hair is glittering (Iliad, xix. 126).
I think she is mainly the confusion of mind coming of
pride, as Eris comes of covetousness; therefore, Homer
makes her a daughter of Jove.   Spenser, under the name
of Até, describes Eris.   I referred to his account of her
in my notice of the Discord on the Ducal Palace of
Venice (remember the inscription there, *Discordia sum,
discordans*).   (Stones of Venice, II. viii. 71.)   But the
stanzas from which Turner derived his conception of her
are these—

> " Als, as she double spake, so heard she double,
>   With matchless eares deformed and distort,
>   Fild with false rumors and seditious trouble,
>   Bred in assemblies of the vulgar sort,
>   That still are led with every light report :

And as her eares, so eke her feet were odde,
And much unlike ; th' one long, the other short,
And both misplast ; that, when th' one forward yode,
The other backe retired and contrárie trode.

' Likewise unequall were her handës twaine ;
That one did reach, the other pusht away ;
That one did make, the other mard againe,
And sought to bring all things unto decay ;
Whereby great riches, gathered manie a day,
She in short space did often bring to nought,
And their possessours often did dismay :
For all her studie was, and all her thought,
How she might overthrow the things that Concord wrought.

" So much her malice did her might surpas,
That even th' Almightie selfe she did maligne,
Because to man so merciful He was,
And unto all His creatures so benigne,
Sith she herself was of His grace indigne :
For all this worlds faire workmanship she tride
Unto his last confusion to bring,
And that great golden chaine quite to divide,
With which it blessed Concord hath together tide."

All these circumstances of decrepitude and distortion
Turner has followed, through hand and limb, with patient
care : he has added one final touch of his own. The nymph
who brings the apples to the goddess, offers her one in
each hand ; and Eris, of the divided mind, cannot choose.

§ 22. One farther circumstance must be noted, in order
to complete our understanding of the picture,—the gloom
extending, not to the dragon only, but also to the fountain
and the tree of golden fruit. The reason of this gloom
may be found in two other passages of the authors from
which Turner had taken his conception of Eris—Virgil
and Spenser. For though the Hesperides in their own
character, as the nymphs of domestic joy, are entirely
bright (and the garden always bright around them), yet
seen or remembered in sorrow, or in the presence of discord, they deepen distress. Their entirely happy character
is given by Euripides :—" The fruit-planted shore of the
Hesperides,—songstresses,—where the ruler of the purple

lake allows not any more to the sailor his way, assigning the boundary of Heaven, which Atlas holds; where the ambrosial fountains flow, and the fruitful and divine land increases the happiness of the gods."

But to the thoughts of Dido, in her despair, they recur under another aspect; she remembers their priestess as a great enchantress; who *feeds the dragon* and preserves the boughs of the trees; sprinkling moist honey and drowsy poppy; who also has power over ghosts; "and the earth shakes and the forests stoop from the hills at her bidding."

§ 23. This passage Turner must have known well, from his continual interest in Carthage: but his diminution of the splendour of the old Greek garden was certainly caused chiefly by Spenser's describing the Hesperides fruit as growing first in the garden of Mammon :—

> "There mournfull cypresse grew in greatest store
> And trees of bitter gall; and heben sad;
> Dead sleeping poppy; and black hellebore;
> Cold coloquintida; and tetra mad;
> Mortal samnitis; and cicuta bad,
> With which th' unjust Atheniens made to dy
> Wise Socrates, who, thereof quaffing glad,
> Pourd out his life and last philosophy.
>
>   *   *   *   *
>
> "The gardin of Prosérpina this hight:
> And in the midst thereof a silver seat,
> With a thick arber goodly over-dight,
> In which she often usd from open heat
> Herselfe to shroud, and pleasures to entreat:
> Next thereunto did grow a goodly tree,
> With braunches broad dispredd and body great,
> Clothed with leaves, that none the wood mote see,
> And loaden all with fruit as thick as it might bee.
>
> "Their fruit were golden apples glistring bright,
> That goodly was their glory to behold;
> On earth like never grew, ne living wight
> Like ever saw, but they from hence were sold;
> For those, which Hercules with conquest bold
> Got from great Atlas daughters, hence began.
>
>   *   *   *   *
>
> "Here eke that famous golden apple grew,
> The which emongst the gods false Até threw."

There are two collateral evidences in the pictures of Turner's mind having been partly influenced by this passage. The excessive darkness of the stream,—though one of the Cyrene fountains—to remind us of Cocytus; and the breaking of the bough of the tree by the weight of its apples—not healthily, but as a diseased tree would break.

§ 24. Such then is our English painter's first great religious picture; and exponent of our English faith. A sad-coloured work, not executed in Angelico's white and gold; nor in Perugino's crimson and azure; but in a sulphurous hue, as relating to a paradise of smoke. That power, it appears, on the hill-top, is our British Madonna: whom, reverently, the English devotional painter must paint, thus enthroned, with nimbus about the gracious head. Our Madonna,—or our Jupiter on Olympus,—or, perhaps, more accurately still, our unknown god, sea-born, with the cliffs, not of Cyrene, but of England, for his altar; and no chance of any Mars' Hill proclamation concerning him, "whom therefore ye ignorantly worship."

§ 25. This is no irony. The fact is verily so. The greatest man of our England, in the first half of the nineteenth century, in the strength and hope of his youth, perceives this to be the thing he has to tell us of utmost moment, connected with the spiritual world. In each city and country of past time, the master-minds had to declare the chief worship which lay at the nation's heart; to define it; adorn it; show the range and authority of it. Thus in Athens, we have the triumph of Pallas; and in Venice the Assumption of the Virgin; here, in England, is our great spiritual fact for ever interpreted to us—the Assumption of the Dragon. No St. George any more to be heard of; no more dragon-slaying possible: this child, born on St. George's Day, can only make manifest the dragon, not slay him, sea-serpent as he is; whom the English Andromeda, not fearing, takes for her lord. The fairy English Queen once thought to command the waves, but it is the sea-dragon now who commands her valleys; of old the Angel of the Sea ministered to them, but now the Serpent of the Sea; where once flowed their clear springs now spreads the black Cocytus pool; and the fair blooming of the Hesperid meadows fades into ashes beneath the Nereid's Guard.

Yes, Albert of Nuremberg; the time has at last come. Another nation has arisen in the strength of its Black anger; and another hand has pourtrayed the spirit of its toil. Crowned with fire, and with the wings of the bat.

Giorgione   W. Holl

79. The Hesperid Ægl̇é

CHAPTER XI

THE HESPERID ÆGLÉ

§ 1. FIVE years after the Hesperides were painted, another great mythological subject appeared by Turner's hand. Another dragon—this time not triumphant, but in death-pang, the Python slain by Ápollo.

Not in a garden, this slaying, but in a hollow, among wildest rocks, beside a stagnant pool. Yet, instead of the sombre colouring of the Hesperid hills, strange gleams of blue and gold flit around the mountain peaks, and colour the clouds above them.

The picture is at once the type, and the first expression of a great change which was passing in Turner's mind. A change, which was not clearly manifested in all its results until much later in his life ; but in the colouring of this picture are the first signs of it ; and in the subject of this picture, its symbol.

§ 2. Had Turner died early, the reputation he would have left, though great and enduring, would have been strangely different from that which ultimately must now attach to his name. He would have been remembered as one of the severest of painters ; his iron touch and positive forms would have been continually opposed to the delicacy of Claude and richness of Titian ; he would have been spoken of, popularly, as a man who had no eye for colour. Perhaps here and there a watchful critic might have shown this popular idea to be false ; but no conception could have been formed by any one of the man's real disposition or capacity.

It was only after the year 1820 that these were determinable, and his peculiar work discerned.

§ 3. He had begun by faithful declaration of the sorrow there was in the world. It is now permitted him to see also its beauty. He becomes, separately and without rival, the painter of the loveliness and light of the creation.

Of its loveliness: that which may be beloved in it, the tenderest, kindest, most feminine of its aspects. Of its light: light not merely diffused, but interpreted; light seen pre-eminently in colour.

Claude and Cuyp had painted the sun*shine*, Turner alone, the sun *colour*.

Observe this accurately. Those easily understood effects of afternoon light, gracious and sweet so far as they reach, are produced by the softly warm or yellow rays of the sun falling through mist. They are low in tone, even in nature, and disguise the colours of objects. They are imitable even by persons who have little or no gift of colour, if the tones of the picture are kept low and in true harmony, and the reflected lights warm. But they never could be painted by great colourists. The fact of blue and crimson being effaced by yellow and gray, puts such effect at once out of the notice or thought of a colourist, unless he has some special interest in the motive of it. You might as well ask a musician to compose with only three notes, as Titian to paint without crimson and blue. Accordingly the colourists in general, feeling that no other than this yellow sunshine was imitable, refused it, and painted in twilight, when the colour was full. Therefore, from the imperfect colourists,—from Cuyp, Claude, Both, Wilson, we get deceptive effect of sunshine; never from the Venetians, from Rubens, Reynolds, or Velasquez. From these we get only conventional substitutions for it, Rubens being especially daring [1] in frankness of symbol.

§ 4. Turner, however, as a landscape painter, had to represent sunshine of one kind or another. He went steadily through the subdued golden chord, and painted Cuyp's favourite effect, " sun rising through vapour," for many a weary year. But this was not enough for him.

[1] There is a very wonderful, and almost deceptive imitation, of sunlight by Rubens at Berlin. It falls through broken clouds upon angels, the flesh being chequered with sunlight and shade.

He must paint the sun in his strength, the sun rising *not* through vapour. If you glance at that Apollo slaying the Python, you will see there is rose colour and blue on the clouds, as well as gold; and if then you turn to the Apollo in the Ulysses and Polyphemus——his horses are rising beyond the horizon,——you see he is not "rising through vapour," but above it;——gaining somewhat of a victory over vapour, it appears.

The old Dutch brewer, with his yellow mist, was a great man and a good guide, but he was not Apollo. He and his dray-horses led the way through the flats, cheerily, for a little time; we have other horses now flaming out "beyond the mighty sea."

A victory over vapour of many kinds; Python-slaying in general. Look how the Python's jaws smoke as he falls back between the rocks:——a vaporous serpent! We will see who he was presently.

The public remonstrated loudly in the cause of Python: "He had been so yellow, quiet, and pleasant a creature; what meant these azure-shafted arrows, this sudden glare into darkness, this Iris message;——Thaumantian;——miracle-working; scattering our slumber down in Cocytus?" It meant much, but that was not what they should have first asked about it. They should have asked simply was it a true message? Were these Thaumantian things so in the real universe?

It might have been known easily they were. One fair dawn or sunset, obediently beheld, would have set them right; and shown that Turner was indeed the only true speaker concerning such things that ever yet had appeared in the world. They would neither look nor hear;——only shouted continuously, "Perish Apollo. Bring us back Python."

§ 5. We must understand the real meaning of this cry, for herein rests not merely the question of the great right or wrong in Turner's life, but the question of the right or wrong of all painting. Nay, on this issue hangs the nobleness of painting as an art altogether, for it is distinctively the art of colouring, not of shaping or relating. Sculptors and poets can do these, the painter's own work is colour.

Thus, then, for the last time, rises the question, what

is the true dignity of colour? We left that doubt a little
while ago among the clouds, wondering what they had
been made so scarlet for. Now Turner brings the doubt
back to us, unescapable any more. No man, hitherto, had
painted the clouds scarlet. Hesperid Æglé, and Erytheia,
throned there in the west, fade into the twilights of four
thousand years, unconfessed. Here is at last one who
confesses them, but is it well? Men say these Hesperides
are sensual goddesses,—traitresses,—that the Graiæ are
the only true ones. Nature made the western and the
eastern clouds splendid in fallacy. Crimson is impure
and vile; let us paint in black if we would be virtuous.

§ 6. Note, with respect to this matter, that the peculiar
innovation of Turner was the perfection of the colour
chord by means of *scarlet*. Other painters had rendered
the golden tones, and the blue tones, of sky; Titian
especially the last, in perfectness. But none had dared
to paint, none seem to have seen, the scarlet and purple.

Nor was it only in seeing this colour in vividness when
it occurred in full light, that Turner differed from preceding painters. His most distinctive innovation as a colourist
was his discovery of the scarlet *shadow*. "True, there is
a sunshine whose light is golden, and its shadow gray;
but there is another sunshine, and that the purest, whose
light is white, and its shadow scarlet." This was the
essentially offensive, inconceivable thing, which he could
not be believed in. There was some ground for the
incredulity, because no colour is vivid enough to express
the pitch of light of pure white sunshine, so that the
colour given without the true intensity of light *looks* false.
Nevertheless, Turner could not but report of the colour
truly. "I must indeed be lower in the key, but that is no
reason why I should be false in the note. Here is sunshine which glows even when subdued; it has not cool
shade, but fiery shade." [1] This is the glory of sunshine.

---

[1] Not, accurately speaking, shadow, but dark side. All shadow
proper is negative in colour, but, generally, reflected light is warmer
than direct light; and when the direct light is warm, pure, and of
the highest intensity, its reflection is scarlet. Turner habitually, in
his later sketches, used vermilion for his pen outline in effects of sun.

§ 7. Now, this scarlet colour,—or pure red, intensified by expression of light,—is, of all the three primitive colours, that which is most distinctive. Yellow is of the nature of simple light; blue connected with simple shade; but red is an entirely abstract colour. It is red to which the colour-blind are blind, as if to show us that it was not necessary merely for the service or comfort of man, but that there was a special gift or teaching in this colour. Observe, farther, that it is this colour which the sunbeams take in passing through the *earth's atmosphere*. The rose of dawn and sunset is the hue of the rays passing close over the earth. It is also concentrated in the blood of man.

§ 8. Unforeseen requirements have compelled me to disperse through various works, undertaken between the first and last portions of this essay, the examination of many points respecting colour, which I had intended to reserve for this place. I can now only refer the reader to these several passages,[1] and sum their import; which

---

[1] The following collected system of the various statements made respecting colour in different parts of my works may be useful to the student :—

1st. Abstract colour is of far less importance than abstract form (Vol. I. Chap. v.) ; that is to say, if it could rest in our choice whether we would carve like Phidias (supposing Phidias had never used colour), or arrange the colours of a shawl like Indians, there is no question as to which power we ought to choose. The difference of rank is vast : there is no way of estimating or measuring it.

So, again, if it rest in our choice whether it will be great in invention of form, to be expressed only by light and shade, as Dürer, or great in invention and application of colour, caring only for ungainly form, as Bassano, there is still no question. Try to be Dürer, of the two. So again, if we have to give an account or description of anything—if it be an object of high interest—its form will be always what we should first tell. Neither leopard spots nor partridge's signify primarily in describing either beast or bird. But teeth and feathers do.

2. Secondly. Though colour is of less importance than form, if you introduce it at all, it must be right.

People often speak of the Roman school as if it were greater than the Venetian, because its colour is "subordinate."

Its colour is not subordinate. It is BAD.

If you paint coloured objects, you must either paint them rightly or wrongly. There is no other choice. You may introduce as little colour as you choose—a mere tint of rose in a chalk drawing, for

is briefly, that colour generally, but chiefly the scarlet, used with the hyssop, in the Levitical law, is the great instance; or pale hues generally—as Michael Angelo in the Sistine Chapel. All such work implies feebleness or imperfection, but not necessarily error. But if you paint with full colour, as Raphael and Leonardo, you must either be true or false. If true, you will paint like a Venetian. If false, your form, supremely beautiful, may draw the attention of the spectator from the false colour, or induce him to pardon it—and, if ill-taught, even to like it; but your picture is none the greater for that. Had Leonardo and Raphael coloured like Giorgione, their work would have been greater, not less, than it is now.

3. To colour perfectly is the rarest and most precious (technical) power an artist can possess. There have been only seven supreme colourists among the true painters whose works exist (namely, Giorgione, Titian, Veronese, Tintoret, Correggio, Reynolds, and Turner); but the names of great designers, including sculptors, architects, and metal-workers, are multitudinous. Also, if you can colour perfectly, you are sure to be able to do everything else if you like. There never yet was colourist who could not draw; but faculty of perceiving form may exist alone. I believe, however, it will be found ultimately that the *perfect* gifts of colour and form always go together. Titian's form is nobler than Dürer's, and more subtle; nor have I any doubt but that Phidias could have painted as nobly as he carved. But when the powers are not supreme, the wisest men usually neglect the colour-gift, and develop that of form.

I have not thought it worth while at present to enter into any examination of the construction of Turner's colour system, because the public is at present so unconscious of the meaning and nature of colour that they would not know what I was talking of. The more than ludicrous folly of the system of modern water-colour painting, in which it is assumed that every hue in the drawing may be beneficially washed into every other, must prevent, as long as it influences the popular mind, even incipient inquiry respecting colour-art. But for help of any solitary and painstaking student, it may be noted that Turner's colour is founded more on Correggio and Bassano than on the central Venetians; it involves a more tender and constant reference to light and shade than that of Veronese; and a more sparkling and gem-like lustre than that of Titian. I dislike using a technical word which has been disgraced by affectation, but there is no other word to signify what I mean in saying that Turner's colour has, to the full, Correggio's "morbidezza," including also, in due place, conditions of mosaic effect, like that of the colours in an Indian design, unaccomplished by any previous master in painting; and a fantasy of inventive arrangement corresponding to that of Beethoven in music. In its concurrence with and expression of texture or construction of surfaces (as their bloom

sanctifying element of visible beauty, inseparably connected with purity and life.

lustre, or intricacy) it stands unrivalled—no still-life painting by any
other master can stand for an instant beside Turner's, when his work is
of life-size, as in his numerous studies of birds and their plumage. This
"morbidezza" of colour is associated, precisely as it was in Correggio,
with an exquisite sensibility to fineness and intricacy of curvature :
curvature, as already noticed in the second volume, being to lines what
gradation is to colours. This subject, also, is too difficult and too little
regarded by the public to be entered upon here, but it must be observed
that this quality of Turner's design, the one which of all is best expres-
sible by engraving, has of all been least expressed, owing to the constant
reduction or change of proportion in the plates. Publishers, of course,
require generally their plates to be of one size (the plates in this book
form an appalling exception to received practice in this respect) ;
Turner always made his drawings longer or shorter by half an inch,
or more, according to the subject ; the engravers contracted or expanded them to fit the books, with utter destruction of the nature of
every curve in the design. Mere reduction necessarily involves such
loss to some extent ; but the degree in which it probably involves it
has been curiously exemplified by the 61st Plate in this volume, reduced
from a pen-drawing of mine, 18 inches long. Fig. 101 is a facsimile of
the hook and piece of drapery, in the foreground, in my drawing, which
is very nearly true to the Turner
curves ; compare them with the
curves either in Plate 61, or in
the published engraving in the
England Series. Plate 80 is
a portion of the foreground of
the drawing of the Llanberis
(England Series), also of its real
size ;[1] and interesting as showing

Fig. 101.

the grace of Turner's curvature even when he was drawing fastest.
It is a hasty drawing throughout, and after finishing the rocks and
water, being apparently a little tired, he has struck out the broken
fence of the watering-place for the cattle with a few impetuous dashes
of the hand. Yet the curvature and grouping of line are still perfectly
tender. How far the passage loses by reduction, may be seen by a
glance at the published engraving.

4. Colour, as stated in the text, is the purifying or sanctifying
element of material beauty.

If so, how less important than form ? Because, on form depends
existence ; on colour, only purity. Under the Levitical law, neither
scarlet nor hyssop could purify the deformed. So, under all natural

------

[1] [Reduced for this edition.]

I must not enter here into the solemn and far-reaching fields of thought which it would be necessary to traverse, in order to detect the mystical connection between life and love, set forth in that Hebrew system of sacrificial religion to which we may trace most of the received ideas respecting sanctity, consecration, and purification. This only I must hint to the reader—for his own following out—that if he earnestly examines the original sources from which our

law, there must be rightly shaped members first ; then sanctifying colour and fire in them.

Nevertheless, there are several great difficulties and oppositions of aspect in this matter, which I must try to reconcile now clearly and finally. As colour is the type of Love, it resembles it in all its modes of operation ; and in practical work of human hands, it sustains changes of worthiness precisely like those of human sexual love. That love, when true, faithful, well-fixed, is eminently the sanctifying element of human life : without it, the soul cannot reach its fullest height or holiness. But if shallow, faithless, misdirected, it is also one of the strongest corrupting and degrading elements of life.

Between these base and lofty states of Love are the loveless states ; some cold and horrible ; others chaste, childish, or ascetic, bearing to careless thinkers the semblance of purity higher than that of Love.

So it is with the type of Love—colour. Followed rashly, coarsely, untruly, for the mere pleasure of it, with no reverence, it becomes a temptation, and leads to corruption. Followed faithfully, with intense but reverent passion, it is the holiest of all aspects of material things.

Between these two modes of pursuing it, come two modes of refusing it—one, dark and sensual ; the other, statuesque and grave having great aspect of nobleness.

Thus we have, first, the coarse love of colour, as a vulgar person's choice of gaudy hues in dress.

Then, again, we have the base disdain of colour, of which I have spoken at length elsewhere. Thus we have the lofty disdain of colour, as in Dürer's and Raphael's drawing : finally, the severest and passionate following of it, in Giorgione and Titian.

5. Colour is, more than all elements of art, the reward of veracity of purpose. This point respecting it I have not noticed before, and it is highly curious. We have just seen that in giving an account of anything for its own sake, the most important points are those of form. Nevertheless, the form of the object is its own attribute ; special, not shared with other things. An error in giving an account of it does not necessarily involve wider error.

But its colour is partly its own, partly shared with other things round it. The hue and power of all broad sunlight is involved in

heedless popular language respecting the washing away of sins has been borrowed, he will find that the fountain, in which sins are indeed to be washed away, is that of love, not of agony.

§ 9. But, without approaching the presence of this deeper meaning of the sign, the reader may rest satisfied with the connection given him directly in written words, between the cloud and its bow. The cloud, or firmament, as we have seen, signifies the ministration of the heavens to man. That ministration may be in judgment or mercy —in the lightning, or the dew. But the bow, or colour of the cloud, signifies always mercy, the sparing of life; such ministry of the heaven as shall feed and prolong life. And

the colour it has cast upon this single thing; to falsify that colour, is to misrepresent and break the harmony of the day: also, by what colour it bears, this single object is altering hues all round it; reflecting its own into them, displaying them by opposition, softening them by repetition; one falsehood in colour in one place, implies a thousand in the neighbourhood. Hence, there are peculiar penalties attached to falsehood in colour, and peculiar rewards granted to veracity in it. Form may be attained in perfectness by painters who, in their course of study, are continually altering or idealizing it; but only the sternest fidelity will reach colouring. Idealize or alter in that, and you are lost. Whether you alter by abasing or exaggerating,—by glare, or by decline, one fate is for you—ruin. Violate truth wilfully in the slightest particular, or, at least, get into the habit of violating it, and all kinds of failure and error will surround and hunt you to your fall.

Therefore, also, as long as you are working with form only, you may amuse yourself with fancies; but colour is sacred—in that you must keep to facts. Hence the apparent anomaly that the only schools of colour are the schools of Realism. The men who care for form only, may drift about in dreams of Spiritualism; but a colourist must keep to substance. The greater his power in colour enchantment, the more stern and constant will be his common sense. Fuseli may wander wildly among gray spectra, but Reynolds and Gainsborough must stay in broad daylight, with pure humanity. Velasquez, the greatest colourist, is the most accurate portrait painter of Spain; Holbein, the most accurate portrait painter, is the only colourist of Germany; and even Tintoret had to sacrifice some of the highest qualities of his colour before he could give way to the flights of wayward though mighty imagination, in which his mind rises or declines from the royal calm of Titian.

as the sunlight, undivided, is the type of the wisdom and righteousness of God, so divided, and softened into colour by means of the firmamental ministry, fitted to every need of man, as to every delight, and becoming one chief source of human beauty, by being made part of the flesh of man : —thus divided, the sunlight is the type of the wisdom of God, becoming sanctification and redemption. Various in work—various in beauty—various in power.

Colour is, therefore, in brief terms, the type of love. Hence it is especially connected with the blossoming of the earth ; and again, with its fruits ; also, with the spring and fall of the leaf, and with the morning and evening of the day, in order to show the waiting of love about the birth and death of man.

§ 10. And now, I think, we may understand, even far away in the Greek mind, the meaning of that Contest of Apollo with the Python. It was a far greater contest than that of Hercules with Ladon. Fraud and avarice might be overcome by frankness and force ; but this Python was a darker enemy, and could not be subdued but by a greater god. Nor was the conquest slightly esteemed by the victor deity. He took his great name from it thenceforth—his prophetic and sacred name—the Pythian.

It could, therefore, be no merely devouring dragon—no mere wild beast with scales and claws. It must possess some more terrible character to make conquest over it so glorious. Consider the meaning of its name, " THE COR-RUPTER." That Hesperid dragon was a treasure-guardian. This is the treasure-destroyer,—where moth and rust doth corrupt—the worm of eternal decay.

Apollo's contest with him is the strife of purity with pollution ; of life with forgetfulness ; of love, with the grave.

§ 11. I believe this great battle stood, in the Greek mind, for the type of the struggle of youth and manhood with deadly sin—venomous, infectious, irrecoverable sin. In virtue of his victory over this corruption, Apollo becomes thenceforward the guide ; the witness ; the purifying and helpful God. The other gods help waywardly, whom they choose But Apollo helps always : he is by name, not only Pythian, the conqueror of death; but Pæan—the healer of the people.

Well did Turner know the meaning of that battle: he has told its tale with fearful distinctness. The Mammon dragon was armed with adamant; but this dragon of decay is a mere colossal worm: wounded, he bursts asunder in the midst,[1] and melts to pieces, rather than dies, vomiting smoke—a smaller serpent-worm rising out of his blood.

§ 12. Alas, for Turner! This smaller serpent-worm, it seemed, he could not conceive to be slain. In the midst of all the power and beauty of nature, he still saw this death-worm writhing among the weeds. A little thing now, yet enough: you may see it in the foreground of the Bay of Baiæ, which has also in it the story of Apollo and the Sibyl; Apollo giving love; but not youth, nor immortality: you may see it again in the foreground of the Lake Avernus—the Hades lake—which Turner surrounds with delicatest beauty, the Fates dancing in circle; but in front, is the serpent beneath the thistle and the wild thorn. The same Sibyl, Deiphobe, holding the golden bough. I cannot get at the meaning of this legend of the bough; but it was, assuredly, still connected, in Turner's mind, with that help from Apollo. He indicated the strength of his feeling at the time when he painted the Python contest, by the drawing exhibited the same year, of the Prayer of Chryses. There the priest is on the beach alone, the sun setting. He prays to it as it descends; flakes of its sheeted light are borne to him by the melancholy waves, and cast away with sighs upon the sand.

How this sadness came to be persistent over Turner, and to conquer him, we shall see in a little while. It is enough for us to know at present that our most wise and Christian England, with all her appurtenances of school-porch and church-spire, had so disposed her teaching as to leave this somewhat notable child of hers without even cruel Pandora's gift.

He was without hope.

True daughter of Night, Hesperid ÆgIé was to him; coming between Censure, and Sorrow,—and the Destinies.

---

[1] Compare the deaths of Jehoram, Herod, and Judas.

§ 13. What, for us, his work yet may be, I know not. But let not the real nature of it be misunderstood any more.

He is distinctively, as he rises into his own peculiar strength, separating himself from all men who had painted forms of the physical world before,—the painter of the loveliness of nature, with the worm at its root: Rose and cankerworm,—both with his utmost strength; the one *never* separate from the other.

In which his work was the true image of his own mind.

I would fain have looked last at the rose; but that is not the way Atropos will have it, and there is no pleading with her.

So, therefore, first of the rose.

§ 14. That is to say, of this vision of the loveliness and kindness of Nature, as distinguished from all visions of her ever received by other men. By the Greek she had been distrusted. She was to him Calypso, the Concealer, Circe, the Sorceress. By the Venetian, she had been dreaded. Her wildernesses were desolate; her shadows stern. By the Fleming, she had been despised; what mattered the heavenly colours to him? But at last, the time comes for her loveliness and kindness to be declared to men. Had they helped Turner, listened to him, believed in him, he had done it wholly for them. But they cried out for Python, and Python came; came literally as well as spiritually; all the perfectest beauty and conquest which Turner wrought is already withered. The cankerworm stood at his right hand, and of all his richest, most precious work, there remains only the shadow. Yet that shadow is more than other men's sunlight; it is the scarlet shade, shade of the Rose. Wrecked, and faded, and defiled, his work still, in what remains of it, or may remain, is the loveliest ever yet done by man, in imagery of the physical world. Whatsoever is there of fairest, you will find recorded by Turner, and by him alone.

§ 15. I say *you* will find, not knowing to how few I speak; for in order to find what is fairest, you must delight in what is fair; and I know not how few or how many there may be who take such delight. Once I could speak joyfully about beautiful things, thinking to be understood;—now I cannot any more; for it seems to me that no one regards them. Wherever I look or travel in England or abroad, I see that men, wherever they can reach, destroy all beauty. They seem to have no other desire or hope but to have large houses and to be able to move fast. Every perfect and lovely spot which they can touch, they defile.[1]

§ 16. Nevertheless, though not joyfully, or with any hope of being at present heard, I would have tried to enter here into some examination of the right and worthy effect of beauty in Art upon human mind, if I had been myself able to come to demonstrable conclusions. But the question is so complicated with that of the enervating influence of all luxury, that I cannot get it put into any tractable compass. Nay, I have many inquiries to make, many difficult passages of history to examine, before I can determine the just limits of the hope in which I may permit myself to continue to labour in any cause of Art.

Nor is the subject connected with the purpose of this book. I have written it to show that Turner is the greatest landscape painter who ever lived; and this it has sufficiently accomplished. What the final use may be to men, of landscape painting, or of any painting, or of natural beauty, I do not yet know. Thus far, however, I *do* know.

§ 17. Three principal forms of asceticism have existed in this weak world. Religious asceticism, being the refusal of pleasure and knowledge for the sake (as supposed) of religion; seen chiefly in the middle ages. Military asceticism, being the refusal of pleasure and knowledge for the sake of power; seen chiefly in the early days of Sparta and Rome. And monetary asceticism, consisting in the refusal of pleasure and knowledge for the sake of money; seen in the present days of London and Manchester.

"We do not come here to look at the mountains," said the Carthusian to me at the Grande Chartreuse. "We do not come here to look at the mountains," the Austrian

---

[1] Thus, the railroad bridge over the Fall of Schaffhausen, and that round the Clarens shore of the lake of Geneva, have destroyed the power of two pieces of scenery of which nothing can ever supply the place, in appeal to the higher ranks of European mind.

generals would say, encamping by the shores of Garda.
"We do not come here to look at the mountains," so the
thriving manufacturers tell me, between Rochdale and
Halifax.

§ 18. All these asceticisms have their bright and their
dark sides. I myself like the military asceticism best, because it is not so necessarily a refusal of general knowledge
as the two others, but leads to acute and marvellous use of
mind, and perfect use of body. Nevertheless, none of the
three are a healthy or central state of man. There is much
to be respected in each, but they are not what we should
wish large numbers of men to become. A monk of
La Trappe, a French soldier of the Imperial Guard, and a
thriving mill-owner, supposing each a type, and no more
than a type, of his class, are all interesting specimens of
humanity, but narrow ones,—so narrow that even all the
three together would not make up a perfect man. Nor
does it appear in any way desirable that either of the three
classes should extend itself so as to include a majority of
the persons in the world, and turn large cities into mere
groups of monastery, barracks, or factory. I do not say
that it may not be desirable that one city, or one country,
sacrificed for the good of the rest, should become a mass
of barracks or factories. Perhaps, it may be well that this
England should become the furnace of the world; so that
the smoke of the island, rising out of the sea, should be
seen from a hundred leagues away, as if it were a field of
fierce volcanoes; and every kind of sordid, foul, or venomous work which, in other countries, men dreaded or dis-
dained, it should become England's duty to do,—becoming
thus the offscourer of the earth, and taking the hyena instead
of the lion upon her shield. I do not, for a moment, deny
this; but, looking broadly, not at the destiny of England,
nor of any country in particular, but of the world, this is
certain—that men exclusively occupied either in spiritual
reverie, mechanical destruction, or mechanical productive-
ness, fall below the proper standard of their race, and enter
into a lower form of being; and that the true perfection of
the race, and, therefore, its power and happiness, are only
to be attained by a life which is neither speculative nor

productive; but essentially contemplative and protective, which (A) does not lose itself in the monk's vision or hope, but delights in seeing present and real things as they truly are; which (B) does not mortify itself for the sake of obtaining powers of destruction, but seeks the more easily attainable powers of affection, observance, and protection; which (C), finally, does not mortify itself with a view to productive accumulation, but delights itself in peace, with its appointed portion. So that the things to be desired for man in a healthy state, are that he should not see dreams, but realities; that he should not destroy life, but save it; and that he should be not rich, but content.

§ 19. Towards which last state of contentment, I do not see that the world is at present approximating. There are, indeed, two forms of discontent: one laborious, the other indolent and complaining. We respect the man of laborious desire, but let us not suppose that his restlessness is peace, or his ambition meekness. It is because of the special connection of meekness with contentment that it is promised that the meek shall "inherit the earth." Neither covetous men, nor the Grave, can *inherit* anything;[1] they can but consume. Only contentment can possess.

§ 20. The most helpful and sacred work, therefore, which can at present be done for humanity, is to teach people (chiefly by example, as all best teaching must be done) not how "to better themselves," but how to "satisfy themselves." It is the curse of every evil nation and evil creature to eat, and *not* be satisfied. The words of blessing are, that they shall eat and be satisfied. And as there is only one kind of water which quenches all thirst, so there is only one kind of bread which satisfies all hunger—the bread of justice, or righteousness; which hungering after, men shall always be filled, that being the bread of Heaven; but hungering after the bread, or wages, of unrighteousness, shall not be filled, that being the bread of Sodom.

§ 21. And, in order to teach men how to be satisfied, it is necessary fully to understand the art and joy of humble

[1] "There are three things that are never satisfied, yea, four things say not, It is enough: the grave; and the barren womb; the earth that is not filled with water; and the fire, that saith not, It is enough!"

life,—this, at present, of all arts or sciences being the one most needing study. Humble life,—that is to say, proposing to itself no future exaltation, but only a sweet continuance; not excluding the idea of foresight, but wholly of fore-sorrow, and taking no troublous thought for coming days; so, also, not excluding the idea of providence, or provision,[1] but wholly of accumulation;—the life of domestic affection and domestic peace, full of sensitiveness to all elements of costless and kind pleasure;—therefore, chiefly to the loveliness of the natural world.

§ 22. What length and severity of labour may be ultimately found necessary for the procuring of the due comforts of life, I do not know; neither what degree of refinement it is possible to unite with the so-called servile occupations of life: but this I know, that right economy of labour will, as it is understood, assign to each man as much as it will be healthy for him, and no more; and that no refinements are desirable which cannot be connected with toil.

I say, first, that due economy of labour will assign to each man the share which is right. Let no technical labour be wasted on things useless or unpleasurable;[2] and let all physical exertion, so far as possible, be utilised, and it will be found no man need ever work more than is

---

[1] A bad word, being only "foresight" again in Latin; but we have no other good English word for the sense into which it has been warped.

[2] I cannot repeat too often (for it seems almost impossible to arouse the public mind in the least to a sense of the fact) that the root of all benevolent and helpful action towards the lower classes consists in the wise direction of purchase; that is to say, in spending money, as far as possible, only for products of healthful and natural labour. All work with fire is more or less harmful and degrading; so also mine, or machine labour. They at present develop more intelligence than rural labour, but this is only because no education, properly so called, being given to the lower classes, those occupations are best for them which compel them to attain some accurate knowledge, discipline them in presence of mind, and bring them within spheres in which they may raise themselves to positions of command. Properly taught, a ploughman ought to be more intelligent, as well as more healthy, than a miner.

Every nation which desires to ennoble itself should endeavour to maintain as large a number of persons as possible by rural and maritime labour including fishing. I cannot in this place enter into consideration of the relative advantages of different channels of industry. Any

good for him. I believe an immense gain in the bodily health and happiness of the upper classes would follow on their steadily endeavouring, however clumsily, to make the physical exertion they now necessarily take in amusements, definitely serviceable. It would be far better, for instance, that a gentleman should mow his own fields, than ride over other people's.

§ 23. Again, respecting degrees of possible refinement, I cannot yet speak positively, because no effort has yet been made to teach refined habits to persons of simple life.

The idea of such refinement has been made to appear absurd, partly by the foolish ambition of vulgar persons in low life, but more by the worse than foolish assumption, acted on so often by modern advocates of improvement, that "education" means teaching Latin, or algebra,

one who sincerely desires to act upon such knowledge will find no difficulty in obtaining it.

I have also several series of experiments and inquiries to undertake before I shall be able to speak with security on certain points connected with education; but I have no doubt that every child in a civilized country should be taught the first principles of natural history, physiology, and medicine; also to sing perfectly, so far as it has capacity, and to draw any definite form accurately, to any scale.

These things it should be taught by requiring its attendance at school not more than three hours a day, and less if possible (the best part of children's education being in helping their parents and families). The other elements of its instruction ought to have respect to the trade by which it is to live.

Modern systems of improvement are too apt to confuse the recreation of the workman with his education. He should be educated for his work before he is allowed to undertake it; and refreshed and relieved while he practises it.

Every effort should be made to induce the adoption of a national costume. Cleanliness and neatness in dress ought always to be rewarded by some gratification of personal pride; and it is the peculiar virtue of a national costume that it fosters and gratifies the wish to look well, without inducing the desire to look better than one's neighbours —or the hope, peculiarly English, of being mistaken for a person in a higher position of life. A costume may indeed become coquettish, but rarely indecent or vulgar; and though a French bonne or Swiss farm-girl may dress so as sufficiently to mortify her equals, neither of them ever desires or expects to be mistaken for her mistress.

or music, or drawing, instead of developing or " drawing out " the human soul.

It may not be the least necessary that a peasant should know algebra, or Greek, or drawing. But it may, perhaps, be both possible and expedient that he should be able to arrange his thoughts clearly, to speak his own language intelligibly, to discern between right and wrong, to govern his passions, and to receive such pleasures of ear or sight as his life may render accessible to him. I would not have him taught the science of music; but most assuredly I would have him taught to sing. I would not teach him the science of drawing; but certainly I would teach him to see; without learning a single term of botany, he should know accurately the habits and uses of every leaf and flower in his fields; and unencumbered by any theories of moral or political philosophy, he should help his neighbour, and disdain a bribe.

§ 24. Many most valuable conclusions respecting the degree of nobleness and refinement which may be attained in servile or in rural life may be arrived at by careful study of the noble writings of Blitzius (Jeremias Gotthelf), which contain a record of Swiss character not less valuable in its fine truth than that which Scott has left of the Scottish. I know no ideal characters of women, whatever their station, more majestic than that of Freneli, in Ulric le Valet de Ferme, and Ulric le Fermier; or of Elise, in the Tour de Jacob; nor any more exquisitely tender and refined than that of Aenneli in the Fromagerie, and Aenneli in the Miroir des Paysans.[1]

§ 25. How far this simple and useful pride, this delicate innocence, might be adorned, or how far destroyed, by higher intellectual education in letters or the arts, cannot be known without other experience than the charity of men has hitherto enabled us to acquire.

All effort in social improvement is paralyzed, because no one has been bold or clear-sighted enough to put and press

---

[1] This last book should be read carefully by all persons interested in social questions. It is sufficiently dull as a tale, but is characterised throughout by a restrained tragic power of the highest order; and it would be worth reading, were it only for the story of Aenneli, and for the last half page of its close.

home this radical question: "What is indeed the noblest tone and reach of life for men; and how can the possibility of it be extended to the greatest numbers?" It is answered, broadly and rashly, that wealth is good; that knowledge is good; that art is good; that luxury is good. Whereas none of them are good in the abstract, but good only if rightly received. Nor have any steps whatever been yet securely taken,—nor, otherwise than in the resultless rhapsody of moralists,—to ascertain what luxuries and what learning it is either kind to bestow, or wise to desire. This, however, at least we know, shown clearly by the history of all time, that the arts and sciences, ministering to the pride of nations, have invariably hastened their ruin; and this, also, without venturing to say that I know, I nevertheless firmly believe, that the same arts and sciences will tend as distinctly to exalt the strength and quicken the soul of every nation which employs them to increase the comfort of lowly life, and grace with happy intelligence the unambitious courses of honourable toil.

Thus far, then, of the Rose.

§ 26. Last, of the Worm.

I said that Turner painted the labour of men, their sorrow, and their death. This he did nearly in the same tones of mind which prompted Byron's poem of Childe Harold, and the loveliest result of his art, in the central period of it, was an effort to express on a single canvas the meaning of that poem. It may be now seen, by strange coincidence, associated with two others—Caligula's Bridge and the Apollo and Sibyl; the one illustrative of the vanity of human labour, the other of the vanity of human life.[1] He painted these, as I said, in the same tone of mind which formed the Childe Harold poem, but with different capacity: Turner's sense of beauty was perfect; deeper,

---

[1] "The Cumæan Sibyl, Deiphobe, was, in her youth, beloved by Apollo; who promising to grant her whatever she would ask, she took up a handful of earth, and asked that she might live as many years as there were grains of dust in her hand. She obtained her petition. Apollo would have granted her perpetual youth in return for her love, but she denied him, and wasted into the long ages—known, at last, only by her voice."—(See my notes on the Turner Gallery.)

therefore, far than Byron's; only that of Keats and Tennyson being comparable with it. And Turner's love of truth
was as stern and patient as Dante's; so that when over
these great capacities come the shadows of despair, the
wreck is infinitely sterner and more sorrowful. With no
sweet home for his childhood,—friendless in youth, loveless in manhood,—and hopeless in death, Turner was what
Dante might have been, without the "bello ovile," without
Casella, without Beatrice, and without Him who gave them
all, and took them all away.

§ 27. I will trace this state of his mind farther, in a little
while. Meantime, I want you to note only the result upon
his work;—how, through all the remainder of his life, wherever he looked, he saw ruin.

Ruin, and twilight. What was the distinctive effect of
light which he introduced, such as no man had painted
before? Brightness, indeed, he gave, as we have seen,
because it was true and right; but in this he only perfected
what others had attempted. His own favourite light is
not Æglé, but Hesperid Æglé. Fading of the last rays of
sunset. Faint breathing of the sorrow of night.

§ 28. And fading of sunset, note also, on ruin. I
cannot but wonder that this difference between Turner's
work and previous art-conception has not been more
observed. None of the great early painters draw ruins,
except compulsorily. The shattered buildings introduced
by them are shattered artificially, like models. There is no
real sense of decay; whereas Turner only momentarily
dwells on anything else than ruin. Take up the Liber
Studiorum, and observe how this feeling of decay and
humiliation gives solemnity to all its simplest subjects;
even to his view of daily labour. I have marked its
tendency in examining the design of the Mill and Lock,
but observe its continuance through the book. There is
no exultation in thriving city, or mart, or in happy rural
toil, or harvest gathering. Only the grinding at the mill,
and patient striving with hard conditions of life. Observe
the two disordered and poor farm-yards, cart, and plough-
share, and harrow rotting away: note the pastoral by the
brook side, with its neglected stream and haggard trees,

and bridge with the broken rail, and decrepit children—
fever-struck—one sitting stupidly by the stagnant stream,
the other in rags, and with an old man's hat on, and lame,
leaning on a stick.   Then the "Hedging and Ditching,"
with its bleak sky and blighted trees—hacked, and bitten,
and starved by the clay soil into something between trees
and firewood; its meanly-faced, sickly labourers—pollard
labourers, like the willow trunk they hew; and the slat-
ternly peasant-woman, with worn cloak and battered bonnet
—an English Dryad.   Then the water-mill, beyond the
fallen steps, overgrown with the thistle: itself a ruin, mud-
built at first, now propped on both sides;—the planks torn
from its cattle-shed; a feeble beam, splintered at the end,
set against the dwelling-house from the ruined pier of the
water-course; the old mill-stone—useless for many a day—
half buried in slime, at the bottom of the wall; the listless
children, listless dog, and the poor gleaner bringing her
single sheaf to be ground.   Then the "Peat Bog," with its
cold, dark rain, and dangerous labour.   And last and chief,
the mill in the valley of the Chartreuse.   Another than
Turner would have painted the convent : but he had no
sympathy with the hope, no mercy for the indolence of
the monk.   He painted the mill in the valley.   Precipice
overhanging it, and wildness of dark forest round; blind
rage and strength of mountain torrent rolled beneath it,—
calm sunset above, but fading from the glen, leaving it to
its roar of passionate waters and sighing of pine-branches
in the night.

§ 29. Such is his view of human labour.   Of human
pride, see what records.   Morpeth tower, roofless and
black; gate of old Winchelsea wall, the flock of sheep
driven *round* it, not through it; and Rievaulx choir, and
Kirkstall crypt; and Dunstanborough, wan above the
sea; and Chepstow, with arrowy light through traceried
windows; and Lindisfarne, with failing height of wasted
shaft and wall; and last and sweetest, Raglan, in utter
solitude, amidst the wild wood of its own pleasance; the
towers rounded with ivy, and the forest roots choked
with undergrowth, and the brook languid amidst lilies
and sedges.   Legends of gray knights and enchanted

ladies keeping the woodman's children away at the sunset.

These are his types of human pride. Of human love: Procris, dying by the arrow; Hesperie, by the viper's fang; and Rizpah, more than dead, beside her children.

§ 30. Such are the lessons of the Liber Studiorum. Silent always with a bitter silence, disdaining to tell his meaning, when he saw there was no ear to receive it, Turner only indicated this purpose by slight words of contemptuous anger, when he heard of any one's trying to obtain this or the other separate subject as more beautiful than the rest. "What is the use of them," he said, "but together?"[1] The meaning of the entire book was symbolized in the frontispiece, which he engraved with his own hand: Tyre at sunset, with the Rape of Europa, indicating the symbolism of the decay of Europe by that of Tyre, its beauty passing away into terror and judgment (Europa being the mother of Minos and Rhadamanthus).[2]

[1] Turner appears never to have desired, from any one, care in favour of his separate works. The only thing he would say sometimes was, "Keep them together." He seemed not to mind how much they were injured, if only the record of the thought were left in them, and they were kept in the series which would give the key to their meaning. I never saw him, at my father's house, look for an instant at any of his own drawings: I have watched him sitting at dinner nearly opposite one of his chief pictures—his eyes never turned to it.

But the want of appreciation, nevertheless, touched him sorely; chiefly the not understanding his meaning. He tried hard one day for a quarter of an hour to make me guess what he was doing in the picture of Napoleon, before it had been exhibited, giving me hint after hint in a rough way: but I could not guess, and he would not tell me.

[2] I limit myself in this book to mere indication of the tones of his mind, illustration of them at any length being as yet impossible. It will be found on examining the series of drawings made by Turner during the late years of his life, in possession of the nation, that they are nearly all made for the sake of some record of human power, partly victorious, partly conquered. There is hardly a single example of landscape painted for its own abstract beauty. Power and desolation, or soft pensiveness, are the elements sought chiefly in landscape; hence the later sketches are nearly all among mountain scenery, and chiefly of fortresses, villages or bridges and roads among the wildest Alps. The pass of the St. Gothard, especially, from his earliest days,

J. M. W. Turner   J. H. Le Keux

82. The Nets in the Rapids

J. Ruskin

J. H. Le Keux

83 The Bridge of Rheinfelden

J. Ruskin

84. Peace

J. H. Le Keux

§ 31. I need not trace the dark clue farther, the reader may follow it unbroken through all his work and life,

had kept possession of his mind, not as a piece of mountain scenery, but as a marvellous road; and the great drawing which I have tried to illustrate with some care in this book, the last he made of the Alps with unfailing energy, was wholly made to show the surviving of this tormented path through avalanche and storm, from the day when he first drew its two bridges, in the Liber Studiorum. Plate 81, which is the piece of the torrent bed on the left, of the real size,[1] where the stones of it appear just on the point of being swept away, and the ground we stand upon with them, completes the series of illustrations of this subject, for the present, sufficiently; and, if compared with Plate 80, will be serviceable, also, in showing how various in its grasp and its delight was this strange human mind, capable of all patience and all energy, and perfect in its sympathy, whether with wrath or quietness. Though lingering always with chief affection about the St. Gothard pass, he seems to have gleaned the whole of Switzerland for every record he could find of grand human effort of any kind; I do not believe there is one baronial tower, one shattered arch of Alpine bridge, one gleaming tower of decayed village or deserted monastery, which he has not drawn; in many cases, round and round, again and again, on every side. Now that I have done this work, I purpose, if life and strength are spared to me, to trace him through these last journeys, and take such record of his best-beloved places as may fully interpret the designs he left. I have given in the three following plates an example of the kind of work which needs doing, and which, as stated in the preface, I have partly already begun. Plate 82 represents roughly two of Turner's memoranda of a bridge over the Rhine. They are quite imperfectly represented, because I do not choose to take any trouble about them on this scale.[1] If I can en-grave them at all, it must be of their own size; but they are enough to give an idea of the way he used to walk round a place, taking sketch after sketch of its aspects, from every point or half-point of the compass. There are three other sketches of this bridge, far more detailed than these, in the National Gallery.

A scratched word on the back of one of them, "Rheinfels," which I knew could not apply to the Rheinfels near Bingen, gave me the clue to the place;—an old Swiss town, seventeen miles above Basle, celebrated in Swiss history as the main fortress defending the frontier toward the Black Forest. I went there the moment I had got Turner's sketches arranged in 1858, and drew it with the pen (or point of brush, more difficult to manage, but a better instrument) on every side on which Turner had drawn it, giving every detail with servile accuracy,

[1] [Reduced for this edition.]

this thread of Atropos.[1] I will only point, in conclusion, to the intensity with which his imagination dwelt always on the three great cities of Carthage, Rome, and Venice—

so as to show the exact modifications he made as he composed his subjects. Mr. Le Keux has beautifully copied two of these studies, Plates 83 and 84; the first of these is the bridge drawn from the spot whence Turner made his upper memorandum; afterwards, he went down close to the fishing house, and took the second; in which he unhesitatingly divides the Rhine by a strong pyramidal rock, in order to get a group of firm lines pointing to his main subject, the tower (compare § 12, p. 190, above); and throws a foaming mass of water away to the left, in order to give a better idea of the river's force; the modifications of form in the tower itself are all skilful and majestic in the highest degree. The throwing the whole of it higher than the bridge, taking off the peak from its gable on the left, and adding the little roof-window in the centre, make it a perfectly noble mass instead of a broken and common one. I have added the other subject, Plate 84,—though I could not give the Turner drawing which it illustrates,—merely to show the kind of scene which modern ambition and folly are destroying, throughout Switzerland. In Plate 83, a small dark tower is seen in the distance, just on the left of the tower of the bridge. Getting round nearly to the foot of it, on the outside of the town, and then turning back so as to put the town walls on your right, you may, I hope, still see the subject of the third plate; the old bridge over the moat, and older wall and towers; the stork's nest on the top of the nearest one; the moat itself, now nearly filled with softest grass and flowers; a little mountain brook rippling down through the midst of them, and the first wooded promontory of the Jura beyond. Had Rheinfelden been a place of the least mark, instead of an early ruinous village, it is just this spot of ground which, costing little or nothing, would have been made its railroad station, and its refreshment-room would have been built out of the stones of the towers.

[1] I have not followed out, as I ought to have done, had the task been less painful, my assertion that Turner had to paint not only the labour and the sorrow of men, but their death. There is no form of violent death which he has not painted. Pre-eminent in many things, he is pre-eminent also, bitterly, in this. Dürer and Holbein drew the skeleton in its questioning; but Turner, like Salvator, as under some strange fascination or captivity, drew it at its work. Flood, and fire, and wreck, and battle, and pestilence, and solitary death, more fearful still. The noblest of all the plates of the Liber Studiorum, except the Via Mala, is one engraved with his own hand, of a single sailor, yet living, dashed in the night against a granite coast,—his body and outstretched hands just seen in the trough of a mountain

Drawn by J. M. W. Turner

Etched by J. Ruskin

Engraved by T. Lupton

86. Dawn after the Wreck

Drawn by J. M. W. Turner   Etched by J. Ruskin   Engraved by T. Lupton

87. The Vale of Zug

Carthage in connection especially with the thoughts and study which led to the painting of the Hesperides' Garden, showing the death which attends the vain pursuit of wealth; Rome showing the death which attends the vain pursuit of power; Venice, the death which attends the vain pursuit of beauty.

How strangely significant, thus understood, those last

wave, between it and the overhanging wall of rock, hollow, polished, and pale with dreadful cloud and grasping foam.

And remember also, that the very sign in heaven itself which, truly understood, is the type of love, was to Turner the type of death. The scarlet of the clouds was his symbol of destruction. In his mind it was the colour of blood. So he used it in the Fall of Carthage. Note his own written words—

> "While o'er the western wave the *ensanguined* sun,
> In gathering huge a stormy signal spread,
> And set portentous."

So he used it in the Slaver, in the Ulysses, in the Napoleon, in the Goldau; again and again in slighter hints and momentary dreams, of which one of the saddest and most tender is a little sketch of dawn, made in his last years. It is a small space of level sea shore; beyond it a fair, soft light in the east; the last storm-clouds melting away, oblique into the morning air; some little vessel—a collier, probably—has gone down in the night, all hands lost; a single dog has come ashore. Utterly exhausted, its limbs failing under it, and sinking into the sand, it stands howling and shivering. The dawn clouds have the first scarlet upon them, a feeble tinge only, reflected with the same feeble blood-stain on the sand. (Plate 86.)

The morning light is used with a loftier significance in a drawing made as a companion to the Goldau, engraved in the fourth volume. The Lake of Zug, which ripples beneath the sunset in the Goldau, is lulled in the level azure of early cloud; and the spire of Arth, which is there a dark point at the edge of the golden lake, is, in the opening light, seen pale against purple mountains. The sketches for these two subjects were, I doubt not, made from the actual effects of a stormy evening, and the next following daybreak; but both with earnest meaning. The crimson sunset lights the valley of rock tombs, cast upon it by the fallen Rossberg; but the sunrise gilds with its level rays the two peaks which protect the village that gives name to Switzerland; and the orb itself breaks first through the darkness on the very point of the pass to the high lake of Egeri, where the liberties of the cantons were won by the battle-charge of Morgarten. (Plate 87.)

Venetian dreams of his become, themselves so beautiful and so frail; wrecks of all that they were once—twilights of twilight!

§ 32. Vain beauty; yet not all in vain. Unlike in birth, how like in their labour, and their power over the future, these masters of England and Venice—Turner and Giorgione. But ten years ago, I saw the last traces of the greatest works of Giorgione yet glowing like a scarlet cloud, on the Fondaco de Tedeschi.[1] And though that scarlet cloud (sanguigna e fiammeggiante, per cui le pitture cominciarono con dolce violenza a rapire il cuore delli

---

[1] I have engraved, at the beginning of this chapter, one of the fragments of these frescoes, preserved, all imperfectly indeed, yet with some feeling of their nobleness, by Zanetti, whose words respecting them I have quoted in the text. The one I saw was the first figure given in his book; the one engraven in my Plate, the third, had wholly perished; but even this record of it by Zanetti is precious. What imperfections of form exist in it, too visibly, are certainly less Giorgione's than the translator's; nevertheless, for these very faults, as well as for its beauty, I have chosen it, as the best type I could give of the strength of Venetian art; which was derived, be it remembered always, from the acceptance of natural truth, by men who loved beauty too well to think she was to be won by falsehood.

The words of Zanetti himself respecting Giorgione's figure of Diligence are of great value, as they mark the first article of Venetian faith: "Giorgione per tale o per altra che vi fosse, contrassegnolla con quella spezie di mannaja che tiene in mano; per altro tanto ci cercava le sole bellezze della natura, che poco pensando al costume, ritrasse qui una di quelle donne Friulane, che vengono per servire in Venezia; non alterandone nemmeno l' abito, è facendola alquanto attempata, quale forse ci la vedea; senza voler sapere che per rappresentare le Virtù, si suole dá pittori belle è fresche giovani immaginare."

Compare this with what I have said of Titian's Magdalen. I ought in that place to have dwelt upon the firm endurance of all terribleness which is marked in Titian's "Notomie" and in Veronese's "Marsyas." In order to understand the Venetian mind entirely, the student should place a plate from that series of the Notomie always beside the best engraving he can obtain of Titian's "Flora."

My impression is that the ground of the flesh in these Giorgione frescoes had been pure vermilion; little else was left in the figure I saw. Therefore, not knowing what power the painter intended to personify by the figure at the commencement of this chapter, I have called her, from her glowing colour, Hesperid Æglé.

genti) may, indeed, melt away into paleness of night, and
Venice herself waste from her islands as a wreath of wind-
driven foam fades from their weedy beach;—that which
she won of faithful light and truth shall never pass away.
Deiphobe of the sea,—the Sun God measures her immortality to her by its sand.   Flushed, above the Avernus
of the Adrian lake, her spirit is still seen holding the
golden bough; from the lips of the Sea Sibyl men shall
learn for ages yet to come what is most noble and most
fair; and, far away, as the whisper in the coils of the shell,
withdrawn through the deep hearts of nations, shall sound
for ever the enchanted voice of Venice.

CHAPTER XII

PEACE

§ 1. Looking back over what I have written, I find that I have only now the power of ending this work,—it being time that it should end, but not of "concluding" it; for it has led me into fields of infinite inquiry, where it is only possible to break off with such imperfect result as may, at any given moment, have been attained.

Full of far deeper reverence for Turner's art than I felt when this task of his defence was undertaken (which may, perhaps, be evidenced by my having associated no other names with his—but of the dead—in my speaking of him throughout this volume[1]), I am more in doubt respecting the real use to mankind of that, or any other transcendent art; incomprehensible as it must always be to the mass of men. Full of far deeper love for what I remember of Turner himself, as I become better capable of understanding it, I find myself more and more helpless to explain his errors and his sins.

§ 2. His errors, I might say, simply. Perhaps, some day, people will again begin to remember the force of the old Greek word for sin; and to learn that all sin is in essence—" Missing the mark;" losing sight or consciousness of heaven; and that this loss may be various in its

[1] It is proper, however, for the reader to know, that the title which I myself originally intended for this book was "*Turner and the Ancients;*" nor did I purpose to refer in it to any other modern painters than Turner. The title was changed; and the notes on other living painters inserted in the first volume, in deference to the advice of friends, probably wise; for unless the change had been made, the book might never have been read at all. But, as far as I am concerned, I regretted the change then, and regret it still.

J. Ruskin

68. Monte Rosa. Sunset

G. Cook

guilt; it cannot be judged by us. It is this of which the words are spoken so sternly, " Judge not ; " which words people always quote, I observe, when they are called upon to " do judgment and justice." For it is truly a pleasant thing to condemn men for their wanderings; but it is a bitter thing to acknowledge a truth, or to take any bold share in working out an equity. So that the habitual modern practical application of the precept " Judge not," is to avoid the trouble of pronouncing verdict by taking, of any matter, the pleasantest malicious view which first comes to hand, and to obtain licence for our own convenient iniquities, by being indulgent to those of others.

These two methods of obedience being just the two which are most directly opposite to the law of mercy and truth.

§ 3. " Bind them about thy neck." I said, but now, that of an evil tree men never gathered good fruit. And the lesson we have finally to learn from Turner's life is broadly this, that all the power of it came of its mercy and sincerity; all the failure of it, from its want of faith. It has been asked of me, by several of his friends, that I should endeavour to do some justice to his character, mistaken wholly by the world. If my life is spared, I will. But that character is still, in many respects, inexplicable to me ; the materials within my reach are imperfect ; and my experience in the world not yet large enough to enable me to use them justly. His life is to be written by a biographer, who will, I believe, spare no pains in collecting the few scattered records which exist of a career so uneventful and secluded. I will not anticipate the conclusions of this writer ; but if they appear to me just, will endeavour afterwards, so far as may be in my power, to confirm and illustrate them ; and, if unjust, to show in what degree.

§ 4. Which, lest death or illness should forbid me, this only I declare now of what I know respecting Turner's character. Much of his mind and heart I do not know; —perhaps never shall know. But this much I do: and if there is anything in the previous course of this work to warrant trust in me of any kind, let me be trusted when I tell you that Turner had a heart as intensely kind, and as

nobly true, as ever God gave to one of His creatures. I
offer, as yet, no evidence in this matter. When I *do* give
it, it shall be sifted and clear. Only this one fact I now
record joyfully and solemnly, that, having known Turner
for ten years, and that during the period of his life when
the brightest qualities of his mind were, in many respects,
diminished, and when he was suffering most from the evil-
speaking of the world, I never heard him say one depre-
ciating word of living man, or man's work; I never saw
him look an unkind or blameful look; I never knew him
let pass, without some sorrowful remonstrance, or endeavour
at mitigation, a blameful word spoken by another.

Of no man but Turner, whom I have ever known, could
I say this. And of this kindness and truth [1] came, I repeat,

---

[1] It may, perhaps, be necessary to explain one or two singular points
of Turner's character, not in defence of this statement, but to show its
meaning. In speaking of his truth, I use the word in a double sense;
—truth to himself, and to others.

Truth to himself, that is to say, the resolution to do his duty by his
art, and carry all work out as well as it could be done. Other painters,
for the most part, modify their work by some reference to public taste,
or measure out a certain quantity of it for a certain price, or alter facts
to show their power. Turner never did any of these things. The
thing the public asked of him he would do, but whatever it was, only
as *he* thought it ought to be done. People did not buy his large
pictures; he, with avowed discontent, painted small ones; but instead
of taking advantage of the smaller size to give, proportionally, less
labour, he instantly changed his execution so as to be able to put
nearly as much work into his small drawings as into his large ones,
though he gave them for half the price. But his aim was always to
make the drawing as good as he could, or as the subject deserved,
irrespective of price. If he disliked his theme, he painted it slightly,
utterly disdainful of the purchaser's complaint. "The purchaser must
take his chance." If he liked his theme, he would give three hundred
guineas' worth of work for a hundred, and ask no thanks. It is true,
exceptionally, that he altered the engravings from his designs, so as to
meet the popular taste, but this was because he knew the public could
not be got otherwise to look at his art at all. His own drawings the
entire body of the nation repudiated and despised: "the engravers
could make something of them," they said. Turner scornfully took
them at their word. If that is what you like, take it. I will not alter
my own noble work one jot for you, but these things you shall have to
your minds;—try to use them and get beyond them. Sometimes, when

all his highest power.   And all his failure and error, deep
and strange, came of his faithlessness.

an engraver came with a plate to be touched, he would take a piece of
white chalk in his right hand and of black in his left : " Which will
you have it done with ? "   The engraver chose black or white as he
thought his plate weak or heavy.   Turner threw the other piece of
chalk away, and would reconstruct the plate, with the added lights or
darks, in ten minutes.   Nevertheless, even this concession to false
principle, so far as it had influence, was injurious to him : he had
better not have scorned the engravings, but either done nothing with
them, or done his best.   His best, in a certain way, he did, never
sparing pains, if he thought the plate worth it : some of his touched
proofs are elaborate drawings.

Of his earnestness in his main work, enough, I should think, has
been already related in this book ; but the following anecdote, which
I repeat here from my notes on the Turner Gallery, that there may be
less chance of its being lost, gives, in a few words, and those his own,
the spirit of his labour, as it possessed him throughout his life.   The
anecdote was communicated to me in a letter by Mr. Kingsley, late of
Sidney College, Cambridge ; whose words I give :—" I had taken my
mother and a cousin to see Turner's pictures ; and, as my mother
knows nothing about art, I was taking her down the gallery to look at
the large Richmond Park, but as we were passing the Sea-storm, she
stopped before it, and I could hardly get her to look at any other
picture ; and she told me a great deal more about it than I had any
notion of, though I have seen many sea-storms.   She had been in
such a scene on the coast of Holland during the war.   When, some
time afterwards, I thanked Turner for his permission for her to see the
pictures, I told him that he would not guess which had caught my
mother's fancy, and then named the picture ; and he then said, ' I did
not paint it to be understood, but I wished to show what such a scene
was like : I got the sailors to lash me to the mast to observe it ; I was
lashed for four hours, and I did not expect to escape, but I felt bound
to record it if I did.   But no one had any business to like the picture.'
' But,' said I, ' my mother once went through just such a scene, and
it brought it all back to her.'   ' Is your mother a painter ?'   ' No.'
' Then she ought to have been thinking of something else.'   These
were nearly his words ; I observed at the time, he used ' record ' and
' painting,' as the title ' author ' had struck me before."

He was true to others.   No accusation has ever been brought
forward against Turner by his most envious enemies, of his breaking
a promise, or failing in an undertaken trust.   His sense of justice was
strangely acute ; it was like his sense of balance in colour, and shown
continually in little crotchets of arrangement of price, or other advantages, among the buyers of his pictures.   For instance, one of my

Faithlessness, or despair, the despair which has been shown already (Vol. III., Chap. XVI. § 31) to be characteristic

friends had long desired to possess a picture which Turner would not sell. It had been painted with a companion; which was sold, but this reserved. After a considerable number of years had passed, Turner consented to part with it. The price of canvases of its size having, in the meantime, doubled, question arose as to what was then to be its price. "Well," said Turner, "Mr. —— had the companion for so much. You must be on the same footing." This was in no desire to do my friend a favour; but in mere instinct of equity. Had the prices of his pictures fallen instead of risen in the meantime, Turner would have said, "Mr. —— paid so much; and so must you."

But the best proof to which I can refer of this character of his mind is in the wonderful series of diagrams executed by him for his lectures on perspective at the Royal Academy. I had heard it said that these lectures were inefficient. Barely intelligible in expression they might be, but the zealous care with which Turner endeavoured to do his duty, is proved by a series of large drawings, exquisitely tinted, and often completely coloured, all by his own hand, of the most difficult perspective subjects; illustrating not only directions of line, but effects of light, with a care and completion which would put the work of any ordinary teacher to utter shame. In teaching generally, he would neither waste his time nor spare it; he would look over a student's drawing, at the Academy,—point to a defective part, make a scratch on the paper at the side, saying nothing; if the student saw what was wanted, and did it, Turner was delighted, and would go on with him, giving hint after hint; but if the student could not follow, Turner left him. Such experience as I have had in teaching, leads me more and more to perceive that he was right. Explanations are wasted time. A man who can see, understands a touch; a man who cannot, misunderstands an oration.

One of the points in Turner which increased the general falseness of impression respecting him was a curious dislike he had to *appear* kind. Drawing, with one of his best friends, at the bridge of St. Martin's, the friend got into great difficulty over a coloured sketch. Turner looked over him a little while, then said, in a grumbling way —"I haven't got any paper I like; let me try yours." Receiving a block book, he disappeared for an hour and a half. Returning, he threw the book down, with a growl, saying—"I can't make anything of your paper." There were three sketches on it, in three distinct states of progress, showing the process of colouring from beginning to end, and clearing up every difficulty which his friend had got into. When he gave advice, it was also apt to come in the form of a keen question, or a quotation of some one else's opinion, rarely a statement of his own. To the same person producing a sketch, which had no

of this present century, and most sorrowfully manifested
in its greatest men; but existing in an infinitely more fatal
form in the lower and general mind, reacting upon those
who ought to be its teachers.

§ 5. The form which the infidelity of England, especially,
has taken, is one hitherto unheard of in human history.

special character: "What are you in *search* of?" Note this expression.
Turner knew that passionate seeking only leads to passionate finding.
Sometimes, however, the advice would come with a startling distinct-
ness. A church spire having been left out in a sketch of a town—
"Why did you not put that in?" "I hadn't time." "Then you
should take a subject more suited to your capacity."

Many people would have gone away considering this an insult,
whereas it was only a sudden flash from Turner's earnest requirement
of wholeness or perfectness of conception. "Whatever you do, large
or small, do it wholly; take a slight subject if you will, but don't
leave things out." But the principal reason for Turner's having got
the reputation of always refusing advice was, that artists came to him
in a state of mind in which he knew they could not receive it. Virtually,
the entire conviction of the artists of his time respecting him was, that
he had got a secret, which he could tell if he liked, that would make
them all Turners. They came to him with this general formula of
request clearly in their hearts, if not definitely on their lips: "You
know, Mr. Turner, we are all of us quite as clever as you are, and
could do all that very well, and we should really like to do a little of
it occasionally, only we haven't quite your trick; there's something in
it, of course, which you only found out by accident, and it is very
ill-natured and unkind of you not to tell us how the thing is done ;—
what do you rub your colours over with, and where ought we to put
in the black patches?" This was the practical meaning of the artistical questioning of his day, to which Turner very resolvedly made no
answer. On the contrary, he took great care that any tricks of execution he actually did use should not be known.

His *practical* answer to their questioning being as follows :—"You
are indeed, many of you, as clever as I am; but this, which you think
a secret, is only the result of sincerity and toil. If you have not sense
enough to see this without asking me, you have not sense enough to
believe me, if I tell you. True, I know some odd methods of colouring. I have found them out for myself, and they suit me. They would
not suit you. They would do you no real good; and it would do me
much harm to have you mimicking my ways of work, without knowledge of their meaning. If you want methods fit for you, find them
out for yourselves. If you cannot discover them, neither could you
use them."

No nation ever before declared boldly, by print and word of mouth, that its religion was good for show, but "would not work." Over and over again it has happened that nations have denied their gods, but they denied them bravely. The Greeks in their decline jested at their religion, and frittered it away in flatteries and fine arts; the French refused theirs fiercely, tore down their altars and brake their carven images. The question about God with both these nations was still, even in their decline, fairly put, though falsely answered. "Either there is or is not a Supreme Ruler; we consider of it, declare there is not, and proceed accordingly." But we English have put the matter in an entirely new light: "There *is* a Supreme Ruler, no question of it, only He cannot rule. His orders won't work. He will be quite satisfied with euphonious and respectful repetition of them. Execution would be too dangerous under existing circumstances, which He certainly never contemplated."

I had no conception of the absolute darkness which has covered the national mind in this respect, until I began to come into collision with persons engaged in the study of economical and political questions. The entire naïveté and undisturbed imbecility with which I found them declare that the laws of the Devil were the only practicable ones, and that the laws of God were merely a form of poetical language, passed all that I had ever before heard or read of mortal infidelity. I knew the fool had often said in his heart, there was *no* God; but to hear him say clearly out with his lips, "There is a foolish God," was something which my art studies had not prepared me for. The French had indeed, for a considerable time, hinted much of the meaning in the delicate and compassionate blasphemy of their phrase "*le bon Dieu*," but had never ventured to put it into more precise terms.

§ 6. Now this form of unbelief in God is connected with, and necessarily productive of, a precisely equal unbelief in man.

Co-relative with the assertion, "There is a foolish God," is the assertion, "There is a brutish man." "As no laws but those of the Devil are practicable in the world, so no impulses but those of the brute " (says the modern political economist) " are appealable to in the world. Faith, generosity, honesty, zeal, and self-sacrifice are poetical phrases. None of these things can, in reality, be counted upon ; there is no truth in man which can be used as a moving or productive power. All motive force in him is essentially brutish, covetous, or contentious. His power is only power of prey : otherwise than the spider, he cannot design ; otherwise than the tiger, he cannot feed." This is the modern interpretation of that embarrassing article of the Creed, " the communion of saints."

§ 7. It has always seemed very strange to me, not indeed that this creed should have been adopted, it being the entirely necessary consequence of the previous fundamental article ;—but that no one should ever seem to have any misgivings about it ;—that, practically, no one had *seen* how strong work *was* done by man ; how either for hire, or for hatred, it never had been done ; and that no amount of pay had ever made a good soldier, a good teacher, a good artist, or a good workman. You pay your soldiers and sailors so many pence a day, at which rated sum, one will do good fighting for you ; another, bad fighting. Pay as you will, the entire goodness of the fighting depends, always, on its being done for nothing ; or rather, less than nothing, in the expectation of no pay but death. Examine the work of your spiritual teachers, and you will find the statistical law respecting them is, " The less pay, the better work." Examine also your writers and artists : for ten pounds you shall have a Paradise Lost, and for a plate of figs, a Dürer drawing ; but for a million of money sterling, neither. Examine your men of science : paid by starvation, Kepler will discover the laws of the orbs of heaven for you ;— and, driven out to die in the street, Swammerdam shall discover the laws of life for you :—such hard terms do they make with you, these brutish men, who can only be had for hire.

§ 8. Neither is good work ever done for hatred, any more than hire ;—but for love only. For love of their country, or their leader, or their duty, men fight steadily ; but for massacre and plunder, feebly. Your signal, " England expects every man to do his duty," they will answer; your signal of Black flag and death's-head, they will not answer. And verily they will answer it no more in commerce than in battle. The cross-bones will not make a good shop-sign, you will find ultimately, any more than a good battle-standard. Not the cross-bones, but the cross.

§ 9. Now the practical result of this infidelity in man, is the utter ignorance of all the ways of getting his right work out of him. From a given quantity of human power and intellect, to produce the least possible result, is a problem solved, nearly with mathematical precision, by the present methods of the nation's economical procedure. The power and intellect are enormous. With the best soldiers, at present existing, we survive in battle, and but survive, because, by help of Providence, a man whom we have kept all his life in command of a company forces his way at the age of seventy so far up as to obtain permission to save us, and die, unthanked. With the shrewdest thinkers in the world, we have not yet succeeded in arriving at any national conviction respecting the uses of life. And with the best artistical material in the world, we spend millions of money in raising a building for our Houses of Talk, of the delightfulness and utility of which (perhaps roughly classing the Talk and its tabernacle together,) posterity will, I believe, form no very grateful estimate;—while for sheer want of bread, we brought the question to the balance of a hair, whether the most earnest of our young painters should give up his art altogether, and go to Australia,—or fight his way through all neglect and obloquy to the painting of the Christ in the Temple.

§ 10. The marketing was indeed done in this case, as in all others, on the usual terms. For the millions of money, we got a mouldering toy: for the starvation, five years' work of the prime of a noble life. Yet neither that picture, great as it is, nor any other of Hunt's, are the best he could have done. They are the least he could have done. By no expedient could we have repressed him more than he has been repressed; by no abnegation received from him less than we have received.

My dear friend and teacher, Lowell, right as he is in

almost everything, is for once wrong in these lines, though
with a noble wrongness :—

> "Disappointment's dry and bitter root,
>   Envy's harsh berries, and the choking pool
>   Of the world's scorn, are the right mother-milk
>   To the tough hearts that pioneer their kind."

They are *not* so ; love and trust are the only mother-
milk of any man's soul.   So far as he is hated and mis-
trusted, his powers are destroyed.   Do not think that
with impunity you can follow the eyeless fool, and shout
with the shouting charlatan ; and that the men you thrust
aside with gibe and blow, are thus sneered and crushed
into the best service they can do you.   I have told you
they *will* not serve you for pay.   They *cannot* serve you
for scorn.   Even from Balaam, money-lover though he be,
no useful prophecy is to be had for silver or gold.   From
Elisha, saviour of life though he be, no saving of life—
even of children's, who " know no better,"—is to be got
by the cry, Go up, thou bald-head.   No man can serve
you either for purse or curse ; neither kind of pay will
answer.   No *pay* is, indeed, receivable by any true man ;
but *power* is receivable by him, in the love and faith you
give him.   So far only as you give him these can he serve
you ; that is the meaning of the question which his Master
asks always, " Believest thou that I am able ? "   And
from every one of his servants—to the end of time—
if you give them the Capernaum measure of faith, you
shall have from them Capernaum measure of works, and
no more.

Do you think that I am irreverently comparing great
and small things ?   The system of the world is entirely
one ; small things and great are alike part of one mighty
whole.   As the flower is gnawed by frost, so every human
heart is gnawed by faithlessness.   And as surely,—as
irrevocably,—as the fruit-bud falls before the east wind, so
fails the power of the kindest human heart, if you meet it
with poison.

§ 11. Now the condition of mind in which Turner did
all his great work was simply this : "What I do must be

done rightly; but I know also that no man now living in
Europe cares to understand it; and the better I do it, the
less he will see the meaning of it." There never was yet,
so far as I can hear or read, isolation of a great spirit
so utterly desolate. Columbus had succeeded in making
other hearts share his hope, before he was put to hardest
trial; and knew that, by help of Heaven, he could finally
show that he was right. Kepler and Galileo could de-
monstrate their conclusions up to a certain point; so far
as they felt they were right, they were sure that after death
their work would be acknowledged. But Turner could de-
monstrate nothing of what he had done;—saw no security
that after death he would be understood more than he had
been in life. Only another Turner could apprehend Turner.
Such praise as he received was poor and superficial; he
regarded it far less than censure. My own admiration of
him was wild in enthusiasm, but it gave him no ray of
pleasure; he could not make me at that time understand
his main meanings; he loved me, but cared nothing for
what I said, and was always trying to hinder me from
writing, because it gave pain to his fellow-artists. To the
praise of other persons he gave not even the acknowledgment of this sad affection; it passed by him as murmur
of the wind: and most justly, for not one of his own
special powers was ever perceived by the world. I have
said in another place that all great modern artists will
own their obligation to him as a guide. They will; but
they are in error in this gratitude, as I was, when I quoted
it as a sign of their respect. Close analysis of the portions
of modern art founded on Turner has since shown me
that in every case his imitators misunderstood him:—that
they caught merely at superficial brilliancies, and never saw
the real character of his mind or of his work.

And at this day, while I write, the catalogue allowed
to be sold at the gates of the National Gallery, for the
instruction of the common people, describes Callcott and
Claude as the greater artists.

§ 12. To censure, on the other hand, Turner was
acutely sensitive, owing to his own natural kindness; he
felt it, for himself, or for others, not as criticism, but as

cruelty. He knew that however little his higher power could be seen, he had at least done as much as ought to have saved him from wanton insult; and the attacks upon him in his later years were to him not merely contemptible in their ignorance, but amazing in their ingratitude. "A man may be weak in his age," he said to me once, at the time when he felt he was dying; "but you should not tell him so."

§ 13. What Turner might have done for us, had he received help and love, instead of disdain, I can hardly trust myself to imagine. Increasing calmly in power and loveliness, his work would have formed one mighty series of poems, each great as that which I have interpreted,— the Hesperides; but becoming brighter and kinder as he advanced to happy age. Soft as Correggio's, solemn as Titian's, the enchanted colour would have glowed, imperishable and pure; and the subtle thoughts risen into loftiest teaching, helpful for centuries to come.

What we have asked from him, instead of this, and what received, we know. But few of us yet know how true an image those darkening wrecks of radiance give to the shadow which gained sway at last over his once pure and noble soul.

§ 14. Not unresisted, nor touching the heart's core, nor any of the old kindness and truth: yet festering work of the worm—inexplicable and terrible, such as England, by her goodly gardening, leaves to infect her earth-flowers.

So far as in it lay, this century has caused every one of its great men, whose hearts were kindest, and whose spirits most perceptive of the work of God, to die without hope: —Scott, Keats, Byron, Shelley, Turner. Great England, of the Iron-heart now, not of the Lion-heart; for these souls of her children an account may perhaps be one day required of her.

§ 15. She has not yet read often enough that old story of the Samaritan's mercy. He whom he saved was going down from Jerusalem to Jericho—to the accursed city (so the old Church used to understand it). He should not have left Jerusalem; it was his own fault that he went out into the desert, and fell among the thieves, and was left for dead. Every one of these English children, in their day, took the desert by-path as he did, and fell among fiends —took to making bread out of stones at their bidding, and then died, torn and famished; careful England, in her pure, priestly dress, passing by on the other side. So far as we are concerned, that is the account *we* have to give of them.[1]

§ 16. So far as *they* are concerned, I do not fear for them;—there being one Priest Who never passes by. The longer I live, the more clearly I see how all souls are in His hand—the mean and the great. Fallen on the earth in their baseness, or fading as the mist of morning in their goodness;—still in the hand of the potter as the clay, and in the temple of their master as the cloud. It was not the mere bodily death that He conquered—that death had no sting. It was this spiritual death which He conquered, so that at last it should be swallowed up—mark the word —not in life; but in victory. As the dead body shall be raised to life, so also the defeated soul to victory, if only it has been fighting on its Master's side, has made no covenant with death; nor itself bowed its forehead for his seal. Blind from the prison-house, maimed from the battle, or mad from the tombs, their souls shall surely yet sit, astonished, at His feet Who giveth peace.

§ 17. Who *giveth* peace? Many a peace we have made and named for ourselves, but the falsest is in that marvellous thought that we, of all generations of the earth, only know the right; and that to us at last,—to us alone,—all the scheme of God, about the salvation of men, has been shown. "This is the light in which *we* are walking. Those vain Greeks are gone down to their Persephone for ever— Egypt and Assyria, Elam and her multitude,—uncircumcised, their graves are round about them—Pathros and careless Ethiopia—filled with the slain. Rome, with her thirsty sword, and poison wine, how did she walk in her

[1] It is strange that the last words Turner ever attached to a picture should have been these :—

"The priest held the poisoned cup."

Compare the words of 1798 with these of 1850.

darkness! We only have no idolatries—ours are the seeing eyes; in our pure hands at last, the seven-sealed book is laid; to our true tongues entrusted the preaching of a perfect gospel. Who shall come after us? Is it not Peace? The poor Jew, Zimri, who slew his master, there is no peace for him: but, for us? tiara on head, may we not look out of the windows of heaven?"

§ 18. Another kind of peace I look for than this, though I hear it said of me that I am hopeless.

I am not hopeless, though my hope may be as Veronese's: the dark-veiled.

Veiled, not because sorrowful, but because blind. I do not know what my England desires, or how long she will choose to do as she is doing now;—with her right hand casting away the souls of men, and with her left the gifts of God.

In the prayers which she dictates to her children, she tells them to fight against the world, the flesh, and the devil. Some day, perhaps, it may also occur to her as desirable to tell those children what she means by this. What is the world which they are to " fight with," and how does it differ from the world which they are to " get on in "? The explanation seems to me the more needful, because I do not, in the book we profess to live by, find anything very distinct about fighting with the world. I find something about fighting with the rulers of its darkness, and something also about overcoming it; but it does not follow that this conquest is to be by hostility, since evil may be overcome with good. But I find it written very distinctly that God loved the world, and that Christ is the light of it.

§ 19. What the much-used words, therefore, mean, I cannot tell. But this, I believe, they *should* mean. That there is, indeed, one world which is full of care, and desire, and hatred: a world of war, of which Christ is not the light which indeed is without light, and has never heard the great " Let there be." Which is, therefore, in truth, as yet no world; but chaos, on the face of which, moving, the Spirit of God yet causes men to hope that a world will come. The better one, they call it: perhaps they might, more wisely, call it the real one. Also, I hear them speak continually of going to it, rather than of its coming to them; which, again, is strange, for in that prayer which they had straight from the lips of the Light of the world, and which He apparently thought sufficient prayer for them, there is not anything about going to another world; only something of another government coming into this; or rather, not another, but the only government,—that government which will constitute it a world indeed. New heavens and new earth. Earth, no more without form and void, but sown with fruit of righteousness. Firmament, no more of passing cloud, but of cloud risen out of the crystal sea—cloud in which, as He was once received up, so He shall again come with power, and every eye shall see Him, and all kindreds of the earth shall wail because of Him.

Kindreds of the earth, or tribes of it![1] the "earth-begotten," the Chaos children—children of this present world, with its desolate seas and its Medusa clouds: the Dragon children, merciless: they who dealt as clouds without water: serpent clouds, by whose sight men were turned into stone;—the time must surely come for their wailing.

§ 20. "Thy kingdom come," we are bid to ask then! But how shall it come? With power and great glory, it is written; and yet not with observation, it is also written. Strange kingdom! Yet its strangeness is renewed to us with every dawn.

When the time comes for us to wake out of the world's sleep, why should it be otherwise than out of the dreams of the night? Singing of birds, first, broken and low, as, not to dying eyes, but eyes that wake to life, "the casement slowly grows a glimmering square;" and then the gray, and then the rose of dawn; and last the light, whose going forth is to the ends of heaven.

This kingdom it is not in our power to bring; but it is, to receive. Nay, it is come already, in part; but not received, because men love chaos best; and the Night, with her daughters. That is still the only question for us, as in the old Elias days, "If ye will receive it." With pains it may be shut out still from many a dark place of cruelty; by sloth it may be still unseen for many a glorious hour. But

[1] Compare Matt. xxiv. 30.

the pain of shutting it out must grow greater and greater:
—harder, every day, that struggle of man with man in the
abyss, and shorter wages for the fiend's work. But it is
still at our choice; the simoom-dragon may still be served
if we will, in the fiery desert, or else God walking in the
garden, at cool of day. Coolness now, not of Hesperus
over Atlas, stooped endurer of toil; but of Heosphorus
over Sion, the joy of the earth.[1] The choice is no vague
nor doubtful one. High on the desert mountain, full
descried, sits throned the tempter, with his old promise—
the kingdoms of this world, and the glory of them. He
still calls you to your labour, as Christ to your rest;—
labour and sorrow, base desire, and cruel hope. So far as
you desire to possess, rather than to give; so far as you
look for power to command, instead of to bless; so far as
your own prosperity seems to you to issue out of contest
or rivalry, of any kind, with other men, or other nations;
so long as the hope before you is for supremacy instead of
love; and your desire is to be greatest, instead of least;—
first, instead of last;—so long you are serving the Lord
of all that is last, and least;—the last enemy that shall be
destroyed—Death; and you shall have death's crown, with
the worm coiled in it; and death's wages, with the worm
feeding on them; kindred of the earth shall you yourself
become; saying to the grave, "Thou art my father;" and
to the worm, "Thou art my mother, and my sister."

I leave you to judge, and to choose, between this labour,
and the bequeathed peace; these wages, and the gift of the
Morning Star; this obedience, and the doing of the will
which shall enable you to claim another kindred than of the
earth, and to hear another voice than that of the grave,
saying, "My brother, and sister, and mother."

---

[1] Ps. xlviii. 2.—This joy it is to receive and to give, because its officers
(governors of its acts) are to be Peace, and its exactors (governors of
its dealings), Righteousness.—Is. lx. 17.

EPILOGUE (1888)

THE republication of this book may seem to break faith with persons who have bought the old editions at advanced prices, trusting my announced resolution that no other should be issued during my lifetime. Had I remained in active health, none could have been; for I should have employed the engravers otherwise, (especially Mr. Allen himself); but I have permitted the re-issue of this early work, to be of what use it may, finding that my plans of better things in the same direction must be abandoned. For the rest, I never encourage the purchase, at advanced prices, of books which their authors wish to withdraw from circulation; and finally, I believe the early editions will never lose their value in the book-market, the original impressions of the plates by Mr. Armytage and Mr. Cousen being entirely beyond imitation by restored plates. Mr. Allen's advertisements are trustworthy as to the cost and pains which have been given to bring the steels up to their first standard,[1] and the adequacy of the impressions obtained to answer the general purposes of the first engraving. But no retouched plate is ever really worth the original one.

Although, as I have said, the book would not have been reprinted if I had been able to write a better to the same effect, I am glad, as matters stand, that the chapters in which I first eagerly and passionately said what throughout life I have been trying more earnestly and resolutely to say, should be put within the reach of readers who care to refer to them.

For the divisions of religious tenet and school to which I attached mistaken importance in my youth, do not in the least affect the vital teaching and purpose of this book: the

---

[1] [This reference is to the plates of the large edition.]

388

claim, namely, of the Personal relation of God to man as the source of all human, as distinguished from brutal, virtue and art. The assertion of this Personal character of God must be carefully and clearly distinguished by every reader who wishes to understand either " Modern Painters " or any of my more cautiously written subsequent books, from the statement of any Christian doctrine, as commonly accepted. I am always under the necessity of numbering with exactness, and frequently I can explain with sympathy, the articles of the Christian creed as it has been held by the various painters or writers of whose work I have to speak. But the religious faith on which my own art teaching is based never has been farther defined, nor have I wished to define it farther, than in the sentence beginning the theoretical part of " Modern Painters " :—

" Man's use and purpose—and let the reader who will not grant me this, follow me no farther, for this I purpose always to assume—is to be the witness of the glory of God, and to advance that glory by his reasonable obedience and resultant happiness."

Nothing is here said of any tradition of Fall, or of any scheme of Redemption ; nothing of Eternal Punishment, nothing of Immortal Life. It is assumed only that man can love and obey a living Spirit ; and can be happy in the presence and guidance of a Personal Deity, otherwise than a mollusc, a beetle, or a baboon.

But I will ask the reflective reader to note besides, that it is said to be the use of man to advance God's glory " by his obedience and happiness,"—not by lectures on the Divine wisdom, meant only to show his own. By his obedience, " reasonable," in submission to the Greater Being because He *is* the greater ; not because we are as wise as He, and vouchsafe to approve His methods of creation. By our happiness, following on that obedience ; not by any happiness snatched or filched out of disobedience ; lighting our lives with lightning instead of sunshine— or blackening them with smoke in the day, instead of receiving God's night in its holiness.

Then, lastly, after the crowning of obedience, and fulfilment of joy, comes the joy of praise,—the " I will magnify

Thee, O God my *King*" of the hundred and forty-fifth Psalm ;—the " My soul doth magnify the Lord, and my spirit hath rejoiced in God my *Saviour*," of the Magnificat ; —the " Bless ye the Lord " of the three Holy Children ;— the " We praise thee, O Lord " of the Archangels with all the Host of Heaven ;—and in the hearts of all, the deepest joy still in the Madonna's thought, For He hath regarded— the lowliness—of His handmaiden,—of His Archangel, or of His first-praying child ;—and perfected praise on the lips of the Babe, as on the harp of David.

He hath regarded their *lowliness*. But not—their *vileness!* The horror and shame of the false Evangelical Religion is in its recommending its souls to God, not for their humility, but their sin ! Not because they cast their crowns before God's throne, but because they strew His earth with their ashes.

All that is involved in these passionate utterances of my youth was first expanded and then concentrated into the aphorism given twenty years afterwards in my inaugural Oxford lectures, " All great Art is Praise ; " and on that aphorism, the yet bolder saying founded, " So far from Art's being immoral, in the ultimate power of it, nothing but Art is moral : Life without Industry is sin, and Industry without Art, brutality " (I forget the words, but that is their purport) : and now, in writing beneath the cloudless peace of the snows of Chamouni, what must be the really final words of the book which their beauty inspired and their strength guided, I am able, with yet happier and calmer heart than ever heretofore, to enforce its simplest assurance of Faith, that the knowledge of what is beautiful leads on, and is the first step, to the knowledge of the things which are lovely and of good report ; and that the laws, the life, and the joy of beauty in the material world of God, are as eternal and sacred parts of His creation as, in the world of spirits, virtue ; and in the world of angels, praise.

CHAMOUNI,

Sunday, September 16th, 1888.

ADDITIONAL NOTES TO VOL. V

PAGE 91.—"*The prettiest pine-glade in Chamouni.*"

Note 1.—The new road to Chamouni has been carried right through it. A cascade on the right, as you ascend, marks the place spoken of in the text,—once as lonely as Corrie-nan-shian. (" Frondes Agrestes," § 47, p. 120.)

Page 115.—"*The finest form you can give a heavy thing will not make it float in a light thing.*"

Note 2.—Compare the old note to § 6 (p. 117); but I had not, when I wrote it, enough reflected on the horrible buoyancy of smoke, nor did I know over what spaces volcanic ashes were diffusible. Will any of my scientific friends now state for me the approximate weight and bulk of a particle of dust of any solid substance, which would be buoyant in air of a given density? (" Cœli Enarrant," p. 22.)

Page 164.—"*The law was given for a foundation; the grace (or mercy) and truth for fulfilment;—the whole forming one glorious Trinity of judgment, mercy, and truth.*"

Note 3.—A great deal of the presumption and narrowness caused by my having been bred in the Evangelical school, and which here fill me with shame and distress in re-reading " Modern Painters," is, to my present mind, atoned for by the accurate thinking by which I broke my way through to the great truth expressed in this passage, which all my later writings, without exception, have been directed to maintain and illustrate. (" Frondes Agrestes," § 76, p. 151.)

Page 345.—"*The Hesperid Ægle.*"

Note 4.—The Hesperid Ægle, from whom this chapter is named, was the daughter of Æsculapius by one of the daughters of the sun. She is the healing power of living light. ("Turner Notes," 1878.)

Page 358.—"*Neither speculative nor productive.*"

Note 5.—"Mechanically" always to be understood; the produce of the earth for daily bread being always gleaned and stored to its last grain. ("Turner Notes," 1878.)

Page 359.—"Can *inherit* anything."

Page 360.—"*Every nation which desires to ennoble itself . . . no difficulty in obtaining it.*"   [In italics.]

Page 366.—"*That they are nearly all made for the sake of some record of human power.*"   [In italics.]

Note 6.—"These italics are put to mark what I wish especially to be noticed. I would not use them in my first text, which I intended to be read as a whole with equal attention. But the then supplementary notes are now of so much more importance to the general public than the text, that I print them in the same type (in "Turner Notes," 1878).

THE END

Printed by BALLANTYNE, HANSON & Co.
Edinburgh & London

Ruskin Reprints

Uniform with this volume

Cloth *limp, Gilt Tops,* **2s. 6d.** ⎫
Leather *limp, Gilt Tops,* **3s. 6d.** ⎭ *per vol. net*

Sesame and Lilies. Three Lectures and long Preface.

The Crown of Wild Olive. Essays on Work, Traffic, and War, etc.

The Two Paths. On Decoration and Manufacture.

Time and Tide. On Laws of Work.

Lectures on Art. Delivered at Oxford in 1870.

A Joy For Ever. On the Political Economy of Art.

The Queen of the Air. A Study of Greek Myths

The Ethics of the Dust. On the Elements of Crystallization.

The Elements of Drawing. With 50 Illustrations.

The Eagle's Nest. On the Relation of Natural Science to Art.

Munera Pulveris. On the Elements of Political Economy.

Frondes Agrestes. Readings in "Modern Painters."

Mornings in Florence

LONDON: GEORGE ALLEN

Ruskin Reprints

Uniform with this volume

Cloth *limp, Gilt Tops,* **2s. 6d.**
Leather *limp, Gilt Tops,* **3s. 6d.** } *per vol. net*

S. Mark's Rest. The History of Venice.

The Stones of Venice. Vol. I. Selections
for Travellers.

The Stones of Venice. Vol. II. Selections
for Travellers.

**The price of the Volumes marked with an
asterisk (*) will, owing to the inclusion of all
the Illustrations, be**

Cloth . . 3s. 6d. net
Leather . 4s. 6d. net

* The Seven Lamps of Architecture

Modern Painters. Vol. I.

Modern Painters. Vol. II.

* Modern Painters. Vol. III.

* Modern Painters. Vol. IV.

Modern Painters (Index). Vol. VI.

Other Volumes to follow

LONDON: GEORGE ALLEN